Component-Level Programming

Peter M. Maurer
Baylor University

Pearson Education, Inc.
Upper Saddle River, New Jersey 07458

Library of Congress Cataloging-in-Publication Data

Maurer, Peter M.
  Component-level programming/Peter M. Maurer.
    p. cm.
  ISBN 0-13-045804-X
  1. Object-oriented programming (Computer science) I. Title.
  QA76.64 .M3855 2003
  005.1'17-dc21

                                                    2002038165

Vice President and Editorial Director, ECS: *Marcia J. Horton*
Acquisitions Editor: *Petra Recter*
Editorial Assistant: *Renee Makras*
Vice President and Director of Production and Manufacturing, ESM: *David W. Riccardi*
Executive Managing Editor: *Vince O'Brien*
Assistant Managing Editor: *Camille Terntacoste*
Production Editor: *Kevin Bradley*
Director of Creative Services: *Paul Belfanti*
Creative Director: *Carole Anson*
Art Director: *Jayne Conte*
Cover Designer: *Bruce Kenselaar*
Art Editor: *Greg Dulles*
Manufacturing Manager: *Trudy Pisciotti*
Manufacturing Buyer: *Lynda Castillo*
Marketing Manager: *Pamela Shaffer*
Marketing Assistant: *Barrie Reinhold*

©2003 by Pearson Education, Inc.
Pearson Education, Inc.
Upper Saddle River, NJ 07458

The author and publisher of this book have used their best efforts in preparing this book. These efforts include the development, research, and testing of the theories and programs to determine their effectiveness. The author and publisher make no warranty of any kind, expressed or implied, with regard to these programs or the documentation contained in this book. The author and publisher shall not be liable in any event for incidental or consequential damages in connection with, or arising out of, the furnishing, performance, or use of these programs.

The screen shots of Visual Basic 6.0, Visual C++ 6.0, Visual Studio 6.0 VB.NET, and VS.NET included in this book are reprinted by permission from Microsoft Corporation.

Printed in the United States of America
10 9 8 7 6 5 4 3 2 1

ISBN 0-13-045804-X

Pearson Education Ltd., *London*
Pearson Education Australia Pty. Ltd., *Sydney*
Pearson Education Singapore, Pte. Ltd.
Pearson Education North Asia Ltd., *Hong Kong*
Pearson Education Canada, Inc., *Toronto*
Pearson Educación de Mexico, S.A. de C.V.
Pearson Education—Japan, *Tokyo*
Pearson Education Malaysia, Pte. Ltd.
Pearson Education, Inc., *Upper Saddle River, New Jersey*

To my wife, Laurie, and my children Laura,
Jennifer, Michael, and Rebecca

Contents

Preface

This book is based on a course in component-level design that I taught at the University of South Florida in the fall of 2000—a course that was taught as a follow-on to a course in object-oriented design. (It is helpful for students to have some knowledge of object-oriented design before studying this material, but it is not essential.) The course was aimed at advanced undergraduates but would also be acceptable as an introductory course at the graduate level.

For a long time, it had been clear that it was necessary to offer courses in component-level design. Component-based languages such as Visual Basic have become widely used as development engines in the commercial world, and computer science students have needed a thorough grounding in such languages. However, a course in Visual Basic, or some other component-based development language, tells only half the story. Such a course will show students how to use preexisting components, but it will not show them how to create their own components.

When developing new component-based applications, it is necessary to combine components with code written in the host language (Visual Basic and others). There is a natural division between the functionality that should be implemented as part of a component and the functionality that should be programmed in the host language. While it is generally preferable to purchase third-party components rather than develop one's own components, there are many applications for which components do not yet exist. For custom software, this tends to be the rule rather than the exception, and there is no reason to suppose that this will change in the future.

Students will discover here the other side of component-based development—namely, the development of the components themselves. This book will show them not only how to develop a wide variety of different components but also how to divide up an application into components and host-level coding.

Chapters 1 through 5 contain the basic material that should be included in every course. The presentation of this material should precede the study of later chapters. Chapters 6 through 18 are relatively independent of one another and can be presented in any order. However, Chapter 7 does serve as the basis for a number of other chapters—in particular, Chapters 8, 9, and 11, and parts of Chapters 10 and 12. I would recommend including the material covered in Chapters 6, 7, and 13 in every course. (Because Chapter 6 presents material that can be used for a substantial number of enjoyable student projects, I prefer to present this material first to enable students to get started with longer projects.) Chapters 19 and 20 contain material for students who plan to do further study in component-level design.

Chapter 13 provides a bridge between component-level software and more typical types of programming. Software that has been developed for a character-based interface such as MS-DOS or the UNIX shell can be converted to component-level software by using the techniques of this chapter. Selection of the other chapters is a matter of taste. I try to include as much of this material as possible.

Chapter 19 can be presented any time after the presentation of Chapter 7. These chapters are actually independent of one another, but the material of Chapter 19 is difficult to motivate without some examples. Chapter 7 and Chapter 13 provide such examples. The flowchart shown here should help in designing a course around this material.

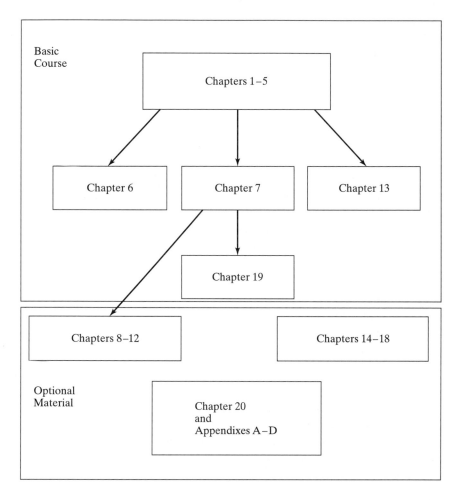

Students will find this course appealing because it enables them to develop the same types of software that they have used on their own computers. Furthermore, it enables them to develop a wide variety of sophisticated-looking software without having to learn all of the details of GUI programming. As courses in component-based development systems become more widely available, the material of this book should become correspondingly more important.

PETER M. MAURER

Chapter 1

Introduction

1. THE COMPONENT REVOLUTION

There have been three major revolutions in the history of computing: the stored-program computer, high-level languages, and component-level programming. The first two revolutions were textbook examples of how revolutions are "supposed" to occur. Great bodies of learned men and women contributed their best ideas, the great universities and research laboratories contributed their very best minds. Principles were elucidated, and the work proceeded along grand designs laid down by great visionaries. The people who participated in these revolutions knew that the world was watching them. They knew that they were making history.

In contrast, the component revolution happened almost by accident. Although there are many component technologies available today, the component revolution is the story of a single technology, the VBX and its heir-designate, the ActiveX control. VBX technology was neither the first nor the best (although these points are debatable), but it was the technology that convinced the world that component-level programming was a good idea.

The term "VBX," which stands for Visual Basic eXtension, was a mechanism for adding new features to the earlier versions of the Visual Basic programming language. To create such an extension, you needed to create a run-time function library with certain standard interface functions. These libraries were stored in files that ended with ".vbx," hence the name. Once a VBX was created, you could add it to a Visual Basic project by copying it onto your hard drive and inserting a reference to it into your Visual Basic project file. In most cases, no complicated installation procedures were needed. Once included in a project, the VBX would provide one or more *custom controls* that could be used by the Visual Basic programmer. The *control* was, and is, the mainstay of Visual Basic programming. A major portion of the VB programming involves adding controls to an application window. Standard controls could be selected from a menu of available controls, and included things like buttons, text boxes, and labels. The custom controls from the VBX could be used in exactly the same manner as

1

the standard controls. They could be added to an application window, and code segments could be added to integrate the functions of the custom control into the program. Multiple noninterfering instances of controls could be created with virtually no effort. Except in rare cases, distinctly different types of custom controls could be integrated into a single program without worrying about compatibility. Very quickly after the introduction of Visual Basic, a stunning variety of custom controls appeared, providing virtually every sort of function from spreadsheets to word processing. Almost anything that was available as an independent program was also available as a VBX custom control. Instead of performing their functions in their own window, they performed them in a subwindow of a Visual Basic application.

The most important point about VBX programming is that it allowed people to program at a new level that went far beyond statement-level programming. To be sure, some statement-level programming was still necessary, but the most complex and detailed portions of a program could now be encapsulated in a collection of VBX components. The statement-level code was used primarily as "glue" to connect components together. Most of the programming practices that were used in VBX-based programs have carried over to ActiveX-based programs, as well as to other component-based technologies.

To understand just how important this revolution has been, it is necessary to realize that programming at "far above the statement level" has been a goal of programming-language theorists for many years. A conventional view was that one could achieve this goal in a series of incremental steps: Start with a conventional programming language, then add new, more powerful primitives to create a more powerful programming language. This new language could then be used as the basis of an even more powerful language. One could continue in this manner until the goal of programming at far above the statement level had been achieved.

Even though the incremental approach seemed reasonable, it never worked. The elusive "next step" never materialized. Many new primitives were introduced, but most of them proved to be of limited usefulness. Many new languages were created, some of which were completely different from conventional languages, but most of them disappeared in less time than it took to create them in the first place. Innovations that were heralded as the awaited "next step" turned out to be less innovative than they first appeared, or too cumbersome for practical use. (Functional languages were one such innovation.)

One useful innovation was the shift from procedural programming to object-oriented programming. Along with this change came a shift in perspective away from new primitives to code reuse. The idea was that one could program at "far above the statement level" not by using new language primitives but by reusing major code elements created by others. In the beginning, there were some spectacular success stories that suggested that there really was something to this idea. One of the more impressive success stories is the graphical user interface (GUI) packages that were developed for MS-DOS programs. Using these packages, one could develop a sophisticated GUI for a program in an environment that was quite hostile to GUI programming, and do it in virtually no time. Unfortunately, there were few other success stories like this, and the disappearance of MS-DOS applications has rendered even this success story irrelevant.

Modern GUI operating systems do have object-oriented development packages, but these packages are generally just wrappers for existing GUI functions.

That is not to suggest that object-oriented programming is unimportant. Nothing could be farther from the truth. Object-oriented programming is an important innovation that permits us to organize programs in a logical and understandable way and to create programs that are much easier to write and to maintain than their procedural counterparts. However, object-oriented programming did not change the way we write code. It changed they way we look at data and our view of the relationship between code and data. But when we write code, we still use assignments, *while* statements, *for* loops, and all the other stuff. Although object-oriented programming made it easier to reuse code, code reuse is a concept that still appears more often in textbooks than in real programs.

Then along came Visual Basic with its VBX components. Suddenly everyone was reusing code, everyone was programming at "far above the statement level," programs were being developed much faster, and they had more features than their object-oriented counterparts. What made all this happen? The answer seems to be "VBX components."

The real question is why did VBX succeed while other, more carefully thought out approaches did not. The answer to this question is important because it will profoundly affect the way we view components. We would like to develop a view of components that is enlightening enough to allow us to develop new component technologies without losing whatever it was that made VBX so successful in the first place. More importantly, if we develop a thorough understanding of the VBX technology and what made it successful, we may discover that this technology is a subset of something more extensive, and ultimately much more useful.

2. ENGINEERING AND COMPUTER SCIENCE

Despite the fact that we like to call ourselves computer scientists, programming is, strictly speaking, not a science but an engineering discipline. Programming does not use the scientific method, but it does use scientific and mathematical principles. Programmers create solutions to problems using the design principles that they have learned. Except in extremely unusual circumstances, they do not formulate hypotheses or conduct experiments to confirm hypotheses.

It is my belief that in our failure to discover the "next level" programming language, we have inadvertently discovered a principle that has been known for many years in other engineering disciplines. Namely, that it is difficult or impossible to design with midlevel parts. When you set out to build a fleet of cars, you don't buy your engines from Mitsubishi, your doors from Ford, your wheels from Chrysler, and your trunk-lids from General Motors. If you did, none of the parts would fit. (Auto manufacturers *do* buy parts from one another, but only for products that were carefully engineered to use these parts.) However, when building your fleet, you *could* buy some cars from Ford, some from Chrysler, some from Mitsubishi, and some from General Motors. You would then be "engineering" your fleet of cars with finished products, not with midlevel parts.

This illustrates another well-known principle that we have rediscovered—namely, that finished products *can* be used as components in larger designs. Before the VBX and other component technologies, the closest thing we had to components was the *subroutine package*. (I use the term in its broadest possible sense.) The standard C library is an example of such a package. One midsize part that can be found in this library is the *quicksort* function. I've used this function many times, but I always have to look up the parameters. I've sometimes found it necessary to fiddle with the prototype to get it to work, and I've found that getting the comparator callback-routine to work properly is something of a black art. All too often I've said to myself, "Oh, it's a short array, I guess I'll just write a quick insertion-sort instead." The point being that using midsize parts is far more demanding than using ordinary primitives, and far more demanding than using finished products.

There are more complex subroutine packages that provide features such as word processing or image analysis. Typically an application that uses package-X must be specifically designed to be a package-X application. The program must conform to the needs of the package, because the package will not or cannot conform to the needs of the program. Needless to say, it is usually not feasible to combine two or more such packages in a single program.

In contrast to subroutine packages, components conform quite easily to the needs of a program. If you decide to add component X to your program, you can do so at virtually any point of the development without having to start over from the beginning. How you use the component is up to you. You seldom have to worry about restructuring your program to conform to the needs of the component. (Most Visual Basic programmers would consider such an idea to be absurd!) When using components it is feasible, and quite reasonable, to combine a word processor, a spreadsheet editor, a Web browser, an animated video player, and an MP3 file player in a single application and expect the whole thing to work.

Despite the fact that a complex subroutine package might provide the same functions as a VBX or other component, the subroutine package is not a finished product. It is a partially engineered solution to some problem that must be combined with additional coding to create a finished product. Components, on the other hand, *are* finished products. Even simple components that provide nothing more than buttons or text boxes are finished products, and despite the extensive support that must be provided by container applications, they are stand-alone programs in their own right.

It is from this perspective that we will begin to examine component-level programming.

3. THE DEFINITION OF A COMPONENT

In this book the term *component* will be defined as an independent program that can readily be used as part of another program. This may be difficult to accept at first, because most components can run only in a host environment, and they place a heavy demand for services from that environment. This seems to contradict the label "independent program." However, it is easy to illustrate that all programs place demands on their environments and that the demands placed by a component are only a matter of degree. A C program running from the UNIX command line (for example) places demands on the UNIX shell. The shell must open the *stdin, stdout,* and *stderr* files for the program. This is a service that goes beyond normal operating system I/O support, memory management, and other run-time services, and not all programs that run in the UNIX environment are provided with this service. While it is true that the demands that a component makes on its environment are more complicated than those made by a command-line program, they are operating system services in the same sense that opening *stdin, stdout,* and *stderr* is an operating system service.

The Visual Basic run-time environment that is included with every Visual Basic program provides extended operating system services that support component instantiation and execution, scheduling and execution of glue code, and the communication interface between glue code and components. Collectively, this collection of extended services constitutes the Visual Basic *component framework.* Every component technology has its own component framework. It is the design of the component framework that defines a particular technology.

4. COMPONENT FRAMEWORKS

Like any other program, a component must be loaded and executed by some external agency. It must be provided with I/O and communication services. It must be able to interact with its environment, with other components, or with both. The design of the component framework defines the basic character of a component technology.

As with components, we can view a component framework from the user's perspective or from the developer's perspective. The *user* of a framework is the Visual Basic programmer, or the Web-page designer—namely, the person who uses the framework to create a new application. The *developer* is the person who designs and builds the framework. These two perspectives are quite different. In the ideal situation, the user is barely aware of the framework, and uses simple programming paradigms to set up the required component interactions. The developer, on the other hand, must be intimately familiar with the implementation details of both the framework and the components themselves. The user's simple view of the world must be translated into the complex world of the underlying implementation.

Standards for component-level programming provide specifications for both the component and the framework. For example, the ActiveX specification describes in detail the services that must be implemented in a module for it to interact properly with its environment, and at the same time specifies those services that must be implemented by a framework to allow it to interact with ActiveX components.

There are two broad categories of component interaction: (1) component-container interaction and (2) component-component interaction. A *container* is an entity that implements the component framework and maintains a collection of one or more components. A Visual Basic program is an example of a container. Mechanisms for component-container interaction have been thoroughly standardized, but component-component interaction is generally reserved for a few specific applications. Generic standards for direct component-component interaction are rare. The most commonly encountered example of direct component-component interaction is the communication between the Visual Basic Data Control and a data-aware component.

At the lowest level, there are two ways that entities can communicate with one another (an *entity* being either a component or a container). The first is *active communication* where *Entity A* calls a subroutine contained in *Entity B*. The second is *passive communication* where *Entity A* modifies a global variable that is also accessible to *Entity B*. Virtually all component technologies use *active* communication, although it is generally possible for the user to *simulate* passive communication when necessary. In active communication, there are several recognized categories of subroutines, some of which are listed below.

Set_Property_P   The user believes that *P* is a variable that is maintained as part of the component's internal state. The *Set_Property_P* function is used to assign a new value to *P*. *P* may be a real variable in the component's internal state, or it may be a virtual property whose value is computed when needed. Setting the value of a virtual property will generally trigger some complex behavior on the part of a component. This function has one parameter—the new value of the property—and no return value. Array properties will have additional parameters to specify array indices. In some technologies, return values are used to indicate the success or failure of a function, in which case the *Set_Property_P* would have an appropriate return value for that purpose.

Get_Property_P   This is the dual of *Set_Property_P*, and used for reading the value of a property. This function has no parameters and one return value—the value of the property *P*. If the property is an array, the function will have one parameter for each array index.

Event_X   An event mechanism allows a component to call a subroutine in another entity, usually the container. The event subroutine can have parameters but generally does not have a return value. The receiving entity does not need to implement the event subroutine, in which case it must substitute a no-op subroutine for it. Event mechanisms are typically the most complex interactions in a component technology.

Initialize_State   This subroutine is called with a parameter that contains initialization data for the component's internal state. The mechanism is generally invisible to the user, although the user may specify the content of the initialization data.

Save_State   This subroutine is called with a parameter that specifies a container for saving initialization data. The data will later be passed to the *Initialize_State* function. Neither the *Initialize_State* function nor the *Save_State* function are strictly necessary.

Method   A method is an arbitrary function that is explicitly called by the user of the component. The function can have input parameters, return values, or both. Implementing input values and return values generally requires a significant amount of effort on the part of the framework developer.

5. PROGRAMMING MODELS

By far the most useful component frameworks are those that support fully programmable containers. The utility of such frameworks depends on the simplicity and effectiveness of the programming model. There are several recognized features that the programming model should support. The most basic is the ability to create instances of components, including multiple noninterfering instances of the same component. The model should support a "data and functions" interface similar to that of object-oriented programming. (In component terminology, data elements of are called *properties*, and function elements are called *methods*.) Although a component instance is not an object in the usual sense, it is convenient for the programmer to treat it as if it were. For example, if *Text* is a property of a component named *Editor*, and there are two instances of *Editor* in the program—*Editor1* and *Editor2*—it should be possible to transfer data from one instance to the other using the following statement, or something similar to it:

```
Editor1.Text := Editor2.Text;
```

If the *Editor* component has a method *Clear* that is used to erase its contents, then it should be possible to invoke this method on a particular instance using a statement similar to the following:

```
Editor1.Clear();
```

In other words, the Property/Method interface should be modeled after the corresponding object-oriented interface.

Finally, the framework should provide an event mechanism that permits the component to communicate with its host. The host programmer would typically declare a subroutine to be the event handler for events of type X, coming from component instance Y. In Visual Basic, the name of the subroutine is used to associate it with the proper instance and event type. Other languages provide less haphazard methods for making such associations.

For many component technologies, the programming interface is polymorphic—that is, the properties, methods, and events that are available depend on the state of the control. Although it is possible to fine-tune the interface in complex ways, the most important distinctions made are based on whether the component is running in *design-mode* or *run-mode*, and whether or not the component is *licensed*. A component is in run-mode when the application is being executed. A component is in design-mode when it is being used to construct a new application. Unlike subroutine packages, a component can be loaded and running while an application is being constructed. This allows the component to respond to design-time changes in its properties. Certain properties may be designated as available only in design-mode, while others may be available only in run-mode. Some components may designate themselves as run-time-only and will refuse to initialize themselves in design-mode.

Commercially available components generally require some form of electronic licensing to enable their full capabilities. Unlicensed components will generally refuse to initialize themselves in design mode, or will run in a restricted "demo" mode. Some components also require a run-time license.

An essential feature found in most existing technologies is the ability for components to define their own interfaces. In other words, the information about what properties, methods, and events are supported by a component can be extracted from the component itself. No independent declarations are required. This permits the container development system to verify the correctness of references to instances of the component without forcing the host programmer to juggle header files.

Although the *Properties/Methods/Events* communication model is nearly universal in component technologies, in the future we may find an entirely different model that is vastly superior. However, as yet no one has suggested anything better. From a technical point of view, the only feature that is *required* is the ability of one entity to call subroutines defined in another.

6. COMPONENT DEVELOPMENT

Although object-oriented design is now considered to be an essential part of component development, earlier technologies were not object-oriented. In fact, component technology and object-oriented technology are quite independent of one another. Nevertheless, there have been considerable benefits gained from the marriage of the two. The most important is the underlying model that is used to represent an instance of a component. Each instance must have an environment that is separate and distinct from every other instance of a component. One could create a separate address space for each component, but this would not permit easy communication between a component and its container, or between two components. Using object-oriented technology, it is possible to provide each instance with its own environment by defining a *support class* to implement the environment. When a new instance of a component is created, a new instance of the support class will be created to maintain the environment. All instance data for the control can be declared as data members of the support class, and all functions that are required to implement the control can be declared as function members of the support class. In the remainder of this book, we will assume that a support class has been defined for each component.

The use of support classes can sometimes be a source of confusion for new component developers. It is easy to forget that there is a distinction between the object model of the control instance and the object model of the support class. Although component properties are usually implemented as data elements of the support class, it is not *necessary* to do so. The support class will generally have many data members that do not represent properties of the component. By the same token, methods will be implemented as function members of the support class but may have declarations that are different from those of the support class member. For example, the support class in ActiveX components is generally defined in C++, while the component interface is defined in IDL (Interface Definition Language). The corresponding function declarations are different, and both are different from the Visual Basic programming model, as the following example shows.

ActiveX Method Declaration (idl):

```
[id(8)] HRESULT GetValue([in] long x, [in] long y,
                    [out, retval] long *ReturnValue);
```

Support-Class Function Definition (C++):

```
STDMETHODIMP CSuppCtrl::GetValue(long x, long y, long *ReturnValue)
```

Visual Basic Usage:

```
X = Instance.GetValue(x, y)
```

In our examples, we will distinguish between the three points of view: (1) interface declaration, (2) container-language usage, and (3) implementation.

Current standards for control development are extremely complex, probably much more so than necessary. However, we must deal with these standards as they exist today, not as we would wish them to be. Fortunately, tools do exist that permit us to build skeleton components that hide most of the messy implementation details. Without such tools, component development would be a daunting task requiring specialized training and experience. With these tools, however, component development is straightforward. We will make use of various tools to simplify development, but the reader is cautioned that these tools could change substantially in the future.

7. CONCLUSION

As with all revolutions, there are some who welcome them and others who wish they had never happened. Regardless of how we feel about it, the component revolution is an accomplished fact. Component-level programming is not "the technology of the future," it is the technology of *today*. Component-level programming has had a profound effect on programming, particularly in the business world, and new developments in the area will continue to affect the future of program development everywhere. It is necessary for us to take the first steps into understanding these new technologies, with the aim of both using them effectively and improving them for the future.

Chapter 2

Visual Basic Programming

1. PREREQUISITES AND OBJECTIVES

You may skip this chapter if

You are already familiar with Visual Basic, Delphi, Visual Age, or some other component-based visual design tool.

Before starting this chapter, you should have

1. A general knowledge of programming.
2. Access to a computer. You should read this chapter while sitting at your computer.

After completing this chapter, you will have

1. A general familiarity with visual component-based programming.
2. A knowledge of how to use existing components to design an application.
3. Some knowledge of Visual Basic.

2. INTRODUCTION

Before you can develop new components, you must have an appreciation of how components are used. Learning Visual Basic is the easiest way to accomplish this. (Other reasonable starting points are the Delphi programming system, and the different JavaBeans visual editors.) Readers who are already familiar with component-based programming may wish to skip this chapter.

Learning Visual Basic is not particularly difficult. You can teach yourself this subject in a few hours. Nevertheless, the whole thing is much easer with a few guidelines. This chapter is intended not to be an extensive course in Visual Basic programming but merely to familiarize you with the fundamentals so you can begin learning on your own.

In this chapter, we will demonstrate how components are used to build applications, and familiarize you with the concepts of properties, events, and methods. The examples will be given in Visual Basic 6.0 and in VB.NET. The two versions of Visual Basic are significantly different, so much so that version 6.0 will probably remain in use for many years, despite being superseded by VB.NET.

3. PROPERTIES

Our first program demonstrates the use of properties. We begin by starting Visual Basic 6.0 and selecting **New Project** from the *File* menu. Then we select **Standard EXE** and click **OK**. (Your copy of Visual Basic may display this dialog automatically upon startup.) Figure 2-1 shows the Visual Basic version 6.0 development environment with the **New Project** dialog box displayed.*

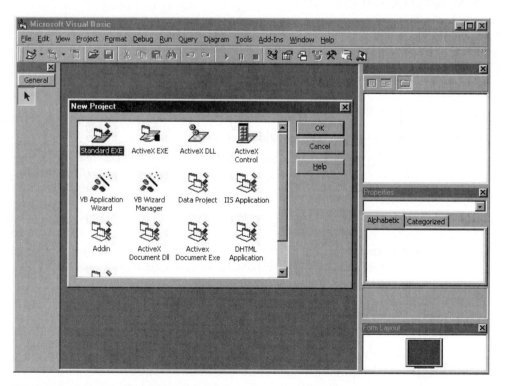

Figure 2-1   Creating a Visual Basic Project

---

*Screen shots reprinted by permission from Microsoft Corporation.

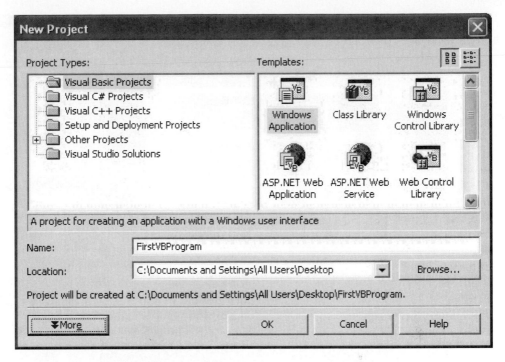

Figure 2-2 VB.NET New Project Dialog Box

The preceding steps will create a new project and display the full development window. To perform the same task in VB.NET, we start Visual Studio (VS.NET) and select **New** and then **Project** from the *File* menu. This will display the dialog box that appears in Figure 2-2. In this dialog box select **Visual Basic Projects** from the list at the left. (This may change the choices that appear in the window at the right.) From the window at the right, choose **Windows Application**. Type the name of the project in the **Name** box, and click **OK**.

At this point, we have a project window with a prototype view of our program's main window. We are going to create an application that does some simple text processing. To accomplish this, we will draw two text boxes into the prototype view of our window, which is entitled **Form1**. To do this in Visual Basic 6.0, we click on 🔲 in the toolbox at the left of the Visual Basic window. This gives us a cross-hairs cursor that will allow us to draw a rectangle on the **Form1** window. Drawing the rectangle will cause a text box to appear in the drawn rectangle. We repeat this process to draw a second text box. We now have two text boxes, as illustrated in Figure 2-3. These text boxes are examples of Visual Basic *controls*. Visual Basic allows us to use several different types of *components*; Visual Basic controls are one such type.

To perform the same task in VB.NET, we must first select the correct section of the toolbox by clicking on **Windows Forms**. This will display the section of the toolbox containing the standard controls, such as text boxes and buttons. We select the text box control by clicking on 🔲 TextBox from this section of the toolbox. As in Visual Basic 6.0,

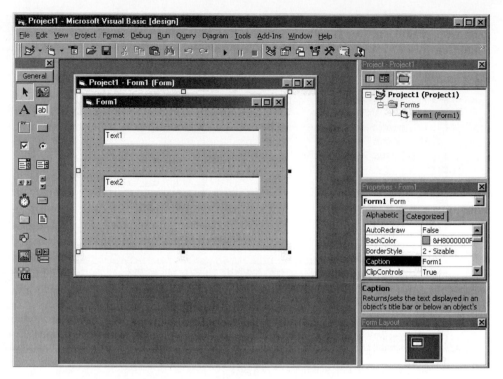

Figure 2-3   Adding Two Text Boxes

selecting this control will give us a cross-hairs cursor that will enable us to draw the two text boxes, shown in the window in Figure 2-4.

Surprisingly enough, we now have a complete, running, Visual Basic Program. We could run it as is, but the results would not be impressive. (If you are following along with this on your own computer, click on ▶ in the upper toolbar, in either version of Visual Basic, to see the program run.) Visual Basic programs are passive. They sit and wait for something to happen, or more correctly, they wait for an *event* to occur. As yet, we have no way to cause events. However, before we proceed to that, let's clean up the existing program. Our two text boxes already have text in them. These labels may be helpful while we are designing our program, but if we don't do something about them, they will also appear when our program runs. What we would like to see when the program runs is two blank text boxes. To achieve this, we must alter the properties of our two controls. This can be done either at design-time, or at run-time during the initialization process. We will do this at design-time.

First, we click on the upper text box to select it. We can tell that the upper text box is selected, because it is now displayed with eight *grab-handles* that allow us to change its size. Figure 2-5 shows the control with the grab-handles displayed.

Next, we go to the properties subwindow on the right-hand side of the Visual Basic window. The properties window is shown in Figure 2-6.

The first thing we see in the properties subwindow is the name of the control and its type. In the window below we see an alphabetic list of the component's properties,

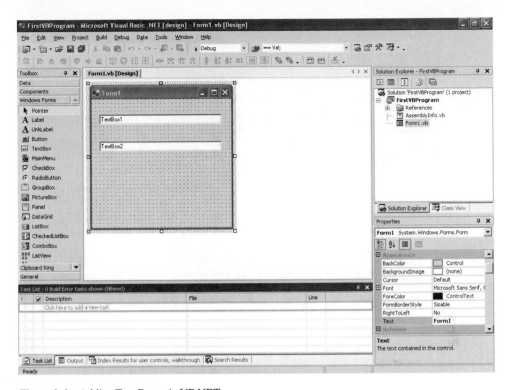

Figure 2-4   Adding Text Boxes in VB.NET

and their current values. On the left is the name of each property supported by the component. *Text* is an example of such a property. Visual Basic adds a number of additional properties, such as *TabIndex*, to those supported by the component. If a component has run-time-only properties, they will not be displayed in this list.

To the right of each property name is the value of the property *for this instance of the component.* Any two components of the same type will have the same list of property names, but the values of these properties will generally be different for each instance of the component. To get rid of the "*Text1*" or "*TextBox1*" label, we must change the value of the *Text* property. (If the *Text* property is not displayed, we must use the scroll bar at the right of the properties list to find it.) We want to delete this label entirely, so we select the label in the properties list, and press **Delete**. In VB.NET you may also need to press **Enter** to confirm the change. As we erase the text from the *Text* property, it also disappears from the text box in the **Form1** window. Even though we are in design mode, the component-instance is loaded and running. It is monitoring the state of its properties, and updating its display accordingly. We use the same procedure to erase the other label. It is important to remember that the *name* of the upper text box is *Text1* or *TextBox1* and the *name* of the lower text box is *Text2* or *TextBox2*. We will use these names in the remainder of our program.

In our simple text-processing example, the user will type some text into the *Text1/TextBox1* text box. We will examine this text and delete each instance of

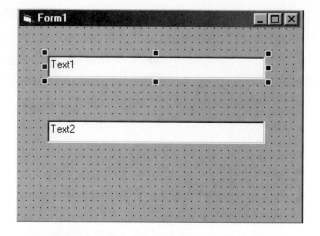

Figure 2-5   Selecting a Component

the letter "e." We will place the result into the *Text2/TextBox2* textbox. The following Visual Basic code will accomplish this in either version of Visual Basic:

```
' Declare Two Work Variables and a Loop Counter
Dim Work1 As String
Dim Work2 As String
Dim I As Integer

' Retrieve the contents of Text1
Work1 = Text1.Text
' Initialize Work2
Work2 = ""
' Examine each character of Text1
For I = 1 To Len(Work1)
```

```
      If Mid$(Work1,I,1) <> "e" Then
          ' Add to Work2 if not equal to "e"
          Work2 = Work2 & Mid$(Work1,I,1)
      End If
  Next I
  ' Save result in Text2
  Text2.Text = Work2
```

This code illustrates several of the most important features of the Visual Basic language. A comment begins with an apostrophe and continues to the end of the line. Variable declarations begin with the keyword **Dim** (for Dimension). The **For** loop, with a loop counter has the form "**For** <loop counter> = <starting value> **To** <ending value>. The body of the loop is terminated by a **Next** statement, which optionally names the counter variable specified in the **For** statement. An **If** statement has the form "**If** <condition> **Then**." The body of the **If** statement is terminated by an **End If** statement. The **Else** body of an **If** statement, if any, is introduced with an **Else** statement. If an **Else** statement is present, only one **End If** statement is used, and it terminates the **Else** body. Assignments are specified with an equal sign. The **Len** function is used to determine the length of a string, while the **Mid$** function is used to extract substrings. The **Mid$** function has three parameters, the first is the source string, the second is the starting position of the substring, and the third is the length of the substring. The first character in a string is position 1. Assignment statements use the typical **+, .−,** *, and **/** symbols to perform arithmetic. Comparison symbols are **=** for equal to, **<>** for not equal to, and the usual **<, >, <=,** and **>=** for the other four comparisons. The logical connectives are **And, Or,** and **Not**. The ampersand, **&**, is used for string concatenation. String constants are enclosed in double quotes, with " " representing the null string. As

Figure 2-6 The Property Sub-Window

in C, **Integer**s are used in place of Boolean variables, with zero representing false, and non-zero representing true. The constants **True** and **False** can be used. They have the numeric values −**1** and **0**, respectively. In addition to **For** loops, there are also **While** loops which have the form "**While** <condition>." The body of the **While** loop is terminated by a **Wend** statement. Code is written one statement per line. Under normal circumstances there cannot be more than one statement per line, nor can a statement be split between lines. (See the Visual Basic *Help* menu for exceptions to this rule.) Capitalization is not significant, so **Abc**, **ABC**, and **aBC** represent the same variable. References to component properties have the form "<instance name>.<property name>," with a period separating the instance name and the property name.

Unfortunately, we still have not answered the most important question: *Where do we put our code?*

As stated above, a Visual Basic program is passive; it responds only to events. Therefore, we must arrange for this code to be executed in response to some event. There are many different kinds of events, but the simplest are those that correspond to keystrokes and mouse clicks. We will arrange for our code to be executed in response to a mouse click. There are many ways to do this, but the simplest is to provide a button so that we have an obvious place to click the mouse, and some visual feedback for the action. A button is a component just like the text box. To create a button, we click on ▣ (Visual Basic 6.0) or **abl Button** (VB.NET) in the toolbox to the left of the Visual Basic window (see Figure 2-7). This will give us the cross-hairs cursor, which we will use to draw a rectangle on the **Form1** window. The result is shown in Figure 2-7. We have made a change so that the label on the button reads "My Button" instead of "Command1" or "Button1." In Visual Basic 6.0, the *Caption* property is used for this purpose, while in VB.NET, the *Text* property is used. The caption of the button is not the same as the *name* of the button, which remains *Command1* or *Button1*.

We want our code to execute whenever somebody clicks this button. To accomplish this, we simply double-click on the button. This will display the code window shown in Figure 2-8. Our code must be placed between the header line that reads "**Private Sub Command1_Click**" or "**Private Sub Button1_Click**" and termination line "**End Sub.**" In Visual Basic, subroutines are declared using the *Sub* keyword followed by the name of the subroutine. The **Private** keyword is optional. Any parameters are placed in parentheses following the function name. Parameter declarations have the same form as a **Dim** statement without the **Dim** keyword, which means that **MyStr As String** and **MyVal As Integer** are legitimate parameter declarations. Multiple parameter declarations are separated by commas. If there are no parameters, a pair of empty parentheses follows the subroutine name. The subroutine body begins immediately following the **Sub** statement, and is terminated by an **End Sub** statement. Subroutines do not return values. (We will discuss function declarations later.) In Visual Basic 6.0, the name of the subroutine is used to associate it with the button *Command1* and the *Click* event. In VB.NET, the *Handles* clause is used for this purpose. (The *Handles* clause permits one subroutine to be used for many different events. In Visual Basic 6.0, one subroutine can handle only one event.)

Once we type our code into this window, we're ready to go. All we need to do is go up to the toolbar and click on ▶. However, before we run our program, it is a good idea to save our project. To do this, we go up to the toolbar and click on 🖫. Unlike some compilers, Visual Basic 6.0 does not automatically save changes before

VB 6.0

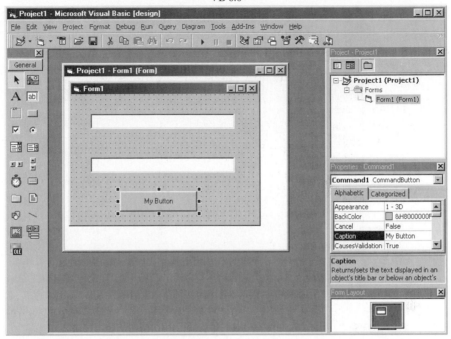

VB.NET

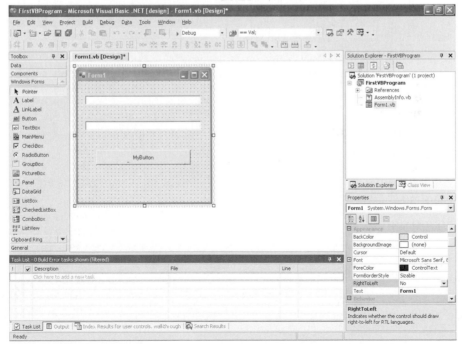

Figure 2-7   Adding a Button

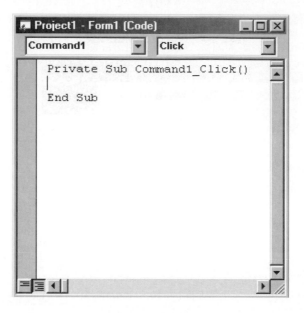

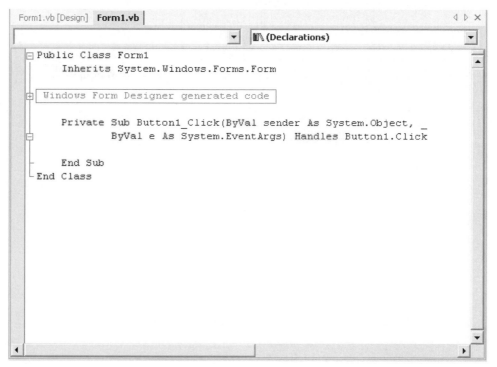

Figure 2-8   The Code Window

running a program. If our program were to blow up for some reason, Visual Basic itself might be terminated, taking all changes with it! (This happens quite often when testing new components.) When saving code, we will be prompted for a project-file name and a form-file name. We will first create a new directory named *Properties* for our project, and then save the form file as *Properties.frm* and the project file as *Properties.vbp*. VB.NET will save our changes before compiling.

Figure 2-9 shows how our program will look once it starts.

To test the program, we type some text in the top text box, and click on *My Button*. The result should look something like Figure 2-10. We now have our first working Visual Basic program.

Figure 2-9 Running the Program

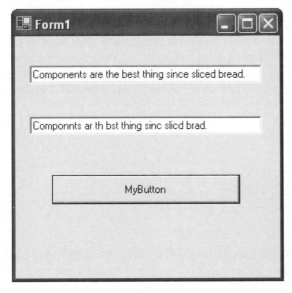

Figure 2-10 Testing the Program

4. EVENTS

Now that we're familiar with Visual Basic programming, we're ready to try something more adventurous. For the next step we will create an application that makes use of events. Because event handling is quite different in Visual Basic 6.0 and VB.NET, we will describe the two programs separately.

4.1 Event Handling in Visual Basic 6.0

We will begin by creating a window that has a button and a red circle. When the button is clicked, we will make the circle flash red and green for 10 seconds. To accomplish this, we will create a new project and will add three components to it. One of these components will be a button, which we already know how to do. The other two will be a Shape and a Timer. To add a shape, we must select ⬚ from the toolbox and draw a rectangle on the **Form1** window. To add a timer, we must select ⏱ from the toolbox, and either draw a rectangle or double-click on the **Form1** window. (The size of the timer component cannot be changed.) We must change several properties of our shape component, which will be named *Shape1*. These properties are the *Shape* property, which must be set to **2–Oval**; the *FillColor* property, which must be set to red (the color we decide to choose from the palette of colors that is offered to us); and the **FillStyle** property, which must be set to **0–Solid**. We must then adjust the boundaries of the oval so it looks round.

We will change the *Caption* property of the *Command1* button to "Flash," and we will check to make sure that the *Interval* property of the *Timer1* component is set to zero. The result should look something like Figure 2-11.

The key to this program is the correct management of the *Timer1* component. This component has only one event called *Timer*, and only one important property called *Interval*. When the *Interval* property is set to something other than zero, the *Timer* component will issue repeated Timer events at regular intervals. The interval at which the events are issued is determined by the *Interval* property. The value of this property is assumed to be the number of milliseconds between events. Thus if *Interval* property is set to 100, ten events are issued every second. If it is set to 1, a thousand events will be issued every second, if it is physically possible to do so. We will use the *Timer* events to flash the color of the circle. Clicking the button will start the process, and we will terminate the process after a fixed number of timer events has occurred. We will set the *Interval* property of *Timer1* to 100 to cause the circle to change color ten times per second, and we will stop the process after 100 *Timer* events have occurred. We will use a global variable to count the events.

To start the process, let us first double-click on the button and put in the code, which will look as follows:

```
Private Sub Command1_Click()
    Timer1.Interval = 100
    Counter = 0
    Shape1.FillColor = 255
End Sub
```

In this subroutine, we first set the *Interval* property of *Timer1* to 100, waking it up. We then set the global variable **Counter** to zero, indicating that zero timer events have occurred.

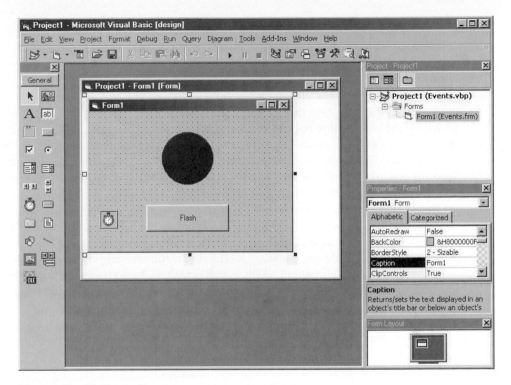

Figure 2-11   The Events Program

Finally, we set the *FillColor* property of *Shape1* to red, to make sure we're starting with the correct color. (The constant 255 specifies the color red; see the Visual *Help* menu for more information about how colors are represented.) It is necessary to define the global variable *Counter*. If we fail to do so, Visual Basic will create a declaration for us making *Counter* a local variable of type **Variant**. This is not what we want, so we must go to the top of the code window, and add the following line *before* the line reading "**Private Sub** Command1_Click( )":

```
Dim Counter As Integer
```

This global variable will be available to all event subroutines. Now let us add the continuing behavior to the program. We do this by double-clicking on the *Timer1* component and creating the following subroutine:

```
Private Sub Timer1_Timer()
    If Counter >= 100 Then
        Shape1.FillColor = 255
        Timer1.Interval = 0
        Exit Sub
    End If
    If (Counter Mod 2) = 0 Then
        Shape1.FillColor = &HFF00&
```

```
    Else
        Shape1.FillColor = &HFF&
    End If
    Counter = Counter + 1
End Sub
```

In this subroutine, the first thing we test for is to see if enough events have occurred. If so, we set the shape color back to red, we set the *Interval* property of *Timer1* to 0, turning it off, and exit the event subroutine using the **Exit Sub** statement. In the **If** statement, we decide whether to set the *FillColor* property of *Shape1* to red or green. The **Mod** operator is actually the remainder operator. This expression will tell us whether the global variable *Counter* contains an even or an odd value. If the value is even, we set the color to green; otherwise we set it to red. This **If** statement also demonstrates how to specify a hexadecimal constant, which begins with **&H** and ends with **&**. Legal digits are 0 through 9 as well as A, B, C, D, E, and F. The constant **&HFF&** is numerically equal to 255, while the constant **&HFF00&** is numerically equal to 65,280.

We now add one finishing touch to this program. To do this, we double-click anywhere in the **Form1** window *except on a component*. This will bring up the code window with the following subroutine:

```
Private Sub Form_Load()
End Sub
```

If we need to initialize our program, this is where we would do it. However, this is not the event we want. What we want is the *Unload* event of the form. The *Load* event occurs when the program starts, while the *Unload* event occurs when the program window disappears. In some cases, the program will not terminate when its window disappears, so we will force this to happen by adding some code to the *Unload* event. We begin by going to the top of the code window, where we see the word "Load" and click on the small button to the right of it. This displays the list of events for the form, as shown in Figure 2-12. We scroll this list down as far as it will go and click on the word "Unload." This will create the subroutine for the *Form_Unload* event. We can now delete the code for the *Form_Load* event, since it doesn't do anything. We must make sure also to delete the **End Sub** statement that terminates the subroutine.

We place one statement, the **End** statement, in the *Form_Unload* subroutine. This statement always forces the termination of the program, regardless of where it is executed. The *Form_Unload* subroutine looks as follows:

```
Private Sub Form_Unload(Cancel As Integer)
    End
End Sub
```

Note that the *Form_Unload* subroutine has one parameter. It is possible for events to have many different parameters, depending on the type of event. In this case, the *Cancel* parameter is used if it is necessary to refuse to close the window. To do this, set *Cancel* to some non-zero value, such as **True**. (If you do this, make sure you have

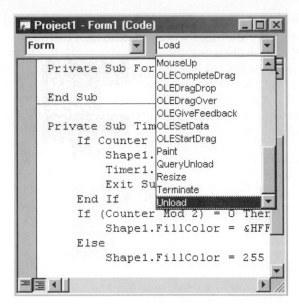

Figure 2-12 Selecting an Event

some other way of terminating your program, since the **X** button in the upper right will no longer work!)

We are now ready to test our program, but it is *absolutely necessary* to save it first. We are in some danger of sending our program into an infinite loop, and if this happens using **Ctrl-Alt-Delete** may be the only way of getting out of it. (In this case the danger is not so great, but in other examples it will be.) If we **Ctrl-Alt-Delete** out of this program, Visual Basic will go with it, destroying any changes since the last save.

We will call our program "Events" and store it in its own directory with appropriately named form and project files. Then, and only then, will we run our program. This should produce a display similar to that of Figure 2-13. Clicking on the *Flash* button should cause the red circle to flash red and green.

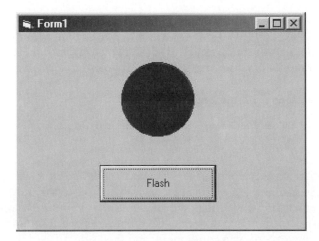

Figure 2-13 Running the Events Program

In addition to defining global variables, we can use the upper part of the code window to define general subroutines that are not associated with any event. To demonstrate how this works, we will change the pair of colors used to flash the circle. Instead of using explicit constants for red and green, we will use two more global variables, of type **Long** to contain the starting color and the flash color. Appropriately enough, we will call these *StartColor* and *FlashColor*. In the event routines, we will replace the explicit constants with references to the correct global variables. Once we finish our changes, we will have the following code:

```
Dim Counter As Integer
Dim StartColor As Long
Dim FlashColor As Long

Private Sub Command1_Click()
    Timer1.Interval = 100
    Counter = 0
    Shape1.FillColor = StartColor
End Sub

Private Sub Form_Unload(Cancel As Integer)
    End
End Sub

Private Sub Timer1_Timer()
    If Counter >= 100 Then
        Shape1.FillColor = StartColor
        Timer1.Interval = 0
        Exit Sub
    End If
    If (Counter Mod 2) = 0 Then
        Shape1.FillColor = FlashColor
    Else
        Shape1.FillColor = StartColor
    End If
    Counter = Counter + 1
End Sub
```

We will use a subroutine to set the values of these two global variables. This subroutine will have two parameters and will be defined as follows:

```
Sub SetColors(SC As Long, FC As Long)
    FlashColor = FC
    StartColor = SC
End Sub
```

This code must immediately follow the line that reads "**Dim** FlashColor **As Long**." As soon as we type the first line of this function, Visual Basic will automatically supply the **End Sub** statement. Now we will add a *Form_Load* subroutine to make sure the global variables start with the correct values. To create this, we double-click anywhere in the **Form1** window, except on a component, and then select *Load* from the list of events. This code also ensures that *Shape1* starts with the correct color. Note that when a subroutine is called in Visual Basic, the parameters are listed without parentheses. The call to *SetColors* would be syntactically incorrect if we placed parentheses around the parameter list:

```
Private Sub Form_Load()
    SetColors &HFF&, &HFF00&
    Shape1.FillColor = StartColor
End Sub
```

Now, to make things more interesting, we will add two more buttons to switch between the "standard" colors and two alternate colors. For the alternate colors, we will use magenta and yellow, with magenta being the starting color. The hexadecimal constants for magenta and yellow are **&HFF00FF&** and **&HFFFF&** respectively. The button to select the alternate colors will be named *Command2*, while the button for the standard colors will be named *Command3*. The captions of these buttons will be *Alternate* and *Standard* respectively. The following is the *Click* event code for these two buttons:

```
Private Sub Command2_Click()
    SetColors &HFF00FF& &HFFFF&
    Shape1.FillColor = StartColor
End Sub

Private Sub Command3_Click()
    SetColors &HFF&, &HFF00&
    Shape1.FillColor = StartColor
End Sub
```

Figure 2-14 shows our new program just after it starts running, while Figure 2-15 shows it after clicking on the *Alternate* button.

In addition to defining our own subroutines, we can also define our own functions. The difference between a subroutine and a function is that a function returns a

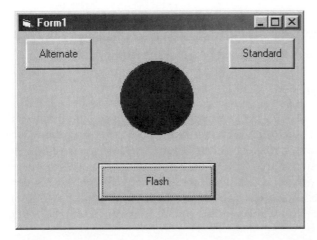

Figure 2-14   The Enhanced Events Program

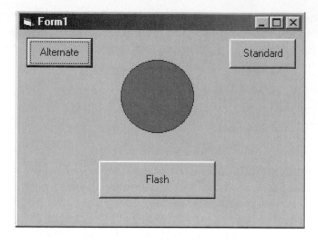

Figure 2-15   Alternate colors

value. The following is a function that squares its two arguments, computes the sum, and returns the result:

```
Function Squareit(X As Integer, Y As Integer) As Integer
    Dim Result As Integer

    Result = (X * X) + (Y * Y)
    Squareit = Result
End Function
```

This function definition (if we had any use for it) must be placed at the top of the code window, as was the definition for *SetColors*. A function must have a declaration of its return type following the parameter list. The result is returned by assigning a value to the function name. The function body is terminated with an **End Function** statement. Similarly, to exit a function in the middle, an **Exit Function** statement is used.

To use this function, we would use a statement similar to the following:

```
X = Squareit(3,5)
```

Unlike subroutines, it is necessary to enclose function parameters in parentheses.

By now you may be getting tired of these silly examples. The next section will allow us to do some things that, at least in some sense, are more useful than flashing colors.

4.2 Event Handling in VB.NET

There are many changes between Visual Basic 6.0 and VB.NET, and many of them will be evident as we develop the VB.NET version of the *Events* program. Because the shape control has been eliminated, we must either provide our own circle control or use something else as a substitute. The easiest alternative is to change the circle to a rectangle and replace it with a label control that has no text. From the **Windows Forms** section of the toolbar, we select two controls: the label **A Label** and the timer ⏱ Timer. The label is drawn on the prototype window, as would any other control. We can do the

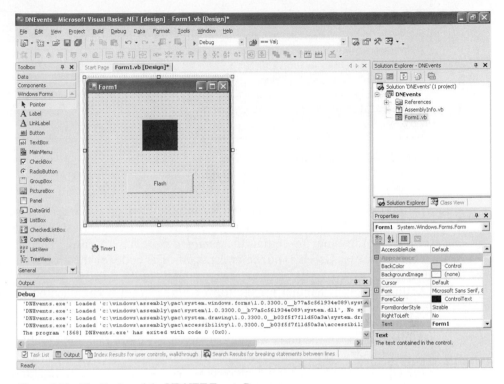

Figure 2-16   The Design of the VB.NET Events Program

same for the timer, but the icon will not appear in the prototype window and will be added instead to the list of nonvisual controls below the prototype window. The usage of the component has not changed, but it no longer consumes valuable screen real estate. After adding a button, we end up with the design illustrated in Figure 2-16.

To create the red square, we simply add a label control and set the *Text* property to the empty string, the border to style to *FixedSingle*, and the *BackColor* to red.

The *Click* event for the button requires some modification in VB.NET, since setting the *Interval* property to zero is no longer the method used to disable it. In fact, it is now illegal to set the *Interval* property of a timer to zero. The *Enabled* property is now used to enable and disable the timer. We no longer use global variables in VB.NET. Anything that would have been specified as a global variable must now be specified as a member of the private class **Form1**. This also holds for event handlers and auxiliary functions. Double-click the button to add an event handler. Like all event handlers in VB.NET, this one has two properties. For now, we can safely ignore them. After adding the event handler *Button1_Click*, we add the counter variable immediately preceding the definition of the event-handler. The *BackColor* property of the label is used to change the color of the square, but colors must be handled differently in VB.NET. When assigning to a color variable, one must use a member of the **Color** class. In this case we will use the constant member **Red**, which will set the background to red. The resultant code appears in Figure 2-17.

```
Dim Counter As Integer
Private Sub Button1_Click(ByVal sender As System.Object, _
    ByVal e As System.EventArgs) Handles Button1.Click
    Timer1.Interval = 100
    Timer1.Enabled = True
    Counter = 0
    Label1.BackColor = Color.Red
End Sub
```

Figure 2-17   Timer Enabling Code

To add the timer *Tick* event handler, we double-click on the timer icon below the prototype window. This code is essentially the same as the Visual Basic 6.0 code, except we will disable the timer by setting the *Enabled* property to **False**, and we will use **Color.Red** and **Color.Green** as our color constants. The code for the *Tick* event is given in Figure 2-18.

Adding an event handler for the form *Unload* event is complicated by the fact that this event no longer exists and has been replaced by the *Closed* event. Furthermore, the mechanism for creating event handlers for form events has also changed.

We first bring up the code window in any convenient fashion. Double-clicking on the prototype window will create an event handler for the form *Load* event. Once the code window has been displayed, we go to the left combo box and display the list, as illustrated in Figure 2-19. Select (**Base Class Events**) from this list. The list of available events will appear in the right-hand drop-down list, as illustrated in Figure 2-20.

```
Private Sub Timer1_Tick(ByVal sender As System.Object, _
    ByVal e As System.EventArgs) Handles Timer1.Tick
    If Counter >= 100 Then
        Label1.BackColor = Color.Red
        Timer1.Enabled = False
        Exit Sub
    End If
    If (Counter Mod 2) = 0 Then
        Label1.BackColor = Color.Green
    Else
        Label1.BackColor = Color.Red
    End If
    Counter = Counter + 1
End Sub
```

Figure 2-18   The VB.NET Tick Event Handler

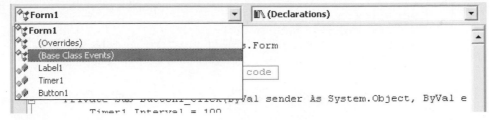

Figure 2-19   Getting at the Form Events

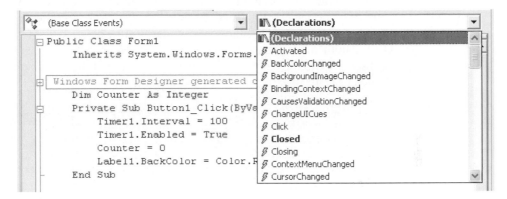

Figure 2-20   The Form Event List

```
    Private Sub Form1_Closed(ByVal sender As Object, _
        ByVal e As System.EventArgs) Handles MyBase.Closed
        End
    End Sub
```

Figure 2-21   The Event Handler for the Closed Event

To create the event handler for the *Closed* event, we select **Closed** from the drop-down list. This will give us the event handler given in Figure 2-21, to which we have added the **End** statement.

Once this final event handler has been added, we can run the program. It is not necessary to save our work because VB.NET automatically saves all files before compiling. (You may also notice that the compile step is now separate, so we can compile our program without running it.)

From here, the development of the enhanced version of the *Events* program proceeds much like the Visual Basic 6.0 enhanced version. The definition of the *SetColors* subroutine is much the same, except for the type declarations of the arguments. This function must be a member of the **Form1** class. The variables *FlashColor* and *StartColor* must also be members of this class. Figure 2-22 shows the new definitions.

```
Dim FlashColor As Color
Dim StartColor As Color
Sub SetColors(ByVal SC As Color, ByVal FC As Color)
    FlashColor = FC
    StartColor = SC
End Sub
```

Figure 2-22   New Definitions

One important difference between Visual Basic 6.0 and VB.NET is the manner in which functions must be called. In Visual Basic 6.0, subroutine arguments must be specified without parentheses, while function arguments must be specified with parentheses. In VB.NET both subroutine arguments and function arguments must be specified with parentheses. Note the call to *SetColors* in the event handlers of Figure 2-23.

The enhanced *Events* program is illustrated in Figure 2-24.

```
Private Sub Button2_Click(ByVal sender As System.Object, _
    ByVal e As System.EventArgs) Handles Button2.Click
    SetColors(Color.Magenta, Color.Yellow)
    Label1.BackColor = Color.Magenta
End Sub

Private Sub Button3_Click(ByVal sender As System.Object, _
    ByVal e As System.EventArgs) Handles Button3.Click
    SetColors(Color.Red, Color.Green)
    Label1.BackColor = Color.Red
End Sub
```

Figure 2-23   Calling Subroutines in VB.NET

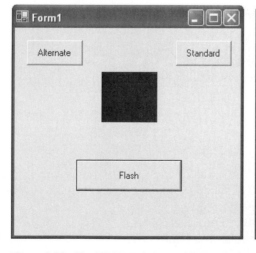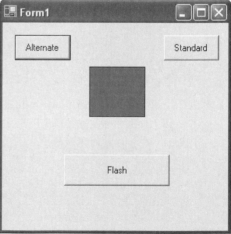

Figure 2-24   The VB.NET Enhanced Events Program

5. METHODS

Methods are simply functions and subroutines that are implemented by a component. (Visual Basic distinguishes functions and subroutines by whether or not a value is returned.) To illustrate the use of a method, we will create our own Web browser. At first this may seem a bit fantastic, but such is the power of component-level programming.

Up to this point, the only components we have used are Visual Basic controls. For this application, we will add an ActiveX control to our project. The first step, of course, is to start Visual Basic and create a new project. To add a new component, we use the Components command of the Project menu, as illustrated in Figure 2-25.

The components command will cause the component selection dialog box to appear. As Figure 2-26 shows, this dialog box contains a list of all ActiveX controls installed on the system. (The list is generally a long one.) It is necessary for us to find the correct control, and click on the check box in front of it to add it to our project. We now want to add *Microsoft Internet Controls* to our project, as indicated in the figure.

Adding this control to our project will cause a new icon to appear in the toolbox on the left of the Visual Basic window. This new icon resembles a globe, as shown in Figure 2-27.

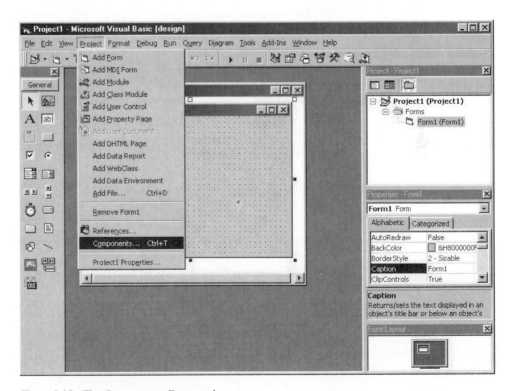

Figure 2-25   The Components Command

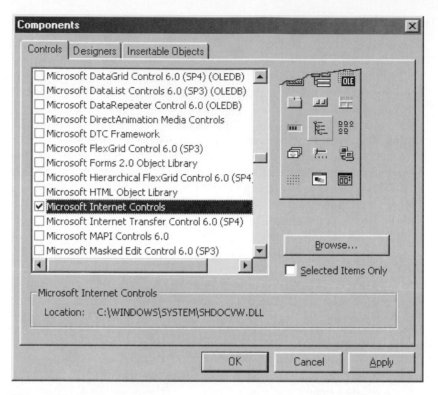

Figure 2-26   The Components Menu

Figure 2-27   The Web Browser
Component Icon

In VB.NET, the procedure for adding the Internet control is slightly different. To add this
component to your project, right-click on the toolbox and select **Customize Toolbox** ...,
as shown in Figure 2-28. Click on the **COM Components** tab as shown in Figure 2-29 and
locate the entry **Microsoft Web Browser**. Click the box in front of this entry, as shown in
Figure 2-29, to add the browser control to your toolbox. The appearance of the control in
the VB.NET toolbox is similar to that of Visual Basic 6.0, as Figure 2-30 shows. Once this
control has been inserted into your toolbox, you can relocate it to the most convenient
section.

    We select the new control from the toolbox, and draw a large instance of it. This
control will be our Web browser window, so it is advantageous for it to be as large as

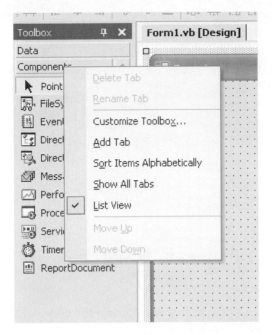

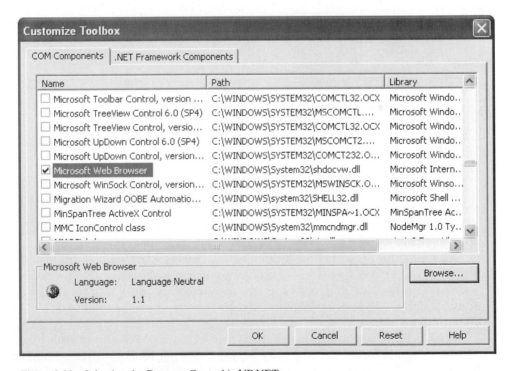

Figure 2-28   Customizing the VB.NET Toolbox

Figure 2-29   Selecting the Browser Control in VB.NET

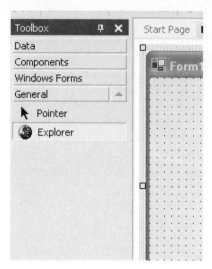

Figure 2-30   The VB.NET Browser Icon

possible. We will also add a button to our project that will contain the code below. (The VB.NET code follows the Visual Basic 6.0 code.)

```
Private Sub Command1_Click()

    WebBrowser1.Navigate "http://cs.baylor.edu/~maurer"

End Sub


Private Sub Button1_Click(ByVal sender As System.Object, _
         ByVal e As System.EventArgs) Handles Button1.Click
    AxWebBrowser1.Navigate("http://cs.baylor.edu/~maurer")
End Sub
```

The *Navigate* method of the **Web Browser** control is used to display a Web page. If your computer is connected to the Internet, you can substitute any URL you wish for http://cs.baylor.edu/~maurer. If you are not connected to the Internet, you should change it so it refers to a file on your system. Figure 2-31 shows the finished VB.NET program, ready to run. The Visual Basic 6.0 version is similar.

Running our program and clicking on the **Navigate** button will produce the results shown in Figure 2-32. The hyperlinks are active, so it is possible to navigate to other pages without leaving our program. The ActiveX control that we added to our project is, in fact, the Internet Explorer display window. It can be used to display many different types of files.

You may have noticed that there are many other ActiveX controls available on the system. Figure 2-33 shows my Visual Basic 6.0 toolbox after adding about three-fourths of my ActiveX controls to a project. (I don't exactly collect these things either.)

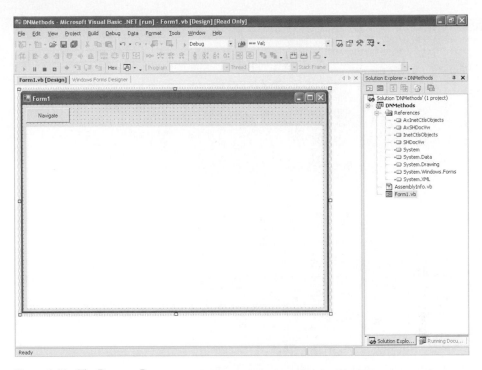

Figure 2-31   The Browser Program

Figure 2-32   Running the Browser Program

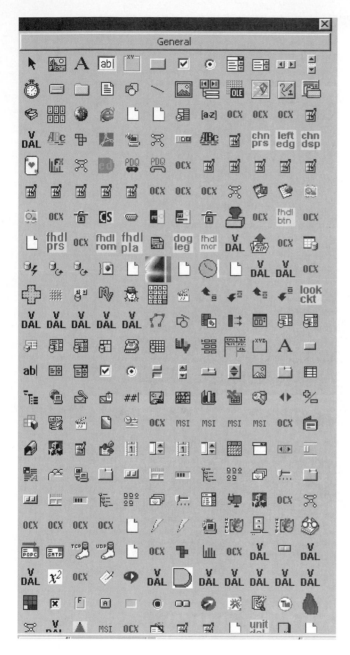

Figure 2-33 A Rather Large Toolbox

6. DATABASE APPLICATIONS

No discussion of Visual Basic would be complete without an example of a database application. Database applications are what convinced the world that Visual Basic was a good idea, and what ultimately created the component-level programming revolution. The techniques for creating database applications have been more or less the same in all versions of Visual Basic, starting with version 3.0. However, VB.NET introduces an enhanced set of procedures that are significantly different from those used in earlier versions of Visual Basic. For simplicity, we will present only the Visual Basic 6.0 version of this program.

Every year (or almost ever year) since 1953, the World Science Fiction Convention has given the Hugo Award for the best science fiction novel of the year. To illustrate an example of a database, we will create a list of Hugo Award winners. The list includes many of the classic science fiction works—from *Rendezvous with Rama* to *Starship Troopers*. The database presents all novels that have won this award along with the year and the name of the author. The information is organized into two tables—one with the names of the books and one with the names of the authors—called *Books* and *Authors* respectively. The database also contains a query named *List* that ties these two tables together and provides a list of books with the names of the authors. Figure 2-34 shows the two tables, and Figure 2-35 shows the query. The database is stored in a file named "hawn.mdb." (If you don't have this file, you can download it from URL http://cs.baylor.edu/~maurer.)

Authors : Table

Auth	FirstNam	MiddleNa	LastName
1	Alfred		Bester
2	Mark		Clifton
3	Frank		Riley
4	Robert	A	Heinlein
5	Fritz		Leiber
6	James		Blish
7	Walter	M	Miller Jr.

Record: 1 of 3

Books : Table

BookID	Title	Year	Author
14	The Moon is a Harsh Mistress	1967	4
15	Lord of Light	1968	9
16	Stand on Zanzibar	1969	12
17	The Left Hand of Darkness	1970	13
18	Ringworld	1971	14
19	To Your Scattered Bodies Go	1972	15
20	The Gods Themselves	1973	16
21	Rendezvous with Rama	1974	17

Record: 1 of 47

Figure 2-34   The Authors and Books Tables

	Year	FirstNam	LastName	Title
	1959	James	Blish	A Case of Conscience
	1960	Robert	Heinlein	Starship Troopers
	1961	Walter	Miller Jr.	A Canticle for Leibowitz
	1962	Robert	Heinlein	Stranger in a Strange Land
	1963	Philip	Dick	The Man in the High Castle
	1964	Clifford	Simak	Way Station

List : Select Query

Record: I◄ ◄   1 ► ►I ►* of 47

Figure 2-35   The List Query

As always, the first step is to create a new Visual Basic project. After doing this, we add a data control to our project, by clicking on 🖳 in the toolbox, and drawing a rectangle. We will change the caption of the resultant data control to *Hugo Awards*, but we will leave its name as *Data1*. The result is shown in Figure 2-36. We must change two other properties of this data control. The first is the *DatabaseName* property. The value field of this property contains a small button when the property is selected. We need to click on this button and locate the file *hawn.mdb* on our hard drive. This associates the data control with the database file. The next property is *RecordSource*. This property cannot be changed until the *DatabaseName* property has a legal value. The value field

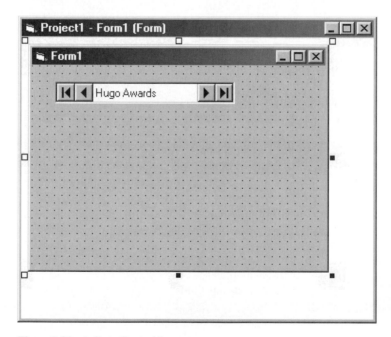

Figure 2-36   A Data Control Instance

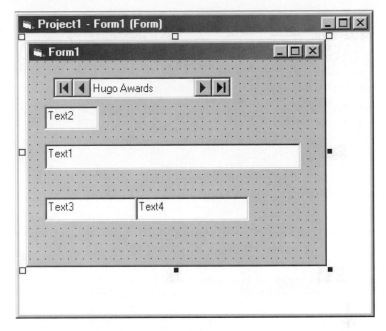

Figure 2-37   A Complete Database Application

of the *RecordSource* property also contains a button when the property is selected. When we click on this button we get a list of the tables and queries contained in *hawn.mdb*. We select the name *List* from this list. We are now ready to hook our data control to other controls.

As was shown in Figure 2-35, the *List* query has four fields, *Year*, *FirstName*, *Last-Name*, and *Title*. We must provide four text boxes, one for each field. The arrangement of these text boxes is arbitrary. The one presented in Figure 2-37 will do just fine.

It is not necessary to change the *Text* property of these four text boxes, since they will be initialized with data from the first record in the *List* query. It is necessary, however, to associate each text box with a field in the database. This is done by hooking the text boxes to the data control using the *DataSource* and *DataField* properties of each text box. Like most of the other properties we have dealt with, the value of the *DataSource* property will have a button in it when the property is selected. Clicking on this button will give us a list of all data controls in the project. In this case, we have only one data control named *Data1*, which we select for each of the four text boxes.

Once the *DataSource* property is set for each of the four text boxes, we can set the *DataField* property of each. The *DataField* property will also have a button in its value field. Clicking on this button will give a list of the fields in the *List* query. (Recall that *Data1* is now hooked into the *List* query.) For *Text2*, we select the field *Year*, for *Text1* we select the field *Title*, for *Text3* we select the field *FirstName*, and for *Text4* we select the field *LastName*. These changes will make no visible change in the appearance of the project. Once they are complete, however, we can run the project to obtain the display shown in Figure 2-38.

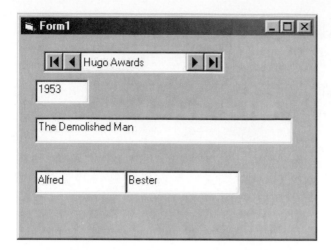

Figure 2-38 The Database
Application Running

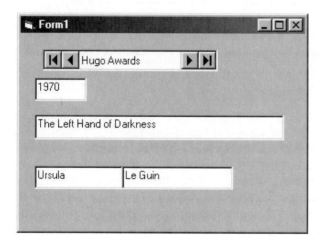

Figure 2-39 The First Le Guin
Award

We can use the buttons on the data control to scroll from one record to the next. As we do this, the contents of the four fields will change. This program is not just a data-display program, however. To demonstrate this, scroll forward to 1970, which will give us the display shown in Figure 2-39.

We will change the author's last name by deleting the space. The result will be "LeGuin." Now scroll forward to 1975. This will give us the display shown in Figure 2-40. Notice how the change appears in this record as well. This is because there is really only one copy of the author's name in the database, and changing it in one place will permanently change it everywhere it is displayed. Changes to any of the four text boxes will be permanently recorded in the database. If we had wanted to, we could have added buttons that would allow us to add and delete records. These changes are left as an exercise for you.

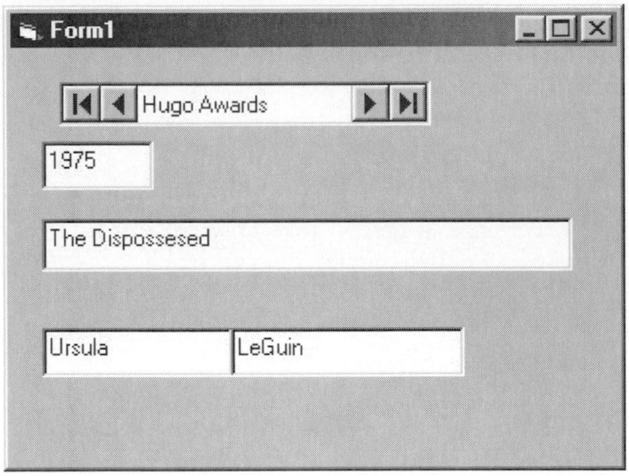

Figure 2-40   The Second Le Guin Award

7. "REAL" PROGRAMMING IN VISUAL BASIC

In recent years there has been much discussion about whether or not Visual Basic is a "real" programming language, or whether it is just a prototyping language. This argument is silly, because Visual Basic is obviously a real programming language. It supports loops, if statements, assignments, functions, and subroutines. Any language that does that is a real programming language.

The real question that comes to mind is this: When creating a new application, can a significant amount of the code be written in Visual Basic, or must we write nearly everything in C++ or some other language and just use Visual Basic to glue things together? My vote would be in favor of developing a significant portion of the code in Visual Basic. Even if there is a performance penalty, it may not be noticeable. If the performance penalty is too great, we can always rewrite the most time-consuming portions of the code in another language. To prove that "real" programming can be done in Visual Basic, we will develop a "real" program directly in Visual Basic. I've put the word "real" in quotes because our real program is actually just an exercise taken from an introductory programming book.

The problem we will solve is a classic one known as the sieve of Eratosthenes: The task is to find all prime numbers between 1 and 1000. Starting with 2, we cross out all multiples of 2, then cross out all multiples of 3, and so forth until we have the desired list of prime numbers. We then display each prime number on a separate line in our text box. The only new thing in this program is setting the *MultiLine* property of the textbox to **True** and the *ScrollBars* property to **3–Both**.

The actual program will be inserted into the *Click* event of our button. Our program is as follows:

```
Private Sub Command1_Click()
    Dim Sieve(1000) As Integer
    Dim I As Integer, J As Integer
```

```
'Set up a list of -Potential- primes
'Zero will indicate that the corresponding index is not prime
For I = 1 To 1000
    Sieve(I) = I
Next I
'One is not prime
Sieve(1) = 0
'The following loop will search for a prime and then cross out
'All of its non-unit multiples. We begin the search with 1.
I = 1
'Using I*I instead of I to terminate the search works,
'And is more efficient than using I.
While I * I <= 1000
    'Find the next prime, if any
    While I * I <= 1000 And Sieve(I) = 0
        I = I + 1
    Wend
    'if we found a prime
    If I * I <= 1000 Then
        'skip the prime itself
        J = I + I
        'cross out all non-unit multiples of the prime
        While J <= 1000
            Sieve(J) = 0
            J = J + I
        Wend
        'continue searching for primes with the next value of I
        I = I + 1
    End If
Wend
'Blank out the textbox
Text1.Text = ""
For I = 1 To 1000
    'if this number is prime, convert it to a string and add it
    'to the textbox. Chr(13) is a return Chr(10) is a linefeed.
    If Sieve(I) <> 0 Then
        Text1.Text=Text1.Text&Format(Sieve(I))&Chr(13)&Chr(10)
    End If
Next I
End Sub
```

Running the "real" program will produce the results shown in Figure 2-41. On my computer, the prime numbers appear instantaneously as soon as the button is clicked.

8. CONCLUSION

A number of visual languages have been introduced over the past several years, of which Visual Basic is by far the most successful. The Visual Basic component interface,

Figure 2-41 Prime Numbers Between 1 and 1000

which is now more or less standard, is the Properties/Methods/Events interface. Once you have familiarized yourself with Visual Basic, you will have a good idea of what the external interface of a component is like. In the remaining chapters, we will describe how to construct this interface and how to construct the internals of a component.

EXERCISES

1. Create a Visual Basic database program to index your CD collection. Make sure that the program will work for both classical and popular music.

2. Use the Visual Basic image control to create a file viewer. Your file viewer should list the contents of a directory and allow a user to select a file. You must then load the selected file into the image control to display it.

3. Access the following Web page, which will install the "cards" ActiveX control on your computer: http://cs.baylor.edu/~maurer/vdal/cardgames/stowers.htm. Use this control to create an implementation of your favorite solitaire game.

Chapter 3

A Brief Survey of Component Technologies

1. PREREQUISITES AND OBJECTIVES

Before starting this chapter, you should have

1. A knowledge of basic definitions (Chapter 1).
2. Familiarity with component-level programming (Chapter 2).

After completing this chapter, you will have

1. A knowledge of what a component is and is not.
2. A knowledge of existing component technologies.

2. INTRODUCTION

Since the beginning of the component revolution, many new component technologies have been introduced. In this chapter, we discuss a number of different technologies, each of which has its own unique features. There are, however, certain features that we insist that every component technology provide. These requirements are given briefly in Figure 3-1.

With the exception of simple controls, all existing component technologies provide these features. We have strong reasons for insisting that all technologies have these features, but the reasons are not necessarily obvious. We insist that a component be a complete, self-contained entity, not a partially constructed solution to some problem. This is the fundamental difference between component-level technologies and

1.	A component must be an independently compiled program. It must not be a function library, it must not be source code.
2.	It must be possible to integrate components to create a larger program, without having access to the source code of the component and without linking the code of the component into the program that uses it.
3.	A component must be embeddable in a container and must provide mechanisms for communicating between the component and its container.
4.	A component technology must support *Properties*, *Methods*, and *Events*, or some equivalent method of communication.
5.	A component technology should provide support for persistent properties. It should be possible to set the value of a property at design time and to have that value be the initial value of the property when the component is activated.
6.	A component should describe its own interface. It should be possible to query the component to determine what *Properties*, *Methods*, and *Events* that it supports.
7.	A component should be usable in a wide variety of different environments.

Figure 3-1   The Key Features of Component Technology

earlier technologies that provide static and dynamic function libraries. If features 1 and 2 are not present, then we are dealing with a function-library technology, not with a component technology. If feature 3 is not present, then we are dealing with application programs, not with components. If feature 4 is not present, then the component technology is useless because communication with components is impossible. Again, we are probably dealing with application programs rather than components.

Features 5, 6, and 7 are not essential, but programming with components is quite difficult without them.

3. SIMPLE CONTROLS

The first components were simple controls designed to be incorporated into dialog boxes. These included standard items such as buttons and text boxes—simple controls that are still in wide use today. Although the underlying implementations are far less sophisticated than more recent technologies, they are true components because they are independent programs that interact with their environment in a predefined way. A simple control has its own window that must be embedded in another window called the *parent* window. The most common method of communication is via messages that are passed between the control and its parent. (There are other implementation styles, but they tend to imitate the basic form in most important respects.)

Message passing can be either active or passive. Each independent program is required to implement a message-processing function. In passive communication, messages are posted to a message queue. The program must then fetch the messages and pass them to the message-processing function. In active communication, a program makes a direct call to another program's message-processing function. In either case, the message must be interpreted to determine what action is necessary.

The message-passing style of communication is quite different from the *Properties/Events/Methods* style of more recent technologies. Message passing is a *request-oriented* mechanism. An entity sends a request to another entity in the form of a message and receives a reply either synchronously through the return value of the messaging function or asynchronously through a return message. The types of requests are generally tailored specifically for the type of component. Asynchronous conditions that arise in the control must be reported to the parent using still other types of messages. Figure 3-2 illustrates the setting of property values for simple controls using messages, while Figure 3-3 illustrates how to retrieve values from the controls. (The details of the message-passing mechanisms need not concern us here.)

```c
// Set Radio Button value
HWND hWndDrawMode = GetDlgItem(IDC_DRAWMODE);
HWND hWndDrawMode1 = GetDlgItem(IDC_DRAWMODE1);
if (DrawMode)
{
    SendMessage(hWndDrawMode,BM_SETCHECK,BST_UNCHECKED,0);
    SendMessage(hWndDrawMode1,BM_SETCHECK,BST_CHECKED,0);
}
else
{
    SendMessage(hWndDrawMode,BM_SETCHECK,BST_CHECKED,0);
    SendMessage(hWndDrawMode1,BM_SETCHECK,BST_UNCHECKED,0);
}

// Set check-box value
HWND hWndMarkPrimary = GetDlgItem(IDC_MARKPRIMARY);
if (MarkPrimary)
{
    SendMessage(hWndMarkPrimary,BM_SETCHECK,BST_CHECKED,0);
}
else
{
    SendMessage(hWndMarkPrimary,BM_SETCHECK,BST_UNCHECKED,0);
}

// Set text-box value
HWND hWndOrientation = GetDlgItem(IDC_ORIENTATION);
wsprintf(TempChar,"%d",Orientation);
SendMessage(hWndOrientation,WM_SETTEXT,0,(long)TempChar);
```

Figure 3-2   Setting Property Values for Simple Controls

```
HWND hWndDrawMode1 = GetDlgItem(IDC_DRAWMODE1);
BOOL DrawMode = SendMessage(hWndDrawMode1,BM_GETCHECK,0,0);

HWND hWndMarkPrimary = GetDlgItem(IDC_MARKPRIMARY);
BOOL MarkPrimary = SendMessage(hWndMarkPrimary,BM_GETCHECK,0,0);

HWND hWndOrientation = GetDlgItem(IDC_ORIENTATION);
SendMessage(hWndOrientation,WM_GETTEXT,20,(long)TempChar);
long Orientation = atol(TempChar);
```

Figure 3-3   Retrieving Property Values for Simple Controls

The operations illustrated in Figures 3-2 and 3-3 correspond to setting and re-trieving property values. In addition to these sorts of messages, there are message codes that correspond to method calls. For example, we can send a message to a text box that will cause it to undo the most recent change.

The container of the control, which is also known as the *parent* of the control, can intercept and process messages from the control. For example, a message is sent to the parent of a button whenever the button is clicked.

Although message passing is a more primitive mechanism than the communica-tion mechanisms used in more recent technologies, it permits direct communication between two entities. In particular, it supports peer-to-peer communication between components, something that is difficult to implement using the *Properties/Events/ Methods* style of communication.

4. VBX

VBX technology is built on top of the message-passing mechanism used by simple con-trols. VBX technology supports properties, events, and (to some degree) methods, and for the most part these are implemented using the message-passing mechanism. One way to read a property value is for the container to send a message to the component requesting the value of the property and supplying the address of the location where the value should be stored. It is also possible to read property values directly without informing the component. Although methods are supported, they must be chosen from a predefined list of names, which include **reset**, **clear**, and **additem**. The parameter lists of these methods are also predefined. A method call is implemented as a special mes-sage to the component, with method operands encoded as operands of the message.

Each VBX component has a message-processing function, which normally ends up being the most important part of the VBX implementation. Figure 3-4 illustrates part of a message-processing function.

The message-processing loop is the starting point for all VBX activity. There are messages that signal the creation and destruction of a component instance, and other messages that are used to pass user input into the component. User input includes mouse clicks, keyboard input, scrolling activity, and a number of other things. These types of messages permit the component to respond directly to user input. In addition

to user input, there are messages that are used to signal property access and separate
messages for accessing the value of a property and for setting its value. These messages
permit the component to exhibit complex behavior in response to property assignments. Other types of messages tell the component when it is necessary to repaint the
window, when it has been resized, and when any other user-controllable property has
been changed. A special message is used to indicate that a method has been executed.
This message will indicate which of the standard functions has been executed, and it
will also supply the parameters for the call.

```
long FAR PASCAL _export SchematCtlProc(HCTL hctl,HWND hwnd,
                        USHORT msg,USHORT wparam,LONG lparam)
{
    LPSCHEMATINFO CtlStruct;
    switch (msg)
    {
        case WM_NCCREATE:
        {
            CtlStruct = (LPSCHEMATINFO)VBDerefControl(hctl);
            … // initialization
        }
        break;
        case WM_NCDESTROY:
        {
            CtlStruct = (LPSCHEMATINFO)VBDerefControl(hctl);
            … // Termination
        }
        break;
        case WM_HSCROLL:
        {
            CtlStruct = (LPSCHEMATINFO)VBDerefControl(hctl);
            … // horizontal scrolling
        }
        break;
        … // other mesages
        case VBM_SETPROPERTY:
        {
            switch (wparam)
            {
                case IPROP_SCHEMAT_ACTION: // property ID
                {
                    CtlStruct = (LPSCHEMATINFO)VBDerefControl(hctl);
                    … // handle property input
                }
                break;
                … // Other properties
```

Figure 3-4   A Control Message-Processing Function

```
        }
    }
    break;
    case VBM_GETPROPERTY:
    {
        switch (wparam)
        {
            case IPROP_SCHEMAT_CELLNAME: // Property ID
            {
                CtlStruct = (LPSCHEMATINFO) VBDerefControl(hctl);
                ...// handle property output
            }
            ... // Other properties
        }
    }
    break;
    case VBM_METHOD:
    {
        CtlStruct = (LPCELLEDITINFO) VBDerefControl(hctl);
        switch (wParam)
        {
            case METH_ADDITEM:
            {
                ... // handle ADDITEM method
            }
            break;
            ... // other methods
        }
    }
    break;
    ... // other messages
    }
}
```

Figure 3-4 (*Continued*)

An important innovation provided by the VBX technology is the *control struct*, which is used to hold the data for a particular instance of a VBX control. One control struct is allocated for each instance of the control. The mechanisms for handling the control struct leave a great deal to be desired, but it is a reasonable way to handle multiple component instances, and it is the basis for more sophisticated object-oriented support mechanisms. Figure 3-5 illustrates a component struct for a simple VBX control.

A VBX component cannot be implemented without a substantial number of calls to functions implemented in the Visual Basic run-time environment. Any program that

```
typedef struct VbFhdlInfo
{
    short Action;
    short Result;
    HLSTR InputString;
    long OutputHandle;
    HLSTR ErrorString;
    HSZ FileName;
    unsigned short InputPosition;
    short InputDone;
    short EOLSent;
    HANDLE CurrData;
    unsigned short DataLen;
    LPVOID EventArgs[2];
}
FhdlInfo;
```

Figure 3-5   A Control Struct

wishes to act as a container for VBX components has to implement this extensive library of functions, which is probably the most serious drawback of the VBX component. In particular, events cannot be implemented without making calls to the Visual Basic run-time environment. Events are fired using the *VBFireEvent* function which identifies the event and supplies its parameters. The event translates into a message that is passed to the container of the component. Figure 3-6 illustrates this process.

Another innovation provided by VBX components is the ability of components to self-identify their properties and events. Each VBX component is required to provide a standard interface function that can be used to extract information about the VBX component. This information includes the names of the components contained in the VBX library (a VBX library can actually contain several independent components) as well as the property and event names of each component. The information also includes a pointer to the message-processing routine for each component. This routine will be called by the container to pass messages to the component.

```
OutMsg = VBCreateHlstr(outbuf,j);  // create VB String
EventArgs[0] = OutMsg; // Put string handle in Args array
VBFireEvent(hctl,IEVENT_VBFHDL_READLINE,EventArgs);

// hctl is the control handle.
// IEVENT_VBFHDL_READLINE is the event ID.
// EventArgs is a pointer to a list of arguments.
```

Figure 3-6   Firing an Event

Although VBX technology is primitive compared with more modern object-oriented technologies like JavaBeans and ActiveX, many of the concepts that originated with VBX technology have become the staple of other, more sophisticated technologies.

5. ACTIVEX

The advent of Windows 95 brought with it a new type of component, the OLE control. Much to the annoyance of Visual Basic developers, it was announced that VBX components would not be supported in 32-bit windows. This meant that the substantial investment that developers had made in VBX components was now wasted money. To maintain the same functionality, it was necessary to purchase entirely new versions of everything. What was even worse was the fact that OLE controls were much slower, much larger, and significantly more expensive than their VBX counterparts. There were many projects that were simply abandoned because it was not economical to upgrade them to 32 bits. Immediately, Microsoft engineers went to work on the problem of making OLE controls smaller and faster. (Since they were third-party products, they had little control over the price.) During this process, new tools and new standards emerged, and at some point the name got changed from OLE to ActiveX.

Despite all the problems, the ActiveX technology has proved to be fundamentally superior to VBX technology. This is immediately apparent when considering the wide variety of ActiveX container applications that have come into existence in recent years. This sort of wide compatibility was difficult or impossible to achieve with VBX components. Even though many programs claimed VBX compatibility, this was generally true only for a small subclass of VBX components. The majority of VBX components could be used with Visual Basic, not with anything else. This was particularly true for data-aware components. The ActiveX specifications provided standards for both components and for containers. These standards permitted the container to access all the features of an ActiveX component, not just a subset. Today, ActiveX technology is the most widely accepted component technology in use.

It is difficult to describe ActiveX technology without saying something about the Component Object Model (COM)—the underlying technology upon which ActiveX is built. COM is a technology for creating and publishing module interfaces. An interface consists of a collection of functions that can be called by an entity wishing to use the interface. Interface functions must be designed according to strict rules; once published, an interface must be immutable.

An ActiveX component is required to implement a number of different interfaces, but the most important of these is the *IDispatch* interface used to implement properties, methods, and events. (Unlike most other interfaces, the *IDispatch* interface has been defined as part of the COM standard.) The dispatch interface defines a number of functions that must be implemented by every ActiveX component, the most important of which is the *Invoke* function that is used to access properties, call methods, and fire events. All interaction with the component is done through the *Invoke* function. Method calls and property accesses are encoded as parameters to the *Invoke* function. The parameters must be decoded by the component to determine the required response.

Events are somewhat more complicated. For a component to fire an event, it must create an *IDispatch* interface that defines the events as methods. This interface must then be implemented by the component's container for the events to be fired.

Fortunately, there are standard function libraries that can handle most of the work of implementing the required interfaces. Even further, a number of design tools have been developed that hide the details of the standard function libraries from the programmer. The programmer must complete the implementation of the properties and methods by supplying the required subroutines to handle them.

When using the standard libraries and design tools, a method is implemented as a single function. Properties can be implemented in two ways: as directly modified properties or as virtual properties. A directly modified property must have a support variable to contain its data, and it may have a notification function to inform the component when the value has been modified. A virtual property has no associated support variable, but it has two functions: one for setting the property value and one for retrieving the property value. A support variable may be used, but it must be managed by the *get* and *set* functions.

Each ActiveX component should have a *support class* to represent instances of the component. (A support class is technically not necessary, but it is quite difficult to get along without one.) Each instance of the support class represents a single instance of the component. The instances of the support class are known as *support objects*. All information unique to an instance of the component is contained in its support object. This includes property values as well as other data. Any functions required by the component are implemented as support class members. This includes property-support functions and method implementations.

We will demonstrate how to create properties and methods using the MFC wizard under Visual C++ 6.0.* The class wizard, illustrated in Figure 3-7, is used for this purpose. The *Automation* tab of the wizard is used to add properties and methods, while the *ActiveX Events* tab is used to add events.

To add a property using the class wizard, we simply click on the *Add Property* button, which brings up the *Add Property* window illustrated in Figure 3-8. Filling in the property name and type and clicking OK will complete the definition of the property. Figure 3-8 shows the *Add Property* window with the property name and type filled in. The property name is *LineWidth* and the type is **long**. In addition to creating the required table entries and ODL statements, the wizard will place a variable, *m_lineWidth*, into the support class definition and will create a function (also a member of the support class), *OnLineWidthChanged*, which will be called whenever a new value is assigned to the property. The value of *m_lineWidth* will be set automatically without any additional programming.

Figure 3-9 illustrates another way to define a property using Get and Set methods. In this case, no variables will be added to the support class, but two functions—*GetVectorCount* and *SetVectorCount*—will be added to the support class. The Set

---

*Visual C++ is a registered trademark of Microsoft Corporation. All screen shots reprinted by permission from Microsoft Corporation.

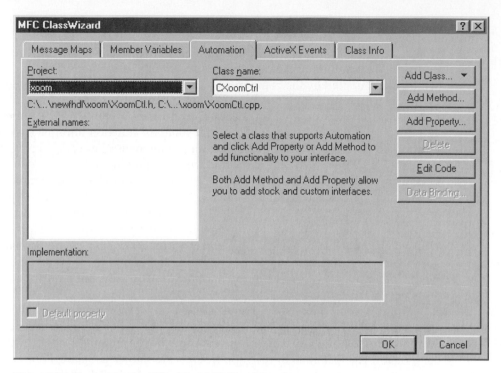

Figure 3-7   The Automation Tab of the MFC Class Wizard

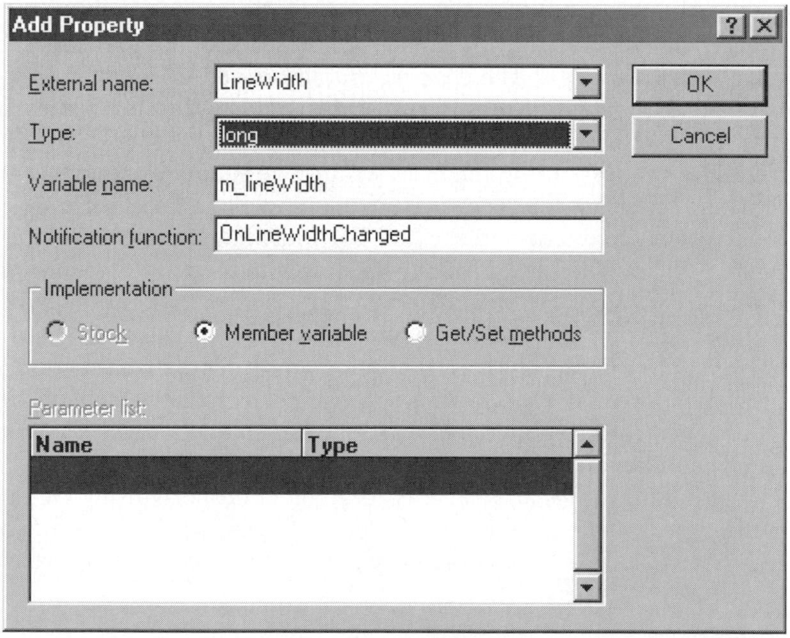

Figure 3-8   Defining an ActiveX Notification Property

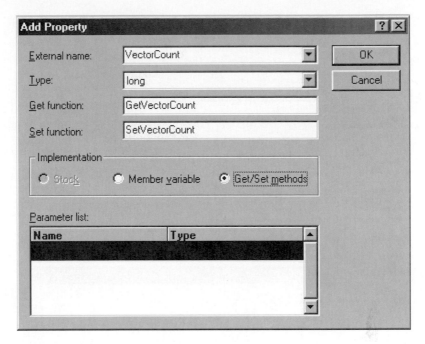

Figure 3-9   Defining a Get and Set ActiveX Property

function will be called to assign a new value to the property and the Get function to retrieve the value of the property. The programmer can implement the value of the property in any convenient way. Read-only and Write-only properties can be created by blanking out the Set and Get function names. Run-time only properties can be implemented by calling the standard *GetNotImplemented* and *SetNotImplemented* functions from the Get and Set routines.

A new method can be added to the component by clicking on the *Add Method* button, which will bring up the *Add Method* window. The programmer must enter the name of the method, its return type, and the names and types of its parameters. Figure 3-10 shows the *Add Method* window with the necessary data filled in.

Once properties and methods have been added, it is necessary to write the bodies of the functions defined by the wizard. This can be done by selecting the appropriate property or method from the class wizard window and clicking on the *Edit Code* button. Figure 3-11 shows the functions defined by the wizard before any code has been added.

The class wizard is also used to define events. The fourth tab of the wizard, illustrated in Figure 3-12, is used for this purpose. Clicking on the *Add Event* button will bring up the *Add Event* window. Defining an event is essentially the same as defining a method, except no return value is required. Figure 3-13 shows the definition of an event *BadInput* with one parameter. The wizard will add a function *FireBadInput* to the support class to permit this event to be fired easily. The body of this function is created by the wizard, not by the programmer.

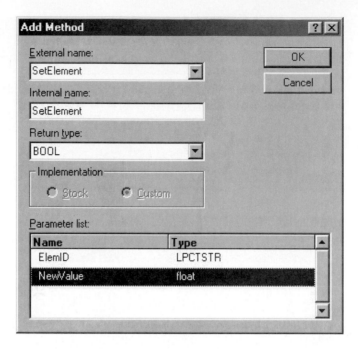

Figure 3-10   Defining an ActiveX Method

```
void CXoomCtrl::OnLineWidthChanged()
{
    // TODO: Add notification handler code
    SetModifiedFlag();
}

long CXoomCtrl::GetVectorCount()
{
    // TODO: Add your property handler here
    return 0;
}

void CXoomCtrl::SetVectorCount(long nNewValue)
{
    // TODO: Add your property handler here
    SetModifiedFlag();
}

BOOL CXoomCtrl::SetElement(LPCTSTR ElemID, float NewValue)
{
    // TODO: Add your dispatch handler code here
    return TRUE;
}
```

Figure 3-11   ActiveX Method and Property Function Bodies

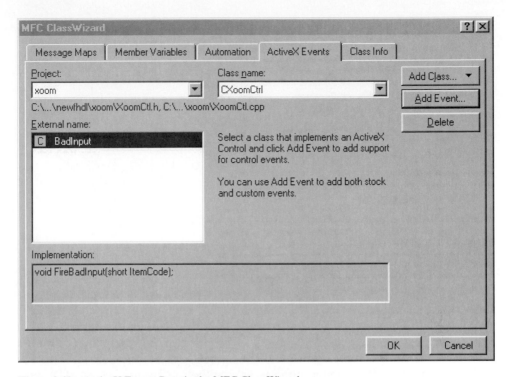

Figure 3-12   ActiveX Events Page in the MFC Class Wizard

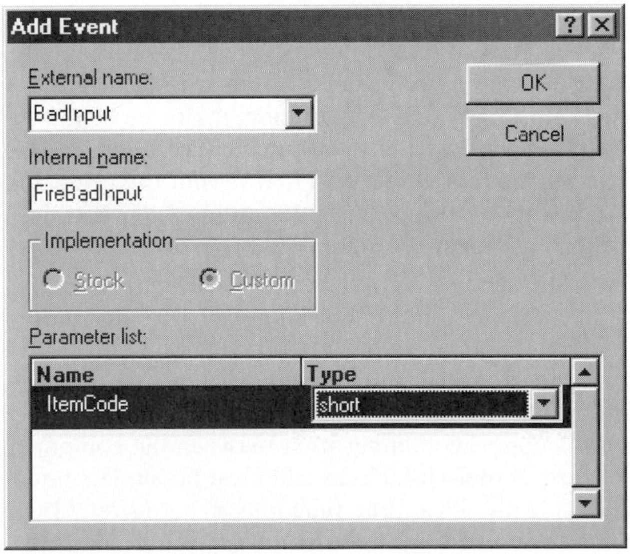

Figure 3-13   Defining an ActiveX Event

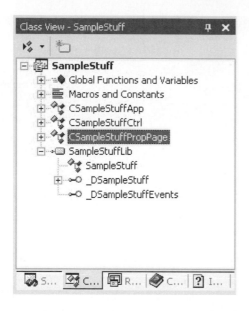

Figure 3-14   The VS.NET Class View

In VS.NET, the functions of the Class Wizard have been integrated into the class view display illustrated in Figure 3-14. The figure illustrates the class view for a project named **SampleStuff**. To add a property or a method, we right-click on **_DSampleStuff** under **SampleStuffLib**, and select the **Add** command from the pop-up menu. This will display two subcommands, **Add Method** and **Add Property**, both of which will display dialog boxes similar to those displayed by Visual C++ 6.0. To add an event, it is necessary to right-click on the class **CSampleStuffCtrl** and select the **Add** command. In addition to the standard **Add Function** and **Add Variable** subcommands, there is also an **Add Event** subcommand that can be used to add events. Again, this subcommand displays a dialog box similar to that displayed by Visual C++ 6.0.

The type-library mechanism allows ActiveX components to be self-describing. The programmer-supplied parameters describing the interface are included as a resource in the ActiveX executable module. Most tools that permit the use of ActiveX components are capable of reading the type library to determine the properties, methods, and events supported by the component.

6. COM/DCOM

COM is the base upon which ActiveX controls are built—which means that every ActiveX control is, by definition, a COM component. However, COM components permit custom interfaces to be used to support communication between the component and its host. *IUnknown* is the simplest of these interfaces and must be implemented by all COM components. The *IUnknown* provides three functions: (1) *AddRef*, (2) *Release*, and (3) *QueryInterface*. The first two functions are used to control access to the interface by incrementing and decrementing a reference count, while the third function, *QueryInterface*, is used to determine the additional interfaces that are provided by the module. When a COM component is instantiated, a pointer to its *IUnknown* interface is automatically provided. This pointer can be used by the container to determine the interfaces supported by the object.

Like C++ classes, one COM interface can be derived from another. In fact, all COM interfaces must be derived from the *IUnknown* interface, so all interfaces must provide the three functions *AddRef, Release*, and *QueryInterface*. Each interface is identified by a globally unique identifier (GUID), and once an interface has been defined and published, it is supposed to be frozen for all time. Any new functionality that is added to a COM interface must be done by creating a new version of the interface with a new name and a new GUID. A published interface is considered a contract, in that its functions, and their behavior, must never change. However, a COM component is free not to implement all functions of an interface. In such cases, the function must still exist, but it must return an error code indicating that it has not been implemented.

The primary difference between COM and ActiveX is that COM allows us to use interfaces beyond the IDispatch interface. In principle, using a COM interface directly is more efficient than using the IDispatch intermediary. However, many tools are unable to use anything other than the IDispatch interface. This requires one to create *dual* interfaces, which provide a set of functions that can be accessed directly, and an *IDispatch Invoke* function for invoking the same functions through the *IDispatch* interface. Dual interfaces must be derived from the *IDispatch* interface. A single declaration of the interface is used, which declares the interface to be a dual interface. Fortunately, the details of such interfaces are handled by the development tools, which means that dual interfaces can be developed in much the same way as ordinary interfaces. A dual interface allows those containers that are able to access COM interfaces directly to do so, but it also provides the *IDispatch* implementation as a "fallback." Of course, one is permitted to use the *IDispatch* interface as the exclusive interface to the COM object.

Unlike ActiveX controls, which must run in the same address space as their containers, COM objects can run in a separate address space from their host. With the DCOM extensions, COM components can even run on a different machine from their host. The lifetime of such components is independent of the lifetime of the host, and a single instance of a component can provide services to several hosts simultaneously. COM and DCOM components can be activated and terminated dynamically, unlike ActiveX components, which (usually) are activated when the client program starts and terminated when the client program terminates.

Properties, methods, and events are supported in the same manner as in ActiveX controls. General interfaces do not support properties directly, but the component designer can define *GetX* and *SetX* functions to create an effective implementation for a property, *X*. For dual interfaces the *GetX* and *SetX* functions are formally identified as implementing a property so the client program can treat *X* as a formal property. Methods are simply defined as interface functions.

As in ActiveX controls, events are implemented using an *IDispatch* interface, which is defined by the control but implemented by the client. Figure 3-15 shows how a COM component named *BackObj* component is used in a Visual Basic program. Before this component can be used, the programmer must add a reference to the component's type library.

```
Dim WithEvents MyCom As BackObj

Private Sub Command1_Click()
    MyCom.Poked = 1
End Sub

Private Sub Command2_Click()
    Text2.Text = MyCom.Square(Text1.Text)
End Sub

Private Sub Form_Load()
    Set MyCom = New BackObj
End Sub

Private Sub MyCom_Ouch(ByVal Poked As Long)
    MsgBox "Hello COM"
End Sub
```

Figure 3-15   Visual Basic Use of COM Components

In Figure 3-15, the *WithEvents* keyword is necessary for the events supported by the component to become available. In addition to providing the variable, *MyCom*, to hold an instance of the *BackObj* component, it is necessary to create the component instance in the *Form_Load* routine. Declaring the *MyCom* variable as a *BackObj* component automatically makes the properties, methods, and events of *MyCom* available to the programmer.

7. JAVABEANS

JavaBeans is probably the most important component technology after ActiveX. The machine independence of Java, and the ability to use this language on Web pages has made it extremely popular. These same factors have contributed to the popularity of the JavaBean technology.

Java is readily adaptable to component-level technology. It is inherently event-oriented, so there are already mechanisms in place for issuing and handling events. It is also inherently object-oriented. A Java program is already an object, and it can be readily incorporated into other programs, almost without change. In fact, it has been said that the only thing you need to do to turn an existing Java object into a JavaBean component is to make all the properties private! This is fairly close to the truth, but to support visual programming some additional features are required.

Java does not support properties in the same way as Visual Basic. In Visual Basic, a property is used as if it were a variable even though it results in a series of function calls. To create a property in a JavaBean, we must supply explicit get and set functions for the property. To access the value of the property, we must call these functions directly. Figure 3-16 shows how to create a text box and assign a value to the text property.

```
vMyTextBox = new com.sun.java.swing.JTextField();
vMyTextBox.setName("MyTextBox");
vMyTextBox.setText("Hello World");
vMyTextBox.setBounds(160, 29, 151, 19);
```

Figure 3-16 Creating a JavaBean Instance

To use the properties and methods of a JavaBean instance, we must call the support class functions directly. The fact that some of these functions implement properties is merely a convention. In a JavaBean, a property is represented by two public support class functions: *setPPP* and *getPPP*. These functions will normally set and retrieve the value of property *PPP*. Although it is possible to use some other naming convention for these functions, this is unwise because both programming tools and other classes will assume that this convention has been followed. A JavaBean method is simply a public function of the support class.

To fire an event, the JavaBean support class must integrate itself into the Java run-time event structure. This structure provides several predefined event categories. To receive events from a JavaBean, container must register with the JavaBean as a listener of events in a particular category. The JavaBean must keep track of all listeners for each category of events that it supports. When an event is fired, the JavaBean must pass an event object to each of its listeners. (A similar procedure is also used to fire events in the ActiveX and COM technologies, but the ActiveX and COM design tools will do the programming for you.)

The creation of a JavaBean can be simplified by inheriting functionality from standard classes and interfaces. For example, there is a serialization interface that can be used to support property persistence. A number of other standard interfaces are available for various purposes.

8. DELPHI COMPONENTS

The Delphi language, which is the visual extension of Object Pascal, allows one to define components that we will call Delphi components. Delphi components are also known as Visual Component Library (VCL) components, but this term has meaning only to Delphi programmers. Delphi is one of the few widely used high-level languages that has incorporated features specifically for designing components. Figure 3-17 shows the definition of an *invisible at run-time* Delphi component. Delphi components can be turned into ActiveX components by placing them inside an ActiveX wrapper.

Compared with other technologies, the definition of a Delphi component is quite simple. The code of Figure 3-17 is quite easy to read, even for those who are not familiar with the Pascal language. This component has two properties, *Size* and *Width*. Note that Delphi provides the keyword **property** for defining properties. A property statement has several parts. If the property has accessor functions, they are declared with the keywords **read** and **write**. These follow the name and type of the property. Accessor

functions are not required. If they are omitted, the property is read and written directly, without notification to the component. In this case the variable containing the value
of the property must be named *Fppp*, where *ppp* is the name of the property. If accessor functions are used, then any variable may be used to hold the value of the property. It is also possible for the property to have a virtual value that is calculated when the
property is accessed.

Delphi provides a fourth access type over and above the **private**, **protected**, and
public access types used by C++. This is the **published** access type, which is used only

```
unit SampleUnit;

interface

uses {standard includes}
  SysUtils, WinTypes, WinProcs, Messages, Classes, Graphics, Controls,
  Forms, Dialogs;

type
  {define event handler}
  TOuchHandler = procedure(Index : Integer) of object;

  TSampleComponent = class(TComponent) {Component Declaration}
  private
    FSize: Integer; {property Size}
    FWidth: Integer; {property Width}
    FOnOuch : TOuchHandler;

    function GetSize: Integer; {Accessor functions (optional)}
    procedure SetSize(NewSize: Integer);

    function GetWidth: Integer;
    procedure SetWidth(NewWidth: Integer);
  protected
    Extra: Integer; {component work variable}
  public
    {width is a run-time only property}
    property Width: Integer read GetWidth write SetWidth;
    function SumIt : Integer;
  published
    {event declaration}
    property OnOuch : TOuchHandler read FOnOuch write FOnOuch;
    {Size is available at design time}
    property Size: Integer read GetSize write SetSize default 3;
  end;

procedure Register;

implementation {declarations of methods and accessor functions}
```

Figure 3-17   A Sample Delphi Component

```
function TSampleComponent.GetSize : Integer;
begin
    GetSize := FSize;
end;

procedure TSampleComponent.SetSize(NewSize : Integer);
begin
    FSize := NewSize;
end;

function TSampleComponent.GetWidth : Integer;
begin
    GetWidth := FWidth;
end;

procedure TSampleComponent.SetWidth(NewWidth : Integer);
begin
    OnOuch(25);
    FWidth := NewWidth;
end;
{method definition}
function TSampleComponent.SumIt : Integer;
begin
    SumIt := FWidth + FSize;
end;

procedure Register;
begin
  RegisterComponents('Samples', [TSampleComponent]);
end;

begin
  Size := 3; {property initialization}
end;

end.
```

Figure 3-17 (*Continued*)

for properties. To be usable, properties must be declared as either **public** or **published**. Public properties are available only at run-time, while published properties are available both at design time and at run-time.

Methods are simply public functions of the support class. The component of Figure 3-17 contains one method called *SumIt*.

Events are both properties and functions. An event type must be declared as a function pointer. This function pointer gives the type of event handler that must be used to process the events. An event handler is not allowed to return a value. (Note that Pascal uses the keyword **procedure** for functions that do not return values, rather than using a void return type.)

To create an event, we declare a variable to hold a pointer to the event handler. The event is then declared as a public property with the event-handler variable as the **read** and **write** accessor functions. To fire the event, we simply call the event as if it were a function, using the parameters declared in the event-handler type. The component declared in Figure 3-17 contains one event, *OnOuch*, which is triggered anytime a new value is assigned to the *Width* property.

Once a Delphi component is created, it must be registered with the Delphi system before it can be used. The *Register* procedure of Figure 3-17 is used for this purpose. Delphi permits components to be laid out visually in a manner virtually identical to that of Visual Basic. Event handlers can be added by double-clicking on a component in the visual layout. Figure 3-18 shows a Delphi program that contains two components, a button and an instance of the sample component defined in Figure 3-17. (This program also has a visual layout that has been omitted for the sake of brevity.)

```
unit Unit1;

interface

uses
  SysUtils, WinTypes, WinProcs, Messages, Classes, Graphics, Controls,
  Forms, Dialogs, Unit2, StdCtrls;

type
  TForm1 = class(TForm)
    SampleComponent1: TSampleComponent;
    Button1: TButton;
    procedure SampleComponent1Ouch(Index: Integer);
    procedure Button1Click(Sender: TObject);
  end;

var
  Form1: TForm1;

implementation

procedure TForm1.SampleComponent1Ouch(Index: Integer);
begin
    MessageBox(GetActiveWindow,'Hello','Debug',MB_OK);
end;

procedure TForm1.Button1Click(Sender: TObject);
begin
    SampleComponent1.Width := 40;
end;

end.
```

Figure 3-18   A Delphi Program Using Components

Regardless of whether accessor functions were declared for the property, a property is accessed as if it were a variable. (Note the assignment in the *Button1Click* event handler.) Unlike Visual Basic, the naming convention used for event handlers is not mandatory. The Delphi programmer can specify the name of a procedure to be used as the handler for a particular event.

9. .NET COMPONENTS

In addition to many new features for creating Web-based applications, Visual Studio.NET (VS.NET) provides the Windows Forms Component. This new type of component can be developed in many different languages, but the most convenient of these at the present time is the C# language that was introduced with VS.NET. C# is quite similar to both C++ and Java and should present no difficulties to programmers of either of these languages.

To create a Windows Forms Component, we derive a new class from the standard class: **System.Windows.Forms.UserControl**. The methods of the component are simply the public functions of this class. A property is defined as if it were a variable, but a special syntax is provided for specifying accessor and mutator functions for the property. Figure 3-19 gives the definition of a property with the external name X.

The class in this figure also provides a private variable, *Xval*, for storing the value of the property, but this is optional. **Get** and **set** are general functions that can be implemented in whatever fashion the programmer chooses. In the **set** function, the keyword **value** is used to designate the new value being assigned to the property. Although creating properties and methods is quite easy in C#, creating events is reasonably complicated. If the event has parameters, the first step is to define a new class to hold the parameters. The new class must be derived from **System.EventArgs**, and must define each parameter as a read-only property. Figure 3-20 gives the definition of a new class that provides two event arguments, x and y.

```
private readonly long Xval = 0;

public long X
{
    get
    {
        return Xval;
    }
    set
    {
        Xval=value;
    }
}
```

Figure 3-19   Defining a Property in C#

```
public class SquareEventArgs : System.EventArgs
{
    public SquareEventArgs()
    {
        xval = 0;
        yval = 0;
    }
    public SquareEventArgs(long newX, long newY)
    {
        xval = newX;
        yval = newY;
    }
    private readonly long xval = 0;
    private readonly long yval = 0;
    public long x
    {
        get
        {
            return xval;
        }
    }
    public long y
    {
        get
        {
            return yval;
        }
    }
}
```

Figure 3-20   A New EventArgs Class

We must next define a deligate function for handling the new event. This declaration is given in Figure 3-21. The delegate declaration serves as a template for event handlers for the new event. The first argument of the delegate must be of type **object**, while the second must have the type of the newly defined **EventArgs** class.

The next step is to add an event declaration, and optionally, a function to fire the event. The event declaration acts like a pointer to the event-handler function, while the event-firing function merely simplifies access to the event handler. Figure 3-22 shows how these are defined. Note that the delegate declaration in Figure 3-21 must be

```
public delegate void SquareEventHandler(object sender,
                                         SquareEventArgs e);
```

Figure 3-21   An Event Delegate

```
public event SquareEventHandler Square;
protected virtual void OnSquare(SquareEventArgs e)
{
   if (Square != null)
   {
      Square(this,e);
   }
}
```

Figure 3-22   Event Declaration and Firing Code

outside the definition of the component class, while the code in Figure 3-22 must be *inside* the class definition.

At this point, Windows Forms Components are so new that very little can be said about their potential for the future. They are reasonably easy to create, and they support the standard properties/methods/events interface. As .NET applications grow, Windows Forms Components will most likely proliferate.

10. CORBA?

Virtually all surveys of component technologies include some description of the CORBA system. This is true despite the fact that CORBA is *not* a component technology. A component is an independent program that can be used as a building block in other programs. Although CORBA objects share many features with components, there is no such thing as a CORBA component.

That being said, it is still important to include CORBA in our discussion of component technologies. This is because CORBA provides features that are becoming increasingly important in component-level programming. In particular, CORBA provides remote access to objects. More important than the remote accessibility is the CORBA view of objects as permanent entities with a lifetime that is independent of their creator. All too often in object-oriented programming we tend to treat our objects as data structures. Specifically, we treat our objects as ephemeral entities that exist only within the confines of a single program. When the program terminates, the objects are destroyed. If we hold to this point of view, we will end up ignoring some of the most powerful aspects of component-level programming.

Due to the complexity of the CORBA standard, we cannot hope to do justice to it here. At best we can hope to give a flavor of how the system works. CORBA allows one to create an object repository that contains one or more objects. Objects have both properties and methods, and they can be as complex as any component. Access to objects is provided by an Object Request Broker (ORB). An ORB provides an application with a reference to an object (*not* a copy of the object). This reference can be used to access the properties and methods of the object. The application does not do this directly, but instead passes the access requests to the ORB. The ORB will then pass the request along to the object. Because the object resides on a single system, and because all access requests are passed to the system that has the object, accesses are system-independent. A program running on an IBM Compatible PC can execute methods on a UNIX system, and vice versa.

CORBA also provides an event mechanism that permits an object to send messages to the application program using the object.

11. CONCLUSION

Although components have much in common with objects, components are not objects. They are independent programs. Even though the most recent technologies support an object-like interface to components, it is possible to create a component technology that does not have such an interface. The technology of simple controls is one example of this. Nevertheless, the marriage between object-oriented technology and component technology has been a good one. In most technologies, once we have learned how to define and use properties, methods, and events, we have mastered the technology.

There are several technologies that are language independent. ActiveX controls, for example, can be developed in C, Pascal, Visual Basic, Java and probably other languages. Other technologies, such as JavaBeans and Delphi components, are tightly bound to one language. JavaBeans and Delphi represent the extremes of language support for component technology. Java provides no language support for JavaBeans. In fact, JavaBeans is more a set of coding conventions for Java objects than a component technology. Delphi, on the other hand, provides integrated support for both the creation and the use of components. This integrated language support makes components easy to build and to use. One advantage of tying a component technology to a single language is the ability to use nonsimple types for properties. In both JavaBeans and Delphi components, properties may have nonsimple types. The same thing applies to method parameters and return values.

When comparing component technologies, it is important to remember that we are at the beginning of the component revolution. Even though some technologies have become quite popular, virtually every existing technology leaves a great deal to be desired. We will discuss this issue further in Chapter 20.

EXERCISES

1. Search the Visual Basic documentation for information on how to access COM components in Visual Basic. (You will need to find information on the **Set** and **With Events** keywords.)

2. Familiarize yourself with the Delphi language, and implement the *Properties* example from Chapter 2.

3. Use the Delphi language to implement the sieve of Eratosthenes example from Chapter 2.

4. Download Visualage for Java (entry-level free edition) from the following Web site: http://www7.software.ibm.com/vad.nsf/data/document4600. Use this software to implement the *Properties* example from Chapter 2.

5. Use Visualage for Java to implement the sieve of Eratosthenes example from Chapter 2.

Chapter 4

Component-Based Application Design

1. PREREQUISITES AND OBJECTIVES

Before starting this chapter, you should have

1. A rudimentary knowledge of component-level programming.
2. Some knowledge of object-oriented programming.

After completing this chapter, you will have

1. A knowledge of how to divide an application into components.
2. A knowledge of component categories.
3. The ability to use component categories as a design tool.

2. INTRODUCTION

A modern graphical user interface (GUI) based program consists of many different parts. At the user-interface level, there is at least a main window and a menu bar. There may also be toolbars, scroll bars, and other sorts of controls. In addition to the external interface, there may be I/O processing routines, internal processing routines, and operating-system interface routines. The process of component-level design is similar to that of any object-oriented design: identify the various distinct parts of a program, develop code for each part, and then integrate the parts. Unlike object-oriented design, component-level design focuses only on the large-scale aspects of the program. The various parts of the program will be implemented as independent components connected with glue logic. The small scale parts of the program will be embedded in the various components, and possibly in the glue logic. The small scale parts of the program will be developed using conventional object-oriented techniques.

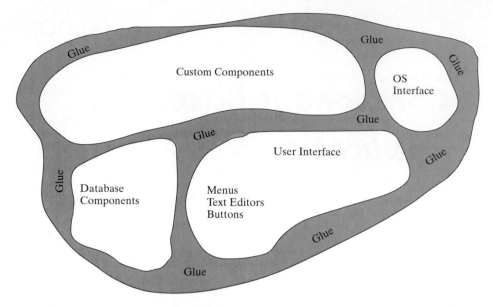

Figure 4-1   A Typical Component-Based Design

As we divide a program into its various parts, we must remember that there are many third-party components available in the marketplace. To speed development, it is necessary to implement as much of the program as possible using these third-party components. In some cases, third-party components and glue logic will be sufficient; however, in most cases, it will be necessary to develop a number of custom components. It is sometimes possible to avoid custom control development by implementing features directly in the glue logic—but except in simple cases, this approach should be avoided.

The first step is to separate program features into a few broad categories, as has been done in Figure 4-1. In this example, existing components are used to create the user interface, the operating system (OS) interface, and the database components. The specialized parts of the program—those that are too complicated to be implemented in glue logic—will be implemented as custom components. Although this sort of breakdown is typical of many applications, there are many others where the breakdown will be somewhat different, and there may be cases where a significant number of the specialized parts of a program will be implemented using existing components.

3. COMPONENT-BASED DEVELOPMENT

Several skills are necessary for effective component-based design: (1) an extensive knowledge of available third-party components; (2) an idea about the typical sorts of services that are provided by third-party components; (3) an awareness of how one typically interacts with them; and (4) an extensive knowledge of the component development process. To create custom components, we must know how the internals of a component are constructed, and we must also know how to create an appropriate interface for interaction between the component and its environment. Finally, we must know how to subdivide an application into components. (At least the portion that will be implemented in custom components.) We must have a good feel for which features should be combined into a single component and which features should be implemented as separate components. The most difficult skill is the ability to design and build a wide variety of different components—a topic that will be the focus of a major portion of this book. The remainder of this chapter will describe the process of breaking an application into components.

4. A DESIGN EXAMPLE

To illustrate the process of breaking down an application into components, it is best to start with a specific example. To that end, we will start with the requirements for a reasonably complex application and create a component-level design for it. The application in question will be a contact-management program. We intend for this to be a specialized product used by a single company. The application will allow the salespeople to list and manage their prospects. We will assume that this application will be a replacement for an existing application, and thus it must be able to read and process the files used by the existing application.

4.1 Application Requirements

The existing application uses a collection of text files, one for each prospect list. Each prospect represents a person with a name, address, telephone number, and e-mail address. Although the prospect files have a rigid format, they are ordinary text files in every other respect. These files have been integrated into other software, so we do not have the option of switching to a database system, even though this would be the ideal solution. The program must be able to open several files simultaneously and integrate them dynamically. Contacts should be displayed in a grid format, as shown in Figure 4-2. Eventually, it will be necessary to add horizontal and vertical scroll bars to this display.

The grid of Figure 4-2 will be the basic means for editing, deleting, and adding entries. The grid will also be used to manage prospects. This will be done by marking several lines for current attention, and then executing a command to create a "current attention" list. The grid will be embedded in a larger window that provides menus and toolbars, resulting in a display that looks similar to that of Figure 4-3. (Remember that this is a preliminary drawing, not a screen shot of the final product.)

Although it is not necessary for us to specify every detail of the application at this point, it is useful to focus on a few low-level technical details. To that end, we will discuss the placing and managing of phone calls. The user must be able to tag entries for current attention and must be able to save multiple current attention lists. The toolbar (or menu) will be used to choose between editing and selecting names for current attention lists. The user must be able to process a current attention list by calling everyone on the list. (The toolbar will be used to invoke this function.) A special window

Last Name	First Name	Phone	E-Mail	Address
Jones	Harry	333-4444	xyz@abc.com	6262 Des
Smith	Helen	719-2391	qed@done.com	1745 Cap
Johnson	Alice	123-4567	eye@ear.com	316 Story
Brown	John	222-3333	ear@eye.com	1732 E 12
White	Allen	555-1212	kxl@ibn.com	1237 East
Fisher	Mary	336-2111	Mary@Fish.com	316 Arlen
Carter	Jimmy	525-3132	Prez@Georgia.com	1225 Harl
King	Larry	211-1111	king@martin.com	404 S 4th

Figure 4-2   A Sample Grid

Prospect File NewCustomer.prs

File Edit Options Help

A B C D E F

Last Name	First Name	Phone	E-Mail	Address
Jones	Harry	333-4444	xyz@abc.com	6262 Des
Smith	Helen	719-2391	qed@done.com	1745 Cap
Johnson	Alice	123-4567	eye@ear.com	316 Story
Brown	John	222-3333	ear@eye.com	1732 E 12
White	Allen	555-1212	kxl@ibn.com	1237 East
Fisher	Mary	336-2111	Mary@Fish.com	316 Arlen
Carter	Jimmy	525-3132	Prez@Georgia.com	1225 Harl
King	Larry	211-1111	king@martin.com	404 S 4th

Figure 4-3   Main Window Design

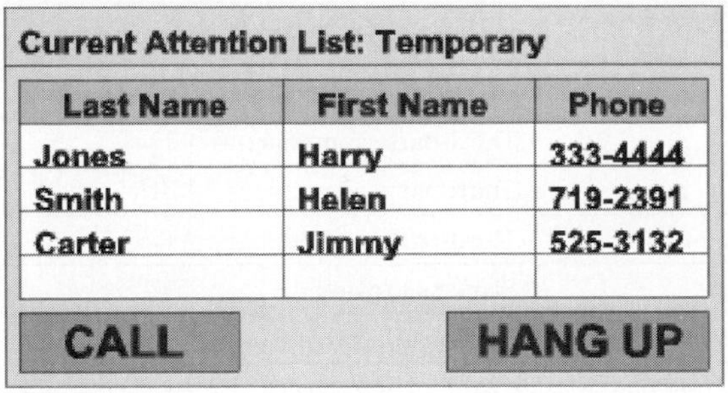

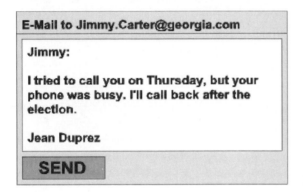

Figure 4-4   Current-Attention-List Window

Figure 4-5   E-Mail Window

similar to that shown in Figure 4-4 will be used for processing current attention lists. This window will enable the user to select a specific prospect and call that person by clicking a button labeled "call." This task will be performed on an office computer equipped with a speaker-phone modem.

Internally, a call involves several steps. The program must first dial the person's number using the computer's modem. Once the call connects, the modem's speaker-phone function must be activated so the salesperson can talk to the prospect. If the call does not connect after four rings, or gets a busy signal, the program must hang up and pop up a special window that enables the salesperson to send e-mail to the prospect. As Figure 4-5 shows, the e-mail window will have a "send" button that sends the e-mail and closes the window.

4.2 Application Design

A preliminary division of this program into components is relatively easy. Although it will be necessary to do a more detailed job before we are finished, a preliminary inspection of the requirements would produce a list similar to the one shown in Figure 4-6. Along with the name of each component (or instance of a component), we have indicated the source of each part.

The breakdown of Figure 4-6 assumes that we have spent some time studying the available third-party controls and have a good knowledge of what is available. (Such knowledge can be obtained by going through the catalogs of a few component clearinghouses—but we won't concentrate on that aspect of things here.) We can use the

Item	Source
Three windows with frames	Development language (VB, Delphi, etc.)
The menu in the main window	Third-party component
The toolbar in the main window	Third-party component
The grid display in the main window	Third-party component
The grid display in the call window	Same as previous
The text editor in the e-mail window	Built-in editor control
A file handler for reading and writing files	*Custom component*
A modem interface for placing calls, detecting rings, busies, and pick-ups	Third-party component
An e-mail interface for sending e-mail	Third-party component
A configuration management tool for keeping track of persistent properties (maybe)	*Custom component*
Buttons and scroll bars	Built-in components
An internal file manager for maintaining open files	*Custom component*

Figure 4-6   Component-Level Program Breakdown

built-in controls provided by our development system to provide windows, buttons, scroll bars, and text editors.

A major part of the program will be provided by third-party components. The entire user interface consists of third-party components and built-in features of the development language. The operating system interface to e-mail functions and to the modem will also be handled by third-party components. Much of what appears to be the functionality of the program will be implemented in glue logic. Specifically, the code implementing things like placing calls will be implemented as event handlers for buttons and the various other components of the program. For example, the Call button of the current attention window might have the Visual Basic code given in Figure 4-7.

This code makes several assumptions about other components. It assumes that there is an array property in the grid component that permits access to the various fields in the row. (Some mechanism to do this must surely be available.) It also assumes that the modem component will handle the dialing function. Let us assume that this is the case, and that the response from the modem is in the form of several different events: *RING, BUSY, CONNECT,* and *ERROR.* The code for the *RING* and *CONNECT* events is given in Figure 4-8.

The major problem in the development of the application is the creation of the customized file management components. File management components are needed because text files must be loaded in their entirety and copied into the grid of Figure 4-2. The grid itself will probably not be suited to storage management. In fact, for some

```
Sub CallButton_Click( )
   Dim Number As String
   ' Get Number from selected row
   Number = DataGrid.FieldOfSelectedRow(2)
   Status = Dialing      ' global with defined variable
   RingCount = 0          ' Number of rings
   ModemComp.Dial  Number
End Sub
```

Figure 4-7   Call Button Handler

```
Sub ModemComp_Ring( )
   ' Global variable initialized to zero at start of call
   RingCount = RingCount + 1
   If RingCount >= 4 Then
      ModemComp.HangUp
      Status = NoCall
      RingCount = 0
      Load EMailWindow
   End If
End Sub
Sub ModemComp_Connect( )
   ModemComp.ActivateSpeakerPhone
   Beep
End Sub
```

Figure 4-8   Ring and Connect Handlers

third-party grids only the visible portion of the grid can be stored in the component. The grid will issue events to obtain new data for scrolling operations.

As files are modified, it will be necessary at some point to write the modified data back to the disk. There needs to be some mechanism for keeping track of whether a file has been modified and for querying the user for saves at appropriate times. As the requirements state, it must be possible to open several files at once and combine them in various ways. In addition, there needs to be a mechanism for handling current call lists.

The first step in creating our custom components is to create an internal representation for prospect files. We will use a linked list for the individual prospect entries, and a header object to contain the linked list. The file name, and other global properties of the file will be contained in the header object. Figure 4-9 illustrates the organization of these objects.

The header object in this figure represents the internal form of a file, and it is proper to think of each header object as a file. All access to the file must go through the header object. The record objects will be protected and available only through accessor and mutator functions. The header object will provide all of the functionality required to manipulate files. There will be functions to access entries, delete entries, add entries, and replace entries. In addition, there will be functions for enumerating entries. Other

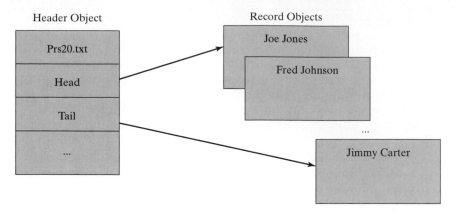

Figure 4-9   Internal Object Design

functions will be used to sort entries into an appropriate order. There will be functions
to combine lists in various ways, purge lists of duplicates, and perform other useful operations. The header object is the heart and soul of our program, and its design will be
completed before proceeding with the remainder of the application.

Once the header object is designed and implemented, we can proceed with the
design of the file-handling components. The types of components that we will create
and the overall structure of the design may be somewhat surprising. To begin with, we
will *not* create a single all-things-to-everyone component. Instead, *we* will create a family of components, each one of which implements a single feature. The overall structure
of the components is shown in Figure 4-10.

The components of Figure 4-10 implement the data management functions of the
application. The file serializer reads and writes text files. It will accept a file name and

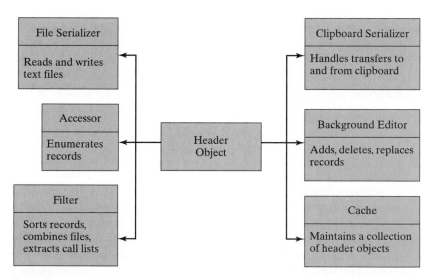

Figure 4-10   Custom Components

return a pointer to a header object (or an error code). It will also accept a pointer to a header object and write the object to a text file. Access to directories and file names will be provided by standard features of our development environment, such as common *Open* and *Save-As* dialog boxes.

The Accessor component gives the glue logic access to the header object. It can be used to enumerate a range of records, or to give access to a specific record. The Background Editor will be used to modify a header object and the records within it. Both the Accessor and the Background Editor will have a pointer to the currently visible file. (It may be advisable to combine these two components into a single component, but at this point we will keep them separate.) The display will be managed through an interaction between the Accessor and the grid component of the main window. Changes to records will be managed through an interaction between the grid component of the main window and the Background Editor component. To make these interactions work, the grid component must issue *Change* events whenever data items change value. The grid must also issue *Scroll* events to obtain new data for the display.

The Cache component will be used to maintain the collection of files that are open but not visible. The Cache will be able to enumerate the names of the files it contains for display on menus. The Filter component will be used to perform major modifications on open files, such as sorting records or combining two lists. It is possible to implement each different type of operation in a separate filter. Access to clipboard cut, paste, and copy operations will be provided by the clipboard Serializer.

As mentioned above, we have created this set of components by implementing each separate feature as a separate component. There are good reasons for doing this. When two features are separated into different components, the coupling between the two features is minimized. The only interaction between the features is through a rigidly defined interface that cannot be subverted. The six components of Figure 4-10 could easily be written by six different individuals, thus maximizing available human resources for the project. Modifying one feature will have minimal impact on other features, because the features are isolated from one another. Adding new features can be done by adding new components, which will also have a minimal impact on existing features. For example, we could add a database feature to our application by adding a database component. Such a component would read a prospect list from a database table and convert it into a header object. Once created, this object could be handled exactly like any other header object. When the user is finished with the object, it could be written back to the database by the same database component.

Although we have said little about the current attention list, we have not really ignored the issue. If we assume that the current attention list and the prospect list have the same internal format, we can handle current attention lists without creating any new components. Note that we are assuming that the filter component is capable of copying selected records from an existing header object into a newly created header object. This will create a new current attention list. A second instance of the Accessor component can be used to serve data for the current attention call window, thus getting two pieces of functionality for the price of one.

It may seem that our technique of subdividing an application into a set of independent features, each of which has minimal functionality, will eventually lead to an essentially unlimited variety of components. Surprisingly this is not the case. In a broad sense, there are only a very few types of components. Consider serializers, for example. Although every serializer does something slightly different, all serializers are pretty much the same. Their interfaces are all roughly identical, they perform similar functions, and the principles of their construction are roughly the same. The same thing can be said of accessors, caches, filters, and background editors. If we categorize components at this level, we will end up with a list of a dozen or so categories. Each category has its own well-defined design methodology, and each provides a specific type of functionality for an application.

Component categorization is an enormously powerful tool for designing component-based applications. We can go through a set of requirements and assign the various features of the application to glue logic, third-party components, and custom components. Each part of the program that is to be implemented as a custom component can be assigned to a particular component category. If a feature does not fit any of the categories, it probably needs to be divided further. When all features have been assigned to one category or another, development can proceed through a set of well-defined design methodologies, one for each category.

Although it is usually desirable to subdivide application features as much as possible, there are cases where different features should be combined into a single component. Third-party components are one such case. When creating a component for the third-party market, it is important to provide as much functionality as possible to make the component more saleable and easier to use. Another case where combining features is useful is when an excessive number of custom components is required for a single application. If you have an application that has hundreds of custom components, you should probably think about combining several features into a single component.

5. COMPONENT CATEGORIZATION

In today's marketplace, there is a bewildering variety of third-party components, a variety that almost defies description. Most attempts to categorize components have focused on applications. There are Web-access components, word-processing components, telephony components, personal information manager components, spreadsheet components, and many, many others. From a component-user's point of view, this sort of categorization makes sense because users are generally looking for a specific set of features for a particular application. A component-developer, however, needs to look at things differently. Is there really any difference between a text editor that is used for word processing and one that is used in a personal information manager? No, not really. There may be some minor differences in features, but the design principles of the two editors will be the same. Since we are focusing on the design of new components, we will adopt a view that is based on internal design principles rather than end use. Viewed from this perspective, there are remarkably few component categories. To simplify things further, we will break our categories into three broad classes: (1) visible components, (2) invisible components, and (3) other types of components.

6. THE VISIBLE COMPONENTS

Visible components are those that normally have a run-time view. Drawing the run-time view is a significant part of the design. In most cases, the end user will be able to interact with the component display using either the keyboard or the mouse, or both. The categories included in this classification are *Models, Editors, Displays, UI Widgets,* and *Decorations*. Although components in these categories normally have run-time displays, it is possible to implement them without one, and it is possible to use them with the run-time display turned off.

6.1 Models

A Model is a component that acts as a wrapper for an object-oriented model of some real-world object. The usual objective in creating a Model is to perform a simulation of some sort. The Model can be used to create games like Parcheesi, chess, or tic-tac-toe. Central to the Model component is an internal object-model that represents the real-world object encapsulated by the Model. The visible display provides a visible rendering of the internal object model. Usually, the end user is capable of interacting with the visible display, either through mouse clicks or keyboard actions. In most cases, the user interaction will be in the form of mouse clicks that are passed to the container as events with informational parameters.

Events are used in two ways: (1) to pass information about user interaction to the component's container and (2) to report exceptional conditions to the component's container. The user winning the game is an example of an exceptional condition.

Properties are used in three ways: (1) as rendering parameters, (2) as model specification parameters, and (3) as model informational parameters. For example, in the tic-tac-toe model, a property could be used to indicate the size of each square. Since this property does not affect the internal object-model, it is a *rendering parameter*. Another property could be used to indicate the number of horizontal and vertical squares in the display (going beyond the traditional 3×3). In reality, this property actually affects only the internal object model; its effect on the display is incidental. Therefore it is a *model specification parameter*. We could use a third property to indicate whether the current state of the model represents a win for one side or the other. The value of this property derives from the current state of the model; its value cannot be changed without changing the model. Therefore it is a *model informational parameter*. When either the model state or the visible rendering is complex, methods can be used instead of properties to implement these three types of functions.

The primary use for methods is as object-model manipulator functions. In the tic-tac-toe model, a method could be used to insert an X or an O in an empty square, or to request that the computer make a move.

In the design of a Model, we generally recommend a *passive object* design philosophy. According to this theory, the component responds *only* to property changes and method calls. User actions are reported to the container as events, but no action is taken in response to them. Responding to user actions is the responsibility of the container, which can elect to call a method or to set a property value in response to the event.

Variations on the Model are the invisible Model, and the Multi-Object Model. Invisible Models are those that require no user interaction or visible display, while multi-object Models are those that can obtain their internal object models from some external source.

6.2 Editors

An Editor has some elements in common with a Model. Like a Model, it has an internal object-model and, it also has a visible display. However, unlike the Model, the Editor is used to create the internal object model and to perform extensive modifications on it. Editors are inherently multi-object in nature. They must be able to save and restore their internal object models. In most cases, persistent storage will be used for this purpose, but semipersistent objects can also be used for this purpose. (A semipersistent object is an object whose lifetime is independent of its creator. See Chapter 19 for more details.) The most important distinction between Models and Editors is the response of the component to end-user actions. In general, an Editor will perform complex actions on its internal state in response to user input. Little or no action will be required on the part of the container.

One of the most important aspects of Editor design is the design of the internal object model. Generally, the internal object model, as represented inside the component, will differ extensively from the data that the Editor stores on persistent storage. For example, a text editor that uses simple text files for external storage may have a complex internal model to facilitate required operations such as adding and deleting lines, scrolling, and searching. Chapter 7 covers object-model design in detail.

Events are used for the monitoring and confirmation of user actions. For example, a **Change** event could be used to signal a user-initiated change in the internal object model. A **Delete** event could be used to alert the container to a pending delete action and to request confirmation of the action. An **OKToSave** event could be used to signal the pending erasure of unsaved changes, either by erasure of the existing object model or by a pending load of a new object model. (These two actions correspond to the *New* and *Open* commands in a file editor.) Events can also be used to monitor the progress of complex changes, such as a *Replace All* command. An **OKToChange** event could be used to confirm each individual change.

Properties are used to provide informational parameters about the display and the internal object model. For example, a **LineCount** property could be used to give the number of text lines in the current object model, while a **FirstVisible** property could be used to indicate the first line visible in the display.

Methods and properties are used to manipulate the state of the internal object model and the state of the display. The **FirstVisible** property mentioned above could also be used to scroll the display to a specific point. A **ScrollTo** method could be used for the same purpose. The general rule about state manipulation is that any operation that can be performed by the user must also be available to the container through properties and methods. If the user can select text, then the container must be able to select text. If the user can draw a new rectangle, then the container must be able to draw a rectangle. There is no consensus about whether properties or methods are best for such state manipulations, but the tendency is to use methods for this purpose because methods generally permit a wider range of parameters to be supplied to the operation.

Methods are also used to perform menu-based operations on the internal object model. In particular, the clipboard operations *Copy, Cut,* and *Paste* are traditionally implemented as menu selections on an *Edit* menu. Since components generally do not have their own menus, methods are used to transmit these menu commands to the component.

It is at least theoretically possible to create an Editor component that has no display or any end-user interaction. For such a component, all editing must be done through the programmatic interface. An example of such a component might be one that permits an HTML document to be created programmatically without external user interaction.

6.3 Displays

A Display component is used to make information visible to the user without providing any editing capability. One important use of Display components is to display information from proprietary file formats that the user is not permitted to edit. Some commercial examples are the Acrobat Reader control, and the PowerPoint viewer control. These components are distributed free of charge. The corresponding editors are commercial products that must be licensed for a fee. In a sense, this type of Display is a restricted form of an Editor. The features of the Display component are generally a subset of those provided by the full product. Because the features of such a Display component are adequately covered in Chapter 7, we will not present a separate discussion of this type of Display component.

A second and more interesting type of Display component is one that is used for the Visualization of data. Visualization is a complex research area in its own right and as such is beyond the scope of this book. However, we will present some simple types of Displays that permit visualization of simple objects. Like Models and Editors, Displays have an internal object-model. Depending on the complexity of the component, the internal model can be something as simple as an array of numbers, or something as complex as a relief map of the United States.

Events are generally used to report exceptional conditions but can also permit some user interaction with the display. If user interaction is permitted, it is generally limited to mouse clicks, which are passed to the container as events, sometimes with informational parameters.

Properties are used to provide informational parameters about the internal object model. For example, a Display component that is used to present a bar graph could provide a property called **LargestBar** that gives the height of the tallest bar. Properties can also be used to modify the display parameters, such as zoom factor and background color, as well as other parameters that are specific to the type of the Display.

Methods are used to supply data to the component. If the data are simple enough, properties can be used for this purpose.

By its very nature, a Display must always have a visible display.

6.4 UI Widgets

User Interface (UI) Widgets are the first and still the most common type of component. There is much discussion about UI Widgets already available. We will repeat much of this information here, but have little additional information to add to it. The only difference in our point of view is that we do not consider data-entry components to be UI Widgets. We prefer to view such components as Editors, because they are substantially different from other types of UI Widgets. In our view, the main purpose of UI Widgets is to translate mouse clicks into more useful types of events.

Although some UI Widgets have an internal object model, many do not. A dropdown list has an internal object model that gives the content of each list item, while a button has no internal object model. (This is an arguable point. Some may consider the caption to be part of a button's internal object model.)

Events are used to report user actions to the container. In some cases, events can also be used for exception reporting.

Properties are used as display parameters to control the size and colors of the display. They can also be used to manipulate the display in limited ways.

Methods are used to supply data for the internal object-model, if any.

Surprisingly, there are examples of invisible UI Widgets. Technically speaking, these components are *transparent* rather than invisible, but they are generally referred to as invisible components. They are used to provide user interaction with objects that do not normally permit such actions. They are typically drawn on top of another object to make that object, or some portion of it, sensitive to mouse clicks.

6.5 Decorations

Decorations are UI Widgets that do not permit user interaction. They are used only to enhance the quality of a display. The most common examples are labels and geometric shapes, but there are more complex types of Decorations. For example, *BeCubed Software* markets a component they call *MhMarque*, which displays a scrolling text banner. A Decoration component does not have to be purely decorative. It can transmit limited amounts of useful information, but it is far less complex than a Display component, or a UI Widget.

Events are generally not used. Properties are used to change the properties of the display. Methods are generally not required.

7. THE INVISIBLE COMPONENTS

The class of invisible components includes those components that do not generally have a visible display or any user interaction. In some component technologies, such as ActiveX, the component will be visible as an icon at design-time but invisible at run-time. In other technologies, such as COM, the component is never visible. Because component-level programming has its roots in visual programming, most users tend to ignore the invisible components. However, the class of invisible components is an emerging area that provides a number of interesting and useful component categories. In some cases, the functions of an invisible component can be combined with those of a visible component. In some cases, it may even be *preferable* to do so. However, because each category of component can be implemented as a separate entity, we prefer to treat each category separately.

There are five main categories of invisible components: (1) Filters, (2) Accessors, (3) Function Libraries, (4) Caches, and (5) Serializers. Because virtually any noninteractive program could be implemented as an invisible component, it is quite difficult to make this list of categories comprehensive. We believe that it is relatively complete but admit to the possibility of some glaring omissions.

7.1 Filters

A Filter is a component that transforms one object into an object of a different type, or into a "better" object of the same type. The objects in question can be files or internal objects. There is virtually no restriction on the types of objects that can be used. If the component operates on internal objects, it is necessary to establish some mechanism for transmitting objects between different components, and for establishing ownership of the objects.

Because many traditional programs can be viewed as filters, it is tempting to simply take a traditional program and place it into a component wrapper and call it a filter. For example, a compiler can be viewed as a program that transforms source files into executable modules, so it may be tempting to convert an existing compiler into a component by embedding the existing implementation in a Filter component wrapper. This is probably not the best way to do it. Because components operate in a different sort of environment from traditional programs, it is not necessary or advisable to consider a file to be the only possible output of a program. (We also use the term *file* to mean console and printer output.) In some cases we might want to consider a linked list, or some other complex object as the output of our Filter component. This permits applications to be broken down into components in some nontraditional ways. Returning to the example of a compiler, we might wish to subdivide it into several components, such as *parser, pre-processor, code generator, optimizer, assembler*, and *linker*. Given sufficient internal memory, there is no need to use files for intermediate storage. We could simply pass complex internal objects from one component to the next. This not only eliminates the need for reading and writing intermediate objects but also allows us to pass input data in a form that is readily accessible to the next stage.

There are two broad categories of filters: (1) *hot* filters and (2) *cold* filters. A cold filter is frozen. Given the same input, it always produces the same output. A hot filter is configurable. Its output depends not only on its input but also on its internal state.

From a component-design point of view, the most important part of a Filter is the programming interface, including the design of the input and output objects. (The design of the internal algorithms is also important, but it spans the range of computer applications and is for the most part beyond the scope of this book.) *Properties* and *methods* are used to transmit objects to the Filter and to retrieve output objects. *Events* are used only to report exception conditions.

In Chapter 11 we give several examples of Filters.

7.2 Accessors

An Accessor is a tool that provides programmatic access at the container level to a complex object. The objects in question are generally difficult or impossible to access in the container's programming technology. An example of an Accessor component is an

HTML component that allows the user to access the tags and content of an HTML file in some reasonable way. Accessor facilities can be added to Model and Editor components.

Methods and properties are used to supply the internal object-model. Properties are also used to access various parts of the object-model, while methods are generally used as iterator functions. Normally, a set of properties will be used to access a subobject within the object-model, and the iterator functions will be used to determine which subobject is currently being accessed by these properties. Accessor components generally have large numbers of properties and methods. Events are used to report errors in the object-model and exception conditions in the iteration process such as **EndOfList** or **NoCurrentObject**.

7.3 Function Libraries

Because existing technology provides many different methods for creating and accessing function libraries, the use of Function Library components is strictly optional. The main reason for embedding a function library in a component is convenience. A component is generally self-defining, so header files and function prototypes are not required. Function libraries are especially useful in Web-based applications, where they can be used to embed useful functions in a Web page.

Function libraries have no internal state, so properties are not required. Function calls are implemented as methods. If desired, events can be used to report exception conditions, but more traditional methods of raising exceptions can also be used. If efficiency is a concern, a standard function library should be used rather than component Function Library.

7.4 Caches

A Cache is a tool used at the container level to store and organize data. It can be used to implement traditional data structures such as stacks, queues, and binary search trees. Access is generally done strictly through the properties, but Accessor functionality can also be added. A drawback of this type of component is that it is generally capable of handling only one type of data. If one needs both a queue of integers and a queue of real numbers, it is generally necessary to implement two different Cache components. Events are used to signal exception conditions, such as **EndOfData**.

7.5 Serializers

A Serializer is a component that accepts semipersistent objects from some source, serializes them, and disposes of them in some fashion, usually by writing them to disk. The Serializer also performs the reverse function of retrieving a serialized object and creating a new semipersistent object from it. A Serializer is the bridge between a file format and a semipersistent object.

In addition to reading and writing objects to disk, a Serializer may write objects to the clipboard, or retrieve them from the clipboard. Since clipboard objects may pass from one address space to another, objects passed through the clipboard must be serialized. A Serializer may also interface with an object storage and retrieval system such as CORBA.

Editors are the most common examples of components that require serialization, but there are many other types of components that could be enhanced with serialization of their internal object models. Although the serialization function for most existing components is built in to the components that require it, there are strong reasons for separating the serialization function from other components. The first reason is encapsulation. Serialization is fundamentally different from the other functions performed by a component. In fact, it is so different that it makes sense to have a separate component to perform this function. The second reason is file-format independence. The use of semipersistent objects frees a component from dependency on a particular file format. Incorporating the serialization function into the component reestablishes this dependency. By separating serialization from other functions, we maintain file-format independence. By encapsulating the serialization functions into a separate component, we also simplify the task of adding new file formats to an application.

8. OTHER TYPES OF COMPONENTS

The types of components described in this section are neither inherently visible nor inherently invisible. They tend to provide functions that are outside the "main stream" of application development (although in some cases the functions they provide are absolutely necessary), or they provide functions that are difficult to classify.

8.1 Service Wrappers

The purpose of a service wrapper is to provide simplified access to operating system services. Many of these components are invisible at run-time, but some of them have a visible user interface. The quintessential example of this type of component is the Microsoft Common Dialogs control. Many of the dialog boxes that appear in programs for the Windows operating system are standard dialog boxes that are provided by an operating system program library. The two most commonly used of these are the *Open File* dialog and the *Save As* dialog. Although most of these dialogs are accessible in Visual Basic and other container applications, they are somewhat difficult to use. The Microsoft *Common Dialogs* component provides a wrapper for these dialogs. To display the *Open* File dialog, the programmer includes a *Common Dialogs* control in his or her program, and then calls the *ShowOpen* method of this control. The control itself is invisible at run-time. Components in this category include wrappers for telecommunications, wrappers for TCP/IP communications, multimedia players, and many others.

8.2 Containers

A Container is a component that is used to hold other components. Any component can be designed as a Container, and component design tools can provide the container functions automatically. It is conceivable that we could design an entire hierarchy of components that are contained within one another, but this has not yet proved useful in practice. A Container can be used as a layout tool, permitting groups of components to be moved or sized as a unit.

One of the most useful types of Containers is the tab control that provides several pages of components and permits the user to switch from page to page by clicking on a tab. Other Containers provide run-time resizable windows and splitter bars that can be used to change the relative sizes of portions of a program's window.

8.3 Miscellaneous Components

In any classification scheme that purports to include all types of components, there will inevitably be a few types of components that do not fit well into the classification scheme. The reader is cautioned that the field of component level design is a highly volatile one, and something that is categorized as "miscellaneous" today could become mainstream tomorrow.

One difficult-to-classify component is the *Universal Data-Aware* component. There are components that can be used to add database functionality to virtually any other component, including those that were not designed for such interaction (see Chapter 2, Section 2.5). Components that permit two other components to communicate with one another are exceedingly rare.

Also in this category are the more complex types of components that can be created using Java and other languages. These languages permit ordinary applications to be embedded in a component wrapper. This can result in a component that contains several other components interacting in a complex way. Such components tend to defy classification.

9. CONCLUSION

The design methodology of this chapter has four distinct phases. The first phase is dividing an application into third-party components, glue logic, and custom components. This phase requires an extensive knowledge of existing third-party components as well as their functionality and interfaces. The second phase is the design of shared objects that will be used by more than one custom component. The third phase is the specification of specific custom components for all application features that are to be implemented in this fashion. The fourth phase is the design of the components themselves.

The classification of components is intended to be used as a design tool for designing the custom components of an application. It focuses on design methodology rather than end use and provides a specific design methodology for each category of component. Using this methodology, the design of a component-level application is a straightforward process that can produce reliable, full-featured applications.

In the remainder of this book, we will look at formal design techniques for specific components and provide a specific design methodology for each category of component.

EXERCISES

1. Examine your favorite MP3 music player. Suggest a component-level design for it.
2. Go to the *EKS* Web site (http://www.kaser.com) and choose your favorite game. Suggest a component-level design for it.
3. Examine your favorite Web browser. Suggest a component-level design for it.
4. Choose a program that you use regularly, other than a game (something like a word processor or a spreadsheet program). Suggest a component-level design for it.
5. Go to a third-party component vendor's site (for example, http://www.vbxtras.com) and categorize 25 of the components you find there according to the scheme presented in this chapter.

Chapter 5

The Implementation of Components

1. PREREQUISITES AND OBJECTIVES

Before starting this chapter, you should have

1. A knowledge of component categories and how they are used to break down an application into components.
2. Some familiarity with object diagrams, UML, or some other notation.

After completing this chapter, you will have

1. A knowledge of how to design a component interface.
2. A knowledge of the passive design philosophy and how it relates to component interface design.
3. The ability to plan and document a component interface.
4. Optionally, a knowledge of how to use the Visual Studio ActiveX design tools.

2. INTRODUCTION

Object-oriented design is an integral part of component development, because components share many features with objects and can be used in much the same way. The main difference is that components are generally broader in scope and have more rigidly defined interfaces. The breakdown into components is typically done only at the highest level. Because components are separately compiled programs, the breakdown is generally not hierarchical. (This may change in the future.)

Component-level design and object-oriented design are actually independent concepts, but it has been found to be useful to tie the two concepts together. The most important feature of this marriage between object-oriented design and component-level programming is the encapsulation of component functionality in a single support class. Each instance of a component has its own support object, which encapsulates all instance-specific data and provides the support functions to handle both user and program input. The encapsulation of data and functionality is necessary to support multiple instances of a component. This encapsulation was necessary for the earlier non–object-oriented technologies as well, but these technologies solved the problem in less elegant ways.

In more recent technologies, the support class is an integral part of the component. This class inherits much of its functionality from standard operating system classes, and it contains the functions and data items necessary to implement the component. In reality, we do not design a component—we design the *support class* of the component. The standard functionality inherited by the support class will perform the low-level operations necessary to integrate the component with its environment. When a component is instantiated, standard functionality built into the component and its environment will create an instance of the support class to encapsulate the details of the component instance. The instances of the support class are called *support objects*. Figure 5-1 shows the relationship between components and the support class. Although there is additional required functionality beyond that of the support class, this functionality is generally invisible to the component developer.

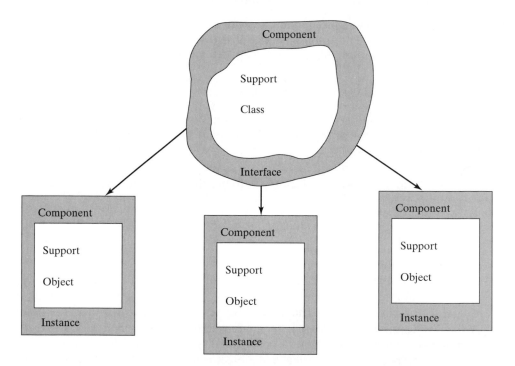

Figure 5-1   Components, Classes, and Instances

As we will demonstrate in later chapters, the design of most types of components involves a significant amount of object-oriented design beyond the design of the support class. In most cases, these classes become aggregates or friends of the support class. Some components serve as mere wrappers for objects, and others require intensive object-oriented design to implement their functionality in a manageable way. No specific object-oriented design methodology is recommended, but it is important to have some familiarity with formal design techniques before proceeding.

3. PROPERTIES, METHODS, AND EVENTS

The interface of a component consists of a set of properties, a set of methods, and a set of events. To document the interface, we need three different types of specifications: (1) property specifications, (2) method specifications, and (3) event specifications. Before proceeding with the details of these specifications, it is important to establish some general rules about how properties, methods, and events are used.

Although a property has much in common with a variable, it is important to remember that it is *not* a variable. The component is capable of monitoring both *read* and *write* accesses to the property, and it is capable of responding to a *read* or *write* request in a complex way. For example, assigning a value to a *FileName* property may cause a file to be written to disk. When documenting a property, it is important to document the actions that will be taken in response to *read* and *write* requests. Properties can be *read-only, write-only*, or *read-write*. Furthermore, it is possible to restrict access to a property to make it *design-time only*, or *run-time only*. A design-time only property can have a value assigned to it by a visual design tool such as Visual Basic, but a value cannot be assigned to the property at run-time. A run-time only property will not be visible to the programmer at design-time, but it will be possible to read it or to change its value at run-time. The formal specification of the property must contain all restrictions on the usage of a property.

The value of a property must be a simple type such as *Short Integer* or *Double Floating Point*, or an array of simple types. (This is a concession to some of the most popular technologies, which do not permit objects as property types. This is a severe restriction that does not exist in all technologies and will probably not exist in any future technology.) If it is necessary to send a set of coordinated values to a component, a method with multiple arguments must be used. However, methods cannot be used at design-time. If it is necessary to supply a coordinated set of values at design-time, the component must be designed to tolerate sets of inconsistent values, because these values must be supplied one at a time. For example, the *Pentomino* component of Chapter 6 has two properties that permit the user to specify the dimensions of the playing surface: The product of the x and y dimensions must be 60, but the component cannot raise an exception when a set of inconsistent values has been specified, because the values must be specified one at a time.

Because properties can trigger complex behavior, it is necessary to make a careful decision about whether a particular feature is to be implemented as a property or as a method. There is no hard-and-fast rule for making such a decision, but there are some guiding principles that will help.

It is wise to consider replacing write-only properties with single-argument methods. A write-only property will not be visible at design-time, because the visual display of a property requires that its value be readable at design-time. If the value assigned to the property is retained by the component after processing and used by the component in other ways, then a property may be a more appropriate implementation than a method. However, if the value is used immediately and then discarded, or not used at all, a method is a more appropriate implementation. By the same token, properties that are both read-only and run-time-only can be replaced by a method with zero arguments.

If you find yourself creating *GetValue* and *SetValue* methods for simple values, you should consider using a property instead (except, of course, for those technologies where properties are specified using *Get* and *Set* functions). It is not necessary for the value of a property to be represented explicitly in the support class. Property values can be computed when they are requested. The choice between property and a method will usually be obvious.

Although events and methods are quite different from one another, people who are just learning about component technology often get confused as to which is which. A method is a function implemented by the component that is called by the container at run-time. An event is a function implemented by the *container* that is called by the *component* at run-time. The container always has the option of doing nothing in response to an event. An event has no behavior defined by the component. If you find yourself thinking about the behavior of an event, you are not thinking about an event; you are thinking about a method. As far as the component is concerned, an event is nothing more than a function call. The body of the function is in the container, not in the component. The primary use for events is to inform the containing program that something important has occurred. The classic example of an event is the *Click* event provided by the standard button component. The button calls the click-event function to inform the host program that the button has been clicked. The Visual Basic programmer (for example) can provide a function body for the click event to perform useful work when the button is clicked. Figure 5-2 summarizes the characteristics of

Property	Method	Event
Can hold simple data items	Valueless	Informs user
Passes simple data items to component	Usually triggers complex behavior	Passes parameters to user
Retrieves simple data items from component	Passes several coordinated data items to component	
Available at design-time	Retrieves simple data items from component	
Design-time assignments are persistent	Not available at design-time	
Sometimes triggers complex behavior		

Figure 5-2   Property, Method, and Event Characteristics

properties, methods, and events. This information can be used to help choose an appropriate implementation for each interface item.

4. THE PASSIVE IMPLEMENTATION STYLE

In this book we recommend a passive style of implementation, an approach that implies that we want to minimize the direct interaction between the program user and the component. Except for Editor components, we believe that components should not directly process mouse or keyboard input. If the user clicks on the component, the mouse click, and possibly its position, should be reported by an event, but beyond that the component should take no action. If the user presses the *Delete* key, a **DeleteRequested** event should be issued, but no direct action should be taken. Over several years of component-based development, we have observed that components that use the passive implementation style are easier both to create and to use than their active counterparts.

The passive implementation style is actually a set of six rules that should be followed when developing a component. In the remainder of this section, we will discuss the individual rules and their impact on component design.

1. *Pass mouse-clicks through the component unprocessed.* We can process the input coordinates to determine the part of the display that has been clicked, but other than this, the component should take no action. The component container may have several modes of operation that are unknown to the component. The mouse click may mean something different depending on the mode. Passing the click through unchanged permits these modes to work properly. A component that actively processes mouse clicks can be used only with the modes that have been designed into it. In most cases, the glue logic will process the mouse click by performing some action on the component. To see how this rule works in practice, imagine a tic-tac-toe component. When the user clicks on a square, an X should be drawn in the square. However, the component does not do this directly. Instead it issues an event indicating which square has been clicked. The glue logic intercepts the event and calls a component method to draw the X. This rule does not apply to Editors, which must interact heavily with the user.

2. *Avoid direct implementation of menu shortcuts.* This especially applies to the *Cut, Paste, Copy*, and *Delete* operations. These are menu shortcuts and should be directed through the menu system by the operating system. Your component is not part of the menu system. This rule applies to all components, even editors. If you find it absolutely necessary to process some menu shortcuts, provide a property that can be used to turn off this processing. If you need *Cut, Paste, Copy*, and *Delete* operations, provide a method for each. These methods must be the only mechanisms for performing these operations. *Cut, Paste, Copy*, and *Delete* operations trigger complex actions that should be implemented at a single site within the component.

3. *Do not issue error messages.* All errors must be reported by using events or return codes. In some cases it is possible to use a status-code property in place of

a return code. If you violate this rule, your component will be much more difficult to internationalize. Any English text will have to be translated and replaced with text in some other language. It is possible to do this without recompiling the component, but the procedures that you must go through to enable this are beyond the scope of this book. Furthermore, what you consider to be an error might not be considered to be an error by the user. Suppose you wanted to write a program that would sort files into three categories: C-Code, PASCAL-Code, and Other. You could use a C-Compiler component and a PASCAL-Compiler component to test for C-Code files and PASCAL-Code files. Since it is not an error for a file to be in the category *Other*, error messages from the compiler components would be an unwanted annoyance. A parser error merely indicates that a file is not of a certain type. It does not indicate an error.

4. *Do not query the user for input.* If it is necessary for you to open a file, implement a **FileName** property, and open a file whenever a new value is assigned to this property. Do not pop up an open-file dialog box. All component input should come through the Property/Method interface (except for Editor components).

5. *Do not ask the user any questions.* This is a special case of the third and fourth rules. Suppose you have implemented a word-processing control and want to provide it with a "Change All With Confirmation" command. When you encounter a match for the input pattern, do not pop up a dialog box saying "Do you want to change this instance?" Instead, issue an event and let the glue logic pop up the dialog box.

6. *Limit keyboard input to shortcuts.* In other words, if it is possible for the user to perform a task using the keyboard, it should be possible to perform the same task using properties and methods. Specifically, if the left arrow can be used to scroll to the left, then there should be a **ScrollLeft** method that does the same thing. The keyboard input must be a shortcut for something that can be done through the property/method/event interface.

Although these six rules govern most situations that you will encounter, it is important to remember that the passive implementation style is a design philosophy, not a set of rules. It is important to follow this design philosophy, even if a particular situation is not covered by the rules.

5. FORMAL SPECIFICATIONS

In any mid- to large-scale software design project, it is important that certain formal specifications be completed before proceeding with the coding. Component-level design is no exception to this rule. We will not invent a new type of formal specification for component internals but will rely instead on those provided by existing object-oriented design methodologies. However, we do recommend a set of formal specifications be completed to describe the interface of the component. Insofar as it is possible, these specifications should be completed before proceeding with the implementation.

Property Design Table		
Name	**Type**	**Function**
Value	Long Integer Default = 0	This property contains the value currently displayed by the component. **Restrictions:** None
ArraySize	Long Integer Default = 20 Minimum = 2 Maximum = 50	When assigned a value, the internal array is destroyed and replaced with a new array. The value of this property determines the size of the array. When read, it returns the current size of the internal array. **Restrictions:** Run-Time Only
QueueSize	Long Integer Default = 0	This property is used to report the size of the internal queue. The queue size changes when the *Push* and *Pop* methods are called. These two methods are responsible for maintaining this value. **Restrictions:** Read Only
Caption	String Default = empty string	The caption will be displayed at the top of the control window both at run-time and design-time.
List	Long Integer Array of size 5 Default = none	This property allows the programmer to store up to five values and retrieve them later. There is no initial value, so an array element should not be read before it is written.

Figure 5-3   The Property Design Table

5.1 Properties

Figure 5-3 shows the property design table, which we will use to give the formal description of properties. Column 1 gives the name of the property. Column 2 gives the type, the default value, and any restrictions on the property value. The type is given in narrative form rather than using a language-specific type specifier. Column 3 contains a narrative description of the property's function, along with any restrictions on its use. If there are no restrictions, the statement **Restrictions: None** may be omitted. A property table entry should be completed for every property before it is implemented.

5.2 Methods

Figure 5-4 shows the Method description diagram that will be used to document all methods. The upper portion of the diagram is used to document the function itself by giving its name, return value, and a narrative description of its function. The second part of the table describes each argument. Column 1 gives the ordinal position of the argument in the argument list. If these numbers are omitted, the arguments are assumed to be described in the order in which they must be specified. Column 2 gives the name of the argument, column 3 gives the type in narrative form, and column 4 gives a description of the argument. Any restrictions on the value of the argument must be listed

Method Description			
Name	Distance		
Return Value	Double Float		
Description	Computes the Pythagorean distance between two points		
Arguments	**Name**	**Type**	**Description**
1	FromX	Double Float	X coordinate of the first point
2	FromY	Double Float	Y coordinate of the first point
3	ToX	Double Float	X coordinate of the second point
4	ToY	Double Float	Y coordinate of the second point

Figure 5-4   A Method Description

Event Description			
Name	SelectSquare		
Description	Provides the row and column of a selected square		
Triggers	Triggered when a user clicks on a square in the component window, or when the *TouchSquare* method is executed		
Arguments	**Name**	**Type**	**Description**
1	Row	Long Integer	Row of the selected square
2	Column	Long Integer	Column of the selected square

Figure 5-5   An Event Description

in the Type column. A method description must be completed for each method before it is implemented.

5.3 Events

Figure 5-5 shows an event description diagram. Except for two lines in the upper section, the diagram is the same as the method description diagram in Figure 5-4. The event description diagram has no return value type, but it does have a *Triggers* description instead. (Although some technologies permit return values for events, this is not universal.) In the Triggers description, it is necessary to document the precise conditions under which the event is fired. The description of the event should describe the event and its intended usage.

6. INDIVIDUAL COMPONENT DEVELOPMENT

In chapters 6 through 10 we will give design methodologies and examples for each different category of component. Many of these chapters are independent of one another, but some of them are closely interrelated and should be read in a specific order. In particular, Chapter 7 introduces the concept of graphical editors through the use of an example called the simple graphical editor. The underlying object structure created to support this editor is complex and can easily serve as a case study in object-oriented design. This object is intended to be passed from component to component, and thus is used by a number of different components introduced in a number of different chapters. The main object is called the **CGraphicList** object. This object contains a number of aggregated objects and provides functions to support adding, deleting, and modifying graphical elements. It also supports undo and serialization facilities, which are used in a number of different components. Figure 5-6 illustrates the usage of this object by the various different components and also indicates in which chapter each component is presented. Like the example of the prospect management program given in Chapter 4, the Simple Graphical Editor (SGE) components show how to develop an application using a series of interrelated components.

Chapters 7, 8, and 9 are exclusively devoted to SGE examples, while Chapters 10, 11, and 12 have a substantial number of other examples. (Chapter 7 contains the introductory material for the SGE family of components, and it is important to read this chapter first.) Because the overall structure of the **CGraphicList** object is developed over several chapters, we include a preview of the entire structure in Figure 5-7.

In this figure, the diamond shape signifies aggregation or inclusion, while the arrowhead signifies inheritance. The range of numbers 1–n specifies a list of objects with at least one element, while the value 0–n specifies a list that may be empty. The left side of the figure is concerned with the representation of graphical objects, while the right side is concerned with the undo facility. Both of these concepts are explained in Chapter 7. The objects **SerRectangle** and **SerCircle** are serial forms of the **CRectangle**

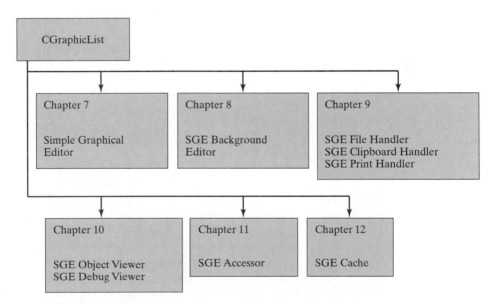

Figure 5-6   Simple Graphical Editor Components

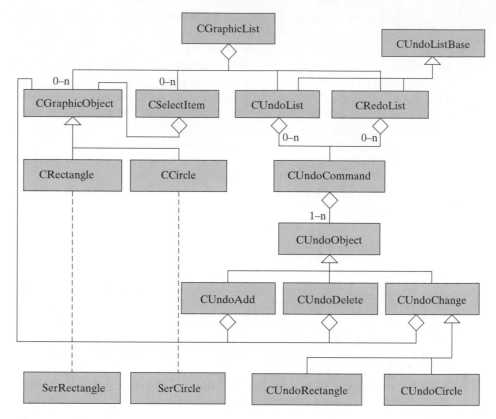

Figure 5-7   CGraphicList Structure

and **CCircle** objects. The **SerRectangle** and **SerCircle** objects are suitable for writing to persistent storage, while the **CRectangle** and **CCircle** objects are not. Serialization and persistent storage are discussed in Chapter 9.

Although a family of components is an extremely powerful development tool, independent components designed to perform a single task without cooperation from other components are equally powerful. Much of the material of Chapters 10, 11, and 12 is devoted to independent components, while Chapter 6 and Chapters 13–18 are entirely devoted to independent components.

7. ACTIVEX DEVELOPMENT*

Although there are many different component technologies, we will focus on a single technology, ActiveX, in the remainder of this book. To describe the process of component

_____

*Although all examples are given in the ActiveX technology, the material in the chapters that follow is designed to be used with virtually any component technology. This section may be skipped by those who do not plan to use the ActiveX technology.

development, it is necessary to give numerous examples. To show the code of an example, we must first select a technology in which to implement it. (The code illustrated in this book is all cut and pasted from running examples. We do not believe in creating "abstract code" merely for the purpose of illustrating a point.) Since all current technologies share the same sorts of features, concentrating on a single technology is not restrictive. To convert our examples into JavaBeans, for example, it is simply a matter of translating our examples into their JavaBeans equivalents. If it is necessary to select a single technology, ActiveX is a reasonable choice. It is the leader in the commercial world, and it allows us to create components that can be used in a wide variety of different applications. An ActiveX control can be used in the Visual Basic, Visual C++, Delphi, and C# languages. It can be placed in a Web page and distributed automatically through the Internet. It can be placed in a Microsoft Word document, a PowerPoint presentation, or an Excel spreadsheet. In addition, ActiveX controls can be developed in many different programming languages. Furthermore, because of the large base of existing ActiveX components, it is unlikely that they will be replaced by newer technologies at any time in the near future.

There is also a price to be paid for this choice. An ActiveX control is complicated, so much so that we must automate much of the development process through the use of development tools. This ties the discussion to a specific set of tools and may tend to give the impression that these tools are the only way to create components. The reader is cautioned that there are many other tools that provide the same functionality as those described here.

The specific set of tools that we will use are the MFC and ATL development packages that have been integrated into the Visual C++ development platform. (As of this writing, version 6.0 is the current version of this platform.) We will use only the MFC tools in this book. ATL is beyond the scope of this book, but we provide some ATL projects on the Web page.

7.1 The MFC Package

The Microsoft Foundation Classes (MFC) package provides wrappers for most of the basic Windows operating system facilities. In particular, it provides a wrapper for ActiveX controls. To create an ActiveX control, start Visual C++, and select the **New** command from the **File** menu. This will display the dialog box shown in Figure 5-8. Type a name in the *Project Name* field and click *OK*.

You will next be shown the dialog box in Figure 5-9. Don't do anything with this; just click **Next**. This will give you the dialog box shown in Figure 5-10. If you want a visible control, do nothing; just click *Finish*. If you want an invisible control, click *Invisible at Run-Time* so that it is checked, and uncheck *Activates When Visible*. Then click on *Finish*. You may now compile your ActiveX control, although to make it interesting, you will need to add a little bit more to it.

You add properties methods and events to your component using the Class Wizard which is accessed from the *View* menu (see Figure 3-7, which illustrates the Class Wizard). The **Automation** tab of the Class Wizard is used to add properties and methods to the control, while the **ActiveX Events** tab is used to add events. Click on the proper button and follow the instructions to create properties, methods, and events. The **Message Maps** tab is used to intercept user input. In most cases the Class Wizard can be used without explicit instructions.

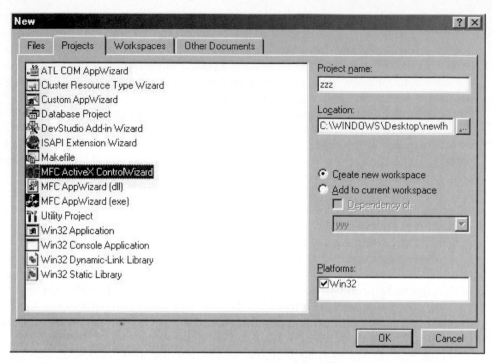

Figure 5-8   Starting a New MFC Project

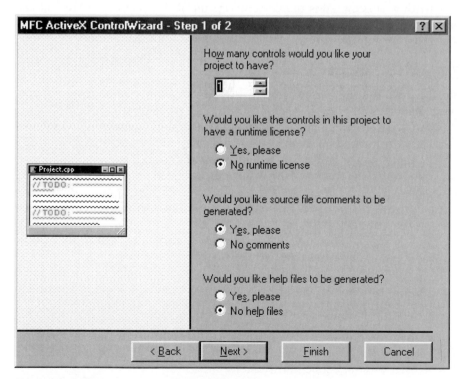

Figure 5-9   MFC ActiveX Control Wizard, Page 1

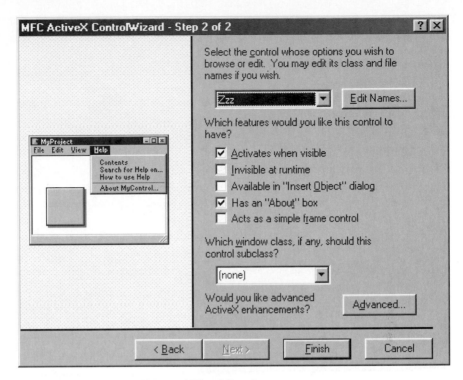

Figure 5-10   MFC ActiveX Control Wizard, Page 2

The function of the Class Wizard, among other things, is to add functions to the support class of your ActiveX control, which is implemented by supplying the bodies of these functions.

One function that is automatically supplied for you is the *OnDraw* function. This function is called anytime the window needs to be redrawn, and whenever your component calls the *CWnd::Invalidate* function. The *OnDraw* function has three parameters: (1) the drawing context of the control window, (2) a rectangle describing the entire window, and (3) a rectangle describing the part of the window that must be redrawn. MFC drawing functions must be used with the drawing context to draw the window.

The process for creating an ActiveX control in VS.NET is quite similar to the procedure used in Visual C++ 6.0. Go to the *File Menu*, select the *New* command and the *Project* subcommand. This will display the dialog box shown in Figure 5-11. From this dialog box, select Visual C++ Projects from the left window, and MFC ActiveX Control from the right window. Type the project name in the *Name* box, and click *OK*.

The VS.NET ActiveX wizard is essentially the same as that for Visual C++ 6.0, but it is organized somewhat differently. Figure 5-12 shows the first page of the wizard. The subsequent pages can be accessed by clicking on the phrases *Application Settings*, *Control Names*, and *Control Settings*. The *Application Settings* page corresponds to page 1 of the VC++ 6.0 wizard, while the *Control Settings* page corresponds to page 2 of the VC++ 6.0 wizard.

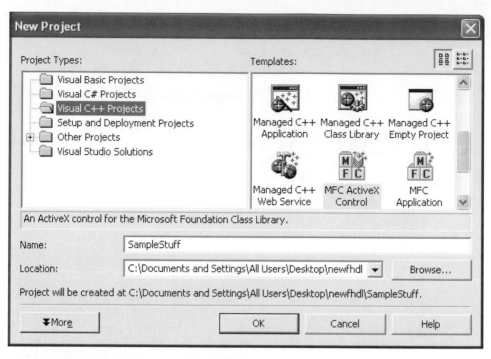

Figure 5-11 Creating an ActiveX Control in VS.NET

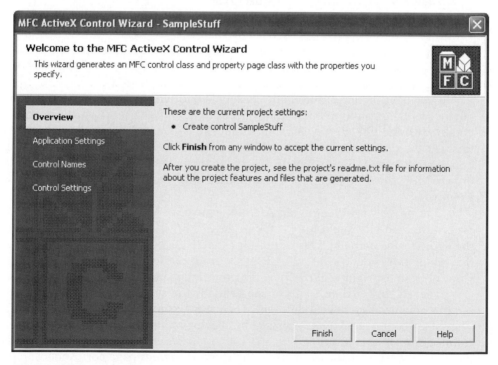

Figure 5-12 The VS.NET ActiveX Wizard, Page 1

As noted in Chapter 3, a number of the Class Wizard functions in VS.NET have moved into the class view window, and others have moved into the property window. (See Chapter 3 for information on creating properties, methods, and events.) To add functions of other types, select the class **C<YourName>Ctrl**, and use the properties window to add the desired function. Figure 5-13 shows how to add a mouse click event handler to a component named **SampleStuff**, while Figure 5-14 shows how to add an

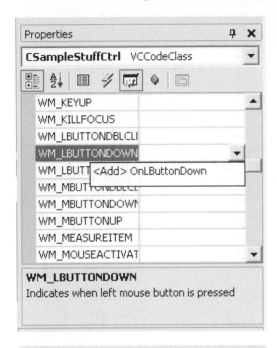

Figure 5-13   Adding a Message Handler in VS.NET

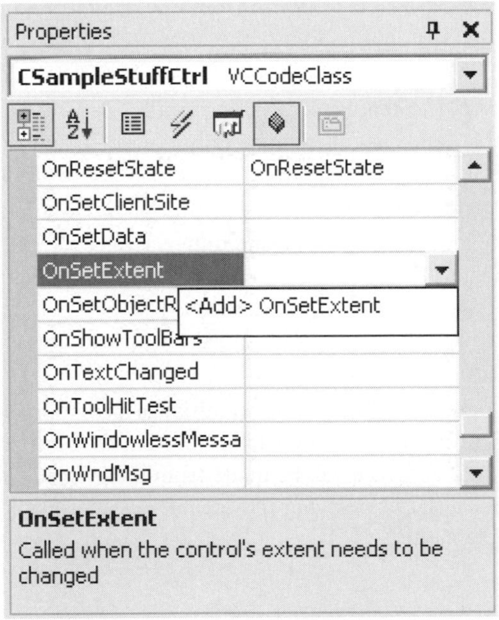

Figure 5-14   Adding an Override in VS.NET

override to the same component. Note the row of icons below the name of the class. To add message handlers, click on the fifth icon from the left; to add an override, click on the sixth icon from the left. In both cases, you can add the desired function by clicking on the suggested function name.

8. CONCLUSION

When dealing with components, the most important implementation skill is determining when to use a property and when to use a method for a particular interface feature. The guidelines presented in this chapter will help, but some practice is necessary. The passive implementation style is an important tool for simplifying component development, because much work is passed off to the glue logic rather than being performed by the component itself. Surprisingly, this implementation style also tends to simplify the glue logic, because the programmer does not have to conform to a set of conventions established by the component.

Documentation and planning are important at all phases of application design. The most important formal specifications for a component are the interface specifications that document the properties, methods, and events. These interface specifications should be completed at the same time as other design documents such as object diagrams and state diagrams.

Once you have mastered the skills of this chapter, and of Chapter 4, you are ready to begin developing your own components.

EXERCISES

1. You are designing a component that needs to read a configuration file. Two different instances of your component may need to use two different files. The configuration file is processed during initialization, but it is also possible to switch from one configuration file to another while a component instance is running. Discuss the best way to implement these features.

2. You are designing a component that needs to read several different files while it is running. These files will be read one at a time, and each file will be fully processed and closed before reading the next. If a specified file cannot be opened, the user should be notified. Discuss the best way to implement these features.

3. You are designing a component that implements a dynamic one-dimensional array. Initially, each instance of the array has a default size. (There is one array per component instance.) The size of the array can be changed dynamically at run-time. Using formal design documents, show how the size of the array will be specified, and show how to access and modify the individual elements of the array.

4. You are designing a random greeting component. The user must initialize a component instance by assigning a number of strings to it. These strings will be stored in an internal list. When the user requests a greeting, a random choice will be made from the internal list of strings and that string will be returned to the user. Using the formal design documents, show how these features should be implemented.

5. You are designing a Parcheesi game simulator that shows the board, the pieces on the board, and the dice. In order to make a move, a player must click on a button marked *Roll* to roll the dice. (Note that in Parcheesi, two dice are rolled, and the player may move one piece the total number of spaces indicated on both dice, or two pieces, one the distance shown on the first die, and the second the distance shown on the second die.) To make a move, the player will first click on a piece to select it and then click on a die to move the piece that distance. The moved piece will remain selected so that it can be moved again. Two custom components are required: one to represent the dice and one to represent the board. Using the formal design documents, describe the portions of the interfaces that permit rolling the dice and making moves.

Chapter 6

Models

1. PREREQUISITES AND OBJECTIVES

Before starting this chapter, you should have

1. A knowledge of programming in C++.
2. A knowledge of component interface design.

After completing this chapter, you will have

1. A knowledge of how to wrap an object model in a component wrapper.
2. The ability to implement simple games and other elementary simulations.
3. A knowledge of the Model-Component design methodology.

2. INTRODUCTION

Of all the different categories of components, the Model is probably the most fun. A Model is used to encapsulate an object-oriented model of some useful object. Interactive puzzles and games can be created using Model components, as well as other more "serious" things. An example of such a Model is the *Towers of Hanoi* component (abbreviated to just *Hanoi* in the text that follows) shown in Figure 6-1.

A Model component contains an internal object model that is manipulated using the methods of the component. Generally, the object model is an integral part of the component, being designed along with the component, and permanently embedded in the component. When the Model component executes, the internal object model is already complete. This approach differs from that taken by an Editor component, which is used to construct the internal object model. The internal object model is not normally saved in permanent storage, but some variants of the Model component permit this.

Most Model components have a display that shows the internal state of the internal object model. In most cases, the user can interact with the internal object model by clicking on various parts of the display.

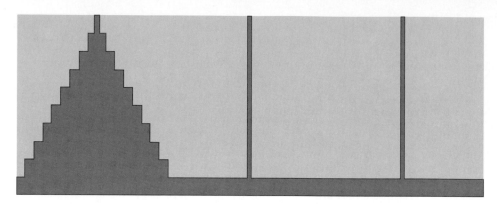

Figure 6-1   The Towers of Hanoi

3. THE DESIGN METHODOLOGY

The design of a Model component proceeds in four stages: (1) the design of the internal object model, (2) the design of the display, (3) the design of the component's manipulator methods, and (4) the design of the user interaction. The design of the internal object model is the most important step. In effect, the internal object model *is* the component. The remaining steps in the design merely provide a wrapper for the internal object model. Properties are used both as model parameters and as display parameters. Model parameters are those that have some effect on the model itself. For example, in the Hanoi component, a model parameter might be the total number of disks in the puzzle. (In Figure 6-1, this parameter would be set to 8.) Display parameters affect only the display. They are a part of the component interface but not a part of the model. An example of a display parameter for the Hanoi component might be the height of each disk. The properties of a Model component are designed both during the design of the internal object model and during the design of the display.

Methods are used for manipulating the model. In the Hanoi component, methods will be used to move a disk from one peg to another and to reset the game to its initial state. Methods are usually wrapper functions for the functions of the internal object model.

Events are used for user interaction. Typically, they are used to report mouse clicks. It is generally necessary to analyze the position of the mouse cursor to determine what part of the model has been clicked. The click event of the Hanoi component will report which peg (if any) has been clicked. Events can also be used to report error conditions. Although we have not done this in the Hanoi model, we could use an event to report an attempt to place a large disk on top of a smaller one.

In the remainder of this chapter we will illustrate the design of a Model component using two games as examples. Model components can also be used for more serious purposes, but games provide a "fun" way to begin learning about component-level design.

4. THE TOWERS OF HANOI

The display of the Hanoi component represents a board with three pegs, on which there are eight disks of different sizes. The disks are stacked pyramid-style on peg 1. The object of the puzzle is to move the stack of disks from peg 1 to peg 2, using peg 3 as a work peg. Disks must be moved one at a time without ever placing a large disk on top of a smaller one. The problem is known to be exponential in the number of disks.

The Hanoi control contains an object-oriented model of the peg-board and the disks. This model was developed without regard to the fact that it would eventually be used in a component, or more specifically, in an ActiveX control. Typical object-oriented-design principles were used, although with somewhat less rigor than we would use for a more "serious" component. As the object model was being created, care was taken to make sure that any program using the model would have a sufficient number of public functions and variables to query the object state and perform the required operations on it.

The design of the model began with the class **CPeg**, which incorporates all of the functionality required to model a peg. The class contains three data items: (1) *Data*, (2) *Slots*, and (3) *Disks*. The *Data* item is a dynamic array of integers representing the size of each disk on the peg. Sizes 1 through 8 would be used for an eight-peg game. The item *Slots* contains the capacity of the peg—i.e., the maximum number of disks the peg can hold—while the item *Disks* contains the current number of disks on the peg. In the *Data* array, the size of the lowest disk is found in array item 0, with the higher indices indicating the disks higher on the peg. If there are k disks on the peg, their sizes will be found in array items 0 through k-1. The three items are protected, because changes to the items must be done in a coordinated way.

The **CPeg** class has four manipulator functions: (1) *AddDisk*, (2) *RemoveDisk*, (3) *Empty,* and (4) *Fill*. The *AddDisk* and *RemoveDisk* functions are used to move disks between pegs, while the *Empty* and *Fill* functions are used during initialization. The *Empty* function removes all disks from a peg, while the *Fill* function places all disks, in order, on the peg. The **CPeg** class also has two accessor functions: (1) *DiskCount*, which returns the current number of disks on the peg, and (2) *DiskSize*, which returns the size of the disk in a particular position on the peg. The **CPeg** class also has a special constructor that is used to construct pegs of a specific size. The definition of the **CPeg** class is shown in Figure 6-2.

The **CPeg** class is a part of the **CBoard** class. Used to encapsulate the functionality of the entire game board, the **CBoard** class contains two protected data items: (1) *NoDisks*, which gives the disk capacity of each peg, and (2) *Pg*, an array of three pegs. There is also a public data item, *Selected*, that indicates which peg, if any, is selected. Any value of *Selected* other than 0, 1, or 2 is used as a "no selection" indicator, so there is no need to make this item protected. The **CBoard** class has a special constructor that is used to create a board of a specific size. The default constructor creates a board with eight disks. There is an *Initialize* function that moves all disks to peg 1 and empties pegs 2 and 3. There are two manipulator functions, *MoveDisk* and *MoveStack*, and three accessor functions *DiskCount(void)*, *DiskCount(long)*, and *DiskSize*. The *MoveDisk* function is used to move a single disk from one peg to another, while the *MoveStack* function is used to move an entire stack of disks starting with the top disk. The

```
class CPeg
{
protected:
    long * Data;
    long Slots;
    long Disks;

public:
    Peg();
    Peg(long NoDisks);
    virtual ~Peg();

    // initialization
    void Empty(void);
    void Fill(void);
    // movement
    long AddDisk(long Size);
    long RemoveDisk();
    // accessor functions
    long DiskSize(long DiskID);
    long DiskCount(void);
}
```

Figure 6-2   The CPeg Class Definition

MoveStack function does not necessarily move *all* disks on a peg. The accessor functions are used to extract information about the disks on a peg, primarily so that the board can be drawn properly. Figure 6-3 presents the definition of the **CBoard** class.

Figure 6-4 shows the implementation of the *AddDisk* and *RemoveDisk* functions. Note that the *Disks* array is treated as a formal stack. This makes sense because disks must be removed in the reverse order from which they were placed on the peg. The *RemoveDisk* function must check for the empty peg error, while the *AddDisk* function must check for peg overflow and stacking a large disk on top of a smaller one.

Figure 6-5 shows the *Empty* and *Fill* functions, which are used by the constructors and by the *Initialize* function. Figure 6-6 shows a **CBoard** constructor and demonstrates how the board is initialized.

Figure 6-7 shows the *MoveDisk* function of the **CBoard** class. This function calls *RemoveDisk* on the *From* peg, and *AddDisk* on the *To* peg. The rest of the code is error checking.

The *MoveStack* function is given in Figure 6-8. This function moves an entire stack of disks from one peg to another. To move a stack of disks, the algorithm uses a source peg, a target peg, and a work peg. To move k disks, k-1 disks are moved to the work peg, then the bottom disk is moved from the source peg to the target peg, and then the k-1 disks are moved from the work peg to the target peg. The k-1 disks are moved using a recursive call to *MoveStack*. If the stack is only one disk high, then a single disk move is used to move the stack. *MoveStack* checks for two errors, invalid peg numbers, and requested number of disks not available.

```
class CBoard
{
protected:
    long NoDisks;
    Peg * Pg[3];
public:
    long Selected;

public:
    Board();
    Board(long DiskCount);
    virtual ~Board();

    void Initialize();
    // movement
    long MoveStack(long From, long To, long Work, long Count);
    long MoveDisk(long From, long To);
    // accessors
    long DiskCount(void);
    long DiskCount(long PegID);
    long DiskSize(long PegID, long DiskID);
};
```

Figure 6-3   The CBoard Class Definition

After the design of the internal object model was completed, the model was embedded in an ActiveX framework. This framework also contains the other three parts of the design: (1) the drawing routine, (2) the manipulator methods, and (3) the user interaction functions. The board is implemented as a single data item, *MyBoard*, of the ActiveX support class.

The drawing routine is straightforward. The bottom of the board and the pegs are drawn as black rectangles, and the disks are drawn as red or blue rectangles with black borders. The pegs are drawn to be "one disk taller" than the maximum number of disks that can be placed on a peg. The distance between pegs is calculated to be half the width of the widest disk plus ten pixels. Ten pixels of space are left on each side of the board. The top of each peg will always touch the top of the control window. The height of each disk is 20 pixels, and the width is its size times 20. Therefore the disk of size 5 is 100 pixels wide. Each disk is drawn as a red rectangle with a black border. If a stack is selected, the top disk in the stack is drawn as a blue rectangle with a black border. We omit the details of the drawing routine, since much of this routine is Windows operating system functions that set drawing modes, background colors, and so forth. During this phase of the design, we added a single property, *BackColor*, which is used to set the background color. The property design table for this property appears in Figure 6-9.

During the third phase of the design, the following manipulator methods were added to permit external manipulation of the model: *Initialize, MoveDisk, Select, De-Select, GetSelect, Solve,* and *Abort*. The formal method descriptions of these methods is given in Figures 6-10 through 6-16. The simplest of these are the *MoveDisk* and

```
long CPeg::RemoveDisk()
{
   if (Disks > 0)
   {
      Disks--;
      return Data[Disks];
   }
   else
   {
      return -1;
   }
}
```

```
long CPeg::AddDisk(long Size)
{
   if (Disks >= Slots)
   {
      return 0; // programming error if we get here
   }
   if (Disks <= 0)
   {
      // first disk on the peg 0=bottom disk position
      Data[0] = Size;
      Disks = 1;
   }
   else
   {
      if (Size > Data[Disks-1])
      {
         return 0; // illegal move
      }
      Data[Disks] = Size;
      Disks++;
   }
   return 1;
}
```

Figure 6-4   The *AddDisk* and *RemoveDisk* Functions

Initialize methods, which are simply wrappers for the *MoveDisk* and *Initialize* functions of the **CBoard** class. Three methods—*Select, DeSelect*, and *GetSelect*—were added to permit the manipulation of the selected peg. These methods use the *Selected* item of the board model, *MyBoard*. The *Select* function sets a specific peg as the selected peg, *DeSelect* clears the selection so no peg is selected, and *GetSelect* returns the current value of the selected peg, if any. *GetSelect* returns a value other than 0, 1, or 2 to indicate that no peg is selected. The final two manipulator methods are *Solve* and *Abort*. *Solve* is used to provide an animated solution of the puzzle, and *Abort* is used to terminate the *Solve* method before completion. Permitting early termination of the *Solve* function is tricky because that function must interrupt itself periodically to allow

```
void CPeg::Empty()
{
    Disks = 0;
}
```

```
void CPeg::Fill()
{
    for (long i=0 ; i<Slots ; i++)
    {
        Data[i] = Slots - i;
    }
    Disks = Slots;
}
```

Figure 6-5   The *Empty* and *Fill* Functions

```
CBoard::CBoard(long DiskCount)
{
    NoDisks = DiskCount;
    Pg[0] = new Peg(NoDisks);
    Pg[1] = new Peg(NoDisks);
    Pg[2] = new Peg(NoDisks);
    Selected = -1;
    Pg[0]->Fill();
    Pg[1]->Empty();
    Pg[2]->Empty();
}
```

Figure 6-6   The CBoard Constructor

```
long CBoard::MoveDisk(long From, long To)
{
    if (From > 2 || From < 0 || To > 2 || To < 0)
    {
        return 0;
    }
    long Disk = Pg[From]->RemoveDisk();
    if (Disk == -1)
    {
        return 0;
    }
    long rv = Pg[To]->AddDisk(Disk);
    if (!rv)
    {
        Pg[From]->AddDisk(Disk);
    }
    return rv;
}
```

Figure 6-7   The MoveDisk Function

```
long Board::MoveStack(long From, long To, long Work, long Count)
{
    if (From > 2 || From < 0 || To > 2 ||
        To < 0 || Work > 2 || Work < 0 ||
        From == To || From == Work || To == Work)
    {
        return 0;
    }
    if (Count <= 0 || Count > Pg[From]->DiskCount())
    {
        return 0;
    }
    if (Count == 1)
    {
        MoveDisk(From,To);
    }
    else
    {
        MoveStack(From,Work,To,Count-1);
        MoveDisk(From,To);
        MoveStack(Work,To,From,Count-1);
    }
    return 1;
}
```

Figure 6-8   The *MoveStack* Function

Property Design Table		
Name	**Type**	**Function**
BackColor	OLE_COLOR Default = White	Specifies the background color for the drawing. This color will fill all empty space in the drawing.

Figure 6-9   BackColor Property Description

Method Description			
Name	Initialize		
Return Value	Void		
Description	Moves all disks to peg 1, clears peg 2 and peg 3, redraws the window.		
Arguments	**Name**	**Type**	**Description**
Void			

Figure 6-10   *Initialize* Method Description

Method Description			
Name	MoveDisk		
Return Value	Void		
Description	Moves the top disk from one peg to another. The parameters specify the source and target peg.		
Arguments	**Name**	**Type**	**Description**
1	From	Long Integer	Source peg 0, 1, or 2.
2	To	Long Integer	Target peg 0, 1, or 2

Figure 6-11 *MoveDisk* Method Description

Method Description			
Name	Select		
Return Value	Void		
Description	Selects a specific peg. Clears selection if selected peg is already selected. Does nothing if operand is invalid.		
Arguments	**Name**	**Type**	**Description**
1	Peg	Long Integer	The peg to be selected, 0, 1, or 2.

Figure 6-12 *Select* Method Description

Method Description			
Name	DeSelect		
Return Value	Void		
Description	Clears the selected peg. No peg is selected after this call.		
Arguments	**Name**	**Type**	**Description**
Void			

Figure 6-13 *DeSelect* Method Description

Method Description			
Name	GetSelect		
Return Value	Long Integer		
Description	Returns the number of the selected peg, or −1 if no peg is selected.		
Arguments	**Name**	**Type**	**Description**
Void			

Figure 6-14 *GetSelect* Method Description

Method Description			
Name	Solve		
Return Value	Void		
Description	Shows an animated solution to the puzzle.		
Arguments	**Name**	**Type**	**Description**
Void			

Figure 6-15   Hanoi *Solve* Method Description

Method Description			
Name	Abort		
Return Value	Void		
Description	Aborts an animated solution of the puzzle.		
Arguments	**Name**	**Type**	**Description**
Void			

Figure 6-16   Hanoi *Abort* Method Description

other portions of the program (such as buttons) to run. It is also necessary to slow the solution process down to provide a reasonable animation. Without some inserted delays, the process would complete too quickly to be visible. The animation is done by changing the state of the model, and then redrawing it. We do not show the intermediate steps as a disk moves from one peg to another.

In creating the *Solve* routine, it was not possible to use the *MoveStack* function of the **CBoard** class, because this function does not (and *should* not) contain the operating system function calls used to redraw the model, delay the drawing, and interrupt the solution process to permit other portions of the program to run. Therefore it was necessary to implement an external *MoveStack* routine that contains all the functionality of the **CBoard** *MoveStack* function, plus the additional operating system calls. This function is called *LMoveStack*, and it interacts with the internal object model using the *MoveDisk* function. Figure 6-17 gives the implementation of *LMoveStack*. This uses the operating system function *CWnd::Invalidate* to redraw the window. To solve the puzzle, it is necessary to call the *Initialize* function to place all disks on peg 1, and then call *LMoveStack* (once) to move all disks from peg 1 to peg 2.

The *Pause* function delays the program the specified number of milliseconds (500=1/2 second), and it also momentarily gives up control of the CPU to let other portions of the program run. The implementation of this function is shown in Figure 6-18. This function does not actually relinquish the CPU but instead finds all pending work for other parts of the program, and dispatches it to the proper program subroutine

```
void CHanoiCtl::LMoveStack(long From,long To,long Work,long Count)
{
    … // Error checking code omitted for brevity.
    if (Count > 1)
    {
        LMoveStack(From,Work,To,Count-1);
        if (AbortSolve)
        {
            return;
        }
        MyBoard->MoveDisk(From,To);
        CWnd::Invalidate();
        Pause(500);
        if (AbortSolve)
        {
            return;
        }
        LMoveStack(Work,To,From,Count-1);
    }
    else
    {
        MyBoard->MoveDisk(From,To);
        CWnd::Invalidate();
        Pause(500);
    }
}
```

Figure 6-17   The *LMoveStack* Function

```
void CHanoiCtl::Pause(long mSec)
{
    MSG msg;

    while (PeekMessage(&msg,NULL,NULL,NULL,PM_REMOVE))
    {
        DispatchMessage(&msg);
    }
    if (AbortSolve)
    {
        return;
    }
    WaitForSingleObject(THandle,mSec);
}
```

Figure 6-18   The *Pause* Function

for processing. This is done through two Windows operating system calls, *PeekMessage* and *DispatchMessage*. During this processing, it is possible for a button to be clicked and for the *Abort* method of the ActiveX control to be called. This will set the Abort-Solve variable to **true**. Once this variable is set to **true**, the *Solve* routine will abort itself without completing its task.

Delays are implemented by waiting for an event that will never occur using the specified delay as a timeout value. This is done using the *WaitForSingleObject* operating system function.

The final phase involves the design of the user interaction. We want the user to be able to solve the puzzle manually by clicking on pegs with the mouse. Ideally, we would like to permit the user to move a disk by dragging it from one peg to another, but because this is relatively complicated, we will settle for something simpler. What we will do is this. We will allow the user to select a peg, and then move the disk from the selected peg to another peg by clicking on the target peg. The selection part has already been implemented, so we need to concentrate only on the movement. For this, we will use a *passive model* method of user interaction. In this type of user interaction, all changes to the internal object model must be performed using manipulator methods. User interactions—mouse clicks and keystrokes—are filtered through the control and passed to the user in the form of events. The control makes no changes to the model in response to user interactions. We will not use keystrokes in our control, but we will use mouse clicks. We will create a single event, *Click2*, which we will fire in response to the user pressing the left mouse button. (We would like to use the name *Click* for our event, but some containers do not respond properly if *Click* is implemented in a nonstandard way.) Our *Click2* event has a single parameter that indicates which peg has been clicked. We do not want it to be necessary for the user to click precisely on the peg, but we do want it to be possible for the user to click anywhere on the stack of disks for the peg. We will return 0, 1, or 2 depending on which peg has been clicked, or −1 if the click is outside the drawing. We use the operating system *CWnd::GetClientRect* to get the rectangle for the control's window. (See Figure 6-19.)

When creating a program for manually solving the Towers of Hanoi puzzle, virtually all of the work can be done in the *Click2* event handler. Figure 6-20 shows the Visual Basic code for implementing the manual solution of the puzzle. In this event handler, we first check to see if a peg is selected. If it is not, then we select the clicked peg. If there is a selected peg but the clicked position is not a valid peg, then we deselect the selected peg. If there is a selected peg and the clicked position is a valid peg, then we deselect the selected peg and move the top disk from the formerly selected peg to the clicked peg.

This completes the design of the Hanoi ActiveX control. The Web site contains the complete code for this component.

5. THE PENTOMINO PUZZLE

Our second example of a Model component is the Pentomino puzzle illustrated in Figure 6-21.

```
void CHanoiCtl::OnLButtonDown(UINT nFlags, CPoint point)
{
    RECT MyPosRect;
    CWnd::GetClientRect(&MyPosRect);
    long ScrWidth = 60*MyBoard->DiskCount()+40;
    long ScrHite = 40+20*MyBoard->DiskCount();
    long x = point.x;
    long y = point.y;
    if (x<MyPosRect.left || x > MyPosRect.left+ScrWidth)
    {
        FireClick2(-1);
    }
    if (y<MyPosRect.top || y>MyPosRect.top+ScrHite)
    {
        FireClick2(-1);
    }
    if (x<MyPosRect.left+20*MyBoard->DiskCount()+15)
    {
        FireClick2(0);
    }
    if (x<MyPosRect.left+40*MyBoard->DiskCount()+25)
    {
        FireClick2(1);
    }
    FireClick2(2);
}
```

Figure 6-19   Firing the *Click2* Event

```
Private Sub HanoiCtl1_Click2(ByVal Pos As Long)
    Dim SelStat As Long

    SelStat = HanoiCtl1.GetSelect
    If SelStat = -1 Then
        HanoiCtl1.Select Pos
    ElseIf Pos = -1 Then
        HanoiCtl1.DeSelect
    Else
        HanoiCtl1.DeSelect
        HanoiCtl1.MoveDisk SelStat, Pos
    End If
End Sub
```

Figure 6-20   Solving the Towers of Hanoi Puzzle Manually

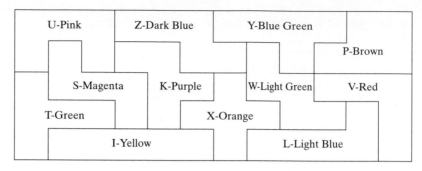

Figure 6-21   The Pentomino Puzzle

The object of this puzzle is to fit 12 odd-shaped pieces into a 5 × 12 rectangle. Each piece consists of five identical squares arranged so that each square shares at least one edge with another square. There are exactly 12 shapes that can be constructed in this fashion. Each shape is designated with a letter that more or less corresponds to the shape. A mechanical version of this puzzle with plastic pieces can be purchased at many game and toy stores. The mechanical version of this puzzle may or may not use a different color for each piece, but on the computer screen, it would be difficult or impossible to see the different shapes in the game board without using a different color for each shape.

In our design of the electronic Pentomino puzzle, we will follow the same methodology that we used for the Towers of Hanoi. We will start with the object model, then design the drawing routine for the model, create manipulator methods, and add the user interface. As a first step in designing the object model, we will select a color to represent each piece. These colors, along with the shape letters, are listed in Figure 6-22.

Shape	Color
U	Pink
T	Green
S	Magenta
I	Yellow
Z	Dark blue
K	Purple
X	Orange
Y	Blue-green
W	Light-green
L	Light-blue
P	Brown
V	Red

Figure 6-22   Shape Color Assignments

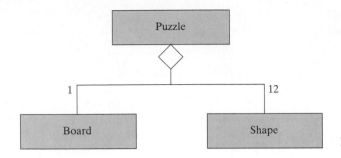

Figure 6-23   Preliminary Object Diagram

5.1 Internal Object Model Design

The object model for the Pentomino puzzle must contain two things: (1) a 5×12 board and (2) a collection of 12 shapes. Eventually, we will need some additional objects to support the solution of the puzzle, but for now let's stick with what we know. This object model is a bit more complex than that for the Towers of Hanoi, so we will use a slightly more rigorous methodology. To that end, we will start with the object diagram shown in Figure 6-23.

We first need to specify how to draw each shape. This will be reasonably complicated because each shape can be drawn in one of eight orientations, not all of which are different for each shape. The orientations are rotations of $0°$, $90°$, $180°$, and $270°$ as well as the mirror image of each rotation. Asymmetric shapes like K have eight orientations, X has one orientation, I has two, and V has four.

The simplest way to model the board is as a 5×12 array of integers. One method of managing the board would be to use the integers 1 through 12 to represent the 12 shapes, and the integer 0 to represent an empty square. However, since the codes we use are arbitrary, it is just as easy to use the shape color as an indicator. (Colors are represented using the low-order 24 bits of a long integer.) We will use the color White (0x00FFFFFF) to represent an empty square. When we draw the board, the color information we need to draw each square will already be in place in the proper position of the board. The information we keep for each shape must permit us to map the color of the shape into the proper position in the 5×12 array. Although we could enumerate the shapes automatically and then enumerate each different orientation of each shape, it is much easier to generate this information manually and simply incorporate it into the source code of the program. Therefore, we will generate a constant list of 12 shapes, and for each shape we will generate a constant list of orientations. In this list, we will list only those orientations that are different from one another.

In describing an orientation for a shape, it may seem necessary to represent all five squares. However this is not true. For each orientation, we will designate one square as the primary square. This square will be implicit and will not be described in the model. The model will contain information on the position of the other four squares with respect to the primary square. For the primary square, we will imagine the shape being embedded in a 5×5 array of squares. The primary square will be the top square in the leftmost column. Figure 6-24 illustrates the primary square for various orientations of the shape K. The selection of the primary square is motivated by the

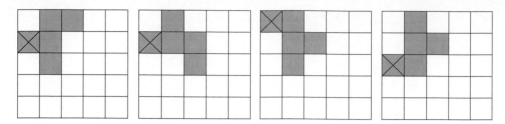

Figure 6-24   Some Orientations for Shape K

algorithm we will use to automatically solve the puzzle. This algorithm will be described fully below. In Figure 6-24, the primary square is designated by a cross through the square.

Each orientation must contain four items of information, each of which will permit a nonprimary square to be positioned with respect to the primary square. For each nonprimary square, we will keep two integers. The first will indicate how many rows to the right we must move to locate the square, and the second will indicate how many rows up or down we must move to locate the square. Negative numbers indicate that the move is in the up direction. Thus for the first orientation of Figure 6-24 we must keep the following pairs of numbers: $(1,-1)$, $(1,0)$, $(1,1)$, $(2,-1)$. We require one class, which we will call the *move class*, to represent a pair of numbers, and another class to represent an orientation. The orientation class must contain an array of four moves. Each shape class must contain a variable-sized array containing the orientations for that shape. In the shape class, we must also have a counter that gives the size of the orientation array. The shape class should also contain the color of the shape. The final puzzle class diagram of our model is shown in Figure 6-25, and the C++ definitions of the

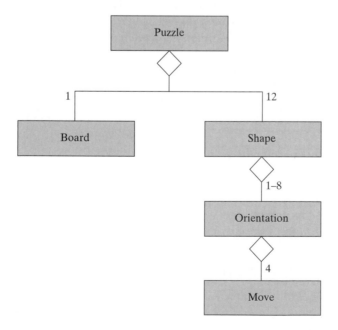

Figure 6-25   Final Puzzle Class Diagram

```
class CSquare                          class COrientation
{                                      {
public:                                public:
   long Over;                             CSquare Square[4];
   long Down;                          };
};
```

```
class CShape                           class CPuzzle
{                                      {
public:                                public:
   char Name;                             CBoard Board;
   COLORREF Color;                        CShape Shapes[12];
   long OrientationCount;              };
   COrientation * Orientations;
};
```

```
class CBoard
{
public:
   void Clear( );
   long AddShape(COrientation &Orientation,
      long StartRow, long StartCol, COLORREF Color);
   long RemoveShape(COrientation &Orientation,
      long StartRow, long StartCol, COLORREF Color);
   long NextEmpty(long StartRow, long StartCol,
      long &NewRow, long &NewCol);
   long NewBoard(long Rows, long Columns);
   COLORREF ** Data;
   long Columns;
   long Rows;
};
```

Figure 6-26   Puzzle Class Definitions

classes are given in Figure 6-26. In keeping with the usual C++ practice, we prefix each class name with the letter *C*. (We have also followed this practice with the Towers of Hanoi and will follow this practice throughout this book.)

For the most part, the class definitions should be no surprise. Note that the array of orientations in the **CShape** class is implemented as a pointer. This element will be dynamically allocated during the initialization phase of the component. Although we indicated that the board would have the dimensions 5×12, the actual implementation of the **CBoard** class allows the board shape to change. To facilitate this, the *Data* element of the board is implemented as a double pointer. This allows it to be accessed as if it were a two-dimensional array, but it also allows it to be reallocated. The default size of 5×12 will be set by the constructor of the class.

The class **CBoard** has been enhanced with four useful functions: (1) *Clear*, which will erase the board to start a new puzzle; (2) *AddShape* and *RemoveShape*, which will allow shapes to be added and deleted from the board; (3) *NewBoard*, which will clear the board and change its size; and (4) *NextEmpty*, which will be used to locate an empty space in the board starting from the upper left and working down each column. (This function will be used as part of the automatic solution of the puzzle.)

Now that we have determined the final object model for the Pentomino puzzle, it is time to address the problem of automatically solving the puzzle. Although it is possible to solve this puzzle manually, it is devilishly difficult to do so—in spite of the fact that there are thousands of different solutions to the puzzle!

To solve the puzzle automatically, we first observe that in a valid solution, all 60 squares must be filled with some shape. We will use the strategy of searching the board for empty squares and attempting to fill each empty square with some shape. As shapes are inserted into the board, they will be marked as *used* so that no shape will be used twice. When an empty square is found, the algorithm will select an unused shape and attempt to fill the empty square with the shape. The algorithm will first place the primary square for the shape into the empty square and then attempt to place the other four squares based on the current orientation of the shape. This attempt can either succeed or fail. If the shape overlaps other shapes already in the board, the placement fails. If the shape overlaps the edge of the board, then the placement fails. Otherwise the placement succeeds. When a placement succeeds, the algorithm will record the details of the placement in a list of successful placements. A solution to the puzzle consists of a list of 12 successful placements.

As anyone who has attempted to solve this puzzle knows, there is more to finding a solution than simply selecting shapes in order and placing them in a rectangle. It is possible to "go down the garden path" to a partial solution that will never lead to a complete solution. This is also true when solving the puzzle automatically. As with a manual solution, it is sometimes necessary to go back to some shape that has already been placed in the board and remove it. When an attempt to fill a square with a particular shape fails, the algorithm will first repeat the attempt with the next orientation of the shape. Once all orientations of a shape have been tried, the algorithm will proceed to the next shape and try the first orientation of that shape. When the list of unused shapes becomes exhausted without filling a square, the algorithm backs up to the last successful placement. That placement is undone, and the attempt is treated as a failed placement attempt. The algorithm will continue with the next orientation or shape for the previously successful attempt.

Those familiar with backtracking algorithms will recognize that this is a blind backtracking algorithm and is inherently exponential (or worse!). If there were a single unique solution to the puzzle, this would probably make the algorithm intractable. However, because there are actually thousands of valid solutions to the puzzle, the algorithm runs quickly.

To keep track of successful placement attempts, we need to record three items of information: (1) the row and column of the square we were attempting to fill, (2) the shape that we used to fill the square, and (3) the orientation we used. We will provide a class to contain these items of data, and will add an array of 12 of these objects to our **CPuzzle** class. We can also use this class to keep track of the current placement attempt. Figure 6-27 shows the enhancement of the class diagram to include a **State** class and Figure 6-28 shows the C++ definition of this class along with the required changes to the **CPuzzle** class. We have added the *Solve* function, which will generate the automatic solution of the puzzle. The array, *ShapesUsed* will keep track of the shapes that

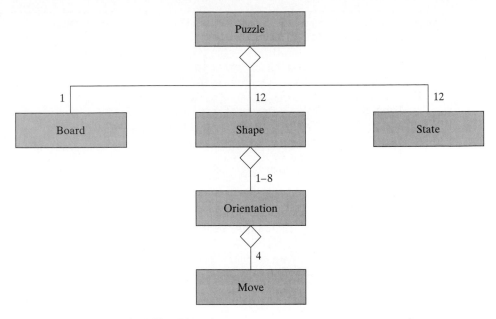

Figure 6-27   The New Final Class Diagram

```
class CState                          class CPuzzle
{                                     {
public:                               public:
    long Column;                          CBoard Board;
    long Row;                             CShape Shapes[12];
    long Shape;                           long ShapeUsed[12];
    long Orientation;                     CState Placements[12];
};                                        long SuccessfulPlacements;
                                          void Solve();
                                      };
```

Figure 6-28   Enhancing the Pentomino Model

have been used, and the variable *SuccessfulPlacements* will keep track of the current location in the *Placements* array.

Apart from the **CPuzzle** *Solve* routine, which we will present later, the most interesting functions in the Pentomino model are the *AddShape* and *RemoveShape* functions of the **CBoard** class. Figure 6-29 gives the code for the *AddShape* function. This function first checks each nonprimary square to make sure it does not fall outside the board or overlap another shape. If the placement is successful, it copies the shape color into each affected square of the board. If the placement is successful, the function returns 1; otherwise it returns zero.

Figure 6-30 shows the code for the *RemoveShape* function. Except for the color references, this routine is identical to the *AddShape* function. The function first tests to

```
long CBoard::AddShape(COrientation &Orientation, long SRow,
      long SCol, COLORREF Color)
{
   ... // error checking code omitted for brevity
   for (long i=0 ; i<4 ; I++)
   {
      long NRow = SRow + Orientation.Square[i].Down;
      long NCol = SCol + Orientation.Square[i].Over;
      if (NRow < 0 || NRow >= Rows || NCol < 0 || NCol >= Columns)
      {
         return 0; // outside the board
      }
      if (Data[NRow][NCol] != RGB(255,255,255))
      {
         return 0; // overlaps another shape
      }
   }
   // successful, so change board colors
   Data[SRow][SCol] = Color;
   for (i=0 ; i<4 ; i++)
   {
      long NRow = SRow + Orientation.Square[i].Down;
      long NCol = SCol + Orientation.Square[i].Over;
      Data[NRow][NCol] = Color;
   }
   return 1;
}
```

Figure 6-29   The *AddShape* Function

see that the shape is really where we claim it is, and then replaces the shape color with the color white, which is coded as RGB(255,255,255).

This completes the design of the object model. Now let us proceed to the next phase of the design.

5.2 Drawing-Routine Design

When constructing the drawing routine, we must be concerned with two things: (1) the appearance of the component, and (2) user interaction with the component. These aspects of the component should be kept in mind when designing the drawing routine.

For the Pentomino puzzle, we obviously want to draw the board that appears in Figure 6-21, but is this all? The object model has two other major parts: the shapes and the solution state. We can easily dismiss drawing the solution state, because it contains no information that is not visually obvious in the drawing of the board. However, we may wish to arrange for drawing the individual shapes in addition to drawing the board. Let us first focus on drawing the board. The routine for drawing the board should look something like the pseudo code of Figure 6-31. (The drawing routine is

```
long CBoard::RemoveShape(COrientation &Orientation, long SRow,
      long SCol, COLORREF Color)
{
   … // Error checking code omitted for brevity
   for (long i=0 ; i<4 ; i++)
   {
      long NRow = SRow + Shape.Square[i].Down;
      long NCol = SCol + Shape.Square[i].Over;
      if (NRow < 0 || NRow >= Rows || NCol < 0 || NCol >= Columns)
      {
         return 0; // Error! shape would be outside the board
      }
      if (Data[NRow][NCol] != Color)
      {
         return 0; // Error! Wrong shape in this position
      }
   }
   Data[SRow][SCol] = RGB(255,255,255);
   for (i=0 ; i<4 ; i++)
   {
      long NRow = SRow + Shape.Square[i].Down;
      long NCol = SCol + Shape.Square[i].Over;
      Data[NRow][NCol] = RGB(255,255,255);
   }
   return 1;
}
```

Figure 6-30   The *RemoveShape* Function

```
for (i=0 ; i<Puzzle.Board.Rows ; i++)
{
   for (j=0 ; j<Puzzle.Board.Columns ; j++)
   {
      Draw Rectangle of Color Puzzle.Board.Data[i][j].
   }
}
```

Figure 6-31   The Pentomino Drawing Routine

much more complicated than this, but the complexity is due to the large number of operating system calls that are required, not to any inherent complexity in the drawing process.)

As Figure 6-31 illustrates, the drawing routine simply draws a bunch of rectangles. The only real problem is determining the size of the rectangle. There are two choices. We can automatically scale the board to fit in the existing control window or we can use fixed-sized squares and require the user to create a control window of the proper size. If we decide to use a fixed size, it is a good idea to use a property value as the "fixed size." This will allow the user to change the size of the squares to fit his or her needs. My preference is to use a fixed size and to specify the size with a property value. However, we need to begin by discussing how to scale the board into the existing window. First, we should set some minimum acceptable window size and draw the window completely white if it is too small. Choosing a minimum window size is somewhat a matter of taste, so we will ignore that problem and proceed under the assumption that the current window size is acceptable.

We must next deal with the *aspect ratio*—the ratio of the height and width—of the window. For our board, the aspect ratio is 5::12. Because it is unlikely that an arbitrary window will have this aspect ratio, we must be careful when scaling our board. We want the entire board to be visible, but we also want to fill as much of the window as possible. Figure 6-32 illustrates the desired appearance of the board for two different aspect ratios.

To find the appropriate square size for a window of height H and width W, we first compute $H/5$ and $W/12$. We must use integer division and ignore the remainder, because we cannot draw partial pixels. The value $H/5$ gives us the square size we must use to fit the board to the height of the window, and $W/12$ gives us the square size we must use to fit the board to the width of the window. To fit the board entirely inside the window, we must choose the minimum of $H/5$ and $W/12$. The minimum of these two values will be used to draw each square.

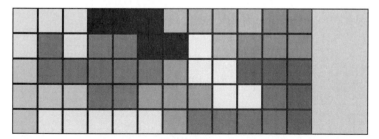

Figure 6-32   Scaling to Fit a Rectangle

To use fixed-sized squares, we first define a property named *SquareSize* of type long. We will provide a variable named *m_squareSize* to contain the value of the property. As with all components, we will define a support class to contain all "global" variables and functions for the component. The variable *m_squareSize* will be added to the support class of the component. Changes to the *SquareSize* property will be monitored. Values that are extraordinarily small or large will be rejected. If the new property value is acceptable, we will force a redraw of the component window.

In addition to drawing the board, we may also wish to draw the list of shapes. However, rather than drawing all shapes and orientations at once, we will provide properties to specify the shape and the orientation to be drawn. Since it is unlikely that the user will want to see both the board and the individual shapes in the same window, we will provide a *DrawMode* property that specifies whether the board or an individual shape is to be drawn. The *DrawMode* property will have one of two values, **0 - Board** and **1 - Shape**. We will use a support-class variable named *m_drawingMode* to hold the value of this property. The new drawing routine will look something like Figure 6-33.

The shape-drawing routine will use the *SquareSize* property and three new properties. The properties *Shape* and *Orientation* will be used to specify the shape and orientation to be drawn, while the *MarkPrimary* property will be used to distinguish the primary square of a shape from the other four squares.

This component has no need to process keyboard input, but we want to allow the user to interact with the display using mouse clicks. When designing user interaction, we want to maintain the *passive model* implementation style, so we will avoid performing complex behavior in response to user input. Instead, we will pass the mouse-click information back to the container through events. We will use two different events, one for each drawing mode. When drawing mode is set to **0 - Board**, we will issue the *Board* event in response to mouse clicks; otherwise we will issue the *Piece* event. The *Board* event will have two parameters, *X* and *Y*, which will be two long integers identifying the square on the board that has been clicked by the user. (If the user clicks off the board, we will not issue an event.) The *Piece* event will also have two parameters, *Shape* and *Orientation*, which are long integers that give the shape number and the orientation number of the shape currently being displayed. (We are jumping ahead a bit in our methodology at this point, but for complex models it is generally impossible to isolate all four phases of the design.)

```
if (m_DrawingMode == 0)
{
    // Board-Drawing Routine;
        ...
}
else
{
    // Shape-Drawing Routine;
    ...
}
```

Figure 6-33   Shape/Board Drawing Routine

Property Design Table		
Name	**Type**	**Function**
DrawMode	Enumerated Default = 0	The value zero will cause the board to be drawn, the value 1 will cause the shape selected by the **Shape** and **Orientation** properties to be drawn. Causes Redraw.
Shape	Long Integer Maximum = 11 Minimum = 0 Default = 0	When **DrawMode** is equal to 1, specifies the shape to be drawn. No function when **DrawMode** is zero. Causes redraw if **DrawMode** is equal to 1. Resets **Orientation** to zero.
Orientation	Long Integer Maximum = Var. Minimum = 0 Default = 0	When **DrawMode** is equal to 1, specifies the orientation of the shape to be drawn. Gets reset to zero when **Shape** changes. Causes redraw when **DrawMode** is equal to 1. Maximum value is one less than the number of orientations of the shape specified by the **Shape** property.
SquareSize	Long Integer Maximum = 100 Minimum = 4 Default = 20	Determines the width and height of the individual squares in both the board display and the individual shape display. Causes Redraw.
MarkPrimary	Boolean Default = True	When DrawMode is equal to 1, a true value will cause an x to be drawn through the primary square of a shape; a false value will cause all squares to be drawn the same.

Figure 6-34   Initial Property Definitions

Figure 6-34 contains the property design table for the properties we have created. We will add entries to this table as we proceed with the program-interface design.

Figure 6-31 suggests that we are equipped to handle boards other than the standard 5×12. However, as yet we have not provided any means for the user or programmer to select any board size other than 5×12. Clearly it would be desirable to add some method of changing the size of the board. We could simply expose the *NewBoard* function of the **CBoard** object, but this would permit board size changes only at run-time. Most programmers would probably prefer to size the board at design-time. If we want to give the programmer this capability, we must add properties that permit the size of the board to be changed. It would be nice if we could change both dimensions at the same time, because this would allow us to verify that the board contained 60 squares.

Unfortunately, we have come to an impasse. The only thing available to the programmer at design-time is properties, but properties can have only simple types. Changing both dimensions of the board simultaneously would require a structure containing two numbers. Since we are forced into a situation where we must permit one dimension to be changed at a time, we must be careful not to generate an error when the board has more than or less than 60 squares. To facilitate the height and width changes, we will add two properties: *BoardWidth* and *BoardHeight*. Figure 6-35 gives the property design table entries for these properties.

Property Design Table		
Name	**Type**	**Function**
BoardWidth	Long Integer Minimum = 3 Maximum = 20 Default = 12	Specifies the number of columns in the board. Causes redraw and puzzle-reset.
BoardHeight	Long Integer Maximum = 3 Minimum = 20 Default = 5	Specifies the number of rows in the board. Causes redraw and puzzle-reset.

Figure 6-35   Board Property Definitions

5.3 The Manipulator Methods and User Interaction

We are finally ready to begin designing our manipulator methods. As we proceed with this, it will become clear that, in the beginning, we did not have a clear idea of how the component would be used. This may require us to go back and make a few changes in the object model and the drawing routine. For complex models, this is to be expected. Although many design methodologies suggest that everything can and should be thought out beforehand, this is simply impossible. However, if we have made good decisions in the beginning, we should be able to incorporate whatever changes are required with a minimum of pain. The true mark of a well-designed object model is not its initial perfection but the ease with which it can be modified to perform new tasks.

The only manipulator method that we have discussed so far is the *Solve* method, which is currently implemented as the *Solve* function of the **CPuzzle** class. Hopefully we will be able to simply provide a wrapper for this routine. To do this, we provide a method named *Solve*, with the initial intention of simply calling Puzzle.Solve(), and forcing a redraw of the control window. However, as we are completing the design document for this method (Figure 6-36), a new approach seems feasible. Why not let the user watch the solution develop by redrawing the control window whenever a shape is added or removed from the board? The user might not always want to watch the solution, so we could provide a new property, *ShowWork*, to permit the user to choose whether to watch the solution of the puzzle develop. Figure 6-36 gives the Method Description for the *Solve* method, and Figure 6-37 gives the property design table entry for the *ShowWork* property.

Unfortunately, adding this new feature will force us to develop a new version of the *Solve* routine that is external to the **CPuzzle** class. The object model of the puzzle does not know about (and *should* not know about) the component's drawing routine. This is the same problem we encountered with the Towers of Hanoi puzzle, and we will have to solve it in much the same way.

Because watching the solution develop might become long and tedious, it might be a good idea to have some means of aborting the solution. We will add an *Abort*

Method Description			
Name	Solve		
Return Value	Void		
Description	Clears the board, marks all shapes as unused, and finds a solution using a blind-backtracking algorithm. If the **ShowWork** property is set to **TRUE**, the control window will be redrawn whenever a piece is successfully placed, or successfully removed.		
Arguments	**Name**	**Type**	**Description**
Void			

Figure 6-36   Pentomino *Solve* Method Description

Property Design Table		
Name	**Type**	**Function**
ShowWork	BOOL Default = TRUE	During automatic solution of the puzzle, specifies whether each successful shape placement or removal will cause a redraw of the board.

Figure 6-37   *ShowWork* Property Definition

method for this purpose, the description of which is given in Figure 6-38. When aborting a solution, we will not clear the board but will leave the partial solution in place.

The next idea that occurs to us is providing some means for allowing the user to solve the puzzle manually. Even though the solution is difficult, there are people who enjoy difficult puzzles, and we should try to accommodate them. Obviously, two methods are needed: one to add a shape to the board and another to remove a shape. (We will not allow users to drag shapes.) Before we can specify the parameters of the *AddShape* and *RemoveShape* functions, we must have a clear picture of how our component will be used and what data will be available when each function is called. We also need to be concerned about the object model, since the **CPuzzle** class has no *AddShape* and *RemoveShape* functions. Because we have made everything public, we could "reach into" the model and call the **CBoard** functions directly, but doing this is usually a mark of bad design. Reaching into a model makes the model difficult to understand and even more difficult to modify.

We will leave the correction of the model to the user, and focus instead on how we expect the model to be used during a manual solution of the puzzle.

Method Description			
Name	Abort		
Return Value	Void		
Description	Aborts the search for a solution. The board is not cleared by this method. It is redrawn with the partial solution in place. Does nothing if solution is not in progress.		
Arguments	**Name**	**Type**	**Description**
Void			

Figure 6-38   *Abort* Method Description

When adding a shape, the most likely scenario is that the program will some-how select a shape and an orientation, and pass these parameters to the *AddShape* function. Since it is "cruel and unusual punishment" to expect the user to provide shape and orientation numbers directly, we must provide some method of obtaining these automatically. We have already designed a drawing mode that will permit indi-vidual shapes and orientations to be displayed, and we have designed an event that will be fired when the shape is clicked. We can use these features to obtain our shape and orientation numbers. We will ask the programmer to provide a second copy of the Pentomino component that will be used to display shapes and orientations. The user should be able to manipulate this display in some fashion to go through the available shapes and orientations and should be able to click on this component to select an orientation of a shape. Once an orientation is selected, the user can click on the square of the board where the shape should be placed. The component displaying the board will then issue an event containing the row and column numbers of the clicked square. The data that will be available for placing a shape will be the shape number, the orientation number, and the row and column numbers. This is sufficient to place a shape in the board. Figure 6-39 gives the design of the *AddShape* method based on these assumptions.

Although the user will specify a shape and an orientation when adding a shape, it would be easiest if the user could remove a shape just by clicking on it. The information available for removing a shape would be just the row and column numbers of the clicked square. This is sufficient, because the color of the board-square can be used to look up the shape, then the shape can be looked up in the list of successful placements

Method Description		
Name	AddShape	
Return Value	Long Integer	Error Code if placement is not successful.
Description	Adds a new shape to the board. The arguments *Shape* and *Orientation* determine the shape to be added. The shape must be currently unused. Adding the shape will cause it to be marked as used. The *Shape* and *Orientation* arguments must be valid. X and Y determine the position of the primary square of the shape orientation. X and Y must be within the board. The new shape must not overlap any existing shapes or extend outside the board. The return value indicates whether adding the shape was successful. This method will add an entry to the list of successful placements.	
Arguments	**Name**	**Type**	**Description**
	Shape	Long Integer	Shape number of the shape to be added.
	Orientation	Long Integer	Orientation number of the shape-orientation to be added.
	X	Long Integer	Column number of the square where the shape is to be added. (Zero based)
	Y	Long Integer	Row number of the square where the shape is to be added.

Figure 6-39 *AddShape* Method Description

Method Description			
Name	RemoveShape		
Return Value	Long Integer	Error code if removal is not successful.	
Description	Removes an existing shape from the board. X and Y must be inside the board and must point to a nonwhite square. The color will be looked up in the list of shapes, then the shape number will be looked up in the list of successful placements. The successful placement will be removed, and the shape will be removed from the board.		
Arguments	**Name**	**Type**	**Description**
	X	Long Integer	Column number of the square where the shape is to be added (zero based).
	Y	Long Integer	Row number of the square where the shape is to be added.

Figure 6-40   RemoveShape Method Description

to find the orientation. Figure 6-40 gives the formal description of the *RemoveShape* method based on these assumptions.

The possibility of adding shapes to the diagram manually raises several questions with regard to the automatic solution of the puzzle. When solving the puzzle automatically, should we clear out all manually placed shapes and start fresh, or should we attempt to build the solution around the manually placed shapes? As with most questions like this, the best answer is to find some way to do both. Let us assume that the method we have already designed, *Solve*, will clear the board before starting. Next, we will create a new method, *Continue*, which will solve the puzzle starting with any manually placed shapes. While we're at it we might as well add a *Clear* method that allows a user to erase the board and start over.

There are still two more problems we need to address. First, what happens if there is no solution with the manually placed shapes in their current positions? Do we include the manually placed shapes in the backtracking, or do we stop and report that there is no solution? Second, what happens if the *Continue* method is called on an aborted solution or on a completely solved board? (Recall that we do not clear the board when the automatic search for a solution is aborted. Instead we display the board with some shapes already in place.)

We will allow the user to determine what happens when no solution can be found for a given manual placement. We will add a property, *RemoveManualOK*, which will be used to indicate whether manually placed shapes should be included in the backtracking process. The *Continue* method will resume a partially completed solution without clearing the board. If the method is called on a complete solution, the last placement will be removed and treated as unsuccessful. The solution will then continue from this point as it does with a partially completed solution. This allows a series of different solutions to be obtained by repeatedly calling the *Continue* method. Figures 6-41, 6-42, and 6-43 contain the formal descriptions of the new properties and methods.

Keeping track of a manual solution requires still more modifications to the object model. At the very least, the **CState** class, which is used to keep track of placed objects, must be modified to indicate whether a placement was manual or automatic. There are

Property Design Table		
Name	**Type**	**Function**
RemoveManualOK	Boolean Default = False	Specifies whether the **Solve** and **Continue** methods are permitted to remove manually placed shapes during the backtracking process. Default is to prevent the automatic removal of manually placed shapes.

Figure 6-41   *RemoveManualOK* Property Description

Method Description			
Name	Continue		
Return Value	Void		
Description	Attempts to find a solution to the puzzle using any manually placed shapes as a starting point. The same blind-backtracking algorithm as the *Solve* method is used to find a solution. A partial solution will be continued from the point where it was aborted. The last placement of a full solution will be backed out and treated as unsuccessful. The backtracking will then proceed from that point If the *ShowWork* property is set to **TRUE**, the control window will be redrawn whenever a piece is successfully placed, or successfully removed.		
Arguments	**Name**	**Type**	**Description**
Void			

Figure 6-42   *Continue* Method Description

Method Description			
Name	Clear		
Return Value	Void		
Description	Remove all shapes from the board, regardless of how they were placed, and display an empty board.		
Arguments	**Name**	**Type**	**Description**
Void			

Figure 6-43   *Clear* Method Description

many acceptable solutions to the problem, one of which can be found on the Web site. We will omit the details of this here because handling manual placements is not substantially different from handling automatic placements.

5.4 The Solve Routine

It would be somewhat of a letdown to conclude this section without showing the routine that automatically finds the solution of the puzzle. Unfortunately, the routine, shown in Figure 6-44, is complicated, and there is no way to simplify it. The basic plan of is to find

```
ClearBoard( );
// Set The Number of Successful Placements to Zero;
SuccessfulPlacements = 0;
for (long i=0 ; i<12 ; i++)
{
        ShapeUsed[i] = false;
}
// Initialize Placements[0] with the first placement attempt,
Placements[0]->Shape=0;
Placements[0]->Orientation=0;
Placements[0]->Column=0;
Placements[0]->Row=0;
DrawBoard( );
while (SuccessfulPlacements < 12)
{
// At this point, the next placement attempt is located in
// Placements[SuccessfulPlacements] For convenience, we will
// retrieve Row, Column, Shape and Orientation from this object.
   CurrentShape = Placements[SuccessfulPlacements]->Shape;
   Orientation = Placements[SuccessfulPlacements]->Orientation;
   X = Placements[SuccessfulPlacements]->Column;
   Y = Placements[SuccessfulPlacements]->Row;
   Success = Board.AddShape(CurrentShape,Orientation,X,Y);
   if (Success)
   {
      // Mark the current shape as Used.
      ShapeUsed[CurrentShape] = true;
      SuccessfulPlacements ++ ;
      if (SuccessfulPlacements >= 12)
      {
         break;  // exit the while statement;
      }
      // Set up next placement attempt. Find Next empty square,
      // starting with the square just filled
      Board.NextEmpty(X,Y,X,Y);
      // Find The Next unused shape;
      CurrentShape = FindFirstUnusedShape( );
      // If CurrentShape >= 12 there is a program error
      // and we should exit
      // Initialize Placements[SuccessfulPlacements] with
      // the proper data
      Placements[SuccessfulPlacements]->Shape=CurrentShape;
      Placements[SuccessfulPlacements]->Orientation=0;
      Placements[SuccessfulPlacements]->Column=X;
      Placements[SuccessfulPlacements]->Row=Y;
   }
   else
   {
```

Figure 6-44   The Pentomino *Solve* Routine

```
        // We will try to create a new placement attempt,
        // backing up if necessary
        RetryPointFound = false;
        // keep backing up until we find something we haven't tried.
        while (!RetryPointFound)
        {
            Placements[SuccessfulPlacements]->Orientation++;
            CurrentOrientation =
                Placements[SuccessfulPlacements]->Orientation;
            CurrentShape = Placements[SuccessfulPlacements]->Shape;
            // First, try the next orientation.
            if (CurrentOrientation < CurrentShape->OrientationCount)
            {
                RetryPointFound = true;
            }
            else
            {
                // If all orientations of the current shape
                // have been exhausted we next try the next
                // unused shape
                CurrentShape = GetNextUnusedShape(CurrentShape);
                if (CurrentShape < 12)
                {
                    RetryPointFound = true
                }
                else
                {
                    // if all shapes have been exhausted, then back up
                    SuccessfulPlacements( );
                    if (SuccessfulPlacements < 0)
                    {
                        // There is no solution exit inner loop
                        break; // before retrying with zero
                    }
                    // Remove The Current Shape From The Board.
                    CurrentShape =
                        Placements[SuccessfulPlacements]->Shape;
                    Orientation =
                        Placements[SuccessfulPlacements]->Orientation;
                    X = Placements[SuccessfulPlacements]->Column;
                    Y = Placements[SuccessfulPlacements]->Row;
                    Board.RemoveShape(CurrentShape,Orientation,X,Y);
                    ShapeUsed[CurrentShape] = false;
                }
            }
        }
    }
    if (SuccessfulPlacements < 0)
    {
```

Figure 6-44   (*Continued*)

```
            // no solution exit main loop
            break;
        }
    }
    // Redraw The Board if ShowWork is true.
    if (m_showWork)
    {
        DrawBoard( );
    }
    // Abort if user has requested it.
    if (UserAbort)
    {
        break;
    }
}
DrawBoard( );
```

Figure 6-44   (*Continued*)

the first empty square starting from the upper left and working down each column. The routine then attempts to fill the empty square with an unused shape. Each unused shape is tried, one by one, until they have all been tried, or until one fits. Each orientation of each shape is tried one by one.

The main loop is used for trial placements. If the trial succeeds, the loop continues with the next empty square and next unused shape. If it fails, the next orientation is tried. If there are no more orientations, the next unused shape is tried. If there are no more unused shapes, the routine backs up to the most recent successful placement and removes it. It then tries the next orientation for *that* shape. This may necessitate backing up even further. If the routine attempts to back up past the first successful placement, then there is no solution.

A modified version of this routine is used for the *Continue* method.

6. VARIANT FORMS OF MODELS

Most Model components follow the pattern developed in the preceding two sections. There is a fixed-object model, which is visible and is manipulated by manipulator methods. There are Model components that do not conform to this pattern. Some Model components have nonfixed object models. Imagine an enhancement to the Pentomino component that permits users to save a partially completed puzzle and come back to it several days later. This is an example of a nonfixed model. Although saving and restoring states is normally associated more with Editor components than with Model components, the Model component does not permit items to be added to or deleted from the internal model. The only additional function that is permitted is saving and restoring the internal state of the model. The state of the model can be obtained either from fixed storage, usually a file of some sort, or through properties and methods. (See the discussion of semipersistent objects in Chapter 19.)

Another type of nonfixed object model is one that is *treated* as fixed by the Model component but is actually modifiable by other components. An example of such a component is a simulator component that was created as part of the FHDL circuit design package. This component is capable of simulating a circuit whose description is passed to it as a semipersistent object. The simulator stimulates the model with input data and produces output data, but the model itself remains unchanged throughout the process. The entire model can be replaced at any time. Other components can be used to edit the model but the simulator component cannot be used for this purpose.

The simulator component is also an example of a Model component that has no visible display. The simulator produces data that is useful internally in the program and can be displayed by other components, but it has no display capabilities of its own. Needless to say, invisible Models are a specialized type of component that perform complex functions that are internal to a program, or produce data that must be massaged in some way before becoming understandable to a user.

The nonfixed object model and the invisible Model are important variations on the general theme of Model components.

7. CONCLUSION

Although a complex program may require many different objects, a Model component should be designed to represent one and only one object. If many objects of the same type are required in a program, each object should be represented by a single instance of the component. It is important to note that providing a component wrapper for an object adds a significant amount of overhead to an object. Because of this, the Model should be used to represent large-scale objects with significant and complex behavior.

The first step in designing a Model is to determine, in broad terms, how the internal object model is to be handled. The first thing we need to determine is whether the model will be visible or invisible. Many useful Models do not require a visible display or any user interaction.

Once we determine whether the model will be visible, we must then determine the source of the model. Specifically, will the object model be permanently embedded in the component, as in the Hanoi and Pentomino controls, or will it be possible to switch between many different object models. If it is not possible to switch between different object models, will it be possible to save and restore the state of the model? If it *is* possible to switch between object models, where will the component obtain them?

In any case, supporting multiple object models is significantly more difficult than using a single embedded object model. Whenever possible, a single embedded object model should be used.

Once we have determined the visibility and the object source, we proceed to object-oriented design of the object model. Any acceptable object-oriented methodology can be used to design the object model, but for complex models it should include object diagrams and a significant amount of planning. Insofar as it is possible, the object-oriented design of the object model should ignore the fact that the model will eventually be embedded in a component.

The design methodology for a Model has three steps that follow the design of the object model. The first of these is the design of the visible interface. Specifically, a drawing routine must be developed for the internal object model. If it will be necessary to redraw the internal object model frequently, the drawing routine must be written in such a way as to permit frequent redraws. In some cases, it is necessary to begin thinking about interaction with the user when the drawing routine is designed. If the internal object model has several different views, it will be necessary to add properties and methods for switching between different views. Anytime properties or methods are added to the component, it is necessary to have a clear idea of how the user will interact with the model to provide the appropriate values for these properties and methods.

If the component has a visible interface, it will usually be necessary to add a few drawing-parameter properties. Such properties are used to control scaling, background colors, borders, three-dimensional shadowing, and other incidental aspects of the drawing. Before adding any drawing parameter, it is necessary to have a precise idea of exactly how that parameter will be used. For example, if a component is designed to blend in with its background, it is unlikely that a border-drawing parameter would ever be used. If a full drawing of the model is too large to fit in a window of reasonable size, then it will be necessary to add scrolling capabilities to the window.

The second step in the design of a Model component is the creation of the programming interface. In most cases the programming interface will consist of a set of manipulator methods that are used to manipulate the model. During this phase of the design, it is necessary to concentrate exclusively on how the component will be used. We should not focus on a particular environment unless that environment is known to cause special difficulties. It is best to go through the exercise of designing a program using the component so that we can visualize where the difficulties will lie. Very often it will be necessary to go back and redo parts of the internal object model and the drawing routine to make them conform with the programming interface.

The final step is the design of the user interaction, which can be integrated with the design of the drawing routine as well as the programming interface. Most user actions will take the form of mouse clicks, which can be associated with various parts of the visible model. Keyboard input is also possible, but for Model components, such input is rare. When designing the user interaction, it is best to adhere to the *passive model* style. In this style, all complex actions in the component are triggered by explicit method calls. Mouse clicks do not cause changes in the model but are simply passed through to the container as events. This style of design permits the container to associate complex actions with certain mouse clicks but does not compel it to do so. The mouse clicks may be used in whatever manner the container chooses, permitting the component to be used in more versatile ways.

Although the Model component is an important part of "serious" programming, it can also be a versatile and fun way to become familiar with component development, because it can be used to create interactive games and puzzles.

EXERCISES

1. Design a Model component for a tic-tac-toe game, and write a Visual Basic program using the Model.

2. Using a Visual Basic program, design a Model component for playing checkers.

3. Correct the problems in the object model of the Pentomino puzzle by changing the appropriate data items from **public** to **protected** and by adding the appropriate functions to the **CPuzzle** class.

4. Make the appropriate changes to the Hanoi component to permit saving and restoring the state of the puzzle in a file.

5. Make the appropriate changes in the Hanoi component to permit the user to change the number of disks. Limit the number of disks to the range 2 through 20.

6. Create a Model component for your favorite game or puzzle. Create a Web page to host your component and make that page available on the Internet.

Chapter 7

Editors

1. PREREQUISITES AND OBJECTIVES

Before starting this chapter, you should have

1. A knowledge of programming in C++.
2. A knowledge of component interface design.

After completing this chapter, you will have

1. A knowledge of how to construct an object model for a graphical editor.
2. The ability to create a full-featured graphical editor with add, modify, delete, and undo facilities.
3. A knowledge of how to design and use multi-event mouse transactions.
4. A knowledge of the Editor-Component design methodology.

2. INTRODUCTION

An editor is similar to a model in that it must have a carefully designed internal object model. However the internal object model must be malleable. It must also be possible to do several things with this model:

1. To create the model dynamically and to alter the model by adding objects to it and deleting objects from it.
2. To select portions of the model and to make changes to the selected portions without affecting the rest of the model.
3. To undo all changes.
4. To create the entire internal object model from scratch, starting with an empty object.
5. To replace an existing internal object model with an entirely new object model.
6. To save and restore the internal object model to persistent storage.

In some cases, design of effective internal object models can be a research topic in its own right. One example of this is a VLSI layout editor. A VLSI layout consists of thousands, or even millions, of rectangles arranged in several different layers. The data can be stored in a simple text file that lists the layer and coordinates of each rectangle. However, the internal object model must provide a means for determining the distance between rectangles, whether certain rectangles overlap, and which rectangles are currently visible in the display. It must be possible to make these determinations without comparing each rectangle with every other rectangle in the model. Several research papers have been written on this topic.

The design of such complex object models is beyond the scope of this book. We will instead present a simple model that permits the editing of objects of modest size. This will allow us to focus on the component-level aspects of the design.

Editors fall into two broad categories: text editors and graphical editors. The internal design of these types of editors is fundamentally different. For a text editor, virtually all changes are made using the keyboard. The mouse is used to move the editing point and to select text. For a graphical editor, virtually all changes are made using the mouse. Existing text-editor components are widely available, and provide a variety of useful features. An example of such a component is the built-in edit box of the Windows operating system. It is possible to create a new text editor by subclassing an existing text editor component and adding new features to it. Because text editing is pretty much the same regardless of how the data is used, it is seldom necessary to create a new text editor from scratch.

On the other hand, graphical editors tend to differ widely from one another. Full-featured graphical editors are not widely available, at least not without substantial cost. Furthermore, a graphical editor that has been designed for one purpose is seldom adaptable to a new one. For example, a graphical editor that has been designed to create circuit schematics is generally not adaptable to the tasks of creating VLSI layouts or animated drawings for cartoons. When it is necessary to create a new type of graphical object, it is generally necessary to create a whole new editor for managing these objects. Because of this, we will concentrate on the problem of creating graphical editors.

3. THE DESIGN METHODOLOGY

A graphical editing program is a complex entity with many independent features. As outlined in Chapters 4 and 5, these features will be implemented in a set of more or less independent components. The Editor component contains those features that are necessary for interacting with the user, and for permitting the user to build complex objects one piece at a time. Four main features should be a part of every graphical editor: (1) the drawing facility, (2) the selection facility, (3) the modification facility, and (4) the undo facility. Figure 7-1 illustrates the breakdown of the Editor component into these facilities. (Other required features, such as file I/O, will be implemented in other components; see Chapter 4 for a breakdown of the different components.)

Although an Editor has heavy user interaction, the most fundamental part of the component is the set of objects used to represent the graphical data. This object is the glue that holds all four facilities together. The functions provided by this set of objects will provide most of the functionality required by the editor. Three of the facilities—Drawing, Selection, and Modification—make use of mouse interaction. The fourth,

Graphical Editor

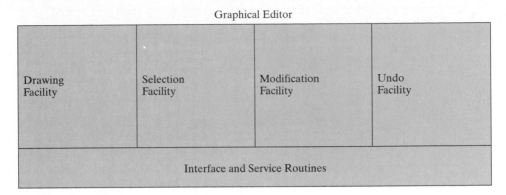

Figure 7-1   Graphical Editor Breakdown

Undo, is implemented entirely in the functions of the underlying object. For mouse interaction, we will make use of a concept called the *mouse transaction*. A mouse transaction consists of a Mouse-Down event signaling the press of a mouse button, several Mouse-Move events signaling motion of the mouse while the button is pressed, and a Mouse-Up event signaling the release of the mouse button. The meaning of each mouse transaction depends on the internal state of the Editor component.

In the remainder of this chapter, we will go through the design of each of the four facilities, and show how each is implemented. We will use a single example called the Simple Graphical Editor (SGE). Sections 7.4 through 7.7 describe the drawing facility, mouse transactions, and the objects required to support the drawing facility. The Selection Facility is described in Section 7.8, and the Modification Facility is described in Section 7.9. Sections 7.10 and 7.11 describe the Undo Facility, which is the most complex of the four.

4. DRAWING OBJECTS

The most important feature of any graphical editor, in terms of user interaction, is its drawing modes. Every graphical editor has a wide variety of drawing modes. For example, consider the icon drawing tool provided by Visual C++. This editor has 21 drawing modes, and 18 different line and fill colors. Each of these drawing modes changes the editing actions performed by mouse clicks and movements. Obviously, it would be to our advantage to start with something much simpler.

To begin with, we will create a simple graphical editor that enables us to draw two different types of objects, circles and rectangles. Once drawn, the circles and rectangles will become the drawing objects manipulated by our editor. We will be able to move them, change their size, or delete them as we chose.

The first step in creating our editor is to create the object model for our drawing objects. Because we want to keep the internal model as simple as possible, we will begin by assuming that our objects will be contained in a linked list. We have two different types of objects, but they have some common properties that should be collected into a base class. We will start our design with the **CGraphicObject** class given in Figure 7-2. Because we anticipate having to remove drawing objects from our linked list, we will make the list doubly linked, with *Next*, and *Previous* pointers. We have added two global properties, *LineColor* and *FillColor*. At this point, the only thing we

```
class CGraphicObject
{
public:
    CGraphicObject * Next;
    CGraphicObject * Prev;
    COLORREF FillColor;
    COLORREF LineColor;

    CGraphicObject( );
    virtual ~CGraphicObject( );

    // each object must draw itself
    virtual void Draw(CDC * Indc) = 0;
};
```

Figure 7-2   The Graphical Object Definition

are concerned with is drawing our objects. (In addition to creation and destruction of course.) We have added a single function called *draw*, because every object must have the ability to be drawn. Because specific shape information is required before we can draw anything, we have made the draw function a pure virtual function. Each drawing object class will be required to define this function.

Next we need to define the specific classes to represent the circles and rectangles. We will derive these classes from **CGraphicObject** to automatically include the common properties. Figure 7-3 illustrates the definition of the **CRectangle** and **CCircle** classes.

To keep things interesting, the **CRectangle** and **CCircle** classes have been designed to be different from the Windows operating system Rectangle and Ellipse drawing objects. The drawing routines, which are quite simple, are shown in Figure 7-4. Each consists of a single drawing function call surrounded by operating system calls to manage the line and fill colors.

```
class CRectangle :                    class CCircle :
      public CGraphicObject                 public CGraphicObject
{                                     {
public:                               public:
    long Left;                            CPoint Center;
    long Top;                             long Radius;
    long Width;
                                          CCircle( );
    long Height;                          virtual ~CCircle( );

    CRectangle( );
    virtual ~CRectangle( );               virtual void Draw(CDC * Indc);
                                      };
    virtual void Draw(CDC * Indc);
};
```

Figure 7-3   The CCircle and CRectangle Classes

```
void CRectangle::Draw(CDC *Indc)
{
    // Set up line and fill colors Pen=Line Brush = Fill
    … // Standard OS calls omitted for brevity
    // draw if not degenerate
    if (Height > 0 && Width > 0)
    {
        Indc->Rectangle(Left,Top,Left+Width,Top+Height);
    }
    // release resources
    … // Standard OS calls omitted for brevity
}
```

```
void CCircle::Draw(CDC *Indc)
{
    // Set up colors, pen=line, brush=fill
    … // Standard OS calls omitted for brevity
    // Draw circle if not degenerate
    if (Radius > 0)
    {
        Indc->Ellipse(Center.x-Radius,Center.y-Radius,
            Center.x+Radius,Center.y+Radius);
    }
    // release resources
    … // Standard OS calls omitted for brevity
}
```

Figure 7-4   Rectangle and Circle Drawing Routines

We must now decide how our object lists will be organized. We could simply add head and tail pointers to the support object, but this would be bad design. Because management of the drawing model is an identifiable subtask of the editor, we should encapsulate all drawing model functionality into a single object. Figure 7-5 gives the definition of the **CGraphicList** class, which will be used for this purpose. The **CGraphicList** class contains the head and tail of the drawing-object list and a count of the objects in the list. This class also defines three functions (in addition to the constructor and destructor): (1) *Draw*, (2) *AddRectangle*, and (3) *AddCircle*. The parameters of these functions anticipate how they will be used. We expect that the user will draw circles and rectangles by sweeping them out with the mouse. Such an operation yields two points: (1) a starting point and (2) an ending point. The first four parameters of *AddRectangle* and *AddCircle* are the coordinates of these two points. The other two parameters are the fill color and the line color. We anticipate that these two parameters will be set for all objects in a manner that is similar to the way that colors are selected in the Visual C++ icon drawing tool. The *Draw* function is supplied with the same parameters that are passed to the *OnDraw* function of an ActiveX control. We anticipate that these parameters will be passed through to the *Draw* function. Figures 7-6, 7-7, and 7-8 present definitions of these functions.

```
class CGraphicList
{
public:
    // Graphic Object List
    CGraphicObject * Tail;
    CGraphicObject * Head;
    long Count; // count of graphic objects

    CGraphicList( );
    virtual ~CGraphicList( );

    // drawing
    void Draw(CDC* pdc, const CRect& rcBounds,
      const CRect& rcInvalid);

    // Adding objects
    void AddRectangle(long x,long y,long xp,long yp,
      COLORREF LineC,COLORREF FillC);
    void AddCircle(long x,long y,long xp,long yp,
      COLORREF LineC,COLORREF FillC);
};
```

Figure 7-5 The **CGraphicList** Class

```
void CGraphicList::Draw(CDC* pdc, const CRect& rcBounds,
const CRect& rcInvalid, long m_handleRadius)
{
    // blank out the drawing area
    pdc->FillRect(rcBounds,
      CBrush::FromHandle((HBRUSH)GetStockObject(WHITE_BRUSH)));
    // Pass the draw request to each object
    for (CGraphicObject * Temp=Head; Temp!=NULL; Temp=Temp->Next)
    {
        Temp->Draw(pdc);
    }
}
```

Figure 7-6 The **CGraphicList** *Draw* Operation

```
void CGraphicList::AddRectangle(long xi, long yi, long xp, long yp,
COLORREF LineC,COLORREF FillC)
{
    // User will sweep out a rectangle with the mouse.
    long x = min(xi,xp);
    long y = min(yi,yp);
    // compute positive height and width
    long w = max(xi,xp) - min(xi,xp);
```

Figure 7-7 The **CGraphicList** *AddRectangle* Function

```
    long h = max(yi,yp) - min(yi,yp);
    // Create object and fill parameters
    CRectangle * Temp = new CRectangle;
    Temp->FillColor = FillC;
    Temp->LineColor = LineC;
    Temp->Left = x;
    Temp->Top = y;
    Temp->Width = w;
    Temp->Height = h;
    // Link object into list
    if (Head == NULL)
    {
        Head = Temp;
    }
    else
    {
        Tail->Next = Temp;
    }
    Temp->Prev = Tail;
    Tail = Temp;
    Count++;
}
```

Figure 7-7   (*Continued*)

```
void CGraphicList::AddCircle(long xi, long yi, long xp, long yp,
COLORREF LineC,COLORREF FillC)
{
    // User will sweep out a rectangle with the mouse
    long x = xi;
    long y = yi;
    // Compute positive width and height
    long w = max(xi,xp) - min(xi,xp);
    long h = max(yi,yp) - min(yi,yp);
    // Minimum of width and height is diameter of circle. Half
    // of this is radius (truncation toward zero for odd diameters)
    long r = min(h,w)/2;
    CCircle * Temp = new CCircle;
    Temp->FillColor = FillC;
    Temp->LineColor = LineC;
    // We must determine the direction of mouse movement from the
    // starting point to determine the quadrant (with starting point
    // as origin) in which the circle lies
    if (xi < xp)
    {
```

Figure 7-8   The **CGraphicList** *AddCircle* Function

```
            Temp->Center.x = x + r; // moving right
        }
        else
        {
            Temp->Center.x = x - r; // moving left
        }
        if (yi < yp)
        {
            Temp->Center.y = y + r; // moving down
        }
        else
        {
            Temp->Center.y = y - r; // moving up
        }
        Temp->Radius = r;
        // Link object into list
        if (Head == NULL)
        {
            Head = Temp;
        }
        else
        {
            Tail->Next = Temp;
        }
        Temp->Prev = Tail;
        Tail = Temp;
        Count++;
}
```

Figure 7-8   (*Continued*)

5. THE DRAWING MODE

To complete the task of drawing circles and rectangles, we must establish a few properties that permit the container, and ultimately the user, to select the proper drawing mode. The user must be able to choose between drawing a circle and drawing a rectangle, and must be able to choose the fill color and line color of each object. For fill and line colors, we establish "current color" modes that will give the fill and line colors for all future objects. Most graphical drawing tools use a similar mechanism. We will create two properties: (1) *FillColor* and (2) *LineColor*. We will choose the member-variable implementation of these properties. Anytime a new object is drawn, we will use the current values of these member variables as our fill and line colors.

To determine whether a circle or a rectangle is to be drawn, we will create a third property, *DrawMode*, that will determine which shape is to be drawn. This property will have a member-variable with the enumerated type *DrawType* illustrated in Figure 7-9.

When a drawing operation commences, the current value of the *DrawMode* property will be used to determine which shape is to be drawn. Additional entries can be added to the *DrawType* enumeration to create additional drawing modes.

```
enum DrawType
{
   DTRectangle = 1,
   DTCircle = 2
};
```

Figure 7-9   The *DrawType* Enumeration

Property Design Table		
Name	**Type**	**Function**
LineColor	OLE_COLOR Default = Black	Specifies the line color for all new drawing objects.
FillColor	OLE_COLOR Default = black	Specifies the fill color for all new drawing objects.
DrawMode	Enum DrawType Default=DTRectangle	Determines whether a circle or a rectangle is to be drawn

Figure 7-10   Property Design Table for LineColor, FillColor, and DrawMode

Figure 7-10 gives the property design table for these three properties.

6. MOUSE OPERATIONS

Objects will be drawn using mouse operations, each of which consists of several mouse messages. Mouse messages are created by the operating system in response to mouse clicks and mouse movement on the part of the user. There are three types of operating system messages for mouse operations. The Mouse-Down and Mouse-Up messages are used to inform the component that a mouse button has been pressed or released. The Mouse-Move message is used to inform the program that the mouse has been moved. All three messages contain the location of the mouse cursor where the action occurred. A mouse operation begins with a Mouse-Down message and ends with a Mouse-Up message. Several Mouse-Move messages may occur between the Mouse-Down and Mouse-Up messages. The following table describes the operations that must take place during the processing of these messages.

Mouse-Down   Determine current drawing mode.

Set internal state to indicate that mouse operation is in progress.

Record starting point.

Perform any additional computations to determine the operation to be executed.

Set internal state to indicate type of operation in progress.

Mouse-Move   Decode internal state to determine the type of operation in progress.

Provide visual feedback about the operation in progress.

Mouse-Up   Decode internal state to determine the type of operation in progress.

Record the ending point.

Perform the requested operation, object creation, change, etc.

Reset internal state to indicate no mouse operation in progress.

Mouse-Move and **Mouse-Up** messages can occur when no mouse operation is in progress. The **Mouse-Move** and **Mouse-Up** processing routines must be designed to ignore such messages. At this point, we have two mouse operations that can be performed: (1) drawing a rectangle and (2) drawing a circle. Thus we require three mouse-state codes: (1) *draw rectangle*, (2) *draw circle*, and (3) *no operation in progress*. Figure 7-11 gives an enumerated data type containing these three codes. Additional codes will be added to this enumeration as development proceeds.

As with the drawing model, we will create a special class **CMouse** to encapsulate the processing of the mouse state. Figure 7-12 contains the definition of the **CMouse**

```
enum MouseDownType
{
    MDNone = 0,
    MDDrawRect = 7,
    MDDrawCirc = 8
};
```

Figure 7-11   The MouseDown Enumeration

```
class CMouse
{
public:
    // Mouse state: MouseDownNone=Mouse is up
    MouseDownType Code;

    // Mouse operation points
    CPoint StartPoint; // Starting point set on mouse down
    CPoint MovePoint; // Intermediate point set on mouse move
    CPoint EndPoint; // Ending point set on mouse up

    CMouse( );
    virtual ~CMouse( );

    // set mouse down code
    void Down(MouseDownType NewCode);
    // set mouse down code to MouseDownNone
    void Up(void);

    void Start(CPoint p); // Set start point
    void Move(CPoint p); // set move point
    void End(CPoint p); // set end point
};
```

Figure 7-12   The CMouse Class

```
// Set mouse starting point and initial move point
void CMouse::Start(CPoint p)
{
    StartPoint = p;
    MovePoint = p;
}
// replace move point
void CMouse::Move(CPoint p)
{
    MovePoint = p;
}
// Set mouse End Point
void CMouse::End(CPoint p)
{
    EndPoint = p;
}
```

Figure 7-13   CMouse Function Definitions

```
// Start mouse operation
void CMouse::Down(MouseDownType NewCode)
{
    Code = NewCode;
}
// End mouse operation
void CMouse::Up()
{
    Code = MDNone;
}
```

Figure 7-14   CMouse *Down* and *Up* Definitions

class. In addition to the variable *Code* which identifies the mouse operation in progress, this class contains the starting point of the mouse operation, the intermediate point for mouse moves, and the ending point of the operation. Functions are provided for setting the mouse state and the various points (see Figures 7-13 and 7-14). The functions are provided both for clarity and to encapsulate operations that are more complicated than simply assigning a value to a single variable. This class will be expanded as the number of mouse operations grows.

7. THE MOUSE-HANDLING ROUTINES

Three mouse-handling routines are required. Since we are using the MFC ActiveX wizard to create our component, we must use the Class Wizard to create our mouse-handling routines. We use the first tab of the wizard, Message Maps, to add message handlers for **WM_LBUTTONDOWN**, **WM_LBUTTONUP**, and **WM_MOUSEMOVE** messages. This will create three functions for us: (1) *OnLButtonDown*, (2) *OnLButtonUp*,

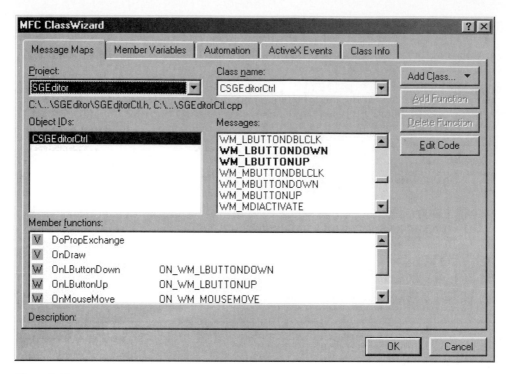

Figure 7-15   Intercepting Mouse Activity

and (3) *OnMouseMove*. Figure 7-15 illustrates how to use the Class Wizard to create these three routines in VC++ 6.0, while Figure 7-16 shows how to create the functions in VS.NET. We will add our message-handling code to these three routines. The first routine to be modified is the *OnLButtonDown* function shown in Figure 7-17.

The *DoXRect* and *DoXCirc* functions that appear in Figure 7-17 are used to draw the outline of the figure while it is being drawn. Both functions draw in XOR mode, so that the sweep rectangle (or sweep circle) can be undrawn and redrawn elsewhere without redrawing the entire screen. (In XOR mode, drawing a figure a second time causes it to be undrawn.) These two functions will make use of the *StartPoint* and *MovePoint* components of the **CMouse** class. Because these functions must have access to the drawing facilities of the support class, they must be added as function members of the support class. These functions will also be used in the *OnMouseMove* function, which appears in Figure 7-18. In the *MDDrawRect* routine, the current rectangle outline is undrawn, the mouse MovePoint is updated with the point from the current mouse-move message, and the rectangle is redrawn in the new position. This process will cause a tracking-rectangle to appear when a new rectangle is being drawn, and it will cause one corner of the tracking rectangle to follow the mouse. The *MDDrawCirc* routine performs a similar function for circles.

The *OnMouseUp* function not only terminates mouse operations but also causes drawing objects to be added to the drawing model. Although the details are somewhat complicated, the fundamental idea is to record the ending mouse position and then to

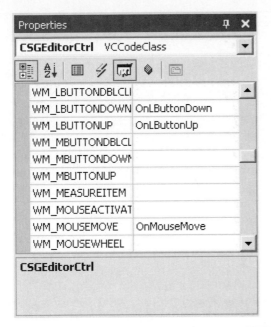

Figure 7-16   Adding Mouse Handlers
in VS.NET

```
void CSGEditorCtrl::OnLButtonDown(UINT nFlags, CPoint point)
{
    // Starting point for all mouse operations
    Mouse.Start(point);
    // Rectangle mode, or Circle mode
    switch (m_drawMode)
    {
        case DTRectangle:
        {
            // begin drawing a new rectangle
            Mouse.Down(MDDrawRect);
            // show the outline of the figure being drawn
            DoXRect( );
        }
        break;
        case DTCircle:
        {
            // begin drawing a new rectangle
            Mouse.Down(MDDrawCirc);
            // show the outline of the circle being drawn
            DoXCirc( );
        }
        break;
    }
    // reflect message back to COleControl
    COleControl::OnLButtonDown(nFlags, point);
}
```

Figure 7-17   Starting a Mouse Operation

```
void CSGEditorCtrl::OnMouseMove(UINT nFlags, CPoint point)
{
    // if mouse is down
    if (Mouse.Code != MDNone)
    {
        switch (Mouse.Code)
        {
            case MDDrawRect:
            {
                // Undraw old rectangle, change the move point,
                // redraw the rectangle
                DoXRect();
                Mouse.Move(point);
                DoXRect();
            }
            break;
            case MDDrawCirc:
            {
                // Undraw old circle, change the move point,
                // redraw the circle
                DoXCirc();
                Mouse.Move(point);
                DoXCirc();
            }
            break;
        }
    }
    // reflect message back to COleControl
    COleControl::OnMouseMove(nFlags, point);
}
```

Figure 7-18   Continuing a Mouse Operation

use the starting and ending mouse positions to set the dimensions of the new drawing object. It is also necessary to undraw the shape outlines created by the *OnMouseMove* function. The routine shown in Figure 7-19 has one (somewhat annoying) complication. Color specifications, as set through properties, are not the same as the color specifications required by the operating system drawing commands. Thus it is necessary to translate the fill color and line color from their property values into values suitable for drawing. This is done using the operating system *OleTranslateColor* function. The function *CWnd::Invalidate* is used to force a redraw of the component's window.

Finally, let us examine the two outline-drawing routines, *DoXRect* and *DoXCirc*. These routines have much in common with the *AddRectangle* and *AddCircle* functions of the **CGraphicList** object, because in both cases we are computing the shape of a drawing object from two mouse-provided points. Both *DoXRect* and *DoXCirc* draw in XOR mode. (In Windows, the actual mode used is NOTXOR.) In XOR mode, the

```
void CSGEditorCtrl::OnLButtonUp(UINT nFlags, CPoint point)
{
   if (Mouse.Code != MDNone) // no action if mouse not down
   {
      // Set ending point for the operation
      Mouse.End(point);
      COLORREF FillC,LineC;
      switch (Mouse.Code)
      {
         case MDDrawRect:
         {
            // Translate colors from OLECOLOR to RGB
            OleTranslateColor(m_lineColor,NULL,&LineC);
            OleTranslateColor(m_fillColor,NULL,&FillC);
            // undraw outline
            DoXRect( );
            // Create a new rectangle drawing object
            Model->AddRectangle(Mouse.StartPoint.x,
                     Mouse.StartPoint.y,Mouse.EndPoint.x,
                     Mouse.EndPoint.y,LineC,FillC);
            // force redraw
            CWnd::Invalidate( );
         }
         break;
         case MDDrawCirc:
         {
            // Translate colors from OLECOLOR to RGB
            OleTranslateColor(m_lineColor,NULL,&LineC);
            OleTranslateColor(m_fillColor,NULL,&FillC);
            // undraw outline
            DoXCirc( );
            // Create a new circle drawing object
            Model->AddCircle(Mouse.StartPoint.x,
                     Mouse.StartPoint.y,Mouse.EndPoint.x,
                     Mouse.EndPoint.y,LineC,FillC);
            // force redraw
            CWnd::Invalidate( );
         }
         break;
      }
      // Don't forget this!
      Mouse.Up( );
   }
   // reflect message back to COleControl
   COleControl::OnLButtonUp(nFlags, point);
}
```

Figure 7-19   Terminating a Mouse Operation

```
void CSGEditorCtrl::DoXRect()
{
    // draw the rectangle outline
    // don't draw degenerate rectangles
    if (Mouse.StartPoint.x != Mouse.MovePoint.x ||
        Mouse.StartPoint.y != Mouse.EndPoint.y)
    {
        // get a drawing context for the control window
        CDC * MyDc = CWnd::GetDC();
        // Set the drawing mode to XOR,
        // line color black, fill color white
        … //Standard system calls omitted for brevity
        // draw the rectangle
        MyDc->Rectangle(Mouse.StartPoint.x,Mouse.StartPoint.y,
                        Mouse.MovePoint.x,Mouse.MovePoint.y);
        // clean up the drawing context & release resources
        … // Standard System calls omitted for brevity
    }
}
```

Figure 7-20   The DoXRect Routine

color black causes background colors to reverse. Thus a black line is always visible regardless of the color of the background. Similarly, the color white is invisible. Thus, setting the fill color to white causes the interiors of rectangles and circles to be transparent. Another advantage of XOR mode is that a figure can be undrawn by simply redrawing it. This permits a single routine to be used for both drawing and undrawing. Figure 7-20 gives the *DoXRect* routine, while Figure 7-21 contains the *DoXCirc* routine.

The *DoXCirc* of Figure 7-21 is fundamentally more complicated than the *DoXRect* routine, because there is no implicit operating system function for drawing circles. Instead we must use the *Ellipse* function. This function inscribes an ellipse inside a rectangle, and has the same parameters as the implicit *Rectangle* function. (We could have saved ourselves a lot of trouble by deciding to draw ellipses instead of circles!)

When we draw a circle, we must convert the rectangle supplied by the mouse points into a square, and then use the *Ellipse* function to inscribe a circle inside the square. To make the drawing of a circle seem natural, we must make sure that one corner of the square is the starting point of the drawing operation. With this restriction, we must then compute the largest square that will fit inside the rectangle drawn by the mouse. We first compute the height and width of the mouse-defined rectangle. Because the mouse can move in any direction from the starting point, we must be careful to compute the height and width as positive numbers. We will do this by subtracting the minimum *x*-coordinate from the maximum *x*-coordinate, and similarly for the *y*-coordinates. The width (and height) of the largest square that will fit in the mouse-defined rectangle

```
void CSGEditorCtrl::DoXCirc()
{
    // draw the circle outline when creating a new circle
    // don't draw circles in degenerate rectangles
    if (Mouse.StartPoint.x != Mouse.MovePoint.x ||
        Mouse.StartPoint.y != Mouse.EndPoint.y)
    {
        CPoint LclPos;
        // get a drawing context for the control window
        CDC * MyDc = CWnd::GetDC( );
        // set the drawing mode to XOR
        // line color to black fill color to white
        … // Standard system calls omitted for brevity

        // Compute a square rectangle that is the largest square
        // contained in the mouse-defined rectangle,
        // with one corner including the start point

        // Compute positive dimensions and compare them
        if (max(Mouse.StartPoint.x,Mouse.MovePoint.x) -
            min(Mouse.StartPoint.x,Mouse.MovePoint.x) >
            max(Mouse.StartPoint.y,Mouse.MovePoint.y) -
            min(Mouse.StartPoint.y,Mouse.MovePoint.y))
        {
            // Vertical dimension is smaller
            // Set horizontal dimension to match vertical
            LclPos.y = Mouse.MovePoint.y;
            // Compute positive diameter in vertical direction
            long Diff = max(Mouse.StartPoint.y,Mouse.MovePoint.y) -
                 min(Mouse.StartPoint.y,Mouse.MovePoint.y);
            // Adjust horizontal diameter + or -
            // depending on direction of mouse movement
            if (Mouse.MovePoint.x < Mouse.StartPoint.x)
            {
                // Mouse is moving up, subtract diameter
                LclPos.x = Mouse.StartPoint.x - Diff;
            }
            else
            {
                // Mouse is moving down, add diameter
                LclPos.x = Mouse.StartPoint.x + Diff;
            }
        }
        else
        {
            // Horizontal dimension is smaller
            // set vertical dimension to match horizontal
            LclPos.x = Mouse.MovePoint.x;
            // Compute positive diameter in horizontal direction
```

Figure 7-21   The *DoXCirc* Routine

```
        long Diff = max(Mouse.StartPoint.x,Mouse.MovePoint.x) -
            min(Mouse.StartPoint.x,Mouse.MovePoint.x);
        // Adjust vertical diameter + or -
        // depending on direction of mouse movement
        if (Mouse.MovePoint.y < Mouse.StartPoint.y)
        {
            // mouse is moving left, subtract diameter
            LclPos.y = Mouse.StartPoint.y - Diff;
        }
        else
        {
            // mouse is moving right, add diameter
            LclPos.y = Mouse.StartPoint.y + Diff;
        }
    }
    // Draw the circle
    MyDc->Ellipse(Mouse.StartPoint.x,Mouse.StartPoint.y,
            LclPos.x,LclPos.y);
    // Clean up drawing context and release resources
    … // Standard system calls omitted for brevity
    }
}
```

Figure 7-21   (*Continued*)

is equal to the minimum of the width and height. We compute this as the diameter of the desired square.

We must next compute the drawing rectangle, which has four coordinates: (1) left, (2) right, (3) top, and (4) bottom. It is not necessary for left to be less than right or for top to be less than bottom, so we will use the mouse starting point for the top and left coordinates. The CMouse MovePoint variable will supply either the right coordinate or the bottom coordinate depending on whether width or height is the minimum dimension. The final coordinate will be computed by adding or subtracting the square diameter to either the top or the left coordinate. The movement of the mouse in the vertical or horizontal direction is used to determine whether to add or subtract. This is necessary to guarantee that the computed square is inside the mouse-defined rectangle.

We are now ready to test our program to see if it draws correctly. The best way to do this is in a Visual Basic project. We first compile our control and then we create a blank Visual Basic project and add an instance of our control to it. We name this instance *Editor*. We also add five buttons named *Rectangle*, *Circle*, *FillColor*, *LineColor*, and *Quit*. To handle changing fill and line colors, we add a common dialogs control named *CDlg*. Figure 7-22 shows the resultant drawing window.

Code for the buttons is given in Figure 7-23. Defined constants *DM_Circle*, and *DM_Rectangle* are used to specify the drawing mode. We should now be able to run the program and create the drawings shown in Figure 7-24.

Figure 7-22   The Drawing Window

```
Private Sub Circle_Click()
    Editor.DrawMode = DM_Circle
End Sub
Private Sub FillColor_Click()
    CDlg.CancelError = True
    On Error GoTo Done
    CDlg.ShowColor
    Editor.FillColor = CDlg.Color
Done:
End Sub
Private Sub LineColor_Click()
    CDlg.CancelError = True
    On Error GoTo Done
    CDlg.ShowColor
    Editor.LineColor = CDlg.Color
Done:
End Sub
Private Sub Quit_Click()
    End
End Sub
Private Sub Rectangle_Click()
    Editor.DrawMode = DM_Rectangle
End Sub
```

Figure 7-23   Visual Basic Code for the Drawing Editor

Figure 7-24   The First Drawings

8. THE SELECTION FACILITY

Now that we have mastered the art of drawing, we will proceed to the next task, selection. In addition to drawing circles and rectangles, we would also like to be able to edit our drawing once it has been created. We would like to be able to delete certain objects, move them, and change their size and color. Naturally, when we make a change, we want to be able to specify the objects to which the change applies. This implies that we must have some method of selecting objects. The typical way to do this is to add another drawing mode, called *Select Mode*. The mouse operations performed in this mode will be used to select objects.

There are two mouse operations we are interested in: (1) clicking on a single object to select it and (2) sweeping out a rectangle to select all objects contained in the rectangle. (We could also consider shift-clicking to add items to or delete items from the selection, but we will leave this as an exercise for interested readers.)

Before worrying about user interaction, we must determine how selected objects are to be represented in the drawing model. The most straightforward approach is to link all selected objects together into a separate chain. However, moving objects from one chain to another can be a complicated process. It is possible to modify the **CSelectObject** class to add another set of pointers for the select chain, but dealing with more than one set of chain pointers per object is difficult and very much prone to error. We will use the simpler alternative of creating a separate class for selected objects and place a pointer to the selected object in this class. This class, **CSelectItem**, is given in Figure 7-25. Since we are not worried about deleting individual items from the selection, we will use a singly linked list for selected items.

```
class CSelectItem
{
public:
    CSelectItem * Next;
    CGraphicObject * Item;

    CSelectItem( );
    virtual ~CSelectItem( );
};
```

Figure 7-25   The Selection Object

To enforce encapsulation of all drawing-related operations, we will add the head of the selection chain to the **CGraphicList** class, the object that represents the drawing model. The following three lines will be added to the **CGraphicList** definition:

```
// Chain of selected objects
CSelectItem * Selection;
long SelCount; // number of selected objects
```

When scanning the list of graphical objects, it might be useful at some point to know whether or not a particular object is selected. Rather than scanning the selection chain to determine whether an object is selected, we will add the following data item to the **CGraphicObject** class to tell us which objects are selected and which are not.

```
BOOL Selected; // true if object is part of selection
```

It will be necessary to add selection-handling functions to the **CGraphicList** class, but before attempting to define such functions, let us first determine the form of the selection-related mouse operations. This will help guide the design of our selection-handling functions.

The first step in designing our mouse operations is to modify the **enum** data type of Figure 7-9 to include a select mode. The modified **enum** type appears in Figure 7-26. This figure also shows the *MouseDownType* with the select operation added.

```
enum DrawType
{
    DTSelect = 0,
    DTRectangle = 1,
    DTCircle = 2
};
enum MouseDownType
{
    MDNone = 0,
    MDSelect = 1,
    MDDrawRect = 7,
    MDDrawCirc = 8
};
```

Figure 7-26   Enhanced Enumerations

```
case DTSelect:
{
   if (Model->Selection != NULL) // if there is a selection
   {
      Model->ClearSelect( );
      Mouse.Down(MDSelect);
      DoXRect( );
   }
   else
   {
      // there is no existing selection
      Mouse.Down(MDSelect);
      DoXRect( );
   }
}
break;
```

Figure 7-27   Starting the *Select* **Mouse** Operation

Next, we must add a *DTSelect* handler to the *OnLButtonDown* function. We will add a new case to the main **select** statement, as illustrated in Figure 7-27. We will use a new *MouseDown* code, *MDSelect*, to indicate that a selection operation is in progress. We will also use the function *DoXRect* to draw the outline of the selection rectangle during the selection operation.

As Figure 7-27 shows, when we start a new selection operation, we clear the existing selection and start a new selection operation. We need to add the *ClearSelect* function to the **CGraphicList** class. We will discuss this function later.

We now need to modify the *OnMouseMove* function to handle the *MDSelect* operation. The added code is illustrated in Figure 7-28. Even though this routine is identical to that for the *MDRectangle* operation, we will resist the temptation to share code between these routines because we may wish to make them different later on.

Finally, we must add an *MDSelect* routine to the *OnLButtonUp* function. This routine must create the new selection. It must also distinguish between clicking on a single object and sweeping out a selection rectangle. Figure 7-29 shows how to terminate the *Select* operation. We first check the mouse starting and ending coordinates, and if they are the same, we treat the selection as a click, and select the clicked object. Otherwise we treat the selection as a rectangle and select all objects in the rectangle.

```
case MDSelect:
{
   DoXRect( );
   Mouse.Move(point);
   DoXRect( );
}
break;
```

Figure 7-28   Continuing the *Select* Operation

```
case MDSelect:
{
    if (Mouse.StartPoint.x == Mouse.EndPoint.x &&
     Mouse.StartPoint.y == Mouse.EndPoint.y)
    {  // Selection is a point
        Model->Select(Mouse.StartPoint);
    }
    else // Selection is a rectangle
    {
        RECT R; // Adjust so top<bottom and left<right
        R.left = min(Mouse.StartPoint.x,Mouse.EndPoint.x);
        R.right = max(Mouse.StartPoint.x,Mouse.EndPoint.x);
        R.top = min(Mouse.StartPoint.y,Mouse.EndPoint.y);
        R.bottom = max(Mouse.StartPoint.y,Mouse.EndPoint.y);
        // Select all objects contained in rectangle R
        Model->Select(R);
    }
    CWnd::Invalidate();
}
break;
```

Figure 7-29   Terminating the *Select* Operation

We need to add two additional functions—*Select(CPoint)* and *Select(RECT &)*—to the
CGraphicList class to handle these selection operations.

  We must now create the three selection handling functions: (1) *Select(CPoint)*,
(2) *Select(RECT &)*, and (3) *ClearSelect*. *ClearSelect*—the simplest—is shown in Figure
7-30. *ClearSelect* deletes all **CSelectItem** objects in the select chain and marks all objects in the select chain as *Not Selected*.

  The two select routines are wrapper routines that are used to pass the selection test
to each object in the list of graphical objects. For *Select(RECT &)*, each object is queried
to determine whether it lies completely within the specified rectangle. For *Select(CPoint)*,
each object is queried to determine whether the specified point lies on the object. Since

```
void CGraphicList::ClearSelect()
{
    // Deselects everything and erases the selection chain
    while (Selection != NULL)
    {
        CSelectItem * Temp = Selection;
        Selection = Selection->Next;
        Temp->Item->Selected = FALSE;
        delete Temp;
    }
    SelCount = 0;
}
```

Figure 7-30   The *ClearSelect* Function

```
void CGraphicList::Select(RECT &R)
{
    // Add all drawing objects inside R to the current selection
    for (CGraphicObject * Temp=Head; Temp != NULL; Temp=Temp->Next)
    {
        if (Temp->Inside(R))
        {
            AddToSelect(Temp);
        }
    }
}
```

Figure 7-31   The *Select(RECT &)* Function

Select(CPoint) is designed to select a single object, the loop exits as soon as an object is found. Both functions use the utility function *AddToSelection(CGraphicObject *)* to add objects to the current selection. *Select(RECT &)* is shown in Figure 7-31, while Figure 7-32 shows *Select(CPoint)*. The utility function *AddToSelect* is shown in Figure 7-33. This function simply creates a new **CSelectItem** object and adds it to the select chain. The select chain is treated as a stack. The object is also marked as being selected.

Now we need to enhance **CGraphicObject** and its derived types, **CCircle** and **CRectangle**, with the necessary query functions. The following three lines must be added to the definition of **CGraphicObject**:

```
// These functions determine when an object is clicked
virtual BOOL Inside(RECT R) = 0;
virtual BOOL Intersect(CPoint point) = 0;
```

Because *Inside(RECT)* and *Intersect(CPoint)* are pure virtual functions, both **CCircle** and **CRectangle** must also define these functions. The tests performed by these functions are straightforward. The **CRectangle** versions of these functions are given in Figure 7-34 and Figure 7-35.

```
void CGraphicList::Select(CPoint p)
{
    // Add the first object containing p to the selection
    for (CGraphicObject * Temp=Head; Temp != NULL; Temp=Temp->Next)
    {
        if (Temp->Intersect(p))
        {
            AddToSelect(Temp);
            break;
        }
    }
}
```

Figure 7-32   The *Select(CPoint)* Function

```
void CGraphicList::AddToSelect(CGraphicObject *NewObj)
{
    // Utility for Select(RECT &) and Select(CPoint) functions
    if (!(NewObj->Selected)) // Don't add something twice!
    {
        CSelectItem * Temp = new CSelectItem;
        Temp->Next = Selection; // Selection is a stack
        Selection = Temp;
        Temp->Item = NewObj;
        NewObj->Selected = TRUE;
        SelCount++;
    }
}
```

Figure 7-33   The AddToSelect Function

```
BOOL CRectangle::Inside(RECT R)
{
    // is this rectangle completely enclosed by R?
    if (Left >= R.left && Left+Width <= R.right &&
        Top >= R.top && Top+Height <= R.bottom)
    {
        return TRUE;
    }
    return FALSE;
}
```

Figure 7-34   The *Inside* Rectangle Function

```
BOOL CRectangle::Intersect(CPoint point)
{
    // Is point in rectangle ?
    if (point.x < Left || point.x > Left+Width ||
        point.y < Top || point.y > Top+Height)
    {
        return FALSE;
    }
    return TRUE;
}
```

Figure 7-35   The *Intersect* Rectangle Function

For **CCircle**, the *Inside* function is also straightforward, because the circle will fall within the specified rectangle if and only if the smallest square containing the circle also falls within the rectangle. This square can be found by adding and subtracting the radius from the x and y coordinates of the center. This routine is given in Figure 7-36.

```
BOOL CCircle::Inside(RECT R)
{
    // is CCircle contained inside of rectangle R?
    if (Center.x-Radius >= R.left && Center.x+Radius <= R.right &&
        Center.y-Radius >= R.top && Center.y+Radius <= R.bottom)
    {
        return TRUE;
    }
    return FALSE;
}
```

Figure 7-36   The *Inside* Circle Function

```
BOOL CCircle::Intersect(CPoint point)
{
    // is point inside circle?
    long x = point.x - Center.x;
    long y = point.y - Center.y;
    // use square of radius to avoid square roots
    long rp = (x*x) + (y*y);
    long rs = Radius * Radius;
    if (rp <= rs)
    {
        return TRUE;
    }
    return FALSE;
}
```

Figure 7-37   The Intersect Circle Function

The *Intersect(CPoint)* function is somewhat more complicated, because we wish to return **TRUE** only when the point lies within the circumference of the circle. To make this determination, we compute the square of the distance of the specified point from the center and compare it with the square of the radius. This routine is illustrated in Figure 7-37.

The changes we have added will enable the end user to select objects either by clicking them or by sweeping out a rectangle around them. The user can also clear the selection by clicking on an empty spot on the drawing surface. However, we have not as yet given the user any way to tell which objects are selected. To do this, we must modify the drawing routine to provide visual feedback about the selection.

The usual way to visually tag selected items is to draw a black rectangle around the selected objects. This is fine for circle objects or for multiple objects when they are selected, but it would not be particularly helpful for rectangles with black borders. To provide useful visual feedback for all selections, we must jump ahead to the next topic.

The usual method for resizing selected objects is to provide a *grab handle*—a small black square drawn on the border of the selected object. When the user clicks and drags one of these grab handles, the size of the object will track the movement of the mouse. Grab handles provide excellent visual feedback for selected objects, even rectangles with black borders.

Many graphical editors provide eight grab handles for each object, one at each corner, and one in the center of each edge of the selection rectangle. Because the four corner grab handles are sufficient to perform all required editing tasks, we will omit the grab handles in the center of each edge. The only thing left to determine is the size of the grab handles. We could simply choose some convenient size and use that for all selections, but it is our practice to make constants of this nature accessible through the properties of the control. Thus we will provide a new integer property, *HandleRadius*, and use the value of that property as the radius (half the width) of the grab handles. We will choose 4, a convenient size, as the default value for this property. Figure 7-38 gives the formal definition of this property.

For the moment, we will use the member variable implementation of this property, but we should seriously consider making the value of *HandleRadius* a member of the **CGraphicList** class. We must now modify the *Draw* function of **CGraphicList** to include the selection rectangle and grab handles. Figure 7-39 gives the new *Draw* routine with the

Property Design Table		
Name	**Type**	**Function**
HandleRadius	Integer Maximum = 30 Minimum = 2 Default = 4	Specifies half the width of the grab handles used to mark the current selection.

Figure 7-38   The *HandleRadius* Property

```
void CGraphicList::Draw(CDC* pdc, const CRect& rcBounds,
        const CRect& rcInvalid, long m_handleRadius)
{
    // blank out the drawing area
    pdc->FillRect( … ); // no change
    // Pass the draw request to each object
    for … // no change
    // if there is a selection, draw the selection rectangle
    // m_handleRadius can be set to zero
    // for printing and metafile creation
    if (Selection != NULL && m_handleRadius > 0)
    {
        // Set line color=black, fill color = hollow
```

Figure 7-39   The Drawing Routine with Drag Handles

```
… // Operating system calls omitted for brevity
// Get the selection rectangle and draw it
RECT R;
GetSelRect(R); // new CGraphicList function
pdc->Rectangle(&R);
// set fill color to black
… // Operating system call omitted for brevity
// draw each handle
pdc->Rectangle(R.left-m_handleRadius,
               R.top-m_handleRadius,
               R.left+m_handleRadius,
               R.top+m_handleRadius);
… // repeat for other three handles
// clean up the drawing object and release resources
… // operating system calls omitted for brevity
    }
}
```

Figure 7-39   (*Continued*)

required modifications. We have added an additional argument, *m_handleRadius,* for passing the value of the *HandleRadius* property to the drawing routine.

The *Draw* routine features a call to a new **CGraphicList** function, *GetSelRect(RECT &),* which is used to get the selection rectangle. This new routine is shown in Figure 7-40.

```
void CGraphicList::GetSelRect(RECT &R)
{
    // returns the smallest rectangle containing the current selection.
    // GetRect is called for each selected object, min TOP, min LEFT,
    // max BOTTOM, and max RIGHT are saved.
    if (Selection != NULL)
    {
        RECT W;
        Selection->Item->GetRect(R);
        CSelectItem * Temp;
        for (Temp=Selection->Next; Temp!=NULL; Temp=Temp->Next)
        {
            Temp->Item->GetRect(W);
            if (W.top < R.top)
            {
                R.top = W.top;
            }
            if (W.bottom > R.bottom)
            {
                R.bottom = W.bottom;
```

Figure 7-40   The *GetSelRect* **Function**

```
          }
        ... // repeat for right and left
      }
    }
    else
    {
      // NULL rectangle if no selection
      R.bottom = 0;
      R.top = 0;
      R.left = 0;
      R.top = 0;
    }
}
```

Figure 7-40   (*Continued*)

The *GetSelRect* function will in turn call a new **CGraphicObject** function, *GetRect(RECT &)*. The *GetRect* function will return the smallest rectangle enclosing a drawing object. As before, we need a new function definition in **CGraphicObject**, and two implementations of the function, one for **CCircle** and one for **CRectangle**. The following line must be added to **CGraphicObject**.

```
// work function used to determine the selection rectangle
virtual void GetRect(RECT &R) = 0;
```

The **CCircle** and **CRectangle** implementations of *GetRect*, presented in Figure 7-41, are straightforward. With these changes, the user cannot only make selections but see them outlined in the control window, as shown in Figure 7-42.

```
void CCircle::GetRect(RECT &R)
{
    // Utility function for computing selection rectangle
    R.left = Center.x - Radius;
    R.right = Center.x + Radius;
    R.top = Center.y - Radius;
    R.bottom = Center.y + Radius;
}
void CRectangle::GetRect(RECT &R)
{
    // Utility function used to get selection rectangle
    R.left = Left;
    R.top = Top;
    R.right = Left + Width;
    R.bottom = Top + Height;
}
```

Figure 7-41   The *GetRect* Functions

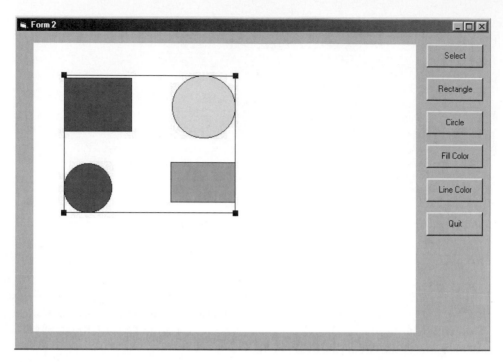

Figure 7-42 Drawing Window with Selection

9. THE MODIFICATION FACILITY

Now that we have the ability to select objects, we can proceed with providing features to allow users to change drawing objects. There are four types of changes we wish to support:

1. The user should be able to move a drawing object to a new location in the drawing window. This should be done by clicking on an object in the current selection and dragging it to a new location. The entire selection should move as a unit.

2. The user should be able to change the size of objects. For rectangles and multiple selections, the user should also be able to change the shape of objects. This should be done by clicking on a grab handle and dragging it.

3. The user should be able to delete selected objects. We will implement this as a *Delete* method, which will be called by the control's container. (Keeping to the "passive object" rule.)

4. The user should be able to change the line and fill colors of selected objects. This will be done when the *LineColor* or *FillColor* property is changed. If there is a current selection when these properties receive a new value, the new value will be applied to all objects in the current selection, as well as to new objects.

Deleting and changing colors is the simplest form of change, so we will dispense with those first. As with all other graphical operations, the changes will be performed by the **CGraphicList** object, and where appropriate, by the drawing objects themselves.

```
void CSGEditorCtrl::Delete()
{
    // Pass deletion request to model
    Model->DeleteSelection();
    CWnd::Invalidate();
}
```

Figure 7-43   The *Delete* Method

We will begin by adding the *Delete* method to our control. The implementation of this function will call the appropriate **CGraphicList** function to perform the operation. The implementation of the *Delete* method is given in Figure 7-43.

The *Delete* method passes the delete request to the **CGraphicList** object using the *DeleteSelection* function. This function is similar to the *ClearSelection* function, except that each selected object is removed from the chain of graphic objects and deleted. Figure 7-44 gives the implementation of this function.

```
void CGraphicList::DeleteSelection()
{
    // delete all selected objects
    if (Selection != NULL)
    {
        // clear selection, but leave select bits set in objects
        while (Selection != NULL) // don't set object selected to false
        {
            CSelectItem * Temp = Selection;
            Selection = Selection->Next;
            delete Temp;
        }
        SelCount = 0;
        CGraphicObject * Temp, *Temp2;
        // Unlink selected objects and delete them
        for (Temp=Head ; Temp != NULL ; Temp = Temp2)
        {
            Temp2 = Temp->Next;
            if (Temp->Selected)
            {
                // unlink
                if (Temp->Prev == NULL)
                {
                    Head = Temp->Next;
                }
                else
                {
```

Figure 7-44   The *Delete Selection* Function

```
                    Temp->Prev->Next = Temp->Next;
                }
                if (Temp->Next == NULL)
                {
                    Tail = Temp->Prev;
                }
                else
                {
                    Temp->Next->Prev = Temp->Prev;
                }
                Count--;
                delete Temp;
            }
        }
    }
}
```

Figure 7-44   (*Continued*)

To implement color changes, we will modify two routines: *OnFillColorChanged* and *OnLineColorChanged*. These routines were created for us when we added the *FillColor* and *LineColor* properties to our control. The color change itself will be performed by the **CGraphicList** object. We pass the color change request to the **CGraphicList** object using the two functions *ChangeSelectLineColor* and *ChangeSelectFillColor*. Figure 7-45 shows

```
void CSGEditorCtrl::OnFillColorChanged()
{
    // if there is a selection we will change
    // the fill color of all selected objects
    COLORREF FillC;
    OleTranslateColor(m_fillColor,NULL,&FillC);
    Model->ChangeSelectFillColor(FillC);
    // During design mode, flags property value for saving
    SetModifiedFlag();
    CWnd::Invalidate();
}
void CSGEditorCtrl::OnLineColorChanged()
{
    // if there is a selection we will change
    // the line color of all selected objects
    COLORREF LineC;
    OleTranslateColor(m_lineColor,NULL,&LineC);
    Model->ChangeSelectLineColor(LineC);
    // During design mode, flags property value for saving
    SetModifiedFlag();
    CWnd::Invalidate();
}
```

Figure 7-45   Color Change Handlers

```
void CGraphicList::ChangeSelectFillColor(COLORREF NewColor)
{
    // Since Fill Color is a property of all drawing objects
    // There is no need for a virtual function to perform the change
    if (Selection != NULL)
    {
        // Modify each object in the selection list
        CSelectItem * Temp;
        for (Temp = Selection ; Temp !=NULL ; Temp = Temp->Next)
        {
            // change the drawing object
            Temp->Item->FillColor = NewColor;
        }
    }
}
void CGraphicList::ChangeSelectLineColor(COLORREF NewColor)
{
    … // Same, except change Temp->Item->LineColor;
}
```

Figure 7-46   Changing Selection Colors

the changes in the *OnFillColorChanged* and *OnLineColorChanged* routines. The routines *ChangeSelectFillColor* and *ChangeSelectLineColor* go through the selection list and change the color of each item in the list. Figure 7-46 shows these routines.

   The move and resize changes are considerably more difficult than deletions and color changes because they must be done in response to mouse operations. The first step is to design the required mouse operations. Because there are four grab handles that are used to do resizing, it is convenient to break the resize operation into four separate operations, one for each grab handle. Thus, five new mouse operations are required. Figure 7-47 shows the definition of the *MouseDownType* enumeration with the five new operations added.

```
enum MouseDownType
{
    MDNone = 0,
    MDSelect = 1,
    MDMove = 2,
    MDUpLeft = 3,
    MDLowLeft = 4,
    MDUpRight = 5,
    MDLowRight = 6,
    MDDrawRect = 7,
    MDDrawCirc = 8
};
```

Figure 7-47   The Complete *MouseDownType* Enumeration

Since each of these mouse operations will start when the control is in select mode (*m_drawMode = DTSelect*), we must determine how to distinguish among the various operations. This determination will be made when processing a Mouse-Down message in select mode. We will make the determination in the following manner. If there is no current selection, the mouse operation is *MDSelect*. If there is a current selection and the user has clicked on one of the grab handles, then the mouse operation will be one of the four resizing operations—*MDUpLeft, MDLowLeft, MDUpRight,* or *MDLowRight*—depending on which grab handle has been clicked. If there is a selection and no grab handle has been clicked but one of the objects in the selection has been clicked, then the new operation will be *MDMove*. If neither a grab handle nor a selected object has been clicked, then the new mouse operation will be *MDSelect* and the current selection will be cleared.

As with other operations that affect the drawing model, we want to pass all operations and tests off to the **CGraphicList** object for handling. In particular, the tests that determine whether a grab handle has been clicked or whether a selected object has been clicked will be passed off to the **CGraphicList** object using two new functions, *PointOnCorner* and *PointOnSelect*. The only parameter required by *PointOnSelect* is the current mouse position, but *PointOnCorner* also requires the handle radius. We will require the *PointOnCorner* function to return a code indicating which grab handle, if any, has been clicked. To simplify coding, we will have *PointOnCorner* return one of the *MouseDownType* codes to indicate which corner has been clicked. Strictly speaking, this is a violation of encapsulation, because we are blending the mouse model with the drawing model, but it saves us from having to do a second decoding of the value returned by *PointOnCorner*.

Visual tracking of the five new mouse operations is somewhat different from that of the existing mouse operations. For existing operations, we use the mouse starting position and its current position to define a rectangle. Our visual tracking uses this rectangle to draw either a rectangle or a circle. For the new operations, we must start with the selection rectangle. The mouse positions are used not to define a rectangle but to determine the distance that the selection rectangle has moved, or the new size of the selection rectangle. For visual tracking, we must start with a rectangle rather than with a point, and we must dynamically compute the size or position of the tracking rectangle. We have added the new function *Rect* to the mouse model to start this operation. We have also added two *RECT* structures named *SRect* and *CRect* to the mouse model. *SRect* and *CRect* will contain the starting tracking rectangle and the current tracking rectangle respectively. The mouse *StartPoint, MovePoint,* and *EndPoint* will be used to recompute the size of the *CRect* structure. The *Rect* function will be used to initialize both the *SRect* and *CRect* structures. Figure 7-48 shows the new Mouse-Down handler for *Select* mode. The *PointOnCorner* and *PointOnSelect* functions are given in Figures 7-49 and 7-50. *PointOnCorner* obtains the selection rectangle and uses the corners of the selection rectangle along with the grab handle radius and mouse point to determine whether a grab handle has been clicked. *PointOnSelect* uses the existing **CGraphicObject** function *Intersect(CPoint)* to determine whether a selected object has been clicked. The mouse tracking routines and object movement routines do not need to know *which* selected object has been clicked.

```
case DTSelect:
{
    if (Model->Selection != NULL) // if there is a selection
    {
        MouseDownType MT = Model->PointOnCorner(point,m_handleRadius);
        if (MT != MDNone) // if mouse on grab handle
        {
            // Resize existing selection
            Mouse.Down(MT);
            RECT R;
            Model->GetSelRect(R);
            Mouse.Rect(R); // use current selection rectangle as start
            // dynamically show resize operation
            DoSRect();
        }
        else if (Model->PointOnSelect(point) != NULL) // mouse on object
        {
            // move existing selection
            Mouse.Down(MDMove);
            RECT R;
            Model->GetSelRect(R);
            Mouse.Rect(R); // use current selection rectangle as start
            // dynamically show movement operation
            DoSRect();
        }
        else
        {
            // delete current selection and create a new one
            Model->ClearSelect();
            Mouse.Down(MDSelect);
        }
    }
    else
    {
        // there is no existing selection, so create a new selection
        Mouse.Down(MDSelect);
    }
}
break;
```

Figure 7-48   The Mouse-Down Handler for *Select* Mode

The function *DoSRect* is used to draw the tracking rectangle. As with other tracking rectangles, this rectangle is drawn in XOR mode, so the rectangle can be undrawn by redrawing it. *DoSRect* draws the rectangle described by the **CRect** structure of the **CMouse** object. In all other respects, *DoSRect* and *DoXRect* are identical.

The **Mouse Move** message handlers for the five new operations undraw the tracking rectangle, recompute its size and position, and redraw it. Five new mouse

```
MouseDownType CGraphicList::PointOnCorner(CPoint p, long w)
{
   // Returns a Mouse-Down code if a handle is clicked, or
   // MDNone(=0) if not on a handle
   RECT R;
   GetSelRect(R);
   if (p.x >= R.left-w && p.x <= R.left+w &&
         p.y >= R.top-w && p.y <= R.top+w)
   {
      return MDUpLeft;
   }
   if (p.x >= R.right-w && p.x <= R.right+w &&
         p.y >= R.top-w && p.y <= R.top+w)
   {
      return MDUpRight;
   }
   if (p.x >= R.left-w && p.x <= R.left+w &&
         p.y >= R.bottom-w && p.y <= R.bottom+w)
   {
      return MDLowLeft;
   }
   if (p.x >= R.right-w && p.x <= R.right+w &&
         p.y >= R.bottom-w && p.y <= R.bottom+w)
   {
      return MDLowRight;
   }
   return MDNone;
}
```

Figure 7-49   The *PointOnCorner* Function

```
CGraphicObject * CGraphicList::PointOnSelect(CPoint p)
{
   // Determines if selection is to be moved by returning an object in
   // the selection upon which point p falls. Returns NULL if none.
   CSelectItem * Temp;
   for (Temp = Selection ; Temp != NULL ; Temp = Temp->Next)
   {
      if (Temp->Item->Intersect(p))
      {
         return Temp->Item;
      }
   }
   return NULL;
}
```

Figure 7-50   The *PointOnSelect* Function

```
case MDMove:
{
    DoSRect();
    Mouse.Move(point);
    // Recompute position of Mouse.CRect
    Mouse.SetCRect();
    DoSRect();
}
break;
case MDUpLeft:
{
    DoSRect();
    Mouse.Move(point);
    // Recompute size of Mouse.CRect
    Mouse.SetUL();
    DoSRect();
}
break;
case MDLowLeft:
{
    … // Same as MDUpLeft, but use Mouse.SetLL to recompute size
}
break;
case MDUpRight:
{
    … // Same as MDUpLeft, but use Mouse.SetUR to recompute size
}
break;
case MDLowRight:
{
    … // Same as MDUpLeft, but use Mouse.SetLR to recompute size
}
break;
```

Figure 7-51   Continuing the Mouse Move and Size Operations

functions are required to recompute the tracking rectangle: (1) *SetCRect*, (2) *SetUL*, (3) *SetLL*, (4) *SetUR*, and (5) *SetLR*. Figure 7-51 shows the Mouse-Move handlers for these five operations.

Figure 7-52 shows the computation of the current tracking rectangle for *MDMove* operations. *CRect*, the current tracking rectangle, is reinitialized with *SRect*, the starting tracking rectangle. The mouse *StartPoint* and *MovePoint* are used to compute the distance the mouse has moved in the *x* and *y* directions. These values, which can be negative, are used to adjust the coordinates of *CRect*. The result is a rectangle that has moved the same distance and in the same direction as the mouse.

The other five tracking routines—*SetUL*, *SetLL*, *SetUR*, and *SetLR*—operate in the same manner as *SetCRect* but move only one corner of the tracking rectangle. The routine *SetUL* is shown in Figure 7-53. *SetLL*, *SetUR*, and *SetLR* are similar.

```
// compute deltas using startpoint and movepoint
// use deltas and SRect as a base to move CRect
void CMouse::SetCRect()
{
    CRect = SRect;
    long Delta = MovePoint.x - StartPoint.x;
    CRect.left += Delta;
    CRect.right += Delta;
    Delta = MovePoint.y - StartPoint.y;
    CRect.top += Delta;
    CRect.bottom += Delta;
}
```

Figure 7-52   The *SetCRect* Function

```
// compute deltas using startpoint and movepoint
// use deltas and SRect as a base to move Upper Left of CRect
void CMouse::SetUL()
{
    CRect = SRect;
    long Delta = MovePoint.x - StartPoint.x;
    CRect.left += Delta;
    Delta = MovePoint.y - StartPoint.y;
    CRect.top += Delta;
}
```

Figure 7-53   The *SetUL* Function

The actual movement or resizing of the selection is done in the Mouse-Up routine shown in Figure 7-54. As with other drawing operations, the move and resize requests are passed off to the **CGraphicList** object. The functions *MoveSelection* and *ScaleSelect* are used for this purpose. The *MoveSelection* requires two parameters—*XDelta* and *YDelta*—that determine the distance to move each selected object. These parameters are computed using the starting and ending mouse positions. Either one of them may be negative.

The **Mouse Up** handlers for the other four operations are identical except for the final computation of the tracking rectangle. The tracking rectangle is undrawn, the final computation is performed, and the starting and ending tracking rectangles are passed to the *ScaleSelect* function. Recall that the starting rectangle is identical to the current selection rectangle.

Because the move and scale operations affect the internal parameters of each selected object, the requests must be passed to each selected object. Figure 7-55 shows the *MoveSelection* routine, which simply passes the move request along to each selected object.

```
case MDMove:
{
    DoSRect();
    // Compute deltas for object movement
    long XDelta = Mouse.EndPoint.x - Mouse.StartPoint.x;
    long YDelta = Mouse.EndPoint.y - Mouse.StartPoint.y;
    Model->MoveSelection(XDelta,YDelta);
    CWnd::Invalidate();
}
break;
case MDUpLeft:
{
    // Scale using Mouse.SRect and Mouse.CRect
    DoSRect(); // Undraw Selection Rectangle
    Mouse.MovePoint = Mouse.EndPoint;
    Mouse.SetUL(); // Final Resize operation
    Model->ScaleSelect(Mouse.SRect,Mouse.CRect);
    CWnd::Invalidate();
}
break;
```

Figure 7-54   Finishing the Mouse Move and Size Operations

```
void CGraphicList::MoveSelection(long x, long y)
{
    if (Selection != NULL)
    {
        // Transmit the move request to each object in the selection
        CSelectItem * Temp;
        for (Temp = Selection ; Temp != NULL ; Temp = Temp->Next)
        {
            Temp->Item->Move(x,y);
        }
    }
}
```

Figure 7-55   The *MoveSelection* Routine

The *ScaleSelect* function of Figure 7-56 is similar to the *MoveSelection* function, except for the computation of the scaling parameters. Scaling cannot be done directly using the starting and ending tracking rectangles. The width and height of each rectangle must be computed to perform the scaling operation. To avoid repeating this computation for each graphical object, the width and height are computed once in the *ScaleSelect* function and passed to each object in the selection. The other four scaling parameters are the upper-left corners of the rectangles. Although the starting rectangle is guaranteed to have *left* < *right* and *top* < *bottom*, these conditions are not guaranteed

```
void CGraphicList::ScaleSelect(RECT &From, RECT &To)
{
    if (Selection != NULL)
    {
        // compute scaling parameters
        long FWid = min(From.right,From.left)-max(From.right,From.left);
        long TWid = min(To.right,To.left)-max(To.right,To.left);
        long FHite = min(From.top,From.bottom)-max(From.top,From.bottom);
        long THite = min(To.top,To.bottom)-max(To.top,To.bottom);
        long FXOrg  = min(From.right,From.left);
        long TXOrg = min(To.right,To.left);
        long FYOrg = min(From.top,From.bottom);
        long TYOrg = min(To.top,To.bottom);
        // Transmit the scaling request to each object in the selection
        CSelectItem * Temp;
        for (Temp = Selection ; Temp != NULL ; Temp = Temp->Next)
        {
            Temp->Item->Scale(FWid,TWid,FHite,THite,
                                FXOrg,TXOrg,FYOrg,TYOrg);
        }
    }
}
```

Figure 7-56   The *ScaleSelect* Function

to hold for the final tracking rectangle. Thus a minimum computation is required to find the upper-left corner of the final tracking rectangle.

The first step in completing the code for the *Move* and *Scale* functions is to add the abstract function definitions of Figure 7-57 to the **CGraphicList** object.

The two movement routines are quite trivial. For circles, the deltas are added to the center coordinates; for rectangles, they are added to the *Left* and *Top* parameters. The two routines are illustrated in Figure 7-58.

Scaling is somewhat more complicated than moving. For each scaling operation, four quantities must be scaled: object height and width, and object distance from the upper left of the selection rectangle in the x and y direction. The new absolute position of the upper left must replace the old upper-left position of the selection rectangle. For circles, we must scale height and width separately even though they are identical. This

```
// each object must move itself, and scale itself
// When multiple objects are scaled simultaneously, the positions
// of some objects may change
virtual void Move(long x, long y) = 0;
virtual void Scale(long FWid,long TWid,long FHite,long THite,
                    long FXOrg,long TXOrg,long FYOrg,long TYOrg) = 0;
```

Figure 7-57   Abstract Function Definitions for *Move* and *Scale*

```
void CCircle::Move(long x, long y)
{
    // Move circle
    Center.x += x;
    Center.y += y;
}
void CRectangle::Move(long x, long y)
{
    // Move the rectangle
    Left += x;
    Top += y;
}
```

Figure 7-58   The *Move* Functions

is because the scaling may be different in the x and y directions, and we must select the minimum of the height and width as the new diameter of the circle. The relocation of the upper left is, in fact, a translation transformation. To perform a translation of a point $p_0 = (x_0, y_0)$ with respect to the two fixed points $p_1 = (x_1, y_1)$ and $p_2 = (x_2, y_2)$, we must compute the new coordinates of p_0 by subtracting the coordinates of p_1 and then adding the coordinates of p_2. Thus the new coordinates of p_0 will be $(x_0 - x_1 + x_2, y_0 - y_1 + y_2)$. After this operation, p_0 will be the same distance from p_2 as it originally was from p_1. Figure 7-59 illustrates this concept. For the *Move* operation, we simplified the operation by precomputing $(x_2 - x_1)$ and $(y_2 - y_1)$. However,

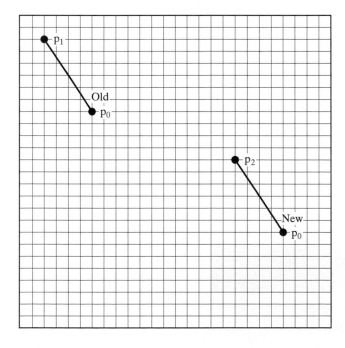

Figure 7-59   Moving p_0 with Respect to p_1 and p_2

when a translation is combined with a scaling operation, the addition and subtraction must be done separately. This is because the scaling operation must be performed on the quantities $x_0 - x_1$ and $y_0 - y_1$.

When scaling a rectangle of size (w_1,h_1) to a rectangle of size (w_2,h_2), where w_x and h_x denote width and height respectively, all objects within the rectangle must be scaled in the same ratio as the rectangles themselves. To maintain the correct relative positions of objects within the scaled rectangle, the distances between objects must also be scaled in the same proportion as the rectangles themselves. Figure 7-60 illustrates this concept. The easiest way to scale the distances between objects inside the rectangle is to scale the distance of each object from the upper-left corner of the rectangle. The x and y directions must be scaled independently of one another.

Figure 7-60 shows two solid rectangles contained within a scaling rectangle of dimensions (w_1,h_1). The dimensions of the rectangles are (c_1,d_1) and (j_1,k_1). The distance of the first rectangle from the upper-left corner of the scaling rectangle is given by (a_1,b_1) and the distance between the upper-left corners of the two rectangles is given by (e_1,f_1). When scaling the objects into the new rectangle of dimensions (w_2,h_2), the ratio of all horizontal dimensions must be equal to w_2/w_1, and the ratio of all vertical dimensions must be equal to h_2/h_1. Thus $w_2/w_1 = a_2/a_1 = c_2/c_1 = e_2/e_1 = j_2/j_1$, and $h_2/h_1 = b_2/b_1 = d_2/d_1 = f_2/f_1 = k_2/k_1$. The two ratios w_2/w_1 and h_2/h_1 need not be the same.

When scaling from a rectangle of width w_1 to a rectangle of width w_2, we must divide each dimension by w_1 and multiply by w_2. To avoid serious problems with round-off error, we must perform the multiplication first. If overflow becomes a problem (which it probably won't), we could switch to floating-point operations for the scaling process. Figure 7-61 shows how these principles are applied to the scaling of rectangle drawing objects.

The scaling of circle drawing objects is essentially the same as scaling rectangle objects, except there is only one value, *Radius*, for both the width and the height of the object. Because of this, we cannot perform a true scaling operation on circles. A circle that is scaled in different proportions along the x and y axis is no longer a circle; it is an ellipse. It will be necessary for us to "fake" the scaling as best we can. We will first

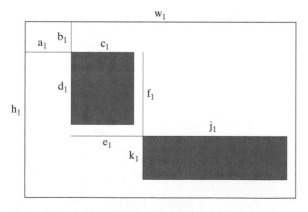
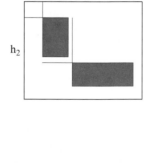

Figure 7-60   Scaling Within a Rectangle

```
void CRectangle::Scale(long FWid, long TWid, long FHite, long THite,
                                long FXOrg, long TXOrg, long FYOrg, long TYOrg)
{
    // Compute the offsets
    long XOff = Left - FXOrg;
    long YOff = Top - FYOrg;
    // Scale the offsets
    XOff *= TWid;
    XOff /= FWid;
    YOff *= THite;
    YOff /= FHite;
    // Compute New Top/Left location
    Left = Xoff + TXOrg;
    Top = Yoff + TYOrg;
    // Scale width and height
    Width *= TWid;
    Width /= FWid;
    Height *= THite;
    Height /= FHite;
}
```

Figure 7-61   The Rectangle Scaling Function

separate the horizontal and vertical scaling operations by performing a separate scaling for width and height. The radius will be used as the starting point for both operations. Once both operations have been performed, we will select the minimum of the new height and width as the new radius. This will cause the scaled circle to fit inside the scaled selection rectangle, but at times circles will appear to move in a peculiar fashion when they are scaled. Figure 7-62 shows how these operations are performed.

```
void CCircle::Scale(long FWid, long TWid, long FHite, long THite,
                            long FXOrg, long TXOrg, long FYOrg, long TYOrg)
{
    // Separate horizontal and vertical radius
    long Width = Radius;
    long Height = Radius;
    // Compute offsets
    long XOff = Center.x - FXOrg;
    long YOff = Center.y - FYOrg;
    XOff *= TWid;
    XOff /= FWid;
    YOff *= THite;
    YOff /= FHite;
    // Recompute center with respect to new upper left
```

Figure 7-62   The Circle Scaling Function

```
    Center.x = XOff + TXOrg;
    Center.y = YOff + TYOrg;
    // Scale the two radii
    Width *= TWid;
    Width /= FWid;
    Height *= THite;
    Height /= FHite;
    // Select the minimum of the two new radii as the true radius
    Radius = min(Width,Height);
}
```

Figure 7-62   *(Continued)*

10. THE UNDO FACILITY

At this point, we have the power to create and edit our drawings as we wish. We can create objects, move them, resize them, change their colors, and delete them. But what happens if we make a mistake? What if we accidentally delete objects that we really wanted to keep? Unfortunately, at this point the only thing we can do is redraw them. We have not provided any method for undoing changes.

Make no mistake, undoing changes is complicated—perhaps even more complicated than drawing and editing objects. It would easy to avoid the problem by claiming that "it's beyond the scope of this book," but undoing edits is an essential and unavoidable part of editing. Providing an editor without an undo facility is cruel and unusual punishment for any user of the editor. Furthermore, there is a right way and a wrong way to implement an undo facility. The wrong way is difficult to implement and difficult to debug, and it is of limited usefulness once you get it working. The right way is relatively easy to implement and is readily adaptable to new situations, but it requires a careful and well thought-out object-oriented design. Since we are on the subject anyway, we might as well learn how to do the job right.

To begin with, the undo facility, as with all other graphical operations, should be an essential part of the graphical model. Since our graphical model is encapsulated in the **CGraphicList** class, undoing edits should be one of the services provided by this class. When we wish to perform an undo operation, we should be able to do so using a function call similar to the following:

```
    Model->Undo();
```

To make this work, we need some means of recording the details of an edit. When the *Undo* function is called, the undo facility will use this information to undo the edit. Our first instinct might be to add several data items to the **CGraphicList** class to keep track of the last editing operation, and perhaps use some type of "last edit code" to determine the nature of the last edit. However, this would be bad design. We must approach this problem in an object-oriented manner. Therefore we will begin by designing an object to encapsulate our undo facility. This object will contain all information about the most recent edit. Figure 7-63 gives the class definition of this object. At this point, we do not know much about this object, but we should at least provide ourselves with the

```
class CUndoObject
{
public:
    CUndoObject * Next;

    CUndoObject();
    virtual ~CUndoObject();
};
```

Figure 7-63   The *Undo* Object

ability to undo more than one edit. We will thus provide a *next* pointer to enable these objects to be chained to one another.

Because we have several different types of edits to undo, a single object will not provide us with everything we need (unless it is very badly designed!). Therefore we will make our **CUndoObject** class into a polymorphic type with virtual functions to perform the required operations. Before we start, we should make a list of every different type of edit, and what actions should be performed to undo the edit. Figure 7-64 gives a list of the editing operations and the required undo actions.

In this figure, we could have separated *Add Object* into *Add Rectangle* and *Add Circle*, but a generic *Delete* operation (performed using the virtual destructor) is all that is required to undo the operation, so it makes sense to combine the two into a single operation. By the same token, we could separate *Delete Object* into two operations *Delete Rectangle* and *Delete Circle*, but this would require us to have some method of determining whether a **CGraphicObject** was actually a **CCircle** or a **CRectangle**. To avoid this problem, we will treat this as a single operation. Similarly, since color changes can be performed without knowledge of the object type, there is no reason to separate these changes. However, the *Move* and *Scale* operations change parameters that are unique to a particular object, so these two actions must be separated into *Move Circle*, *Move Rectangle*, *Scale Circle*, and *Scale Rectangle*.

The principles of object-oriented design would direct us to create a separate class for each of the eight edits we have identified. There is nothing to prevent us from proceeding along these lines, but we can simplify our object-oriented design by combining similar edits into a single object. This will require more work to be performed for each

Editing Functions	Action
Add Object	Delete the object
Delete Object	Re-add the object
Line Color Change	Restore previous color
Fill Color Change	Restore previous color
Move	Restore Center or Top and Left
Scale	Restore Center and Radius or Top, Left, Width, and Height

Figure 7-64   Undo Actions for Editing Functions

undo operation and consume more storage than is actually required, but the penalties are not severe and it will simplify our programming task. Therefore, we will combine the two color changes into a single **CUndoChange** class. This class will provide the ability to undo all color changes. We will use this as the base object for all changes except *add* and *delete*. This will enable us to combine color changes with scaling and moving, should we desire to do so.

Next we will combine operations that affect the internal parameters of a single object. Thus we will combine *Move Circle* with *Scale Circle* and *Move Rectangle* with *Scale Rectangle*. The resultant **CUndoCircle** and **CUndoRectangle** classes will provide the ability to undo any change to their respective drawing objects.

We will provide two separate classes, **CUndoAdd** and **CUndoDelete**, to handle *Add Object* and *Delete Object* edits. The resultant class structure is shown in Figure 7-65. Figure 7-66 gives the preliminary declarations of these classes.

In the **CUndoChange**, **CUndoCircle**, and **CUndoRectangle** classes, we have provided storage space for both new and old parameters. This may seem like overkill (and perhaps it is), but we anticipate using these classes for both *undo* and *redo* operations, and having both old and new parameters will be a convenience in such a situation. To simplify the creation of these three types of objects, we have provided a "split" constructor for the class. The first half of the constructor is a conventional constructor with a single parameter. This parameter must be a pointer to the affected object. The second half of the constructor is the *Finish* function. When constructing a **CUndoCircle** object (for example), one passes the address of the affected object to the constructor *before any changes are made*. The constructor will initialize the old parameters using the values contained in the affected object. Once all changes have been made to the affected object, the *Finish* function is called to initialize the new parameters from the same object. The split constructor greatly simplifies the code required to create an **CUndo** object.

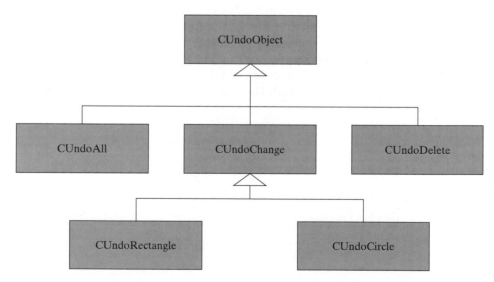

Figure 7-65 Class Diagram for Undo Operations

```
class CUndoAdd: public CUndoObject          class CUndoDelete : public CUndoObject
{                                           {
public:                                     public:
    // Affected object                          // Affected Object
    CGraphicObject * Obj;                       CGraphicObject * Obj;

    CUndoAdd();                                 CUndoDelete();
    CUndoAdd(CGraphicObject * NewObj);          CUndoDelete(CGraphicObject * NewObj);
    virtual ~CUndoAdd();                        virtual ~CUndoDelete();
};                                          };
```

```
            class CUndoChange : public CUndoObject
            {
            public:
                // The affected object
                CGraphicObject * Obj;

                // Old and New colors
                COLORREF NLineColor;
                COLORREF OLineColor;
                COLORREF NFillColor;
                COLORREF OFillColor;

                CUndoChange();
                CUndoChange(CGraphicObject * NewObj);
                void Finish(CGraphicObject * NewObj);
                virtual ~CUndoChange();
            };
```

```
class CUndoCircle : public CUndoChange      class CUndoRectangle : public CUndoChange
{                                           {
public:                                     public:
    // New and Old circle parameters.           // New and Old Rectangle parameters.
    CPoint NCenter;                             long NLeft;
    CPoint OCenter;                             long OLeft;
    long NRadius;                               long NTop;
    long ORadius;                               long OTop;
                                                long NWidth;
    CUndoCircle();                              long OWidth;
    CUndoCircle(CCircle * NewObj);              long NHeight;
    void Finish(CCircle * NewObj);              long OHeight;
    virtual ~CUndoCircle();
};                                              CUndoRectangle();
                                                CUndoRectangle(CRectangle * NewObj);
                                                void Finish(CRectangle * NewObj);
                                                virtual ~CUndoRectangle();
                                            };
```

Figure 7-66   Undo Class Declarations

At this point, we can design the virtual functions for our polymorphic type. Because we intend to use the same objects for undo and redo operations, we need two virtual functions, *Undo* and *Redo*. We begin by adding the following two lines to the definition of **CGraphicObject**:

```
virtual void Undo(CGraphicList *Model) = 0;
virtual void Redo(CGraphicList *Model) = 0;
```

We have included a pointer to the **CGraphicList** model as an argument to each of these functions, in case the *Undo* and *Redo* operations need to access components of the model. (**CUndoAdd** and **CUndoDelete** may have to access the head and tail of the drawing object chain.)

We will include definitions of these functions in each of the five classes defined in Figure 7-66. The functions for the **CUndoChange**, **CUndoCircle**, and **CUndoRectangle** classes are straightforward. The code for **CUndoRectangle** is given in Figure 7-67. The code for the other two classes is similar.

The functions for the **CUndoAdd** and **CUndoDelete** classes is somewhat more complicated. The *Undo* function for the **CUndoAdd** class must delete the affected object from the list of graphical objects. Because the *Add Object* operation is subject to a *Redo*, we must not delete the affected object but keep it in the **CUndoAdd** object until the operation can no longer be redone. Figure 7-68 demonstrates the unlinking and saving of the object.

```
void CUndoRectangle::Undo(CGraphicList *Model)
{
  // Specialize type of Obj
  CRectangle * TObj = (CRectangle *)Obj;
  TObj->Height = OHeight;
  TObj->Width = OWidth;
  TObj->Left = OLeft;
  TObj->Top = OTop;
  // Reflect back to base class for color restore
  CUndoChange::Undo(Model);
}

void CUndoRectangle::Redo(CGraphicList *Model)
{
  // Specialize type of Obj
  CRectangle * TObj = (CRectangle *)Obj;
  TObj->Height = NHeight;
  TObj->Width = NWidth;
  TObj->Left = NLeft;
  TObj->Top = NTop;
  // Reflect back to base class for color restore
  CUndoChange::Redo(Model);
}
```

Figure 7-67 Rectangle *Undo* and *Redo* Functions

```
void CUndoAdd::Undo(CGraphicList *Model)
{
    // Undo ADD must remove the new object from the model's
    // Object list. The object is not deleted, but left in the
    // Undo object, which will now be placed on the REDO chain
    if (Obj->Prev == NULL)
    {
        Model->Head = Obj->Next;
    }
    else
    {
        Obj->Prev->Next = Obj->Next;
    }
    if (Obj->Next == NULL)
    {
        Model->Tail = Obj->Prev;
    }
    else
    {
        Obj->Next->Prev = Obj->Prev;
    }
    Model->Count-;
}
```

Figure 7-68   The **CUndoAdd** *Undo* Function

```
void CUndoAdd::Redo(CGraphicList *Model)
{
    // Insert the new object back into the model's object list
    if (Model->Head == NULL)
    {
        Model->Head = Obj;
    }
    else
    {
        Model->Tail->Next = Obj;
    }
    Obj->Prev = Model->Tail;
    Model->Tail = Obj;
    Model->Count++;
}
```

Figure 7-69   The **CUndoAdd** *Redo* Function

When an *Add Object* operation is redone, the affected object is simply added to the tail of the model's chain of drawing objects. This is the location from which it was deleted. Figure 7-69 illustrates how to add the object back into the chain.

```
void CUndoDelete::Undo(CGraphicList *Model)
{
    if (Obj->Prev == NULL)
    {
        Model->Head = Obj;
    }
    else
    {
        Obj->Prev->Next = Obj;
    }
    if (Obj->Next == NULL)
    {
        Model->Tail = Obj;
    }
    else
    {
        Obj->Next->Prev = Obj;
    }
    Model->Count++;
}
```

Figure 7-70   The **CUndoDelete** *Undo* Function

When a *Delete Object* operation is performed, we will require that the routine removing the object from the chain leave the *Prev* and *Next* pointers intact. We want this to be done so that an *Undo* operation can add the object back into the chain at the precise point from which it was deleted. This is done to preserve the Z-Order of the drawing objects. (The Z-Order determines which objects appear on top of others.) Figure 7-70 contains the *Undo* routine for the CUndoDelete object.

To redo a *Delete Object* operation, we simply remove the affected object from the chain of drawing objects. We take care not to change the *Prev* and *Next* pointers because the operation can be undone once more. Figure 7-71 shows the *Redo* function for the **CUndoDelete** class.

At this point, it appears that we are ready to implement the *Undo* and *Redo* operations for **CGraphicList**, the modeling object. However, there are still a few things we have not thought about. For example, when undoing an *Add Object* operation, what happens if the object is selected? We did not do anything about deleting the object from the select chain. When we undo a *Delete Object* operation, what if the object was part of the selection when it was deleted? (This is usually the case!) Should the object be added back into the selection? At this point, it is best to avoid the problem entirely and insist that our high-level *Undo* and *Redo* functions clear the selection before calling the low-level functions. This means that there will never be a selection when a low-level *Undo* or *Redo* function is executed, and that objects are never added to the selection by these functions.

But there is still another problem we have not addressed. What about changes that affect more than one object? When a user selects ten objects and moves them and

```
void CUndoDelete::Redo(CGraphicList *Model)
{
    // Re-Remove object from model's object list
    if (Obj->Prev == NULL)
    {
        Model->Head = Obj->Next;
    }
    else
    {
        Obj->Prev->Next = Obj->Next;
    }
    if (Obj->Next == NULL)
    {
        Model->Tail = Obj->Prev;
    }
    else
    {
        Obj->Next->Prev = Obj->Prev;
    }
    Model->Count--;
}
```

Figure 7-71   The **CUndoDelete** *Redo* Function

then requests an *Undo* operation, all ten objects should go back to their original positions. There are some editors that do not take this view. I have used editors that require each individual change of a multi-object change to be separately undone. Using such an editor is not a pleasant experience. Since we do not wish to create unpleasant software, we must work on our object model a bit more to find some method of undoing multi-object changes all at once.

The solution to this problem is surprisingly simple. We will make *all* Undo operations multi-object operations. When a single object is changed, we will create a multi-object undo that affects a single object. To accomplish this, we will design an **Undo Command** object, which will contain a linked list of **Undo** objects that must be undone or redone as a unit. For single-object changes, the linked list will contain a single **Undo** object. We will encapsulate this functionality in the **CUndoCommand** class whose definition is given in Figure 7-72.

The *Undo* and *Redo* functions shown in this figure will simply pass the *undo* request along to each object in the list of **Undo** objects. We have added a *Prev* pointer to this class to permit **Undo Command** objects to be deleted from both ends of an **Undo Command** chain. The *PushUndo* function will be used to build the **CUndoCommand** object one **Undo** object at a time. The code for this function is given in Figure 7-73. Since the order of the **Undo** objects in an **Undo Command** does not matter, this function will treat the List data item as the head of a stack and simply push the new object onto the stack.

```
class CUndoCommand
{
public:
        CUndoCommand * Next;
        CUndoCommand * Prev;

        // Head of a linked list of UNDO objects. Treated as a stack
        CUndoObject * List;
        long Count;      // Number of UNDO objects in List.

        CUndoCommand();
        virtual ~CUndoCommand();

        // Will be "passed along" to every object in the list
        void Undo (CGraphicList * Model);
        void Redo(CGraphicList * Model);

        // Add a new UNDO object to the List
        void PushUndo(CUndoObject * Obj);
};
```

Figure 7-72   The CUndoCommand Class Definition

```
void CUndoCommand::PushUndo(CUndoObject *Obj)
{
    // Push an undo object onto the command object's list
    Obj->Next = List;
    List = Obj;
    Count++;
}
```

Figure 7-73   The *PushUndo* Function

We are now ready to begin the high-level design of our *Undo* facility. We will organize **Undo Command** objects into a linked list, and design a header object to encapsulate the functionality of the list. We anticipate having two lists: an *Undo* list and a Redo list. When an operation is undone, we will pop an element off the *Undo* list, perform the *Undo* operation, and push the element onto the head of the *Redo* list. We will reverse these steps for *Redo* operations. When a new object is added to the *Undo* chain, we will clear the *Redo* chain. Our *Undo* facility inherently provides for unlimited undos, but to limit storage use we will build in a user selectable limit for undo operations. We will also provide a means for the user to select unlimited undos and to make this the default. The definition of our **Undo List** header object is given in Figure 7-74.

Because the **CUndoListBase** object provides a convenient place to encapsulate the **Undo Command** creation, we have added a number of useful functions to this object. The *NewCommand* function will create an empty **Undo Command** and push it onto the head of the list. The empty command can be populated with **Undo** objects using the *PushUndo* function, which pushes an **Undo** object into the command at the head of the chain. These two functions can be used to create a multi-object **Undo Command**. Single-object **Undo Commands** can be created using the *PushCommand(CUndoObject)*

```
class CUndoListBase
{
public:
    long Limit;   // Maximum number of undo commands
    long Count;   // Current Number of undo commands
    // Command Chain
    CUndoCommand * Head;
    CUndoCommand * Tail;

    CUndoListBase();
    virtual ~CUndoListBase();
    // Create an empty command and add to head of chain
    void NewCommand(void);
    // Add an UNDO object to the command at the head of the chain
    void PushUndo(CUndoObject * Obj);
    // Add a pre-created undo command to the head of the chain
    void PushCommand(CUndoCommand * Cmd);
    // Create an empty command, add it to the head of the chain, and
    // insert an undo object into it.
    void PushCommand(CUndoObject * Obj);
    // Remove command from head of chain and return it
    CUndoCommand * PopCommand(void);
};
```

Figure 7-74   The CUndoListBase Class Definition

function. This function creates an empty **Undo Command**, pushes it onto the head of the chain, and then pushes the **CUndoObject** into the new command. Moving commands from one list to another can be accomplished using the *PopCommand*, and *PushCommand(CUndoCommand)* functions. The *Limit* data item contains the maximum number of **Undo Commands** in the list. If this item contains zero, the number of **Undo Commands** is unlimited. The *PushCommand* functions and the *NewCommand* function enforce the *Undo* limit by deleting items from the end of the chain when the limit is exceeded.

   Another useful function, which is missing from Figure 7-74, is the *Clear* function, which deletes all **Undo Commands** in the list. We deliberately omitted this function from the definition of **CUndoListBase**, because there is another problem that we have not yet considered. When an **Undo** object is deleted, either because it is deleted from the end of the list or because the list is cleared, what should we do with the affected object? For **CUndoChange** objects, and those objects derived from it, the problem is nonexistent. We simply ignore the affected object. However, for **CUndoAdd** and **CUndoDelete** objects the problem is serious. When we delete a **CUndoDelete** object from the *Undo* list, we should delete the affected object, because that object is no longer part of the drawing. We should *not* delete the affected object from **CUndoAdd** objects, because these objects *are* part of the drawing. The real problem arises when we delete these objects from the *Redo* list. When we delete a **CUndoDelete** object from the *Redo* list, the affected object has been reinserted into the drawing and must not be deleted. When we delete a **CUndoAdd** object from the *Redo* list, the affected object has been permanently removed from the diagram and must be deleted. This is exactly the reverse of the situation for the *Undo* list. The problem is complicated by the fact that we are dealing with a polymorphic type and have no easy way of determining the type of the object we are dealing with.

Believe it or not, there is a nice, object-oriented way of dealing with this problem using polymorphic types. We will begin by adding the following two function definitions to the definition of **CUndoObject**, the base object for all **Undo** objects:

```
virtual void UndoDelete(void) = {return;};
virtual void RedoDelete(void) = {return;};
```

We did not make these functions pure virtual functions, because for most derived objects we want these routines to default to No-Ops. For the **CUndoDelete** object, we will override the *UndoDelete* function. For the **CUndoAdd** object, we will override the *RedoDelete* function (see Figure 7-75). In all other cases, we will allow these functions to default to No-Ops.

Next, we will convert **CUndoListBase** to a polymorphic type and derive two new types from it. We will add the following function definition to the definition of **CUndoListBase**:

```
// Delete Affected Object for ADD or DELETE undos
virtual void DeleteObj(CUndoCommand *Cmd) = 0;
```

This function is pure virtual, because it must be redefined in the derived types.

The two derived classes, **CUndoList** and **CRedoList**, do nothing more than provide specializations for the *DeleteObj* function. The definitions of these classes are given in Figure 7-76.

The purpose of the *DeleteObj* function is to delete the affected objects from the appropriate **Undo** objects. This function will be called on a command just before it is deleted. For the **CUndoList** class, the *DeleteObj* function will pass an *UndoDelete* request to each object in the Undo Command's object list. For the **CRedoList** class, the function will pass a *RedoDelete* request to each object. The *UndoDelete* request will cause the affected object to be deleted from *Delete Object* undos and will have no effect on the others. The *RedoDelete* request will delete the affected object from *Add Object* undos and have no effect on the rest. The two *DeleteObj* functions are listed in Figure 7-77.

```
void CUndoDelete::UndoDelete()
{
    delete Obj;
}
void CUndoAdd::RedoDelete()
{
    delete Obj;
}
```

Figure 7-75 *UndoDelete* and *RedoDelete* Overrides

```
class CUndoList : public CUndoListBase        class CRedoList : public CUndoListBase
{                                             {
public:                                       public:
    CUndoList();                                  CRedoList();
    virtual ~CUndoList();                         virtual ~CRedoList();
    virtual void                                  virtual void
        DeleteObj(CUndoCommand *Cmd);                 DeleteObj(CUndoCommand *Cmd);
};                                            };
```

Figure 7-76   CUndoList and CRedoList Class Declarations

```
void CUndoList::DeleteObj(CUndoCommand *Cmd)
{
    CUndoObject * Temp;
    for (Temp = Cmd->List ; Temp != NULL ; Temp=Temp->Next)
    {
        Temp->UndoDelete();
    }
}
void CRedoList::DeleteObj(CUndoCommand *Cmd)
{
    CUndoObject * Temp;
    for (Temp = Cmd->List ; Temp != NULL ; Temp=Temp->Next)
    {
        Temp->RedoDelete();
    }
}
```

Figure 7-77   The *DeleteObj* Functions

Now that we have the *DeleteObj* function defined, we can use it to create the *Clear* function, which can be defined as part of the **CUndoListBase** class. Figure 7-78 shows the code for this function.

We can use the *Clear* function as part of the destructor of the **CUndoListBase** class, but we must use care when doing so. The destructor calling order is to first call the destructor of the derived class and then the destructor of the base class. Because **CUndoListBase** has a pure virtual function, there can be no objects of this type, so the call to *DeleteObj* in the *Clear* function seems safe. However, once the destructor for the base class is called, the object is technically no longer a member of either derived class, because the derived class, or that part of the object that made it a member of the derived class, has already been destroyed. This makes the call to *DeleteObj* a call to a pure virtual function, which is illegal. Therefore, we must place the call to the *Clear* function in the destructors of the derived classes, as illustrated in Figure 7-79.

We can now focus on the remainder of the **CUndoListBase** functions. The two functions *PushCommand(CUndoCommand)* and *PopCommand* will be used to manage

```
void CUndoListBase::Clear()
{
    CUndoCommand * Temp, * Temp2;
    for (Temp = Head,Temp2 = NULL; Temp != NULL ; Temp = Temp2)
    {
        Temp2 = Temp->Next;
        DeleteObj(Temp);
        delete Temp;
    }
    Count = 0;
    Head = NULL;
    Tail = NULL;
}
```

Figure 7-78   The **CUndoListBase** *Clear* Function

```
CUndoList::~CUndoList()          CRedoList::~CRedoList()
{                                {
    Clear();                         Clear();
}                                }
```

Figure 7-79   Destructors for the *Undo* Lists

the contents of the *Undo* and *Redo* lists. These two functions are an essential part of
the undo facility, because they will be used to move **Undo Command** objects from one
list to another and to provide the most recent **Undo Command** for processing. We will
also use the *PushCommand(CUndoCommand)* function to enforce the *Undo* limit. We
will localize the handling of the *Undo* limit in this function and pass all other types of
requests to this function for processing.

The code for the *PushCommand(CUndoCommand)* function is given in Figure
7-80. The first part of this function takes the **CUndoCommand** argument, pushes it
onto the head of the command stack, and increments the *undo* count. A stack *must* be

```
void CUndoListBase::PushCommand(CUndoCommand *Cmd)
{
    // Add a preconstructed UNDO command object to the list
    Cmd->Next = Head;
    Cmd->Prev = NULL;
    if (Tail == NULL)
    {
        Tail = Head;
    }
```

Figure 7-80   The *PushCommand(CUndoCommand)* Function

```
    Head = Cmd;
    Count++;
    // The only place the UNDO limit is enforced
    if (Limit > 0)
    {
        while (Count > Limit)
        {
            CUndoCommand * Temp = Tail;
            DeleteObj(Temp);  // implemented in CUndoList and CRedoList
            // Unlink object from tail
            Tail = Tail->Prev;
            if (Tail != NULL)
            {
                Tail->Next = NULL;
            }
            else
            {
                Head = NULL;
            }
            delete Temp;
            Count--;
        }
    }
}
```

Figure 7-80   (*Continued*)

used to maintain the list of **Undo Commands**, because edits must be undone in reverse order from which they were performed.

If the undo limit is less than or equal to zero, processing stops at this point. Otherwise the undo count is compared with the undo limit. While the undo count exceeds the limit, commands are removed from the tail of the list and destroyed. The virtual function *DeleteObj* is used to delete the affected objects from the appropriate types of **Undo Objects**. The undo count is decremented for each undo command that is destroyed.

The *PopCommand* function unlinks an object from the head of the chain and returns a pointer to it. If the list is empty, *PopCommand* returns NULL. This fact is not necessarily obvious in the code, but *PopCommand* always returns the head of the list, and if the list is empty, then the head will contain the NULL pointer. The code for the *PopCommand* function is given in Figure 7-81.

The remaining functions are quite simple. The *PushCommand(CUndoObject)* function of Figure 7-82, which is used to create single-object commands, creates a new **CUndoCommand** object, pushes the **CUndoObject** argument into the new **CUndoCommand** object, and then uses the *PushCommand(CUndoCommand)* function to put the new **Undo Command** object on the undo command list. Using the *PushCommand(CUndoCommand)* function guarantees that the undo limit will be enforced for this operation.

```
CUndoCommand * CUndoListBase::PopCommand()
{
    // Standard POP operation
    // This is the first step in any UNDO/REDO operation
    CUndoCommand * rv = Head;
    if (Head != NULL)
    {
        Head = Head->Next;
        Count--;
        if (Head != NULL)
        {
            Head->Prev = NULL;
        }
        else
        {
            Tail = NULL;
        }
    }
    return rv;
}
```

Figure 7-81   The PopCommand Function

```
void CUndoListBase::PushCommand(CUndoObject *Obj)
{
    CUndoCommand * Cmd = new CUndoCommand;
    Cmd->PushUndo(Obj);
    PushCommand(Cmd); // NOT a recursive call!!!
}
```

Figure 7-82   The *PushCommand(CUndoObject)* Function

The *NewCommand* and *PushUndo* functions are used to create multi-object *undo* commands. The *NewCommand* (see Figure 7-83) function creates an empty **CUndoCommand** object and calls the *PushCommand(CUndoCommand)* function to push the new **CUndoCommand** onto the command list. The *PushCommand (CUndoCommand)* function will enforce the *undo* limit for this operation. The

```
void CUndoListBase::NewCommand()
{
    CUndoCommand * Cmd = new CUndoCommand;
    PushCommand(Cmd);
}
```

Figure 7-83   The *NewCommand* Function

```
void CUndoListBase::PushUndo(CUndoObject *Obj)
{
    if (Head != NULL)
    {
        Head->PushUndo(Obj);
    }
}
```

Figure 7-84   The *PushUndo* Function

PushUndo function (see Figure 7-84) is used to add **Undo** objects to the empty **Undo Command** object. This function adds an **Undo** object to the **Undo Command** at the head of the command list. If the command list is empty, the request is ignored.

Now we are finally ready to add the *Undo* and *Redo* processing functions to our main modeling class, the **CGraphicList** class, and to our editor component. We must first add the following three lines to the definition of **CGraphicList**:

```
// UNDO/REDO management
CRedoList RedoList;
CUndoList UndoList;
```

Now we must implement the *Undo* and *Redo* functions for the **CGraphicList** class. We've already done most of the work, so these functions are quite simple. Figure 7-85 gives the implementations of these functions. These functions are quite similar. They

```
void CGraphicList::Undo()
{
    if (UndoList.Head != NULL)
    {
        // Clear the current selection
        ClearSelect();
        // Remove command from head of UNDO list
        CUndoCommand * Cmd = UndoList.PopCommand();
        // Request Undo
        // Request will be transmitted to all undos in the command
        Cmd->Undo(this);
        // Put command on REDO list
        RedoList.PushCommand(Cmd);
    }
}
void CGraphicList::Redo()
{
    if (RedoList.Head != NULL)
    {
        // Clear the current selection
        ClearSelect();
```

Figure 7-85   The *CGraphicList Undo* and *Redo* Functions

```
        // Remove command from head of REDO list
        CUndoCommand * Cmd = RedoList.PopCommand();
        // Request Redo
        // Request will be transmitted to all undos in the command
        Cmd->Redo(this);
        // Put command on UNDO list
        UndoList.PushCommand(Cmd);
    }
}
```

Figure 7-85   (*Continued*)

first clear the selection (recall that we assumed this would be done in the *Undo* and *Redo* operations), then they pop an **Undo Command** off the appropriate list, perform the requested operation, and push the command onto the other list.

As a final step, we add the *Undo* and *Redo* methods to our component. These methods simply call the *Undo* and *Redo* functions of the modeling object. The formal description of these methods is given in Figure 7-86, and their implementations are given in Figure 7-87.

Method Description			
Name	Undo		
Return Value	Void		
Description	Undoes the most recent editing operation, and adds the edit action to the redo list.		
Arguments	**Name**	**Type**	**Description**
Void			

Method Description			
Name	Redo		
Return Value	Void		
Description	Redoes the last *Undo* operation. If an editing operation has been performed since the last Undo operation, then *Redo* is no longer possible.		
Arguments	**Name**	**Type**	**Description**
Void			

Figure 7-86   *Undo* and *Redo* Method Descriptions

```
void CSGEditorCtrl::Undo()
{
    // pass the undo request to the model
    Model->Undo();
```

Figure 7-87   *Undo* and *Redo* Method Implementations

```
    CWnd::Invalidate(); // redraw window
}
void CSGEditorCtrl::Redo()
{
    // pass the redo request to the model
    Model->Redo();
    CWnd::Invalidate(); // redraw window
}
```

Figure 7-87   (*Continued*)

11. CREATING UNDO OBJECTS

Our undo facility is now fully implemented and accessible to the users of our control. However, there is one important thing that we have not yet done. We have not provided any way to create **CUndo** objects. Compared with everything else we have done, this is a relatively minor task. We have implemented constructors and other functions to do most of the work, so it is just a matter of using these functions in the right places. Let's start by modifying the *AddCircle* and *AddRectangle* functions of the **CGraphicList** class. To modify *AddRectangle*, we will add the lines of code shown in Figure 7-88 to the end of the function. At this point, the variable *Temp* contains a pointer to the newly created **CRectangle** object.

The code in Figure 7-88 will also work for the *AddCircle* function, so we add the same code to the end of that function as well. We are now able to undo the *AddRectangle* and *AddCircle* operations.

Our next step is to modify the *ChangeSelectFillColor* function. This change will be more complicated because we must create a multi-object **CUndoCommand**, and we must use a split constructor to create the **Undo** objects. Figure 7-89 gives the modified code for the *ChangeSelectFillColor* function. Note that the *Finish* function is called *after* the affected object has been changed, while the **new** statement is executed *before* the affected object has been changed. Also note the use of the *NewCommand* and *PushUndo* functions to create a multi-object **Undo Command**. The changes to the function *ChangeSelectLineColor* are identical to those shown in Figure 7-89.

We can now undo color changes and then modify the *DeleteSelection* routine. (It is especially important to be able to undo deletes!) Figure 7-90 shows the modified code for this function. For brevity, long segments of unchanged code have been omitted from the figure.

```
    // Create UNDO ADD and push onto undo list
    CUndoAdd * TempUndo = new CUndoAdd(Temp);
    UndoList.PushCommand(TempUndo);
    // Redos must be cleared at this point
    RedoList.Clear();
```

Figure 7-88   Creating an Undo

```
void CGraphicList::ChangeSelectFillColor(COLORREF NewColor)
{
    if (Selection != NULL)
    {
        // Create a new UNDO command
        UndoList.NewCommand();
        // Redos must be cleared at this point
        RedoList.Clear();
        // Modify each object in the selection list
        CSelectItem * Temp;
        for (Temp = Selection ; Temp !=NULL ; Temp = Temp->Next)
        {
            // Create an undo object
            CUndoChange * TempUndo = new CUndoChange(Temp->Item);
            // change the drawing object
            Temp->Item->FillColor = NewColor;
            // finish the undo object
            TempUndo->Finish(Temp->Item);
            // Insert undo object into command at head of UNDO chain
            UndoList.PushUndo(TempUndo);
        }
    }
}
```

Figure 7-89   Modifying the *FillColor* Change Handler

```
void CGraphicList::DeleteSelection()
{
    // delete all selected objects
    if (Selection != NULL)
    {
        // clear selection, but leave select bits set in object
        … // code omitted, no change from existing implementation
        // Create a new undo command
        UndoList.NewCommand();
        // Clear the redo list now
        RedoList.Clear();
        // Search the list for objects with the select tag set to true
        // Unlink such objects
        for (Temp=Head ; Temp != NULL ; Temp = Temp2)
        {
            Temp2 = Temp->Next;
            if (Temp->Selected)
            {
```

Figure 7-90   The Modified *DeleteSelection* Routine

```
                    // unlink object
                    … // Code omitted, No change from existing implementation
                    // delete statement is removed
                    // create an undo object and link it into
                    // The undo command at the head of the UNDO list.
                    CUndoDelete * TempUndo = new CUndoDelete(Temp);
                    UndoList.PushUndo(TempUndo);
                }
            }
        }
    }
```

Figure 7-90   (*Continued*)

Now only two functions are left: *MoveSelection* and *ScaleSelect*. Unfortunately, these two functions present something of a problem. They cannot create an **Undo** object directly because some objects in the selection chain require a **CUndoRectangle** object and some require a **CUndoCircle** object. There is no reasonable way for the *MoveSelection* and *ScaleSelect* functions to construct these objects. We will solve this problem by passing the construction of the **Undo** objects to the **CRectangle** and **CCircle** classes. We will insist that the functions *Move* and *Scale* of these classes return an **Undo** object. We could also ask these functions to push the **Undo** object onto the Undo list, but this would be bad design for two reasons. First, the **CRectangle** and **CCircle** classes cannot access the *Undo* list directly. An additional item would have to be added to the function parameter lists. Second, this forces the *Move* and *Scale* functions to make assumptions about how they will be used, and it also restricts the way that we can use these functions. Therefore, we will perform the **CUndo** object creation in the *Move* and *Scale* routines but perform the list management in the *MoveSelection* and *ScaleSelect* functions. Figure 7-91 shows the required modifications to the *MoveSelection* function. The changes to the *ScaleSelect* function are identical. The

```
void CGraphicList::MoveSelection(long x, long y)
{
    if (Selection != NULL)
    {
        // Create a new undo command at the head of the UNDO list
        UndoList.NewCommand();
        // Clear the REDO list
        RedoList.Clear();
        // Transmit the move request to each object in the selection
        CSelectItem * Temp;
        for (Temp = Selection ; Temp != NULL ; Temp = Temp->Next)
        {
```

Figure 7-91   The Changes to the *MoveSelection* Function

```
        // Object Move now returns undo object.
        CUndoObject * TempUndo = Temp->Item->Move(x,y);
        // Push object into command at head of UNDO List
        UndoList.PushUndo(TempUndo);
      }
    }
}
```

Figure 7-91   (*Continued*)

```
CUndoObject * CRectangle::Move(long x, long y)
{
    // Create UNDO object
    CUndoRectangle * rv = new CUndoRectangle(this);
    // Move the rectangle
    Left += x;
    Top += y;
    // Finish UNDO object
    rv->Finish(this);
    return rv;
}
```

Figure 7-92   The Changes to the *CRectangle Move* Function

changes to the **CRectangle** *Move* function are shown in Figure 7-92. The changes to the other three functions are identical. These changes complete the implementation of our *Undo* facility.

12. REMAINING ISSUES

We have now completed the implementation of our Simple Graphical Editor (SGE) control. This may seem like a strange statement, because we certainly have not implemented everything that is required in a graphical editing program. We have no way to open or save files. We have no way to cut and paste things using the clipboard. We have no way to print our drawings. How can we say that the control is finished if we haven't implemented these things?

The simple answer to this question is that a component is not the same thing as a finished program. Even if we were to implement the missing features listed in the previous paragraph, we would still not have a complete graphical editing program. We have no menus or toolbars or any of the other things that go into creating a well-designed program. Nor is there any conceivable reason for adding toolbars and menus to our control. These things can be handled much better by toolbar and menu components, and *should* be handled in this manner.

I insist that certain tasks—opening and saving files; cutting, copying, and pasting; and printing—are things that are best left to other components. We have completed the task we set out to perform. It is now time to pass the remaining tasks off to other components. At first glance, this seems impossible. All of these functions require intimate interaction with our main modeling object, the **CGraphicList** object. This object is internal to our editor component. How can we expect other components to access this object?

What we need is a change in viewpoint. We have been treating the **CGraphicList** object as if it were an integral part of our graphical editor. Instead, let us begin treating this object as a project in its own right. In fact, we have been careful to encapsulate all graphical functions into the **CGraphicList** object, so the coupling between the **CGraphicList** object and the SGE is quite loose. We could take all code for the **CGraphicList** object and its subobjects and compile it as a separate project. We could create either an object library or a dynamic link library out of it, and use the resultant library as a resource for the SGE project. In fact, if you examine the C++ code for our project, you will see that this is exactly what we have done. By doing this, we enable other projects to use the **CGraphicList** object.

To give other components access to the **CGraphicList** object contained in the Editor, we simply provide a property that returns the address of the SGE's modeling object. This will enable us to pass the address of the modeling object to any other component that needs it. Unfortunately, there is not an elegant way to do this. In fact, passing pointers around in this fashion is dangerous, and probably should not be done without operating system support. But *there is not any operating system support for doing this*, so we will have to cross our fingers and hope for luck. Later on, we will revisit this subject and attempt to lay down some rules that will remove some of the dangers. For now though, we will forge ahead and add the *ModelHandle* property to our control. Figure 7-93 gives the property design table description of this property, and Figure 7-94 shows how it is implemented. Note that we treat the property type as a long integer. This is also dangerous, because memory sizes are becoming larger and larger, and there is no guarantee that an address will fit in a long integer in future releases of the Windows operating system.

In addition to illustrating the *ModelHandle get* and *set* functions, Figure 7-94 also demonstrates how to make a property invisible at design time. The *GetAmbientProperty* operating system function will tell us whether we are in run mode or design mode. The *GetNotSupported* operating system function indicates that the property is not supported in this mode. This feature is absolutely necessary for this property: If a designer accidentally types in a non-zero value for this property, the control's drawing routine will immediately blow up, taking the entire programming environment with it.

Property Design Table		
Name	**Type**	**Function**
ModelHandle	Long Integer Maximum = N/A Minimum = N/A Default = None	Provides the address of the modeling object cast to a long integer. When a new value is assigned to this property, the existing modeling object is destroyed and replaced with the new object. NULL values are ignored.

Figure 7-93 *ModelHandle* Property Description

```
long CSGEditorCtrl::GetModelHandle()
{
   BOOL UMode;
   GetAmbientProperty(DISPID_AMBIENT_USERMODE,VT_BOOL,&UMode);
   if (UMode)
   {
      return (long)Model; // run time
   }
   else
   {
      GetNotSupported();// design time
      return 0;
   }
}
```

```
void CSGEditorCtrl::SetModelHandle(long nNewValue)
{
   CGraphicList * NewModel = (CGraphicList *)nNewValue;
   if (NewModel != NULL)
   {
      delete Model;
      Model = NewModel;
   }
   CWnd::Invalidate();
}
```

Figure 7-94 *ModelHandle* Implementation

Method Description			
Name	NewDrawing		
Return Value	Void		
Description	Destroys the existing drawing and replaces it with a new empty drawing.		
Arguments	**Name**	**Type**	**Description**
Void			

Figure 7-95 *NewDrawing* Method Description

The possibility of replacing an existing drawing with a new drawing suggests two new features for our control. The first is that there should be some way for a user to erase the existing drawing and replace it with an empty drawing. To accomplish this, we will provide the *NewDrawing* method, which clears the existing drawing and starts over with an empty drawing window. Figure 7-95 gives the method description, and Figure 7-96 gives the implementation of the method.

The second feature is actually an essential feature of all editors, the need for which has not been obvious until now. Even though we have not as yet provided a means for saving files, we plan to provide such a feature in the future. When the drawing

```
void CSGEditorCtrl::NewDrawing()
{
   // new drawing. Delete old model, create new empty model
   delete Model;
   Model = new CGraphicList;
   CWnd::Invalidate(); // redraw window
}
```

Figure 7-96 *NewDrawing* Implementation

model is replaced using either the *NewDrawing* method or the *ModelHandle* property, it should be possible to test whether the existing drawing needs to be saved. The way to do this is to provide a "dirty flag" that indicates that the drawing model has been modified. This should be an integral part of the drawing model, so we will add a data item *Dirty* to the **CGraphicList** class. This item will have the type **BOOL**, and will be initialized to **FALSE**. Any time the model is changed, *Dirty* will set to **TRUE**. Adding the code for this is relatively easy, because the dirty flag must be set anytime the *Redo* list is cleared. If we search for the statement "RedoList.Clear," we will locate all the places in the code where *Dirty* must be assigned **TRUE**.

To provide access to the dirty flag, we will add a new property, *Dirty*, to the control. This property will return the value of the dirty flag and will allow the dirty flag to be reset to **FALSE**. The property design table entry for this is shown in Figure 7-97.

There are two final issues that are raised by the possibility of other components having access to the SGE drawing model. Since other components can access the model, other components can change the model. There is no automatic way to notify the SGE that its window needs to be redrawn, so we will provide a method that forces a redraw of the control window. The *Redraw* method description is given in Figure 7-98.

Property Design Table		
Name	**Type**	**Function**
Dirty	BOOL Default = FALSE	Returns the current value of the dirty flag. A new value can be assigned to set the dirty flag to **TRUE** or **FALSE**

Figure 7-97 The Dirty Flag Property Description

Method Description			
Name	Redraw		
Return Value	Void		
Description	Forces a redraw of the control's window		
Arguments	**Name**	**Type**	**Description**
Void			

Figure 7-98 The *Redraw* Method Description

Method Description			
Name	ReleaseModel		
Return Value	Void		
Description	Replaces the current drawing with an empty drawing. A new drawing is created to replace the old, but the old drawing is not deleted. The control retains no pointer to the old drawing.		
Arguments	**Name**	**Type**	**Description**
Void			

Figure 7-99   *ReleaseModel* Method Description

```
void CSGEditorCtrl::ReleaseModel()
{
    // release ownership of existing model
    // replace with new empty model
    Model = new CGraphicList;
    CWnd::Invalidate();
}
```

Figure 7-100   *ReleaseModel* Implementation

Because drawing models can be passed around to other controls, and because the SGE always deletes its existing model before installing or creating a new one, there is the possibility of creating dangling references in other components. To avoid this, we will provide a method that tells the SGE to forget about its drawing model and not delete it. The description of the *ReleaseModel* method is given in Figure 7-99, and its implementation is given in Figure 7-100.

13. A REVIEW OF THE METHODOLOGY

The design of a graphical editor breaks down into several distinct steps that have been elaborated in the preceding sections. At this point, we will summarize these steps and describe the documentation that should be produced for each step.

Four facilities that must be present in every graphical editor: (1) Drawing, (2) Selection, (3) Modification, and (4) Undo. The first three require the use of mouse operations, which should be encapsulated into a single object. All mouse information should be recorded in this object, and accessor functions should be used to read and write this information. If efficiency is a concern, **inline** functions can be used. A separate document describing all mouse operations should be developed during the design of the Drawing, Selection, and Modification facilities.

13.1 The Drawing Facility

A complete object model of the drawing must be developed during the design of this facility. Separate objects should be designed for each different type of drawing object, and these should be combined into a polymorphic type that represents a generic drawing object. There may be as many levels in the hierarchy as are needed. Each object must be able to draw itself.

Drawing modes must be designed, usually one mode for each different type of drawing object. Each of these drawing modes will normally have an associated mouse operation. A mouse operation has three parts: (1) initiation, (2) movement, and (3) termination. Each part of each mouse operation must be clearly described in the documentation of the operation. Documentation of the initiation part must clearly describe the conditions that cause the operation to be initiated. A Mouse-Down event is just one of these conditions. There are normally other conditions that must be met as well. The object used to encapsulate mouse operations should contain a code indicating that a mouse operation is in progress. The initiation documentation should clearly indicate the code used for the operation.

The documentation for the movement portion of a mouse operation must describe the tracking information that will be displayed while the operation is in progress. Finally, the documentation for the termination part must describe the objects that will be created or modified as a result of the operation. The documentation of each mouse operation must be reviewed carefully before coding begins.

A header object must be designed to encapsulate all drawing objects. This object provides the means for organizing drawing objects. In many cases, a single linked list will not be an acceptable method for doing this. Indeed, some highly technical papers have been written on the subject of organizing graphical information. This problem must be solved in the context of the editing operations that must be performed on the graphical objects. For editors that are designed to handle large-scale objects, this is the most critical part of the design, the details of which are beyond the scope of this book.

The dirty flag should be incorporated into the design of the header object from the beginning.

13.2 The Selection Facility

The selection facility must include a selection drawing mode and one or more mouse operations. Because most selection drawing modes are also used by the modification facility, the method used to distinguish between selection operations and modification operations must be clearly documented. The mouse operations must be documented as described in the preceding section.

An object or set of objects must be designed to manage the selection. Normally, the header object used to manage the drawing will also manage the selection, and it will generally organize the selection objects in the same way that it handles the drawing objects. The data items used to organize the selection (primarily pointers) *should not* be incorporated into the graphical objects themselves, but should instead be organized into a separate selection object. This will tend to minimize programming errors.

13.3 The Modification Facility

The modification facility consists of a collection of mouse operations and a collection of methods. The mouse operations must be thoroughly documented as described in the preceding sections. The mouse operations will be used to move objects or parts of objects and to change the size or shape of objects. Object parameters will be changed using methods. One or more *Delete* methods should be used to delete objects or parts of objects. There should be one or more methods that allow new models to be created and one or more methods replacing the existing model with a different one. The entire structure of the modification facility should be mapped out and documented before proceeding with coding.

Graphical objects must perform their own changes. All objects must be provided with the ability to move and scale themselves. Other more specialized types of changes can be made specific to the particular object.

13.4 The Undo Facility

The undo facility should be encapsulated in a polymorphic type with a header object responsible for the overall organization. The undoheader objects must be incorporated into the header object for the graphical model. There are three types of undo operations: (1) *Add*, (2) *Delete*, and (3) *Change*. Each of these should be handled by a separate object or a collection of separate objects. The class structure of the objects that handle changes will mirror the class structure of the graphical objects. The class structure of the undo facility should be clearly documented before coding begins. The general overall structure will be similar to that presented in this chapter.

14. CONCLUSION

Although the Simple Graphical Editor is missing some important features, it is a relatively complete implementation of the user interface for drawing simple objects. The object-oriented design of the component allows new types of drawing objects to be added with a minimum of effort. Encapsulation of the drawing functions into a single object allows that object to be shared among several components and to be used as a resource in other projects.

Two additional features that are found in most graphical editors are scrolling and scaling. Although these features can be added without much effort, they are tied quite closely to the graphical environment in which they are implemented. In developing the Simple Graphical Editor, we tried to keep most functions as general as possible to permit the project to be retargeted to other technologies. Although there are some dependencies on the Windows operating system, these are minimal and can be replaced by similar features found in other graphical environments. The same is not true for scaling and scrolling. Scrolling depends heavily on the messages produced by the standard Windows scroll bar. Other graphical environments might not produce the same type of messages. Drawing a scaled or scrolled window can be done quite simply in the Windows operating system by using the Window and Viewport coordinate functions. Such functions may not be available in other graphical environments, or might be provided in a very different form.

Nevertheless, those who learn the material of this chapter will have a firm grounding in the principles of graphical editing and should be able to develop a wide range of graphical editors by adhering to these principles.

EXERCISES

1. Add a new type, *Line*, to the Simple Graphical Editor. Integrate this new type into the drawing, editing, selection, and undo facilities. Begin by making a list of all new classes that need to be created, then make a list of all classes, enumerated types, and functions that must be changed to incorporate this type. Finally, make the required changes to the Simple Graphical Editor and test it thoroughly. *Hint:* The most difficult step will be click-selecting a line. The simplest procedure is to use the rectangle defined by the line's endpoints as the click area. This will, however, produce undesirable results. Another procedure is to first check that the click point is inside the rectangle, and then determine the distance of the click point from the line. (The distance formula computes the distance from the entire line, not just the segment drawn on the screen.) Assume that the endpoints of the line are $p_1 = (x_1,y_1)$ and $p_2 = (x_2,y_2)$, and that the click point is $p_0 = (x_0,y_0)$. The first step is to compute the slope using the formula $(y_2 - y_1)/(x_2 - x_1)$. The distance to the line can then be determined as the square root of $d^2 = [slope*(x_0 - x_1) - (y_0 - y_1)]^2/(slope^2 + 1)$. There is no need to take the square root. You can determine that the mouse is "close" to the line by comparing d^2 to the square of some fixed tolerance, such as 2. You must arrange the divisions and multiplications to avoid round-off error, or you must use floating-point calculations. Remember that you must be "inside the box" for the distance formula to work.

2. The data items of each object in this chapter are declared to be public. Change the code to make them protected. Several alterations to the code will be necessary. Check your changes against those on the Web site. (The Web site project declares all data items to be protected.)

3. Create a graphical editor that enables users to draw fixed-sized triangles and stars. (The orientation should also be fixed.) You should use the Simple Graphical Editor as the basis for your project.

4. Read the Visual C++ documentation, and figure out how scroll bars work. Add scroll bars to the Simple Graphical Editor window, and use the information from the scroll bars to scroll the display. (This would make a good term project.)

5. Implement a scaling facility that allows the display to be scaled to 100% (normal size), 200% (double size), and 50% (half size). This can be done in such a way as to allow any percentage of scaling. Implement the facility in the most general way possible. (This would make a good term project.)

6. Add a new graphical object of your choice to the Simple Graphical Editor project.

Chapter 8

Background Editors

1. PREREQUISITES AND OBJECTIVES

Before starting this chapter, you should have

1. A knowledge of programming in C++.
2. A knowledge of component interface design.

After completing this chapter, you will have

1. A knowledge of background editing—what it is and why it is used.
2. The ability to create background editors for complex objects.
3. A knowledge of the background editor design methodology.

2. INTRODUCTION

A background editor is an editor with no visible interface. This style of editor is sufficiently different from a graphical editor that it could be considered a separate kind of component. In a background editor, all editing operations must be performed using properties and methods. These facilities can also be built in to a graphical editor, and depending on the aims of the project it may be preferable to do so. If one wishes to create a third-party product that will be sold to developers for creating their own programs, then it is advantageous to implement as many features as possible in a single component. This will make the product more attractive and simplify the distribution of the third-party software. On the other hand, if the aim is to create a versatile set of tools and to distribute only those functions that are actually required by an application, then it is advantageous to separate all independent functions into separate components.

Developing a Background Editor based on an existing graphical editor is reasonably easy because much of the functionality will already be implemented. Some of the required methods may already be in place. For example, the delete function will normally already be implemented as a method. To complete the implementation, it is necessary to provide methods for those operations that were performed graphically in the graphical editor. In this chapter, we will illustrate the process of creating a Background Editor by presenting the design of such an editor for the simple graphical editor.

3. THE METHODOLOGY

The methodology for creating the Background Editor is straightforward. We first make a list of those operations that are performed through the graphical interface. These are (typically) drawing, selecting, moving, and resizing objects. Because objects are not visible, there must be some facility for enumerating individual objects and their parameters. This is normally the function of an Accessor component, and we will assume the existence of such in the remainder of this chapter. By making such an assumption, we can confine ourselves to implementing the graphical editing functions as component methods.

An attractive alternative is to build the Accessor facility directly into the Background Editor, and integrate its function with editing functions such as move, resize, and delete. Of course, all of this functionality could also be built into the Editor itself.

4. THE SGE BACKGROUND EDITOR

Like the Simple Graphical Editor (SGE), the Background Editor will have an internal object model but will have no serialization functions. This implies that there must be some means for accessing the internal model and passing it to other components. We will implement a property named *ModelHandle* that can be used to obtain the address of or to replace the internal object model. Figure 8-1 shows the property design table entry for this property.

We provide a *ReleaseModel* method that is identical to that of the SGE. For brevity, we will omit the formal description and definition of properties and methods that are identical to those of the SGE. These include the *Delete*, *Undo*, *Redo*, and *NewDrawing* methods, and the *LineColor*, *FillColor*, and *Dirty* properties.

The **CGraphicList** object will be used for the internal object model of the Background Editor. This will permit internal object models to be shared by these two components and will greatly reduce the development time for the Background Editor. During the development of this component, we may discover that certain convenient

Property Design Table		
Name	**Type**	**Function**
ModelHandle	Long Integer Maximum = N/A Minimum = N/A Default = None	Provides the address of the modeling object cast to a long integer. When a new value is assigned to this property, the existing modeling object is destroyed and replaced with the new object. NULL values are ignored.

Figure 8-1   The *ModelHandle* Description

functions are missing from the **CGraphicList** model. Because this model is now shared between two projects, we have chosen to treat the development of the **CGraphicList** object as a separate project. The functions of the **CGraphicList** object and its aggregates will be made available to both projects as a compile-time function library. (This approach should be used for all objects that are used by more than one project.) Since our objects are physically shared between components, we must make sure to recompile *both* components when the internal object model changes.

The first new methods that we will add are the *AddRectangle* and the *AddCircle* methods. The definitions of these methods are given in Figures 8-2 and 8-3, and their implementations are given in Figures 8-3 and 8-4.

The implementations of *AddRectangle* and *AddCircle* require two new functions—*NewRectangle* and *NewCircle*—to be added to the **CGraphicList** model. The

Method Description			
Name	AddRectangle		
Return Value	Void		
Description	Adds a rectangle with the given *Left, Top, Height*, and *Width* parameters. The current line and fill colors are used to create the new object. If there is no existing object model, this method does nothing.		
Arguments	**Name**	**Type**	**Description**
1	NewLeft	Long Integer	*X* coordinate of the upper left corner of the new rectangle.
2	NewTop	Long Integer	*Y* coordinate of the upper left corner of the new rectangle.
3	NewWidth	Long Integer	Width of the new rectangle.
4	NewHeight	Long Integer	Height of the new rectangle.

Figure 8-2   *AddRectangle* Method Description

Method Description			
Name	AddCircle		
Return Value	Void		
Description	Adds a circle with the given *Center* and *Radius*. The current line and fill colors are used to create the new object. If there is no existing object model, this method does nothing.		
Arguments	**Name**	**Type**	**Description**
1	NewCenterX	Long Integer	*X* Coordinate of the center of the new circle.
2	NewCenterY	Long Integer	*Y* Coordinate of the center of the new circle.
3	NewRadius	Long Integer	Radius of the new circle.

Figure 8-3   *AddCircle* Method Description

```
// Add a rectangle
void CSGEPEditCtrl::AddRectangle(long NewLeft, long NewTop,
                                 long NewWidth, long NewHeight)
{
    if (Model != NULL)
    {
        COLORREF FillC;
        COLORREF LineC;
        OleTranslateColor(m_lineColor,NULL,&LineC);
        OleTranslateColor(m_fillColor,NULL,&FillC);
        Model->NewRectangle(NewLeft,NewTop,NewWidth,NewHeight,
                            LineC,FillC);
    }
}
```

Figure 8-4   *AddRectangle* Implementation

existing functions were designed under the assumption that they would be given two mouse points that defined the upper left and lower right of a rectangle containing the new object. Two new functions that allow the object parameters to be supplied directly are now needed. Figures 8-4 and 8-5 show the implementations of the *AddRectangle* and *AddCircle* methods, while Figures 8-6 and 8-7 show the implementation of the two new functions. These functions make use of the existing undo facility. These routines also use special constructors for the **CCircle** and **CRectangle** objects. (These constructors were omitted from the figures of Chapter 7 to simplify the presentation.)

At this point, it is necessary to implement the methods that handle the selection. For the moment, we will ignore the problem of creating the selection and concentrate on the functions that manipulate it. The first method we will add is the *ClearSelect* method, which is a wrapper for the *ClearSelect* function of the **CGraphicList** model. The description of this method is given in Figure 8-8, and its implementation is given in Figure 8-9.

```
// Add a circle
void CSGEPEditCtrl::AddCircle(long NewCenterX, long NewCenterY,
                              long NewRadius)
{
    if (Model != NULL)
    {
        COLORREF FillC;
        COLORREF LineC;
        OleTranslateColor(m_lineColor,NULL,&LineC);
        OleTranslateColor(m_fillColor,NULL,&FillC);
        Model->NewCircle(NewCenterX,NewCenterY,NewRadius,LineC,FillC);
    }
}
```

Figure 8-5   *AddCircle* Implementation

```
void CGraphicList::NewRectangle(long NewLeft, long NewTop,
        long NewWidth, long NewHeight, COLORREF LineC, COLORREF FillC)
{
   // Create a new rectangle from a list of its internal parameters
   CRectangle * Temp = new CRectangle(NewLeft,NewTop,NewWidth,
                                      NewHeight,LineC,FillC);
   // Link new rectangle into model's object chain
   if (Head == NULL)
   {
      Head = Temp;
   }
   else
   {
      Tail->Next = Temp;
   }
   Temp->Prev = Tail;
   Tail = Temp;
   Count++;
   // Create an ADD OBJECT Undo and add it to the Undo chain
   CUndoAdd * TempUndo = new CUndoAdd(Temp);
   UndoList.PushCommand(TempUndo);
   // Redo list must be cleared
   RedoList.Clear();
   // Model has been modified
   Dirty = TRUE;
}
```

Figure 8-6   *NewRectangle* Implementation

```
void CGraphicList::NewCircle(long NewCenterX, long NewCenterY,
        long NewRadius, COLORREF LineC, COLORREF FillC)
{
   // Create a new circle from its list of internal parameters
   CCircle * Temp = new CCircle(NewCenterX,NewCenterY,
                               NewRadius,LineC,FillC);
   // Link the circle into the model's object chain
   if (Head == NULL)
   {
      Head = Temp;
   }
   else
   {
      Tail->Next = Temp;
   }
   Temp->Prev = Tail;
}
```

Figure 8-7   *NewCircle* Implementation

```
    Tail = Temp;
    Count++;
    // Create an ADD OBJECT Undo and link it into the UNDO chain
    CUndoAdd * TempUndo = new CUndoAdd(Temp);
    UndoList.PushCommand(TempUndo);
    // Clear the REDO List
    RedoList.Clear();
    // The model has been modified
    Dirty = TRUE;
}
```

Figure 8-7   (*Continued*)

Method Description			
Name	ClearSelect		
Return Value	Void		
Description	Deselects all selected objects. If there is no internal object model, then this method does nothing.		
Arguments	**Name**	**Type**	**Description**
Void			

Figure 8-8   *ClearSelect* Method Description

```
// deselect everything
void CSGEPEditCtrl::ClearSelect()
{
    if (Model != NULL)
    {
        Model->ClearSelect();
    }
}
```

Figure 8-9   *ClearSelect* Implementation

We can now add the *MoveSelect* and *ScaleSelect* methods, which are also wrappers for the corresponding **CGraphicList** methods. The method descriptions for these are shown in Figures 8-10 and 8-11, and their implementations are shown in Figures 8-12 and 8-13.

As a final step, it is necessary to provide a method for creating a selection as well as some sort of enumeration and query facilities to allow the user of the component to determine what drawing objects are contained in the internal model. While it is simple enough to implement such a facility, these functions are more properly part of an Accessor component. Therefore, we will make the following assumptions:

Method Description			
Name	MoveSelect		
Return Value	Void		
Description	Moves the selection the distance specified by the *NewX* and *NewY* parameters. These parameters are deltas, not absolute coordinates. Their values can be negative. The selection rectangle does not change size during this operation.		
Arguments	**Name**	**Type**	**Description**
1	NewX	Long Integer	The distance, in the *X* direction, that the upper left corner of the selection rectangle will move.
2	NewY	Long Integer	The distance, in the *Y* direction, that the upper left corner of the selection rectangle will move.

Figure 8-10   *MoveSelect* Method Description

Method Description			
Name	ScaleSelect		
Return Value	Void		
Description	Changes the size of the selection rectangle, using the *NewWidth* and *NewHeight* parameters. These parameters are absolute sizes. The upper-left corner of the selection does not move.		
Arguments	**Name**	**Type**	**Description**
1	NewWidth	Long Integer	The new width of the selection rectangle.
2	NewHeight	Long Integer	The new height of the selection rectangle.

Figure 8-11   *ScaleSelect* Method Description

```
// move selection, NewX and NewY are deltas, not absolute postions
void CSGEPEditCtrl::MoveSelect(long NewX, long NewY)
{
    if (Model != NULL)
    {
        Model->MoveSelection(NewX,NewY);
    }
}
```

Figure 8-12   *MoveSelect* Implementation

```
// Scale selection
void CSGEPEditCtrl::ScaleSelect(long NewWidth, long NewHeight)
{
    RECT R1,R2;
    if (Model != NULL)
    {
        Model->GetSelRect(R1);
        R2 = R1;
        R2.right = R2.left + NewWidth;
        R2.bottom = R2.top + NewHeight;
        Model->ScaleSelect(R1,R2);
    }
}
```

Figure 8-13   *ScaleSelect* Implementation

1. An Accessor component for the **CGraphicList** object has already been created, and the Accessor is able to enumerate the objects contained in a **CGraphicList** model.

2. The accessor can provide the address of each of these objects on demand, and this pointer will be cast to a long integer.

3. The Accessor component and the Background Editor share the same internal object model. In most cases, it may be more convenient to implement the enumeration and query features directly in the Background Editor. However, background editing and accessing are two separate functions, and in our examples we wish to encapsulate separate functions as separate components.

To create a selection, it is necessary to use an accessor to enumerate the subobjects of the graphical model and to pass the addresses of the selected objects to the background editor. We will use the *AddToSelect* method for this purpose. Figure 8-14

Method Description			
Name	AddToSelect		
Return Value	Void		
Description	Converts the *Handle* parameter into a drawing object pointer, validates the pointer, and if valid, adds the object to the selection chain. To be valid, the object pointer must exist in the chain of drawing objects of the internal object model.		
Arguments	**Name**	**Type**	**Description**
1	Handle	Long Integer	Pointer to a graphical drawing object, cast to a long integer.

Figure 8-14   *AddToSelect* Method Description

```
// get model handle from Accessor, send to this function
// Add handle to selection
long CSGEPEditCtrl::AddToSelect(long Handle)
{
    if (Model != NULL)
    {
        CGraphicObject * Addr = (CGraphicObject *)Handle;
        if (Model->IsLegalObject(Addr))
        {
            Model->AddToSelect(Addr);
            return 0;
        }
        return 1;
    }
    return 0;
}
```

Figure 8-15   *AddToSelect* Implementation

```
BOOL CGraphicList::IsLegalObject(CGraphicObject *Obj)
{
    // Look up object in graphical object list.
    // Return TRUE if found, FALSE otherwise.
    for (CGraphicObject * Temp = Head; Temp != NULL ; Temp=Temp->Next)
    {
        if (Temp == Obj)
        {
            return TRUE;
        }
    }
    return FALSE;
}
```

Figure 8-16   *IsLegalObject* Implementation

shows the method description of the *AddToSelect* method. This method has one argument, *Handle*, which is assumed to contain the address of a drawing object. This drawing object must be contained in the Background Editor's internal model. Since it is unwise to assume that the address is valid, the *Handle* pointer is validated by looking it up in the component's list of graphical drawing objects. If the pointer is invalid, it is ignored. To validate the *Handle* address, a new function, *IsLegalObject*, has been added to the **CGraphicList** model. Figure 8-15 shows the implementation of the *AddToSelect* method, and Figure 8-16 shows the implementation of the new function *IsLegalObject*.

This completes the implementation of the background editor.

5. CONCLUSION

A Background Editor is usually much simpler than its graphical counterpart, but it can have a number of uses. For example, a background editor can be used to implement a tutorial program for its graphical counterpart. A single internal model can be shared between a background editor and the graphical editor. The background editor can be used to create a sample drawing that can then be completed by a student.

A Background Editor can also be used to create a project wizard for its graphical counterpart. The project wizard could receive a number of design parameters from a user and then create a partially completed project based on those parameters.

In many cases, the background editing and enumeration facilities will be incorporated into the graphical editor itself.

EXERCISES

1. Modify the Background Editor by adding enumeration and query methods and properties. Use the modified component to test adding, moving, scaling, recoloring, and deleting graphical objects. Pass the internal object model to the Simple Graphical Editor for viewing.

2. Incorporate the Background Editor functions into the Simple Graphical Editor, including the enumeration and query facility described in the preceding exercise.

Chapter 9

Serializers

1. PREREQUISITES AND OBJECTIVES

Before starting this chapter, you should have

1. A knowledge of programming in C++.
2. A knowledge of component interface design.

After completing this chapter, you will have

1. Rudimentary knowledge of semipersistent objects.
2. A knowledge of how to handle file I/O, clipboard operations, and printing.
3. A knowledge of the Serializer-Component design methodology.

2. INTRODUCTION

Serialization is the process of writing an object, or a collection of objects, to a persistent medium such as a file. There are three distinct types of serialization: (1) saving and restoring files, (2) copying to and from the clipboard, and (3) printing.

Serialization mechanisms are widely available in different object packages and languages. The MFC class system provides serialization mechanisms for many different kinds of objects. Serialization mechanisms are also available in Java and other languages, but these generic mechanisms may not be suitable for complex objects containing pointers and many aggregate objects. This chapter will explain how to design a serialization mechanism from scratch. We begin by showing how to make a set of classes serializable and finish by giving examples of the three types of serialization. We will use the Simple Graphical Editor (SGE) as a basis for this material.

3. THE METHODOLOGY

The serialization components themselves are relatively simple. For serialization operations like writing files, we pass the component a **CGraphicList** pointer. For deserialization operations like reading files, we pass a file name to the component and receive an **CGraphicList** pointer in return. Most of the work will be performed by functions built into the **CGraphicList** object and its aggregates. Each graphical object will know how to serialize itself. Serialization consists of extracting all nonpointer information into a buffer. If it is necessary to retain pointers, they must be converted into a machine-independent form (usually a binary index of some sort). Type codes, which can be omitted in polymorphic objects, must be included in the serialized data. One or more deserialized objects will be stored in a buffer and written to persistent storage.

Unlike serialization, which is done by member functions of the graphical objects, deserialization must be done, at least in part, by a global function. The individual objects, like rectangle and circle, have to be identified before they can be turned into internal objects of the correct type. The remainder of this chapter illustrates the serialization process with three different types of serializers for the Simple Graphics Editor.

4. THE SGE SERIALIZATION FUNCTIONS

For a serialization mechanism to conform to the philosophy of object-oriented design, each object must serialize itself. This can mean many things. In some cases, it means that when an object is provided with an archive pointer, it will write its state to that archive. This forces a great deal of functionality into the object, since it must be capable of dealing with all required types of archives.

We do not want to force this much functionality into our objects. Instead, our goal is to provide a serialization mechanism that converts data into a form that can be used for many different purposes. To keep the serialization mechanism as simple as possible, we will provide the component with a storage area and expect it to serialize itself into that storage area.

We must modify the **CGraphicList** project so that the **CGraphicList** object and its subobjects serialize themselves. The general mechanism for doing this is shown in Figure 9-1. In this routine, a **CGraphicList** object is serialized into a string variable. The

```
void CGraphicList::SSerialize(CString &S)
{
    S.Empty();
    CGraphicObject * Temp;
    // Serialize each graphical object
    for (Temp = Head ; Temp != NULL ; Temp = Temp->Next)
    {
        CString T;
        Temp->SSerialize(T);
        S += T;
    }
}
```

Figure 9-1   Serializing the CGraphicList Object

CGraphicList object passes the serialization request to each graphical object, and accumulates the results in its own string variable. Our objects are so simple that no header information is required. However, if this were the case, such information would be added to the **CGraphicList** string variable before adding the information from the graphical objects. (*Note:* **CString** is an MFC string type that permits strings to be expanded without a fixed limit. The overloaded $+=$ operator concatenates new data onto the end of an existing string.)

At times we may not want to serialize only selected portions of the object. The function *SSerializeSelect* in Figure 9-2 passes the serialization request to selected objects only.

To serialize the graphical objects **CCircle** and **CRectangle**, we first add the following pure virtual function definition to the definition of **CGraphicObject**:

```
virtual void SSerialize(CString &rv) = 0;
```

Adding this definition forces us to add an *SSerialize* function to both the **CCircle** and **CRectangle** classes.

Each graphical object is required to serialize its internal state as a human-readable line of text, and it is required to terminate that line with a **return** character and a **line-feed**. To permit deserialization, the first character of the line will be used to identify the type of the object. (Some means of identifying objects is required in any serialization mechanism.) The letter "C" will be used to identify circles, and the letter "R" will be used to identify rectangles. Figure 9-3 shows the *SSerialize* function for the **CCircle** class. (*Note:* The *Format* function of the **CString** class works like the standard C function *sprintf*. The overloaded + operator is used for concatenation.) Strictly speaking, the **CGraphicObject** class should implement its own *SSerialize* function for serializing fill and line colors. The **CCircle** class would then call its base-class function before serializing its own data. Due to the simplicity of our class structure, we have elected to serialize the entire object in the **CCircle** and **CRectangle** functions. Figure 9-4 gives the implementation of the **CRectangle** *SSerialize* function.

This completes the serialization mechanism of the **CGraphicList** object. The string created by the **CGraphicList** *SSerialize* function can be written to a text file. The full implementation of the **CGraphicList** object also includes a binary serialization mechanism. This mechanism is a bit more difficult to implement, but the reverse operation, the

```
void CGraphicList::SSerializeSelect(CString &S)
{
    S.Empty();
    CSelectItem * Temp;
    for (CTemp = Selection ; Temp != NULL ; Temp = Temp->Next)
    {
        CString T;
        Temp->Item->SSerialize(T);
        S += T;
    }
}
```

Figure 9-2   Serializing the Selection

```
void CCircle::SSerialize(CString &rv)
{
    // String serializer
    rv = "C ";
    CString Work;
    Work.Format("%8.8x",FillColor);
    rv += Work + " ";
    Work.Format("%8.8x",LineColor);
    rv += Work + " ";
    Work.Format("%d",Center.x);
    rv += Work + " ";
    Work.Format("%d",Center.y);
    rv += Work + " ";
    Work.Format("%d",Radius);
    // Line Terminator
    rv += Work + "\r\n";
}
```

Figure 9-3   Serializing the CCircle Object

```
void CRectangle::SSerialize(CString &rv)
{
    // String serialization function
    rv = "R ";
    CString Work;
    Work.Format("%8.8x",FillColor);
    rv += Work + " ";
    Work.Format("%8.8x",LineColor);
    rv += Work + " ";
    Work.Format("%d",Left);
    rv += Work + " ";
    Work.Format("%d",Top);
    rv += Work + " ";
    Work.Format("%d",Width);
    rv += Work + " ";
    Work.Format("%d",Height);
    // Line Terminator
    rv += Work + "\r\n";
}
```

Figure 9-4   Serializing the CRectangle Object

deserialization mechanism, is reasonably simple. The string deserialization mechanism, on the other hand, is quite complicated.

The binary serialization mechanism uses the two structures shown in Figure 9-5. These structures are also used by the string deserialization mechanism for temporary storage. This allows both deserialization mechanisms to use the same special constructors

```
struct SerRectangle                      struct SerCircle
{                                        {
   long Type;                               long Type;
   COLORREF FillColor;                      COLORREF FillColor;
   COLORREF LineColor;                      COLORREF LineColor;
   long Left;                               long CenterX;
   long Top;                                long CenterY;
   long Width;                              long Radius;
   long Height;                          };
};
```

Figure 9-5   Binary Serialization Structures

to create **CCircle** and **CRectangle** objects. Beyond showing these structures, we will not discuss the binary serialization mechanism.

The deserialization function is quite long, but repetitive. Figure 9-6 shows the important parts of this function. The caller of this function is required to break the serialized string into individual lines and to pass the lines one at a time to the *SDeserialize* function. The *SDeserialize* function will return NULL if a format error is found; otherwise it will return a pointer to a **CGraphicObject**. The *GetWord* function is used to parse the input string into white-space delimited words. This function is straightforward and its implementation is omitted for brevity.

```
CGraphicObject * SDeserialize(CString LineIn)
{
   // Each input consists of a line
   // The first character of the line determines the type of object
   // The remaining parameters are space delimited words on the line
   CString Work;
   if (LineIn[0] == 'C')
   {
      // First copy all parameters into a serialization object
      SerCircle C;
      // Get word will find the first word starting at Pos
      // set Pos to skip type code
      int Pos = 1; // int is required for CString indexing
      // First Parameter: Fill Color
      // GetWord changes Pos
      Work = GetWord(LineIn, Pos);
      if (Work.IsEmpty())
      {
         return NULL; // Empty means NO WORD FOUND: Format Error!
      }
      Work = "0x" + Work;
```

Figure 9-6   The *SDeserialize* Function

```
        C.FillColor = strtol(Work,NULL,0); // color in hex
        … // Repeat for Line Color
        // Third Parameter: Center.x
        Work = GetWord(LineIn,Pos);
        if (Work.IsEmpty())
        {
            return NULL; // Empty means NO WORD FOUND: Format Error!
        }
        C.CenterX = atol(Work);
        … // Repeat for the other two parameters
        // Now create the circle structure
        CCircle * rv = new CCircle(C);
        return rv;
    }
    else if (LineIn[0] == 'R')
    {
        … // Same as for CCircle
    }
    else
    {
        // Invalid type code
        return NULL;
    }
}
```

Figure 9-6   (*Continued*)

5. THE SGE FILE HANDLER

To write a file, we must have both a file name and something to write into the file. Thus the SGE file handler needs at least two properties, one to supply the file name and one to supply the content. Figure 9-7 gives the description of two properties—*FileName* and *ModelHandle*—which are used for this purpose.

We must next provide methods that perform the functions required to read and write files. The *Open* method will open the file specified by the *FileName* property,

Property Design Table		
Name	**Type**	**Function**
ModelHandle	Long Integer Maximum = N/A Minimum = N/A Default = None	Provides the address of the modeling object cast to a long integer. NULL values are ignored.
FileName	String Default = Empty String	Contains the file name of the file to be read or written. This property will also be set by the *SaveAs* and *OpenFile* properties.

Figure 9-7   *ModelHandle* and *FileName* Property Descriptions

Method Description			
Name	Open		
Return Value	Long		
Description	Reads the file specified by *FileName*, creates a **CGraphicList** object, and makes the object available in the *ModelHandle* property. If the file cannot be read, an error code is returned; otherwise a success code is returned.		
Arguments	**Name**	**Type**	**Description**
Void			

Method Description			
Name	Save		
Return Value	Long		
Description	Serializes the model specified by *ModelHandle*, and writes the serialized data to the file specified by *FileName*. If the file cannot be written, an error code is returned; otherwise a success code is returned.		
Arguments	**Name**	**Type**	**Description**
Void			

Figure 9-8   *Open* and *Save* Method Descriptions

read and deserialize its contents, and create a new model that will be available through the *ModelHandle* property. The *Save* method will serialize the contents of the object specified by the *ModelHandle* property and write the serialized data to the file specified by the *FileName* property. (Any existing file will be overwritten.) Figure 9-8 gives the method definitions of these two methods.

Figure 9-9 contains the implementations of the *Open* and *Save* methods. Two utility functions—*ReadModel* and *SaveModel*—perform the actual *read* and *write* operations.

```
long CSGEFileCtrl::Open()
{
    // We need a file name to open
    if (m_fileName.IsEmpty())
    {
        return FILE_NAME_EMPTY;
    }
    // Read a new model from the specified file
    return ReadModel();
}
long CSGEFileCtrl::Save()
{
    // Must have a file name to save
```

Figure 9-9   *Open* and *Save* Implementations

```
    if (m_fileName.IsEmpty())
    {
        return FILE_NAME_EMPTY;
    }
    // Must have a model to save
    if (Model == NULL)
    {
        return MODEL_IS_NULL;
    }
    // Save model to specified file
    return SaveModel();
}
```

Figure 9-9   (*Continued*)

The *Open* and *Save* methods check that the file name is not empty, while the *Save* method also checks that the model handle is not NULL.

In addition to these two methods, we will also create a *SaveAs* method, which supplies a file name as a parameter, and an *OpenFile* method, which also supplies a file name. The names supplied by either of these methods replace the current value of the *FileName* property. The definitions of these two methods are given in Figure 9-10. The

Method Description		
Name	OpenFile	
Return Value	Long	
Description	Reads the file specified by the *NewFileName* parameter, creates a **CGraphicList** object, and makes the object available in the *ModelHandle* property. If the file cannot be read, an error code is returned; otherwise a success code is returned.	
Arguments	**Name**	**Type**	**Description**
1	NewFileName	String	Supplies the name of the file to be read. This must not be the empty string.

Method Description		
Name	SaveAs	
Return Value	Long	
Description	Serializes the model specified by *ModelHandle*, and writes the serialized data to the file specified by *FileName*. If the file cannot be written, an error code is returned; otherwise a success code is returned.	
Arguments	**Name**	**Type**	**Description**
1	NewFileName	String	Supplies the name of the file to be written. This must not be the empty string.

Figure 9-10   *OpenFile* and *SaveAs* Method Descriptions

implementations, which are virtually identical to those of the *Open* and *Save* methods, are not shown here.

Finally, we will create a *Backup* method that can be used to create a backup copy of a file before the file is rewritten. This is done by renaming the existing file with a *.bak* suffix. Figure 9-11 gives the method description of this property, while Figure 9-12 gives the implementation. The implementation uses a utility function, *RenameFile*, to do the actual renaming.

The real work of the component is done by the *SaveModel, ReadModel*, and *RenameFile* functions. The *RenameFile* function is straightforward and will be omitted. The implementation of the *SaveFile* function is given in Figure 9-13. The real work of this routine is done by the serialization facility of the **CGraphicList** object.

The *ReadModel* function is longer and more involved than the *SaveModel* function. The main difficulty is breaking the input data into lines, which then must be passed to the deserialization function. To do this, characters must be examined one at a time. However, for efficiency reasons we cannot read one byte at a time. Instead, a character buffer is used to hold data read from the file. This data is scanned one byte at a time, and a line of data is accumulated in the line buffer. When an end-of-line character is found, the line is passed to the deserialization function, and the resultant data structure is chained into the model being built. When the buffer is completely processed,

Method Description			
Name	Backup		
Return Value	Long		
Description	Serializes the model specified by *ModelHandle*, and writes the serialized data to the file specified by *FileName*. If the file cannot be written, an error code is returned; otherwise a success code is returned.		
Arguments	**Name**	**Type**	**Description**
Void			

Figure 9-11   *Backup* Method Description

```
long CSGEFileCtrl::Backup()
{
    // renames specified file with a new suffix (000, 001, ...)
    // Must have a file to rename
    if (m_fileName.IsEmpty())
    {
        return FILE_NAME_EMPTY;
    }
    // turn the existing file into a backup copy
    return RenameFile();
}
```

Figure 9-12   The *Backup* Method Implementation

```
long CSGEFileCtrl::SaveModel()
{
    // called by Save and SaveAs functions
    // Open specified file. If file exists, overwrite
    HANDLE SF = CreateFile(m_fileName,GENERIC_WRITE,0,NULL,
            CREATE_ALWAYS,FILE_ATTRIBUTE_NORMAL,NULL);
    if (SF == INVALID_HANDLE_VALUE)
    {
        // specified file can't be opened for writing
        return FILE_OPEN_ERROR;
    }
    unsigned long BytesWritten;
    CString S;
    // Serialize the drawing as a string,
    //and write the string to the open file
    Model->SSerialize(S);
    WriteFile(SF,S,S.GetLength(),&BytesWritten,NULL);
    // Close the file
    CloseHandle(SF);
    S.Empty();
    // Zero return indicates all OK
    return 0;
}
```

Figure 9-13   The *SaveModel* Implementation

it is replenished by reading the file. When the end of the file is reached, any data remaining in the line buffer is passed to the deserialization function, and the process terminates. Figure 9-14 gives the implementation of the *ReadModel* function. *ReadModel* uses a new **CGraphicList** function, *AddObject*. This function inserts a graphical object into the linked list of graphical objects, without using the undo facility. Since an entirely new model is being built, it would be inappropriate to permit the individual object insertions to be undone.

```
long CSGEFileCtrl::ReadModel()
{
    // Attempt to open file for reading
    HANDLE RF = CreateFile(m_fileName,GENERIC_READ,FILE_SHARE_READ,
                    NULL,OPEN_EXISTING,FILE_ATTRIBUTE_NORMAL,NULL);
    if (RF == INVALID_HANDLE_VALUE)
    {
        // If file does not exist, or other error
        return FILE_OPEN_ERROR;
    }
    // create a new model empty model
```

Figure 9-14   The *ReadModel* Function

```
Model = new CGraphicList;
static char Buffer[1000];
unsigned long BytesRead = 0;
unsigned long BufferBytes = 0;
unsigned long BP = 0;
unsigned long FileLength = GetFileSize(RF,NULL);
CString S;
S.Empty();
// The following loop will read the file in 1000 byte chunks
// Each chunk will be scanned one byte at a time, searching for
// the end of a line. Once a full line has been accumulated, the
// line will be passed to the SDeserialize function to create a
// drawing object. The SDeserialize is a global function that is
// provided with the model.
while (BytesRead < FileLength)
{
    ReadFile(RF,Buffer,1000,&BufferBytes,NULL);
    if (BufferBytes <= 0)
    {
        // Number of bytes read is zero (or less?)
        // This must be a read error, so shut down
        // the process and report an error
        CloseHandle(RF);
        delete Model;
        Model = NULL;
        return FILE_FORMAT_ERROR;
    }
    // Scan the current chunk looking for EOL
    // For chunks after the first, there will normally
    // be some bytes left from the last chunk in CString S.
    while (BP < BufferBytes)
    {
        // accumulate current byte into S
        S += Buffer[BP];
        if (Buffer[BP] == '\n')
        {
            // If EOL found, deserialize the line,
            // erase the string
            // add the deserialized object to the model
            CGraphicObject * Obj = SDeserialize(S);
            S.Empty();
            if (Obj == NULL)
            {
                // NULL return from SDeserialize indicates a
                // format error. Delete the model, close the file
                // and report an error.
                delete Model;
```

Figure 9-14   (*Continued*)

```
                    Model = NULL;
                    CloseHandle(RF);
                    return FILE_FORMAT_ERROR;
                }
                // Add object to model WITHOUT UNDO or setting Dirty bit
                Model->AddObject(Obj);
            }
            // go to next character
            BP++;
        }
        // go to next chunk
        BytesRead += BufferBytes;
    }
    if (!S.IsEmpty())
    {
        // if there are leftover bytes in S after the last EOL was found
        // it is probably an unterminated line. Go ahead and process it.
        CGraphicObject * Obj = SDeserialize(S);
        S.Empty();
        if (Obj == NULL)
        {
            // NULL return from SDeserialize indicates a
            // format error. Delete the model, close the file
            // and report an error.
            delete Model;
            Model = NULL;
            CloseHandle(RF);
            return FILE_FORMAT_ERROR;
        }
        // Add object to model WITHOUT UNDO or setting Dirty bit
        Model->AddObject(Obj);
    }
    // zero return indicates all OK
    return 0;
}
```

Figure 9-14   *(Continued)*

6. THE SGE CLIPBOARD HANDLER

The SGE clipboard handler will make use of the serialization and deserialization functions developed for the SGE file handler. The Windows clipboard supports several standard types of data, and permits programs to define their own data types. To add data to the clipboard, it is necessary to create a memory block, insert the clipboard data into the memory block, and pass the memory block to the clipboard. Standard operating system functions are used to allocate the memory block and pass it to the clipboard. Like the file handler, the clipboard handler must have a *ModuleHandle* property that supplies the data to be placed on the clipboard. Figure 9-15 contains the description of this property.

Property Design Table		
Name	**Type**	**Function**
ModelHandle	Long Integer Maximum = N/A Minimum = N/A Default = None	Provides the address of the modeling object cast to a long integer. NULL values are ignored.

Figure 9-15   Clipboard Handler Property Descriptions

The clipboard handler also requires three methods: (1) *Copy*, which will copy the current selection to the clipboard, (2) *Cut*, which will do the same but will delete the selection on completion of the copy, and (3) *Paste*, which will insert the clipboard data into the drawing. If there is a current selection, the pasted data will replace the selection. Figure 9-16 gives the method descriptions of the three methods.

Method Description			
Name	Copy		
Return Value	Void		
Description	Copies the current selection to the clipboard. If *ModelHandle* is NULL, does nothing.		
Arguments	**Name**	**Type**	**Description**
Void			

Method Description			
Name	Cut		
Return Value	Void		
Description	Copies the current selection to the clipboard, and then deletes the current selection. If *ModelHandle* is NULL, does nothing.		
Arguments	**Name**	**Type**	**Description**
Void			

Method Description			
Name	Paste		
Return Value	Void		
Description	Pastes the clipboard data into the selection. If the clipboard is empty, or *ModelHandle* is NULL, does nothing. If there is a current selection, it is deleted before the paste operation is done.		
Arguments	**Name**	**Type**	**Description**
Void			

Figure 9-16   *Copy, Cut,* and *Paste* Method Descriptions

```
void CSGEClipCtrl::Copy()
{
    // called by copy and cut
    DoCopy();
}
```
```
void CSGEClipCtrl::Cut()
{
    long rv = DoCopy();
    // Don't delete the selection unless the copy was successful
    if (rv)
    {
        Model->DeleteSelection();
    }
}
```

Figure 9-17   *Cut* and *Copy* Implementations

The implementations of *Cut* and *Copy* are similar and are given in Figure 9-17. These methods use a utility function, *DoCopy*, to copy the selection to the clipboard. *DoCopy* returns a success/failure code that is used by the *Cut* method to determine whether it should delete the current selection. The return code is ignored by the *Copy* method.

The implementation of the *DoCopy* function is given in Figure 9-18. This function first serializes the selection; if the serialized selection is not empty, it opens the clipboard, clears it, creates a memory block, copies the serialized data into the memory

```
long CSGEClipCtrl::DoCopy()
{
    CString Buffer;
    if (Model != NULL)
    {
        // Serialize each object, and accumulate the data in Buffer
        Model->SSerializeSelect(Buffer);
        // If there was something to serialize, put it in the clipboard
        if (!Buffer.IsEmpty())
        {
            // can't use MFC functions, control might not have a window.
            if (!::OpenClipboard(::GetActiveWindow()))
            {
                // Couldn't get the clipboard
                return 0;
            }
            ::EmptyClipboard();
            // Add first format to clipboard: Private format allowing us
            // to paste objects from the clipboard into a drawing
```

Figure 9-18   The *DoCopy* Function

```
        HGLOBAL Mem = GlobalAlloc(GMEM_MOVEABLE,Buffer.GetLength()+1);
        if (Mem == NULL)
        {
            // couldn't allocate memory, return error
            ::CloseClipboard();
            return 0;
        }
        char *MemAddr = (char *)GlobalLock(Mem);
        memcpy(MemAddr,Buffer,Buffer.GetLength()+1);
        GlobalUnlock(Mem);
        // clipboard now owns memory block
        ::SetClipboardData(ClipID,Mem);
        // Done with clipboard.
        ::CloseClipboard();
    }
  }
  // All OK
  return 1;
}
```

Figure 9-18   (*Continued*)

block, passes the memory block to the clipboard with a private data type, and finally closes the clipboard. The private data type is created when the file handler component is instantiated, and it is destroyed when all programs referring to the type terminate and the clipboard does not contain data of this type. The process of copying data to the clipboard consists of a set of standard Windows operating system function calls. *DoCopy* returns 1 if the operation was successful and 0 otherwise.

The implementation of the *Paste* method is shown in Figure 9-19. This function is similar to the deserialization function used by the SGE file manager. The clipboard is

```
void CSGEClipCtrl::Paste()
{
    HGLOBAL Mem;

    if (Model == NULL)
    {
        // can't paste to nothing
        return;
    }
    if (!IsClipboardFormatAvailable(ClipID))
    {
        // Nothing to paste -- no data available
        return;
    }
    // can't use MFC functions, this control might not have a window.
```

Figure 9-19   The *Paste* Method Implementation

```
if (!::OpenClipboard(::GetActiveWindow()))
{
    // can't paste because we can't get the clipboard
    return;
}
Mem = ::GetClipboardData(ClipID);
if (Mem == NULL)
{
    // There was supposed to be data, but we couldn't get it
    ::CloseClipboard();
    return;
}
// paste replaces current selection
Model->DeleteSelection();
char *Buffer = (char *)GlobalLock(Mem);
long BP = 0;
long BufferBytes = GlobalSize(Mem);
CString S;
S.Empty();
// clear redos
Model->ClearRedo();
// This must be called before the Model->InsertObject function
// is called. InsertObject will place all redos into the empty
// command created by NewUndoCommand
Model->NewUndoCommand();
// Scan the clipboard data one byte at a time looking for EOLs
// Accumulate characters in CString S
// when an EOL is found, pass the line to SDeserialze
// SDeserialize is a global function provided with the model
while (BP < BufferBytes)
{
    S += Buffer[BP];
    if (Buffer[BP] == '\n')
    {
        S.Empty();
        CGraphicObject * Obj = SDeserialize(S);
        // Test for format error. We will ignore
        // any bad lines and paste what we can.
        // (Bad lines indicate an error in DoCopy)
        if (Obj != NULL)
        {
            // Add object with UNDO and dirty bit set
            Model->InsertObject(Obj);
        }
    }
    BP++;
}
```

Figure 9-19   (*Continued*)

```
    // release the clipboard memory block
    GlobalUnlock(Mem);
    // if there is data left in S, it must be an unterminated line
    // attempt to process it.
    if (!S.IsEmpty())
    {
        CGraphicObject * Obj = SDeserialize(S);
        S.Empty();
        if (Obj != NULL)
        {
            Model->InsertObject(Obj);
        }
    }
    // release the clipboard
    ::CloseClipboard();
}
```

Figure 9-19   (*Continued*)

queried for the proper type of data, the private type used by the *DoCopy* function. If data is present, the address and size of the memory block are obtained from the clipboard. The block is scanned one character at a time looking for end-of-line characters. The content of each line is accumulated in the line buffer. When a complete line has been found, it is passed to the deserialization function to create a drawing object. This drawing object is inserted into the model using a new **CGraphicList** function *InsertObject*. The *InsertObject* function uses the undo facility, so a *Paste* operation can be undone.

7. THE SGE PRINT CONTROL

The SGE print control is the simplest of our three serializers. It provides two properties, *ModelHandle* and *PrintDC*. (See Figure 9-20 for the formal descriptions.) Once a model has been passed to the control through the *ModelHandle* property, the contents

Property Design Table		
Name	**Type**	**Function**
ModelHandle	Long Integer Maximum = N/A Minimum = N/A Default = None	Provides the address of the modeling object cast to a long integer. NULL values are ignored.
PrintDC	Handle to a Printer Drawing Context.	Provides the drawing context for a print operation. The print operation is performed immediately. The drawing context handle is discarded after the print operation is complete. **Restrictions:** Write-Only, Run-Time Only

Figure 9-20   Print Handler Property Descriptions

of the drawing can be printed by assigning a printer drawing context handle through the *PrintDC* property. The Windows operating system uses the same method for printing as is used for drawing. A drawing context is created for the desired printer. Just like a window drawing context, the printer drawing context encapsulates the standard drawing functions and translates them into printer commands. To print a drawing, we can use the same drawing routine that we use to display the drawing on the screen.

In most cases the printer drawing context will be obtained from another ActiveX control—the Microsoft Common Dialogs control, for example. The print control will not retain a copy of this drawing context, since printer drawing contexts are usually temporary items that become invalid after a period of time. Each time a print operation is performed, a new drawing context handle must be supplied.

The biggest problem with printing is scaling. Our drawing routine runs in TEXT mode, which translates drawing coordinates into screen coordinates without scaling. Therefore the two points (10, 10) and (10, 20) will be in the same vertical column, 10 pixels apart. If this mode is used for printing, the drawings will be tiny. All control windows have an assumed resolution of 100 pixels per inch, while printers have a resolution of 300 to 600 dots per inch (DPI) and more. (The actual resolution of the window varies with the screen resolution.) The difference in physical resolution will cause printed drawings to appear much smaller than they appear on the screen. Thus it is necessary to scale printer drawings to make them the proper size.

The general problem of scaling is discussed in Chapter 7. A similar technique is used to scale an entire drawing. Let us assume that we want to scale a drawing from R_1 DPI to R_2 DPI. A point (x, y) must be transformed to $(xR_2/R_1, yR_2/R_1)$. If integer arithmetic is used, the multiplication must be performed first to avoid problems with round-off error. We could modify the drawing routines of the **CGraphicList** model to add scaling parameters, but this is not the best way to solve the problem. In fact, if we expand the **CGraphicList** model to include text, this scaling method will no longer work. The size of text is determined by the size of the font being used. There are no size parameters in the drawing commands.

Fortunately, the Windows operating system provides a mechanism that can be used to scale and translate *all* drawing operations. To use this mechanism, we must use the *anisotropic* drawing mode, which allows drawings to be scaled by different amounts in the *x* and *y* directions. Two functions are used to control scaling: *SetWindowExt* and *SetViewportExt*. The *SetWindowExt* function of the drawing context object (**CDC**) has two parameters that give the *x* and *y* resolution of the drawing parameters that are supplied to the drawing functions. In our case, we will use 100 for each of these parameters. The *SetViewportExt* function of the CDC object supplies the *x* and *y* resolutions of the device. If we were printing on a 600 DPI printer, we would use 600 for each of these parameters. The **CDC** object has a query function, *GetDeviceCaps*, that can supply the *x* and *y* resolutions of the device to which it is attached. Translation, which is not required by our print routine, is handled by the functions *SetWindowOrigin* and *SetViewportOrigin*.

Figure 9-21 shows how all of this is put together into a drawing routine and contains the implementation of the *SetPrintDC* function. One line, the call to the **CGraphicList** *Draw* routine, does the actual printing. The other lines are used for scaling and for issuing the required operating system function calls.

```
void CSGEPrintCtrl::SetPrintDC(OLE_HANDLE nNewValue)
{
    // We don't (and shouldn't!) save the device context.
    // We simply use it for printing and throw it away.
    // This could also be a method.
    // Attach the hDC to a CDC
    CDC Thing;
    CDC * MyDc = &Thing;
    MyDc->Attach((HDC)nNewValue);
    // Save current context
    MyDc->SaveDC();
    if (Model == NULL)
    {
        // Nothing to print
        return;
    }
    // Set up DOCINFO structure
    DOCINFO MyDoc;
    MyDoc.cbSize = sizeof(DOCINFO);
    MyDoc.fwType = 0;
    MyDoc.lpszDatatype = NULL;
    MyDoc.lpszDocName = "Simple Graphics Editor";
    MyDoc.lpszOutput = NULL;
    // Get the document rectangle
    CRect MyRect;
    Model->GetRect(MyRect);
    if (MyRect.top > 0)
    {
        MyRect.top = 0;
    }
    if (MyRect.left > 0)
    {
        MyRect.left = 0;
    }
    // Get the horizontal and vertical pixels per inch for scaling
    // Each dimension is scaled separately
    // For a 600 DPI printer, PixX and PixY will get the value 600.
    long PixX = MyDc->GetDeviceCaps(LOGPIXELSX);
    long PixY = MyDc->GetDeviceCaps(LOGPIXELSY);
    // Start a document and a page
    MyDc->StartDoc(&MyDoc);
    MyDc->StartPage();
    // This stuff MUST DEFINITELY follow StartDoc and StartPage calls
    // MM_ANISOTROPIC allows independent scaling of X and Y dimensions.
    MyDc->SetMapMode(MM_ANISOTROPIC);
    // The WindowExt and ViewportExt provide a scaling function
    // WindowExt is the divsor, ViewportExt is the multiplier
```

Figure 9-21   The Printing Routine

```
// WindowOrg and ViewportOrg provide a translation of coordinates
// WindowOrg is the subtractor, ViewportOrg is the adder
// Without this scaling, most printers would print 1/3 to 1/6 the
// proper size.
MyDc->SetWindowOrg(0,0);
MyDc->SetWindowExt(100,100);
MyDc->SetViewportOrg(0,0);
MyDc->SetViewportExt(PixX,PixY);
// Call the model drawing function
Model->Draw(MyDc,MyRect,MyRect,0);
// Finish the page
MyDc->EndPage();
MyDc->EndDoc();
// restore previous context
MyDc->RestoreDC(0);
// detach context from CDC
MyDc->Detach();
}
```

Figure 9-21   (*Continued*)

8. CONCLUSION

As our examples show, serializers are simple components that perform simple operations. It would have been possible to implement these operations directly in the Simple Graphical Editor. There are, however, compelling reasons for not doing so. The first of these is versatility. Using serializers, it is possible to implement many different file formats for the same editor, without complicating the design of the editor. Each of these file formats would be handled by its own Serializer. By the same token, once a Serializer is created, it can be used with several other components. The three components developed in this chapter could be used with both the SGE and the SGE Background Editor. By implementing the serializers as separate components, we provide file handling, clipboard access, and printing to both components at the same time.

It is probably most tempting to incorporate the clipboard and printing facilities into the SGE. These facilities are simple and easily implemented. The reason we have chosen to separate them into separate components is related to the concept of isolation of function. Component-level programming provides a means for completely isolating a facility to eliminate unwanted coupling between features. Other than sharing the same base object, there should be no coupling between drawing, file I/O, clipboard operations, and printing. By isolating these facilities into separate components, we guarantee that there are no "sneak paths" between these features.

EXERCISES

1. Create a text-file serializer that can be used to read the entire contents of a text file into a string. The component will have two properties, *FileName* and *Contents*. *FileName* will be persistent; *Contents* will not be persistent and will be run-time only. Once *FileName* has a

value, the file can be read by reading the *Contents* property and can be written by writing the *Contents* property. When the file is written, it must be completely replaced by the new value of *Contents*.

2. Modify the component of Exercise 1 to permit incremental reads and writes. Add a property *BlockSize* to determine the number of bytes read for each *Read* operation. Add two methods—*StartRead* and *StartWrite*—to initiate incremental reading and writing, and a third—*StartBlockMode*—to return to reading and writing the entire file at once. Block mode will be the default state. The *StartRead* and *StartWrite* functions initiate incremental read and write modes. When in incremental read mode, reading the value of *Contents* reads the next block. When in incremental write mode, writing a new value to *Contents* will append the value to the end of the file. In incremental read mode, writing the value of *Contents* is illegal and will cause an event to be fired. In incremental write mode, reading the value of *Contents* is legal and will retrieve the last string assigned to *Contents*. The current contents of the file is erased when *StartWrite* is called.

3. Modify the component of Exercise 2 to permit random access reads and writes. The design of the component, including any new properties and methods, is your responsibility.

Chapter 10

Displays

1. PREREQUISITES AND OBJECTIVES

Before starting this chapter, you should have

1. A knowledge of programming in C++.
2. A knowledge of component interface design.

After completing this chapter, you will have

1. A knowledge of how to create an object viewer from an existing graphical editor.
2. Familiarity with the principles of object viewers and file viewers, and a knowledge of the differences between them.
3. A knowledge of the Viewer-Component design methodology.

2. INTRODUCTION

A display component permits the viewing of an entity without permitting the entity to be edited or changed. There are three types of viewers: (1) file viewers, (2) object viewers, and (3) Visualization components. Examples of file viewers include the Adobe Acrobat PDF file viewer and the Microsoft PowerPoint viewer. These components allow PDF files and PowerPoint files to be viewed in a Web page, but no editing facilities are provided.

Object viewers are similar to file viewers in that they permit the internal state of an object to be viewed without providing the ability to manipulate the object. Unlike file viewers, object viewers cannot be used in isolation because they depend on other components for object creation. An object viewer can be combined with a serialization component to create a file viewer program.

Visualization components are fundamentally different from file and object viewers, both of which are designed in much the same way as Editor components. In fact, many file and object viewers are based on existing editors, with the editing facilities omitted or disabled. Visualization components, on the other hand, are based on model components. In most cases file and object viewers provide only a static view of their internal objects, while Visualization components typically provide a more dynamic display.

In the following sections we provide examples of all three types of display components. The SGE object viewer and the SGE debug viewers are both object viewers. The text file viewer is a file viewer, and the quicksort visualizer is a visualization component. (Visualization is a major research area in its own right and beyond the scope of this book.)

3. THE METHODOLOGY

Creating a viewer based on an existing Editor component is quite simple. One simply copies the Editor component and strips out all features that permit the user to change the underlying file or object. Saving files, if available, must also be disabled. We will demonstrate this procedure by creating an object viewer based on the Simple Graphical Editor.

The design methodology for displays depends on what kind of display is being created. If an object viewer is being designed as a complement for a graphical editor, we can simply make a copy of the editor and disable the editing features. This is essentially what was done for the SGE object viewer.

When we do not have an editor to start with, the procedure is a bit more systematic. The methodology for object and file viewers is somewhat different than that for visualizers, so we will cover these topics separately. The first step in creating an object or file viewer is to specify the visible elements of the file or object. In many cases it is undesirable or impossible to display every detail of a file or an object. We must determine what portions of the data are most important and specify those portions to be the visible portions of the file or object.

The next step is to define a display format. In most cases, the display format will be dictated somewhat by the structure of the object or file. Text files should be displayed as text, and graphical objects should be displayed graphically. It is only in rare cases that we would deviate from the "natural" method of viewing a file. (As an example of such a case, we present the SGE Debug Viewer, which presents graphical objects in text form for debugging.)

The final design step is to define the transformations that will convert data from its internal form into visible objects on the screen. In many cases, this is the most demanding part of the design. The first two steps are relatively simple, because it will generally be obvious which portions of the object or file should be displayed, and the display format will generally also be obvious. The real work of creating the component is in designing and implementing the data transformations.

Visualizers differ from other viewers in two important ways. The first is in the source of the input data. Unlike object and file viewers, which accept data from the outside world, the data used by many visualizers is entirely self-contained. For example, a visualizer that shows the opening of a flower bud may display successive frames of data from an internal cache. It is also possible to go to the other extreme with data that streams in continuously over a long period of time. For example, a visualizer might be used to display a graph of temperature data for the latest 24-hour period. The data for such a component will probably be presented as periodic observations of the current temperature.

The second way that visualizers differ from other viewers is in how they determine the visual format of the data. Consider the example of the temperature graph. We could present a jagged line representing the temperature fluctuations, or we could represent different temperatures as different colors and present the observations as a multicolored strip.

The transformation routines used to convert data from internal form to a visible display are the final and most complex step. Most effective visualizers use some form of animation, which must be managed very carefully. Visualization is a science in its own right and is, for the most part, beyond the scope of this book. We will present a simple example to illustrate the principles of visualizer design.

4. THE SGE OBJECT VIEWER

Our first example is an object viewer for the **CGraphicList** object. This component has one property, *ModelHandle*, and one method, *Redraw*. Figure 10-1 gives the property definition for the *ModelHandle* property while Figure 10-2 gives the method description for the *Redraw* method. The implementations of these are straightforward and will not be included here.

Property Design Table		
Name	**Type**	**Function**
ModelHandle	Long Integer Maximum = N/A Minimum = N/A Default = None	Provides the address of the modeling object cast to a long integer. NULL values are ignored. Assigning a value to this property causes a redraw of the control window.

Figure 10-1   *ModelHandle* for the CGraphicList Viewer

Method Description			
Name	Redraw		
Return Value	Void		
Description	Redraws the control window. If *ModelHandle* is null, the window is filled with a white rectangle.		
Arguments	**Name**	**Type**	**Description**
Void			

Figure 10-2   Method Description for the *Redraw* Method

```
void CSGEViewCtrl::OnDraw(
        CDC* pdc, const CRect& rcBounds, const CRect& rcInvalid)
{
    if (Model != NULL)
    {
        // we don't have a handle-radius, so make one up
        Model->Draw(pdc,rcBounds,rcInvalid,4);
    }
    else
    {
        // blank window if no model
        pdc->FillRect(rcBounds,
                CBrush::FromHandle((HBRUSH)GetStockObject(WHITE_BRUSH)));
    }
}
```

Figure 10-3 *OnDraw* Implementation for the CGraphicList Viewer

The component consists of little more than a drawing routine. Since virtually all of the drawing functionality is embedded in the **CGraphicList** object, this routine is almost trivial. The implementation of the *OnDraw* function is given in Figure 10-3. It is virtually identical to that of the Simple Graphical Editor.

The *ModelHandle* method is used to pass addresses of **CGraphicList** objects to the viewer. The value of this property is retained by the component. If other components change the model, the *Redraw* method must be called to redraw the component window. Alternatively, a new value can be assigned to the *ModelHandle* property. This does not cause the current model to be deleted.

5. THE SGE DEBUG VIEWER

Our next example is a component that is used only for debugging purposes. It is an object viewer that takes a **CGraphicList** object and displays its contents in human readable form. It is intended to be used for debugging applications that modify the **CGraphicList** object. Adding this component to a debugging program for such a component allows the programmer to monitor the contents of a **CGraphicList** object owned by another component.

This component has much in common with the file handler component described in Chapter 9. It requires each object in the **CGraphicList** model to provide its own debugging information. The **CGraphicList** object will use this facility to organize information about its subobjects. The **CGraphicList** object will accumulate this information into a single string, add information about itself, and return the entire string as the debugging information for the model. To implement this facility, each class in the **CGraphicList** model will have a function named *GetDebugInfo* that will be used to provide a human-readable dump of the corresponding objects' contents. There are many classes in the **CGraphicList** model, and the *GetDebugInfo* functions are quite similar to one another. For that reason, we will provide the implementations of only a few of these functions.

```
CString CGraphicList::GetDebugInfo()
{
    // Dump the entire model for debugging purposes
    CString rv;
    CString rv2;
    // Dump the main modeling object
    rv.Format("%8.8x GRAPHICLIST Dirty=%d,Count=%d,Head=%8.8x,\
                    Tail=%8.8x,SelCount=%d,Selection=%8.8x\r\n",
                    this,Dirty,Count,Head,Tail,SelCount,Selection);
    // Dump all graphical objects
    rv += "\r\n---Graphical Objects---\r\n";
    CGraphicObject * Temp;
    for (Temp = Head ; Temp != NULL ; Temp=Temp->Next)
    {
        rv2 = Temp->GetDebugInfo();
        rv += rv2;
    }
    // Dump the selection list
    rv += "\r\n---Selection List--—\r\n";
    CSelectItem * Stemp;
    for (STemp = Selection ; STemp != NULL ; STemp = STemp->Next)
    {
        rv2 = STemp->GetDebugInfo();
        rv += rv2;
    }
    // Dump the UNDO/REDO lists
    rv += "\r\n-—Undo/Redo Lists-—\r\n";
    rv2 = UndoList.GetDebugInfo();
    rv += rv2;
    rv += "\r\n";
    rv2 = RedoList.GetDebugInfo();
    rv += rv2;
    return rv;
}
```

Figure 10-4   The **CGraphicList** *GetDebugInfo* Function

Figure 10-4 gives the implementation of the **CGraphicList** *GetDebugInfo* function. This function has the responsibility for collecting information about all subobjects in the model.

The *GetModelInfo* function of the **CGraphicList** model collects information about the graphical objects, the selection, and the undo/redo lists. The debug information for each object shows the address of the object in hex to allow visual coordination between the objects and the dump of other objects that contain pointers. Figure 10-5 shows the debug information for the **CSelectItem** class. The dump of the *Item* address can be coordinated with the addresses of the graphical objects shown in the dump.

```
CString CSelectItem::GetDebugInfo()
{
    CString rv;
    rv.Format("%8.8x Select Item: Item=%8.8x, Next=%8.8x\r\n",
              this,Item,Next);
    return rv;
}
```

Figure 10-5 The CSelectItem *GetDebugInfo* Function

```
CString CUndoList::GetDebugInfo()
{
    // Dump object for debugging
    CString rv;
    CString rv2;
    rv.Format("%8.8x UNDOLIST ",this); // \r\n intentionally omitted.
    // Get the rest of the information from the base class
    rv2 = CUndoListBase::GetDebugInfo();
    return rv+rv2;
}
```

Figure 10-6 The CUndoList GetDebugInfo Function

Figure 10-6 shows the implementation of the **CUndoList** *GetDebugInfo* function. This function calls the base class function for most of its information. This function is provided to permit **CUndoList** objects to be distinguished from **CRedoList** objects. The base-class function is shown in Figure 10-7. This function also dumps the contents of the **CUndoCommand** chain, by calling the *GetDebugInfo* function of each object in the chain. This object dumps the contents of its **CUndo** object chain by calling the *GetDebugInfo* function of every object in its **CUndo** object chain. Figure 10-8 gives an example of a *GetDebugInfo* function for an **CUndo** object.

Like the **CGraphicList** viewer, the debug viewer has one method and one property. The names and descriptions of these are identical to those of Figures 10-1 and 10-2, so we will omit their descriptions and implementations. Most of the work done in the debug viewer is encapsulated in the **CGraphicList** *GetDebugInfo* function. For the implementation, we will subclass the standard Windows operating system text box control, which gives us the ability to display multiline text and to scroll through the text using horizontal and vertical scroll bars.

The first step in creating a subclassed control is done when creating the project. Figures 10-9 and 10-10 show the second page of the MFC ActiveX wizard. At the bottom of this page is a combo-box labeled *"Which window class, if any, should this control subclass?"* We have selected *"EDIT"* from the list of available controls that will make our control a special case of the *EDIT* control, which is also known as the *Text Box* control.

```
CString CUndoListBase::GetDebugInfo()
{
    // dump contents for debugging
    CString rv;
    CString rv2;
    // Meant to be concatenated to the end of an existing line
    rv.Format("Count=%d, Limit=%d, Head=%8.8x, Tail=%8.8x\r\n",
                ,Count,Limit,Head,Tail);
    // dump contents of command list
    for (CUndoCommand * Temp = Head ; Temp != NULL ; Temp=Temp->Next)
    {
        rv2 = Temp->GetDebugInfo();
        rv += rv2;
    }
    return rv;
}
```

Figure 10-7   The CUndoListBase GetDebugInfo Function

```
CString CUndoAdd::GetDebugInfo()
{
    // Dump information for debugging
    CString rv;
    CString rv2;
    rv.Format("    %8.8x UNDOADD Obj=%8.8x\r\n",this,Obj);
    rv2.Format("                Links: Next=%8.8x\r\n",Next);
    return rv+rv2;
}
```

Figure 10-8   The CUndoAdd GetDebugInfo Function

There is one important additional function that is added to your component when subclassing a Windows operating system control. That is the *PreCreateWindow* function. This function can be modified to change the properties of the control. When we subclass a Windows control, our component ends up being a special case of that control. When we set standard Windows operating system properties in the *PreCreateWindow* function, we are setting the properties of our own window. We wish our component to be a multiline text box and we wish it to have vertical and horizontal scroll bars. None of these properties are default, so we must set them in the *PreCreateWindow* function. Figure 10-11 shows how this is done.

Because our control is a subclassed text box, the standard text box drawing routine will eventually be used to draw the control window. The *OnDraw* routine of our component can add steps before and after the standard text box drawing routine is called. To invoke the standard drawing routine, the *DoSuperclassPaint* function must be called at some point in the *OnDraw* routine. In our case, we will simply make sure

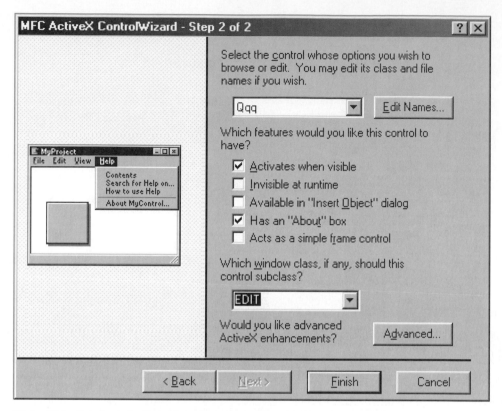

Figure 10-9   Subclassing a Control

that the text box contains the proper text before it is drawn. We will use the *GetDebugInfo* function of the **CGraphicList** class to obtain the text box contents, and we will insert this text into the text box using the *SendMessage* Function. If there is no model, we will delete all text from the text box using the same function. (See Chapter 3 for more discussion of the *SendMessage* function.) The design of the *OnDraw* function, shown in Figure 10-12, completes the design of the debug viewer.

6. THE TEXT FILE VIEWER

We will next give an example of a file viewer. To keep things simple, we will create a viewer for simple text files. This viewer will allow us to scroll through a text file of virtually any size, regardless of whether it fits completely in memory, but it will provide no editing capabilities. To permit very large files to be viewed, we will read in only that portion of the file that is currently visible in the control window. We will use the default system font to display the text and will not allow the user to change fonts. Each line in the text file will be displayed on a separate line of the display. We will not process special characters like **tab**.

The main problem that we must deal with is locating lines in the text file. Because such lines are of variable length, the position of a particular line can be determined

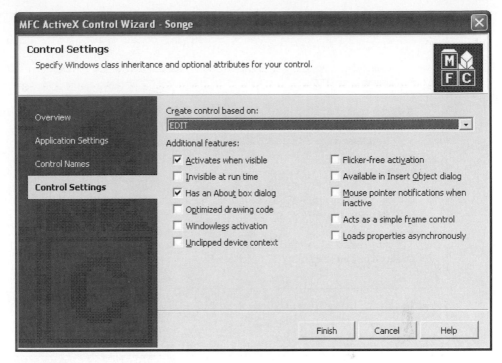

Figure 10-10   Subclassing in VS.NET

```
BOOL CSGEDebugCtrl::PreCreateWindow(CREATESTRUCT& cs)
{
    cs.lpszClass = _T("EDIT");
    // required additions to make EDIT control MULTILINE and to add
    // scroll bars. The other two lines are provided by the wizard.
    cs.style |= ES_MULTILINE | WS_HSCROLL | WS_VSCROLL;
    return COleControl::PreCreateWindow(cs);
}
```

Figure 10-11   The *PreCreateWindow* Function

only by reading all characters that precede it. Because the file is not read completely into memory, this would require an enormous amount of I/O when scrolling long distances through the file. To solve this problem, we will create a line indexing array. When a file is first opened, we will read the entire file and note the starting position and length of each line. We will accumulate this information into an array that will allow us instant access to any line in the file. (For exceptionally large files, we may want to keep less information than this, but that is a different component.)

The functionality of our line-list array will be encapsulated in a single class, **CLineList**, which is shown in Figure 10-13. Initially, data will be accumulated in a linked list, and then the linked list will be reorganized into an array.

```
void CSGEDebugCtrl::OnDraw(
        CDC* pdc, const CRect& rcBounds, const CRect& rcInvalid)
{
    // Remember we are a subclassed multi-line text box
    if (Model != NULL)
    {
        // dump the model into Txt, and feet Txt to the TEXT control
        CString Txt = Model->GetDebugInfo();
        SendMessage(WM_SETTEXT,0,(long)((LPCTSTR)Txt));
    }
    else
    {
        // If no model, blank the text control
        SendMessage(WM_SETTEXT,0,(long)(""));
    }
    // required function call for subclassed controls
    DoSuperclassPaint(pdc, rcBounds);
}
```

Figure 10-12   The **Debug Viewer *OnDraw*** Routine

```
class CLineList
{
public:
    CLineElement * Array;
    long Count;

    BOOL ArrayDone;
    CLineLink * Tail;
    CLineLink * Head;

    CLineList();
    virtual ~CLineList();

    void AddLine(long NewPos,long NewLen);
    void MakeArray(void);
    long GetCount(void);
    long GetLength(long LineNumber);
    long GetPosition(long LineNumber);
};
```

Figure 10-13   The CLineList Class

In Figure 10-13, the data items *Array* and *Count* are used to maintain the line-list array, while the data items *Head* and *Tail* are used for the initial accumulation of information. The *AddLine* function is used to accumulate data into the linked list, while the *MakeArray* function is used to reorganize the linked list into an array. Access to the array is given by the functions *GetCount*, *GetLength*, and *GetPosition*. The class

```
class CLineLink
{
public:
    CLineLink * Next;

    long Length;
    long Position;

    CLineLink();
    CLineLink(long NewPos, long NewLen);
    virtual ~CLineLink();
};
```

Figure 10-14   The CLineLink Class

CLineLink, shown in Figure 10-14, is used to create the linked list. The definition of this class is straightforward.

The line-list array is an array of **CLineElement** objects, the class definition of which is given in Figure 10-15. The definition of this class is reasonably straightforward, except for the overloaded assignment operator, which is used to simplify the creation of the array from a linked list of **CLineLink** objects.

Figure 10-16 shows how line information is accumulated into a linked list with the *AddLine* function. The *ArrayDone* variable of the **CLineList** class is used to determine whether an array has been built from the accumulated data. If it has, then accumulating new data is not allowed. The file must be read through completely when it is first opened. The *AddLine* function maintains the value of the *Count* data item.

Figure 10-17 shows how data is moved from the linked list to the array, using the *MakeArray* function. Making an array is illegal if there is already an array, or if no data has been accumulated. The linked list is destroyed as data is moved into the array.

The *GetPosition* and *GetLength* functions are given in Figure 10-18. These functions will return −1 if there is no array, or if the array bounds have been violated.

```
class CLineElement
{
public:
    long Length;
    long Position;

    CLineElement();
    virtual ~CLineElement();

    CLineElement & operator=(const CLineLink &x);
};
```

Figure 10-15   The CLineElement Class

```
void CLineList::AddLine(long NewPos, long NewLen)
{
    if (ArrayDone)
    {
        return;
    }
    CLineLink * Temp = new CLineLink(NewPos,NewLen);
    if (Head == NULL)
    {
        Head = Temp;
    }
    else
    {
        Tail->Next = Temp;
    }
    Tail = Temp;
    Count++;
}
```

Figure 10-16   The *AddLine* Function of the **CLineList** Class

```
void CLineList::MakeArray()
{
    if (ArrayDone)
    {
        return;
    }
    if (Count <= 0)
    {
        return;
    }
    Array = new CLineElement[Count];
    long i = 0;
    CLineLink * Temp;
    for (Temp = Head, *Temp2=NULL ; Temp != NULL ; Temp=Temp2,i++)
    {
        Temp2 = Temp->Next;
        Array[i] = *Temp;
        delete Temp;
    }
    Head = NULL;
    Tail = NULL;
    ArrayDone = TRUE;
}
```

Figure 10-17   The *MakeArray* Function

```
long CLineList::GetPosition(long LineNumber)
{
    if (!ArrayDone)
    {
        return -1;
    }
    if (LineNumber < 0)
    {
        return -1;
    }
    if (LineNumber >= Count)
    {
        return -1;
    }
    return Array[LineNumber].Position;
}
long CLineList::GetLength(long LineNumber)
{
    if (!ArrayDone)
    {
        return 0;
    }
    if (LineNumber < 0)
    {
        return 0;
    }
    if (LineNumber >= Count)
    {
        return 0;
    }
    return Array[LineNumber].Length;
}
```

Figure 10-18   *GetPosition* and *GetLength* Functions

Property Design Table		
Name	**Type**	**Function**
InputFile	String Default = Empty	Supplies the name of the text file to be viewed. A full path name is usually supplied. **Restrictions:** Run-Time Only

Figure 10-19   The *InputFile* Property

To allow the user to specify a file to be viewed, we provide a property called *InputFile*. Its property table is given in Figure 10-19. This property is not available at design-time. When a new value is assigned to *InputFile*, the existing file, if any, is closed and its line-list array is deleted. The *SetInputFile* function is used to create the new line-list array. The file is kept open while being viewed to prevent any other program from writing new data to the file and invalidating the line-list array. Figure 10-20 shows the implementation of the *SetInputFile* function.

The *SetInputFile* function first closes any existing file and deletes the line-list object for the file. It then opens the new file and creates a new line-list object. It reads the

```
void CTextViewerCtrl::SetInputFile(LPCTSTR lpszNewValue)
{
    m_inputFile = lpszNewValue; // Record file name
    if (FileOpen) // Close existing file, if any
    {
        CloseHandle(FileHandle);
        FileOpen = FALSE;
    }
    if (LL != NULL) // delete existing line list, if any
    {
        delete LL;
        LL = NULL;
    }
    LL = new CLineList; // create new line list
    FileHandle = CreateFile(m_inputFile,GENERIC_READ,FILE_SHARE_READ,
                  NULL,OPEN_EXISTING,FILE_ATTRIBUTE_NORMAL,NULL);
    if (FileHandle == INVALID_HANDLE_VALUE)
    {
        … // Report open error
    }
    else // file opened correctly
    {
        FileOpen = TRUE;
        char * Buffer = new char[10000]; // create I/O buffer
        long CharCount = 0;
        long Pos = 0;
        unsigned long BytesRead;
        // Read first chunk of file
        BOOL Success = ReadFile(FileHandle,Buffer,10000,&BytesRead,NULL);
        if (!Success)
        {
            … // report I/O Error
        }
        while (BytesRead > 0) // Process chunks until EOF
        {
            unsigned long i;
            char * tc;
            // examine each character
            for (i=0,tc=Buffer ; i<BytesRead ; i++,tc++)
            {
                CharCount++; // length of current line
                if (*tc == '\n') // If EOL found, record line pos & len
```

Figure 10-20 The *SetInputFile* Function

```
            {
                LL->AddLine(Pos,CharCount);
                Pos += CharCount;
                CharCount = 0;
            }
        }
        // get next chunk
        Success = ReadFile(FileHandle,Buffer,10000,&BytesRead,NULL);
        if (!Success)
        {
            … // Report I/O Error
        }
    }
    if (CharCount > 0) // process an unterminated line, if any
    {
        LL->AddLine(Pos,CharCount);
    }
    delete [] Buffer; // release I/O buffer
    LL->MakeArray();
}
// Set scrolling parameters
VMax = LL->GetCount()-1;
VPos = 0;
HPos = 0;
CWnd::SetScrollRange(SB_VERT,0,VMax);
CWnd::SetScrollPos(SB_HORZ,HPos);
CWnd::SetScrollPos(SB_VERT,VPos);
CWnd::Invalidate();
}
```

Figure 10-20   (*Continued*)

file in 10,000 byte chunks and processes each chunk looking for linefeed characters. Characters are examined one at a time and counted. When a linefeed is found, the position and length of the line is added to the line-list object. Once all data has been read, the file is left open to prevent other programs from changing it. If there is an unterminated line at the end of the file, the position and length of this line are recorded at this point. Finally, a new array is created by the line-list object, and scrolling parameters are set for both scroll bars.

The viewer component allows the user to scroll data up and down as well as to the right and left. This function is not performed automatically by the Windows operating system, but must be explicitly programmed into our component. The first thing we must do is add horizontal and vertical scroll bars to our component window. Figure 10-21 shows how this is done. (Use the first tab of the Class Wizard to add this function to a component.)

We now need to add functions to process the messages created by the scroll bars. The scroll bars do not control the window directly. Their only function is to send messages

```
BOOL CTextViewerCtrl::PreCreateWindow(CREATESTRUCT& cs)
{
    cs.style |= WS_HSCROLL | WS_VSCROLL;
    return COleControl::PreCreateWindow(cs);
}
```

Figure 10-21   Adding Scroll Bars to a Component Window

Message	Action
SB_BOTTOM	Set *VPos* to its maximum value.
SB_TOP	Set *VPos* to zero.
SB_LINEDOWN	If *VPos* is less than the maximum, increment its value by one.
SB_LINEUP	If *VPos* is greater than zero, decrement its value by one.
SB_PAGEDOWN	Increment *VPos* by the number of lines in the window minus one. If *VPos* is greater than the maximum, set it to the maximum.
SB_PAGEUP	Decrement *VPos* by the number of lines in the window minus one. If *VPos* is less than zero, set it to zero.

Figure 10-22   Vertical Scrolling Actions

to the component. The handling of these messages is entirely up to the component. We add two variables, *VPos* and *HPos*, to the support class to keep track of the current scrolling position. When we receive a message from one of the scroll bars, we will change the value of either *VPos* or *HPos* and redraw the window. The drawing routine will use the *VPos* and *HPos* variables to position text within the window and to determine which lines to read from the file. Messages from the vertical scroll bar are handled by the function *OnVScroll*. Rather than providing code for this function, we will list the scroll-bar messages processed by the routine and the action taken for each. This information is presented in Figure 10-22. The horizontal scrolling actions are virtually identical to the vertical ones.

The *OnDraw* routine is given in Figure 10-23. This function first determines the pixel height and width of the window by calling the operating system function *GetClientRect*. Next, the *GetTextExtent* function is used on a sample string to determine the height of a line and the average width of a character in the current font. This information is used to compute the height of the window in lines and the width of the window in average-width characters. This information is saved in the support class variables *VPage* and *HPage*, which will be used by the horizontal and vertical scrolling routines. (The first drawing of the window will precede the first use of the scroll bars.)

Vertical scrolling is accomplished by using the *VPos* variable as the starting index for reading lines from the current file. A sufficient number of lines will be read to fill the display. Each line is displayed as it is read. Horizontal scrolling is done using the standard operating system function *SetWindowOrg*. Each line will be drawn at *x*-position

```
void CTextViewerCtrl::OnDraw(
        CDC* pdc, const CRect& rcBounds, const CRect& rcInvalid)
{
   pdc->FillRect(rcBounds,
            CBrush::FromHandle((HBRUSH)GetStockObject(WHITE_BRUSH)));
   if (FileOpen)
   {
      RECT DispRect;
      CWnd::GetClientRect(&DispRect);
      long DispHeight = DispRect.right - DispRect.left;
      long DispWidth = DispRect.bottom - DispRect.top;
      CSize TextSize =
            pdc->GetTextExtent("ABCDEFGHIJKLMNOPQRSTUVWXYZ"
                                 "abcdefghijklmnopqrstuvwxyz");
      long LineHeight = TextSize.cy;
      long CharWid = TextSize.cx / 52;
      DispLines = DispHeight / LineHeight;
      DispChars = DispWidth / CharWid;
      VPage = DispLines - 1;
      HPage = DispChars - 1;
      pdc->SaveDC();
      long OldHMax = HMax;
      HMax = 0;
      pdc->SetWindowOrg(HPos*DispChars,0);
      for (long i=0,DrawPos=0 ; i<DispLines && i+VPos < LL->GetCount();
                i++,DrawPos+=LineHeight)
      {
         long Pos = LL->GetPosition(i+VPos);
         unsigned long Len = LL->GetLength(i+VPos);
         if ((unsigned long)HMax < Len-1)
         {
             HMax = Len-1;
         }
         if (Pos != -1 && Len != 0)
         {
            unsigned long BytesRead;
            char * Buffer = new char [Len+1];
            SetFilePointer(FileHandle,Pos,NULL,FILE_BEGIN);
            BOOL rv = ReadFile(FileHandle,Buffer,Len,&BytesRead,NULL);
            if (rv && BytesRead == Len)
            {
                Buffer[Len] = '\0';
                pdc->TextOut(0,DrawPos,Buffer);
            }
            delete Buffer;
         }
```

Figure 10-23   The Text Viewer *OnDraw* Function

```
        }
        if (HMax != OldHMax)
        {
            CWnd::SetScrollRange(SB_HORZ,0,HMax);
        }
        pdc->RestoreDC(0);
    }
}
```

Figure 10-23   (*Continued*)

zero. By setting the window origin to a value larger than zero, different parts of the line will be clipped. The horizontal page size used by the scroll bar will be set by the *OnDraw* routine after the length of each line has been determined.

The complete code for the text file visualizer is available at the Web site.

7. THE QUICKSORT VISUALIZER

The quicksort visualizer is based on a generic class that can be used to produce a visual animation of virtually any sorting algorithm. The control displays the list of items to be sorted as an array of vertical bars, with the height of each bar representing the value of the item in the list. Figure 10-24 shows the visualization of an unsorted list. When the

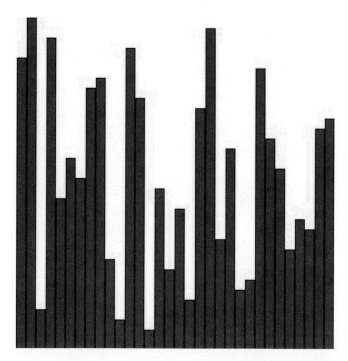

Figure 10-24   An Unsorted List

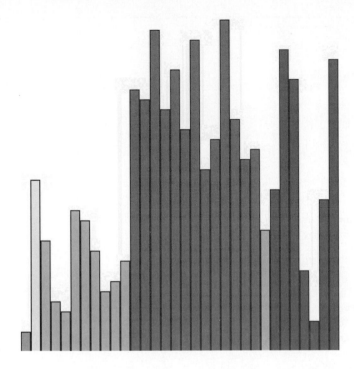

Figure 10-25   Quicksort in Progress

list is sorted, the bars will be arranged in a stair-step fashion. During the course of the sort, the bars will be moved, and their color will be changed to illustrate the role that they are playing in the sort algorithm.

Figure 10-25 shows the sort operation in progress, with the various shades of gray illustrating the progress of the operation. The Web site has a more colorful display.

The quicksort visualizer has several methods and properties that control the animation. The user can select the number of bars and set the speed of the animation. The *Sort* method is used to begin the animation. The user can randomize the list to repeat the animation or presort the list to demonstrate the difference in speed between a presorted list and a randomized list.

Internally, the animation is built using a "standard" sort animation object called **CSortAnimator**. This object has been used to create many different sort animations. It controls the drawing of the list and provides functions for changing bar colors and for moving bars around in the list. Figure 10-26 gives the definition of this class. The general methodology for using this class is to first take a sort algorithm, "right out of the book," and then modify it slightly to conform to the requirements of the class. In many respects, the objects of this class act like arrays of integers, but there are some differences. Figure 10-27 shows a textbook version of an iterative quicksort algorithm with the required changes.

Although the *Sort* function in Figure 10-27 provides a complete animation of the Quicksort algorithm, it will happen much too fast for the user to see. Furthermore, the color changes that indicate the status of each bar have not yet been inserted. The color of each bar is limited to a fixed set of colors given by the **ColorType** enumeration of

```
class CSortAnimator
{
public:
    // Bar Dimensions in pixels
    // BarHeight[I] = BarNumber[I]*BarIncrement+MinBarHeight
    long BarIncrement;
    long MinBarHeight;
    long BarWidth;
    // Bar array
    long Size;
    long * Values;
    ColorType * Colors;
    long GetSize(void);
    long SetBarCount(long Bars);
    long SetBarColor(long BarNumber,ColorType Color);
    // Temp Array
    long TempCount;
    long * Temps;
    ColorType * TempColors;
    long GetTempCount(void);
    long SetTempCount(long NewTempCount);
    long SetTempColor(long TempID,ColorType Color);
    // Sorting
    long TempSize(long TempID); // bar size in temp storage
    long BarSize(long Bar); // retrieve bar size
    long operator[](long x); // retrieve bar size
    long MoveTempToBar(long TempID, long Bar); // temp storage mgmt
    long MoveBarToTemp(long Bar,long TempID); // temp storage mgmt
    long SwapBars(long BarA,long BarB);
    // Drawing
    long Draw(CDC *Mydc, const CRect& rcBounds, const CRect& rcInvalid);
    // Initialization
    long Randomize(void);
    long Initialize(void);
    // Color Decoding
    COLORREF GetColor(ColorType Color); // internal utility function
    // creation and Destruction
    CSortAnimator();
    virtual ~CSortAnimator();
};
```

Figure 10-26 The CSortAnimator Class

Figure 10-28. The enumeration is used to simplify the programming of the sort algorithm and to provide a *None* color to indicate that a bar is currently invisible. This color
enumeration is used with the *SetBarColor* function to further enhance the animation.

To slow down the animation so that the user can see it, the component provides a
Sync function that will redraw the component window and then wait for a user-specified

```
void CQuickSortCtrl::Sort()
{
    long SFirst[32],SLast[32],SSize=0; // private stack
    long n = L.GetSize();
    SFirst[SSize] = 0; // push entire list on stack
    SLast[SSize] = n-1;
    SSize++;
    while (SSize>0) // while stack not empty
    {
        SSize--; // pop a sub-list off the stack
        long First = SFirst[SSize];
        long Last = SLast[SSize];
        while (First < Last) // split the sublist
        {
            long SP,i; // SP is the split point
            for (i=First+1,SP=First ; i<=Last ; i++)
            {
                // L is the CSortAnimator Object
                if (L[i] < L[First]) // L[First] is the pivot point
                {
                    SP++;
                    L.SwapBars(i,SP);
                }
            }
            L.SwapBars(First,SP);
            // Stack Shortest, process longest immediately
            // Empty lists must be stacked
            if ((Last-SP) > (SP-First))
            {
                SFirst[SSize] = SP+1;
                SLast[SSize] = Last;
                SSize++;
                Last = SP-1;
            }
            else
            {
                SFirst[SSize] = First;
                SLast[SSize] = SP-1;
                SSize++;
                First = SP+1;
            }
        }
    }
}
```

Figure 10-27   Adapted Quicksort

```
enum ColorType
{
    None = 0,
    Red = 1,
    Green = 2,
    Blue = 3,
    Yellow = 4,
    Cyan = 5,
    Magenta = 6,
    Black = 7,
    White = 8
};
```

Figure 10-28   The ColorType Enumeration

number of milliseconds. Although this function is not part of the **CSortAnimator** class, it is a standard part of all sort animations created using the class. This is done by embedding the Sync function and the **CSortAnimator** class in a project template, and using the template to generate several animations. Because the *Sync* function simply calls a series of operating system functions, we will not present the code for it. For interested readers, the complete code can be found on the Web site.

The completely instrumented version of the quicksort algorithm is given in Figure 10-29.

```
void CQuickSortCtrl::Sort()
{
    long SFirst[32],SLast[32],SSize=0;
    long n = L.GetSize();
    SFirst[SSize] = 0;
    SLast[SSize] = n-1;
    SSize++;
    for (long x = 0 ; x<n ; x++)
    {
        L.SetBarColor(x,White);
    }
    Sync();
    while (SSize>0)
    {
        SSize--;
        long First = SFirst[SSize];
        long Last = SLast[SSize];
        while (First < Last)
        {
```

Figure 10-29   The Fully Instrumented Quicksort Algorithm

```
    for (x=First ; x<=Last ; x++)
    {
        L.SetBarColor(x,Red);
    }
    Sync();
    long SP,i;
    L.SetBarColor(First,Yellow);
    Sync();
    for (i=First+1,SP=First ; i<=Last ; i++)
    {
        if (L[i] < L[First])
        {
            L.SetBarColor(i,Cyan);
            Sync();
            SP++;
            L.SwapBars(i,SP);
            Sync();
        }
        else
        {
            L.SetBarColor(i,Magenta);
            Sync();
        }
    }
    L.SwapBars(First,SP);
    Sync();
    L.SetBarColor(SP,Green);
    Sync();
    if ((Last-SP) > (SP-First))
    {
        for (x=SP+1 ; x<=Last ; x++)
        {
            L.SetBarColor(x,White);
        }
        Sync();
        SFirst[SSize] = SP+1;
        SLast[SSize] = Last;
        SSize++;
        Last = SP-1;
    }
    else
    {
            for (x=First ; x<=SP-1 ; x++)
            {
                L.SetBarColor(x,White);
            }
```

Figure 10-29 (*Continued*)

```
              Sync();
              SFirst[SSize] = First;
              SLast[SSize] = SP-1;
              SSize++;
              First = SP+1;
         }
     }
     if (First == Last)
     {
         L.SetBarColor(First,Green);
         Sync();
     }
   }
   Sync();
}
```

Figure 10-29   (*Continued*)

Because the **CSortAnimator** class is used for many different sort animations, it contains features that are not used by the quicksort animation. There is a facility for demonstrating the use of temporary variables to hold list elements. (This is especially useful for Merge Sort, and Radix Sort.) The bars representing temporary variables are drawn horizontally across the top of the control window. There is also a facility for pre-sorting a list and another for randomizing it.

The implementation of most of the **CSortAnimator** functions should be obvious. To illustrate the general methodology, we present the implementation of two of these functions in Figure 10-30.

For the most part, the properties and methods of the component simply provide access to the functions of the internal **CSortAnimator** object. The exception is the *Interval* property, which is used to set the delay used by the *Sync* function. The property design table is given in Figure 10-31, and the method descriptions are given in Figure 10-32.

8. A REVIEW OF THE METHODOLOGY

The design methodology for displays depends on what kind of display is being created. If an object viewer is being designed as a complement for a graphical editor, we can simply make a copy of the editor and disable the editing features. This is essentially what was done for the SGE object viewer.

An object viewer that is not associated with an interactive editor must be more carefully designed. Such displays are quite similar to file viewers, the only difference being in the source of the input data. The first step in the design of either type of viewer is to specify the visible elements of the component. Once the visible elements have been specified, along with any required scaling and scrolling features, we must design the transformation routines that will convert the object or file into the visible display. In some cases, this is nothing more than a simple display of the data contained in the

```
long CSortAnimator::SwapBars(long BarA, long BarB)
{
    if (BarA >= 0 && BarA < Size && BarB >= 0 && BarB < Size)
    {
        long Temp = Values[BarA]; // Swap Bars and colors
        Values[BarA] = Values[BarB];
        Values[BarB] = Temp;
        ColorType CTemp = Colors[BarA];
        Colors[BarA] = Colors[BarB];
        Colors[BarB] = CTemp;
        return 1;
    }
    else
    {
        return 0; // at least one index is illegal
    }
}
```

```
long CSortAnimator::operator[](long x)
{
    if (x >= 0 && x < Size) // return bar size if index legal
    {
        return Values[x];
    }
    else
    {
        return 0;
    }
}
```

Figure 10-30   Two CSortAnimator Functions

object or file. In most cases, however, some computation will be required to convert the source data into a form suitable for display. In fact, the major portion of the design of a Display consists of transforming input data into visible form.

The design of a visualizer is similar to that of an object or file viewer, but there are some additional aspects that must be considered. The design of the visible elements is generally quite complicated and is for the most part beyond the scope of this book. The transformation of data into visible form is extremely complicated, in many cases representing a major development effort. (This is true even for the simple example presented above.) The input data to a visualizer is likely to be handled somewhat differently than it would be for object or file viewers. In some cases, the data will be entirely contained within the component. In other cases, the data will be presented piecemeal as it becomes available. (Imagine a historical display of temperature data.) In other cases, the data may be streamed, with the component firing events to request new data. The design of a visualizer may involve each of these aspects.

The first step in designing a visualizer is to determine the source, type, and input style of the data being visualized. The next step is to select (or design) the visualization

Property Design Table		
Name	**Type**	**Function**
Interval	Long Integer Maximum = 10000 Minimum = 0 Default = 500	Delay in milliseconds for each discrete operation performed by the animation.
BarIncrement	Long Integer Maximum = None Minimum = None Default = 20	The difference in height between two successive bars when the list is sorted. Units are in pixels.
BarWidth	Long Integer Maximum = None Minimum = None Default = 20	The width in pixels of each bar.
MinBarHeight	Long Integer Maximum = None Minimum = None Default = 20	The height in pixels of the shortest bar.
BarCount	Long Integer Maximum = None Minimum = None Default = 32	The number of bars in the list. Setting this property causes the list to be presorted.

Figure 10-31   Property Design Table for the Quicksort Animator

Method Description			
Name	Initialize		
Return Value	Void		
Description	Presorts the list and redraws the window. Bar color is set to red for each bar. The control window is redrawn.		
Arguments	**Name**	**Type**	**Description**
Void			

Method Description			
Name	Randomize		
Return Value	Void		
Description	Randomizes the list, and sets the bar color of each bar to red. The control window is redrawn.		
Arguments	**Name**	**Type**	**Description**
Void			

Figure 10-32   Method Descriptions for the Quicksort Animator

Method Description			
Name	Sort		
Return Value	Void		
Description	Starts the sort animation process. This method is not interruptible, and will not return until the animation is complete.		
Arguments	Name	Type	Description
Void			

Figure 10-32 (*Continued*)

method used to represent the data. The final and most complicated step is to design the routines that transform the input data into the visible display. In some cases, the visualizer will perform some sort of simulation based on the input data. In such cases, it is necessary to design the timing behavior of the component. We must determine how often the view will be updated and how the information will be presented. Will smooth animations be provided, or just successive views of the data? It is also necessary to determine what transformations will be performed on the input data for each successive update of the display. These questions can be quite complicated and are beyond the scope of this book.

9. CONCLUSION

Display components are extremely useful for many different applications. There are three broad categories of Displays: (1) file viewers, (2) object viewers, and (3) visualizers. File and object viewers are designed in much the same way. If an editor exists for the file or object, then it can be used as the basis for a viewer; otherwise the transformation of data into visible form is the major part of the design of the viewer. Visualizers are usually more complicated than viewers. They can be used for a number of purposes. In fact, the visualization of data is an important field in its own right. The visualizer component is an important way to package a visualization algorithm for public use. We should expect to see new and better visualizer components appearing in the future.

EXERCISES

1. Create a visualizer (or a pair of visualizers) that will demonstrate the difference between linear search and binary search.
2. Create a visualizer that will demonstrate how binary fan-in works. (Binary fan-in is a parallel algorithm for adding up a list of numbers.)
3. Create a viewer for INI files (see Chapter 17 for the format). Display only one section at a time, with the title at the top.
4. Create a viewer for BMP files. See the Visual C++ help menu for the format of these files.

Chapter 11

Accessors

1. PREREQUISITES AND OBJECTIVES

Before starting this chapter, you should have

1. A knowledge of programming in C++.
2. A knowledge of component interface design.

After completing this chapter, you will have

1. A knowledge of the Accessor-Component design methodology.

2. INTRODUCTION

The accessor component gives programmatic access to an object that is either inaccessible or accessible only through great difficulty in the base language. An example of such an object is an HTML document. Even though such a document is nothing more than a text file, it has a highly complex structure. It is possible to parse an HTML file in virtually any language, but it is a daunting task. There are Accessor components that permit one to download an HTML page and analyze its structure automatically. One can enumerate tags, links, and sections and perform other complex operations. These things can also be done through brute-force programming, but it is neither an easy nor a pleasant task to do so.

Another type of accessor is one that is designed to give access to a semipersistent object that has been created by another component. Such an object may or may not be accessible in the base language. Even if the object is accessible, the Accessor can provide additional functions that simplify certain types of access.

In this chapter we will present two examples of accessor components: an object Accessor and a file accessor. Object Accessor functions are reasonably straightforward, and are often incorporated into another component, such as an editor or a viewer.

3. THE METHODOLOGY

The two main parts of an Accessor are data elements and enumerators. Individual data items such as integers, floating-point numbers, and strings are presented through a set of data access properties. An accessor for an object should have a property for each simple data member of the object. For data elements that are arrays of simple objects, the preferred method is to use an array property, but it is also possible to use an enumerator. Subobjects are normally associated with an enumerator, but if there is a single instance of the subobject that is always present, then simple properties can be used as though the data elements of the subobject belonged to the parent object.

Enumerators must be used for arrays and linked lists of subobjects. There are two styles of enumerators: the parallel-array enumerator and the first/next enumerator. In the parallel-array enumerator, the data members of an object are treated like a set of parallel arrays, one array for each data member. The component should be supplied with a count property that gives the size of the parallel arrays. This sort of access gives maximum accessibility but can be extremely slow for linked lists.

The first/next enumerator is implemented with two methods: one that initializes the enumeration to the first element of the list or array and one that advances the enumeration to the next element. A set of simple (nonarray) properties are used to access the data members of the current object. The content of these properties changes when the first/next functions are executed. Some mechanism must be provided for signaling the end of the enumeration. The best way is to provide the *First/Next* functions with a return code that indicates whether all items have been exhausted. Other methods are to provide a *Done* property or an *EndOfList* event. The sections that follow illustrate this methodology with two examples, the SGE Accessor and a text file Accessor.

4. THE SGE ACCESSOR

In our first example, we will present an accessor for the SGE internal object. We will limit our accessor functions to the list of graphical objects, but we could easily expand the functionality of this component to include the selection and the undo/redo lists. Before proceeding with the development of the accessor component, it is necessary to add some additional functionality to the **CGraphicList** model. Because the accessor must provide the type and parameters of each graphical object, it is necessary to enhance each object with functions to provide this information. Furthermore, it is necessary to enhance the **CGraphicList** with functions that give external access to the list of graphical objects. Due to the simplicity of our requirements, the only new function required by the **CGraphicList** object is *GetHead*, which will return the first element in the list of graphical objects. Each of the classes **CGraphicObject, CCircle**, and **CRectangle** must have three new virtual functions: (1) *GetType*, (2) *GetParms*, and (3) *GetParmCount*. Rather than return parameters by name, each object will create an array of long integers and place all of its parameters into the list. This is done to avoid overcomplicating the object structure and the accessor component interface. The **CGraphicObject** functions are pure virtual. For **CCircle** and **CRectangle**, the

```
long * CRectangle::GetParms()
{
    // The Accessor provides lists of parameters for each object
    // It does not name them individually
    long * rv = new long[4];
    rv[0] = Left;
    rv[1] = Top;
    rv[2] = Width;
    rv[3] = Height;
    return rv;
}
```

Figure 11-1   The **CRectangle** *GetParms* Function

GetParmCount and *GetType* functions return constants that are appropriate for the object. The *GetParms* function is slightly more complicated. Figure 11-1 illustrates this function for **CRectangle**; that of **CCircle** is similar.

It would have been possible to include line and fill colors in the list of parameters created by the *GetParms* routine, but since these are properties of all objects, it is more straightforward to provide explicit accessor properties for them.

The design of the SGE accessor follows a pattern that is similar for all accessors. A set of methods is provided to iterate through a list of objects, and a set of properties is provided to access the object members. Because we do not wish to provide editing capabilities in the accessor, all properties are read-only. It is a common practice to combine accessor functionality with that of a background editor to provide both access and editing capability. Figure 11-2 gives the description of the SGE accessor methods.

The methods described in this figure are typical of those used to traverse a linked list of objects. The *FirstObject* function starts the iteration while the *NextObject* continues the iteration. Iterator methods generally occur in pairs in this fashion. The iterator variable is contained in the component itself. Other function pairs can be used to provide other types of access. For example, a pair of reverse-order functions or functions for accessing only circles can be provided. In some cases a single *NextObject* method can be provided, with the *FirstObject* method determining the subsequent operation of the *NextObject* function. This technique produces fewer programming errors, but permits only one iteration to be performed at a time. The *FirstObject* function is given in Figure 11-3. Figure 11-4 shows the implementation of the *NextObject* method.

Figure 11-5 gives the property design table for the SGE accessor component. Since the design of these properties is straightforward, we will not discuss them individually. The properties give us the number of objects and of parameters for each object, the values of the parameters, and individual access to the global properties of each object. Default values are returned if there is no current model or no current object.

The implementations for the properties listed in Figure 11-5 are straightforward. The only unusual feature is the *Parm* property, which is an array of integers. When the *Parm* property was declared, it had a single parameter named *ParmNumber*. The implementation of the property uses this parameter to look up the property value in the property array. Figure 11-6 shows the implementation of the *GetParm* function for the

Method Description			
Name	FirstObject		
Return Value	Long Integer		
Description	Begins the iteration process with the first element of the list of graphical objects. If the list is empty, this function returns 0; otherwise it returns 1. If this function returns zero, then the accessor properties have undefined values; otherwise they return the properties of the first object in the list.		
Arguments	Name	Type	Description
Void			

Method Description			
Name	NextObject		
Return Value	Long Integer		
Description	Begins the iteration process with the first element of the list of graphical objects. If there is no next object, this function returns 0; otherwise it returns 1. If this function returns zero, then the accessor properties have undefined values; otherwise they return the properties of the first object in the list. There are several conditions under which there is no next object: no internal object model has been supplied, the *FirstObject* function has never been called, there is no current object, and there is a current object but it is the last object in the list.		
Arguments	Name	Type	Description
Void			

Figure 11-2   The *FirstObject* and *NextObject* Method Descriptions

```
long CSGEAccessorCtrl::FirstObject()
{
   // returns zero if end of list found, one otherwise
   if (Model == NULL)
   {
      CurrentObject = NULL;
      // End of list found
      return 0;
   }
   CurrentObject = Model->GetHead();
   if (CurrentObject == NULL)
   {
      // List is Empty
      return 0;
   }
   else
   {
```

Figure 11-3   The *FirstObject* Method Implementation

```
        if (Parms != NULL)
        {
            delete [] Parms; // clean up any previous access
        }
        // Get object parameters, parm count, and type
        ParmCount = CurrentObject->GetParmCount();
        Parms = CurrentObject->GetParms();
        Type = CurrentObject->GetType();
        // object is usable
        return 1;
    }
}
```

Figure 11-3   (*Continued*)

```
long CSGEAccessorCtrl::NextObject()
{
    if (Model == NULL || CurrentObject == NULL)
    {
        return 0;
    }
    // go to next object in list
    CurrentObject = CurrentObject->Next;
    if (CurrentObject == NULL)
    {
        // clean up if end of list is found
        if (Parms != NULL)
        {
            delete [] Parms;
            Parms = NULL;
        }
        ParmCount = 0;
        Type = 0;
        // end of list found
        return 0;
    }
    else
    {
        // extract object type, parm count and parameters
        ParmCount = CurrentObject->GetParmCount();
        Parms = CurrentObject->GetParms();
        Type = CurrentObject->GetType();
        // object is usable
        return 1;
    }
}
```

Figure 11-4   The *NextObject* Implementation

Property Design Table		
Name	**Type**	**Function**
ModelHandle	Long Integer Maximum=N/A Minimum=N/A Default=0	Provides the address of the modeling object cast to a long integer. NULL values are ignored. **Restrictions:** Run-Time Only
ItemCount	Long Integer Maximum=N/A Minimum=0 Default=0	A count of the number of graphic objects in the current model; use zero if there is no model. **Restrictions:** Read-Only
Type	Long Integer Maximum=2 Minimum=0 Default=0	A numeric value indicating the type of the current object. 0=No current object 1=Rectangle 2=Circle **Restrictions:** Read-Only
Parm	Long Integer Array Maximum=N/A Minimum=N/A Default=NONE	An array of properties for the current object. If there is no model or no current object, then this array has zero size. Size is given by the *ParmCount* property. **Restrictions:** Read-Only
ParmCount	Long Integer Maximum=N/A Minimum=0 Default=0	The number of elements in the *Parm* array; use zero if there is no model or no current object. **Restrictions:** Read-Only
ObjectHandle	Long Integer Maximum=N/A Minimum=N/A Default=0	The address of the current object cast to a long integer; use NULL if there is no current object or no model. **Restrictions:** Read-Only
FillColor	Color Default=Black	The *FillColor* of the current object; use black if there is no current object or no model. **Restrictions:** Read-Only
LineColor	Color Default=Black	The *LineColor* of the current object; use black if there is no current object or no model. **Restrictions:** Read-Only
Selected	Boolean Default=FALSE	Returns **TRUE** if there is a model, a current object, and the object is selected. Returns **FALSE** otherwise. **Restrictions:** Read-Only

Figure 11-5   Properties of the SGE Accessor

```
// read-only property array
long CSGEAccessorCtrl::GetParm(long ParmNumber)
{
    // property array must exist, and ParmNumber must be legal
    if (Parms != NULL && ParmNumber > -1 && ParmNumber < ParmCount)
    {
        return Parms[ParmNumber];
    }
```

Figure 11-6   The *GetParm* and *GetSelected* Property Implementations

```
    return 0;
}
// read-only property
BOOL CSGEAccessorCtrl::GetSelected()
{
    if (CurrentObject != NULL)
    {
        // extraction not required: part of all graphic objects
        return CurrentObject->Selected;
    }
    return FALSE;
}
```

Figure 11-6   (*Continued*)

property array and the implementation of the *GetSelected* function for the *Selected* property for contrast.

5. A TEXT FILE ACCESSOR

The text file Accessor component will allow a text file to be treated as an array of lines. The component has three properties: one to supply the file name, one to give the number of lines in the file, and one that will act as the array of lines. The property design table is given in Figure 11-7.

For the implementation of the text file Accessor, we will make use of the **CLineList** class developed in Chapter 10 for the text file viewer. When a new file name is supplied by assigning a value to the *InputFile* property, the file is opened, it is completely read, and an array is created that gives the starting position and length for each line in the file. These actions are identical to those taken for the text file viewer. (See Chapter 10 for the details.)

Property Design Table		
Name	**Type**	**Function**
InputFile	String Default=Empty	Provides the name of the text file to be indexed. **Restrictions:** Run-Time Only
LineCount	Long Integer Maximum=N/A Minimum=0 Default=0	Counts number of lines in the current file; zero if there is no file. **Restrictions:** Read-Only
Line	String Array Default=Empty Str.	Functions as an array of lines for the current file. If there is no current file, then this array has zero size. Size is given by the *LineCount* property. **Restrictions:** Read-Only

Figure 11-7   The Text File Accessor Property Design Table

```
Private Sub Command1_Click()
    Dim S1 As String, S2 As String, S3 As String
    Dim LineCount As Integer
    File1.InputFile = "tarzn10.txt"
    LineCount = File1.LineCount
    S1 = File1.Line(35)
    S2 = File1.Line(457)
    S3 = File1.Line(228)
    ...
End Sub
```

Figure 11-8   Text File Accessor Usage

When the property *Line* is accessed, the appropriate line is read from the file, using the data accumulated when the value was initially assigned to the *InputFile* property. An example of the usage of this component is given in Figure 11-8. This Visual Basic subroutine opens a text file, retrieves the total number of lines in the file, and then retrieves the text of three selected lines.

6. A REVIEW OF THE METHODOLOGY

The preceding sections have illustrated the design methodology for accessor components. The methodology differs, depending on whether you are designing an object accessor or a file accessor. For an object accessor, it is necessary to start with a complete description of the object to be accessed. The first step is to separate the fixed parts of the object from the repeating parts. Each part must be further separated into items with simple and complex types. (An item with a complex type is either a structure or another object.) A read-only property is created for each item with a simple type.

If a repeating item is an array of a simple type, then a read-only array property is provided for the item. If the repeating item is a linked list or an array of complex items, then iterator methods must be provided to select a single item from the repeating group. If the repeating item is an array, a read-only selection property can be used instead of the iterator methods. (A selection property sets the current index for the array.)

This process is repeated in a recursive fashion for items with complex types. For polymorphic types, two different approaches are possible. The first is to supply accessor methods and properties for each of the different derived types. In most cases, this will be the preferable approach. The second approach is to gather, where possible, the unique parameters of each object into an array, but this can be done only if all items have the same type. In this respect the SGE Accessor is the exception rather than the rule. As is to be expected, providing accessor properties and methods for each derived type can be quite cumbersome.

A list of exception conditions should be developed during the process of creating the accessor properties and methods. For each exception condition, the technique for reporting the condition must be documented. In some cases, the exception condition will be reported using the return value of a method. In other cases it will be reported by firing an event. Events must be designed for each condition that is to be reported. If the user program is expected to take an action that is unique to the particular exception condition, then the condition should have its own event; otherwise it is possible to group several conditions together into a single event. In any case, the parameters of the event should give information about how and why the exception condition occurred.

7. CONCLUSION

Accessors can simplify programs that must deal with complicated objects or file structures. A significant portion of the code required to access parts of objects or files can be hidden within the Accessor component, allowing the programmer to deal with simple properties and methods. Although independent Accessors are common, it is equally common to see Accessor functionality added to other types of components.

EXERCISES

1. Integrate the SGE Accessor features into the Simple Graphical Editor and the SGE Background Editor.
2. Pick your favorite example from this book (other than those found in this chapter), and add accessor features to it.
3. Design an accessor for some object that you designed as part of a project for some other course.
4. Design an accessor for BMP files. See the Visual C++ help file for the format of these files.

Chapter 12

Caches

1. PREREQUISITES AND OBJECTIVES

Before starting this chapter, you should have

1. A knowledge of programming in C++.
2. A knowledge of component interface design.

After completing this chapter, you will have

1. A knowledge of how to enhance a program's storage facilities with Cache components.
2. A knowledge of the Cache-Component design methodology.

2. INTRODUCTION

In its simplest form, a cache is simply a place to store data. In that respect, it provides little more functionality than a variable. Caches become useful and interesting when they are equipped with additional capabilities. Regardless of the internal complexity of a cache, it can generally be used as if it were a simple variable. This allows the Cache designer to enhance the host language (Visual Basic or whatever) with "variables" that provide new powerful capabilities. In this chapter, we will give several examples and then elaborate the design principles that were used to create the examples.

3. THE METHODOLOGY

The process of designing a Cache component consists of four steps: (1) specifying the input view or input format of the data, (2) specifying the output view or output format of the data, (3) designing the internal storage mechanisms, and (4) specifying the access methods for the output. If the Cache is simply a data repository, the input and output view will be the same. However, if the Cache transforms the data in some way, then the

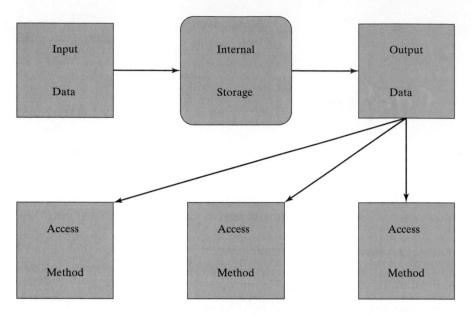

Figure 12-1   Cache-Component Structure

two may be quite different. Even a simple sorter provides different views of its input data. The input is a collection of unrelated data items, while the output is an ordered list of items. Even more substantial transformations are possible.

The internal storage problem can be quite complicated. The most popular Cache component is the Visual Basic Database component that uses a relational database for data storage. The Cache components that we will deal with in this chapter use much simpler data storage techniques. The access methods determine how data is returned to the containing program. Many different techniques are possible. We can use the various enumerators described in Chapter 11, or we can use a stacklike "pop" access through a single variable. Figure 12-1 shows the relationship between the various parts of the design. The remainder of this chapter illustrates cache design principles through several examples.

4. TWO SIMPLE CACHES

The simplest nontrivial data structures that we deal with in elementary computer science are stacks and queues. Using components to implement stacks and queues can greatly simplify the programs that use them. Figure 12-2 shows how stack and queue components would be used in a Visual Basic program.

In this figure, the stack cache acts as if it were a variable named *Stack1.Value*. Pushes and pops are done by assigning values to the variable or by accessing the variable. If we need to look at the top of the stack without popping, we could add a *Peek* property to the component and permit references of the form *Stack1.Peek* or *Stack1.Peek(10)*.

The unfortunate drawback of building such components is that a different component is required for each different data type. We can solve this problem by using a

```
Stack1.Value = 1
Stack1.Value = 2
Stack1.Value = 3
' Messages in Three Two One order
MsgBox Stack1.Value
MsgBox Stack1.Value
MsgBox Stack1.Value
Queue1.Value = 1
Queue1.Value = 2
Queue1.Value = 3
' Messages in One Two Three order
MsgBox Queue1.Value
MsgBox Queue1.Value
MsgBox Queue1.Value
```

Figure 12-2   Using Stack and Queue Caches

dynamic type such as the Visual Basic Variant, or by using generic pointers. These techniques are beyond the scope of this book.

The first step in designing the integer Stack and Queue components is to create an object to implement the data structures. In both cases, we will use a linked list to hold the data items. Figure 12-3 shows the definition of the **CHold** class, the list element. The list elements will be managed by the **CHolderList** object, which is declared to be a friend of the CHolder object. **CHolderList** will have two different implementations, one for the Stack component and one for the Queue component. We will present the queue implementation and then describe the differences between the queue and the stack. The declaration of the **CHolderList** class is given in Figure 12-4.

The primary queue management is done with the *AddValue* and *PopValue* functions. *AddValue* inserts a new integer into the queue, while *PopValue* removes an integer and returns its value. These two functions are given in Figure 12-5.

The **CHolderList** class has three additional functions: (1) *IsEmpty*, which can be used to determine whether there are items in the queue, (2) *GetCount*, which returns

```
class CHolderList;
class CHolder
{
    friend CHolderList;
protected:
    CHolder * Next;
    long Value;
public:
    CHolder();
    CHolder(long NewValue);
    virtual ~CHolder();
};
```

Figure 12-3   The CHolder Class

```
class CHolderList
{
protected:
    CHolder * Tail;
    CHolder * Head;
    long Count;
public:
    // List management functions
    void Clear(void);
    long GetCount(void);
    BOOL IsEmpty(void);
    long PopValue(void);
    void AddValue(long NewValue); // Insert into queue
    // Constructor and Destructor
    CHolderList();
    virtual ~CHolderList();
};
```

Figure 12-4   The CHolderList Class

```
void CHolderList::AddValue(long NewValue)
{
    CHolder * Temp = new CHolder(NewValue);
    if (Head == NULL)
    {
        Head = Temp;
    }
    else
    {
        Tail->Next = Temp;
    }
    Tail = Temp;
    Count++;
}
long CHolderList::PopValue()
{
    if (Head == NULL)
    {
        return 0;
    }
    long rv = Head->Value;
    CHolder * Temp = Head;
    Head = Head->Next;
    delete Temp;
    Count--;
    if (Head == NULL)
```

Figure 12-5   The *AddValue* and *PopValue* Functions

```
    {
        Tail = NULL;
    }
    return rv;
}
```

Figure 12-5   *(Continued)*

the number of items in the queue, and (3) *Clear*, which empties the queue. These functions are given in Figure 12-6.

In the Queue component, the *AddValue* and *PopValue* functions are encapsulated in the Get and Set routines for the *Value* property. The component has two read-only properties that give access to the *GetCount* and *IsEmpty* functions, and a method that gives access to the *Clear* function. Figure 12-7 gives the property design table for the Queue component; Figure 12-8 contains the method description of the *Clear* method.

The Stack component is identical to the Queue component in all respects except one—namely, the implementation of the *AddValue* function of the **CHolderList** class. Figure 12-9 shows the implementation of this function. Although no other changes are required, the *Tail* element of the **CHolderList** class could be eliminated for efficiency.

```
BOOL CHolderList::IsEmpty()
{
    if (Head == NULL)
    {
        return TRUE;
    }
    return FALSE;
}
long CHolderList::GetCount()
{
    return Count;
}
void CHolderList::Clear()
{
    while (Head != NULL)
    {
        CHolder * Temp = Head;
        Head = Head->Next;
        delete Temp;
    }
    Count = 0;
    Tail = 0;
}
```

Figure 12-6   The *IsEmpty*, *GetCount*, and Clear Functions

Property Design Table		
Name	**Type**	**Function**
Value	Long Integer Default=Empty	Inserts values into and extracts values from the queue. **Restrictions:** Run-Time Only
Count	Long Integer Maximum=N/A Minimum=0 Default=0	Returns the number of items currently in the queue. **Restrictions:** Read-Only
Empty	Boolean Default=Empty Str.	Returns **True** if the queue is empty; otherwise returns **False** **Restrictions:** Read-Only

Figure 12-7   The Queue Property Design Table

Method Description			
Name	Clear		
Return Value	Void		
Description	Deletes all elements from the queue.		
Arguments	**Name**	**Type**	**Description**
Void			

Figure 12-8   The **Queue** *Clear* Method

```
void CHolderList::AddValue(long NewValue)
{
    CHolder * Temp = new CHolder(NewValue);
    Temp->Next = Head;
    Head = Temp;
    Count++;
}
```

Figure 12-9   The Stack *AddValue* Function

5. THE RANDOMIZER CACHE

Although Stack and Queue components can be used to conveniently store large quantities of data, we can create more interesting examples by enhancing their internal structure. For example, suppose we modify the Queue component so that it returns values in random order. We could use such a component to deal bridge hands, as illustrated in Figure 12-10. (See the cards component in Chapter 14 for an example of how the output of the randomizer might be used.)

In Figure 12-10, each card in the deck is numbered from 1 to 52. These values are inserted into the randomizer Cache, and then placed in four different hands. Because the randomizer Cache returns values in random order, each hand will be dealt at random.

```
Dim West(13) As Integer, East(13) As Integer
Dim South(13) As Integer, North(13) As Integer
For I = 1 To 52
    Randomizer1.Value = I
Next I
For I = 1 To 13
    West(I) = Randomizer1.Value
    East(I) = Randomizer1.Value
    North(I) = Randomizer1.Value
    South(I) = Randomizer1.Value
Next I
```

Figure 12-10   Dealing Bridge Hands

To create the randomizer Cache, we start with the **CHolder** and **CHolderList** classes used by the Stack and Queue components. The **CHolder** class will not be modified, but we will make the appropriate changes to the **CHolderList** class to perform the randomization. The external interface of the randomizer Cache is identical to that of the Stack and Queue components. The changes to the **CHolderList** class definition are given in Figure 12-11. A new data item, *Dirty* has been added along with a new internal utility function, *Randomize*.

The two functions of the **CHolderList** class, *PopValue* and *AddValue*, have been modified to perform the randomization. The data item *Dirty* will be initialized to **FALSE** by the **CHolderList** constructor. When *AddValue* is called, it sets the *Dirty* item to **TRUE**. When *PopValue* is called, it tests the value of *Dirty*, and if it is **TRUE**, then it calls the *Randomize* function. The *Randomize* function will randomize the order of the

```
class CHolderList
{
protected:
    BOOL Dirty;
    CHolder * Tail;
    CHolder * Head;
    long Count;
    void Randomize(void);
public:
    void Clear(void);
    long GetCount(void);
    BOOL IsEmpty(void);
    long PopValue(void);
    void AddValue(long NewValue);
    CHolderList();
    virtual ~CHolderList();
};
```

Figure 12-11   The Randomizer CHolderList Class

```
void CHolderList::Randomize()
{
    if (Count <= 1) // nothing to do
    {
        return;
    }
    // Create the sorting arrays
    long * Array = new long [Count];
    long * Random = new long [Count];
    long i = 0;
    for (CHolder * Temp = Head ; Temp != NULL ; Temp=Temp->Next, i++)
    {
        Array[i] = Temp->Value;
        Random[i] = rand();
    }
    // Sort both arrays using insertion sort
    for (i=1 ; i<Count ; i++)
    {
        long j = i=1;
        long x = Array[i];
        long y = Random[i];
        for ( ; j>=0 && Random[j]>y ; j--)
        {
            Array[j+1] = Array[j];
            Random[j+1] = Random[j];
        }
        j++;
        Array[j] = x;
        Random[j] = y;
    }
    // insert values back into the linked list
    for (Temp = Head,i = 0 ; Temp != NULL ; Temp=Temp->Next, i++)
    {
        Temp->Value = Array[i];
    }
    // destroy the two arrays
    delete [] Array;
    delete [] Random;
}
```

Figure 12-12   The *Randomize* Function

list, and set Dirty to **FALSE**. The only significant change to the implementation of the **CHolderList** class is the *Randomize* function, which is given in Figure 12-12.

The *Randomize* function creates two arrays: (1) *Array*, to hold the values from the linked list, and (2) *Random*, to hold a random number. Once the values of these arrays have been filled in, the two arrays are sorted in parallel using the value of *Random* as the key. Once the sort is complete, the values from *Array* are inserted back into the linked list, and the two arrays are destroyed.

6. THE WORD-EXTRACTOR CACHE

Although in most cases the data retrieved from a cache will be identical to the data inserted into the cache, useful components can be created by adopting two different views of the data, one for input and one for output. For caches of this type, there is some overlap in functionality between the Cache component and a Filter component (see Chapter 13), but the function of a Cache component is more restricted. As an example, let us consider the word-extractor Cache. The input to this cache will be a line of text; however, the data will be accessed as an array of words rather than as a line of text.

To parse the words of the line of text, we will use a technique similar to the one that we used in the text file Accessor (see Chapter 11). For each word in the line, we will keep track of the position and the length of the word using the **CWordLink** class of Figure 12-13.

To avoid having to search the list of **CWordLink** objects each time a word is requested, we will reorganize the list into an array of **CWordElement** objects. The **CWordElement** class is given in Figure 12-14.

The word-list functionality will be encapsulated into the **CWordList** class of Figure 12-15, which will do most of the work. This class will be used with an external string variable. An external routine must parse the string variable and identify the position and length of each word. Once a word is located, the *AddElement* function of **CWordList** must be used to add the word into the **CWordLink** chain of objects. Once

```
class CWordLink
{
public:
    CWordLink * Next;
    long Position;
    long Length;
    // Construction and Destruction
    CWordLink(long NewPos, long NewLen);
    CWordLink();
    virtual ~CWordLink();
};
```

Figure 12-13   The CWordLink Class

```
class CWordElement
{
public:
    CWordElement & operator=(const CWordLink &x);
    long Length;
    long Position;
    CWordElement();
    virtual ~CWordElement();
};
```

Figure 12-14   The CWordElement Class

```
class CWordList
{
public:
    // The array
    CWordElement * Array;
    long Count;
    // The linked list
    CWordLink * Tail;
    CWordLink * Head;
    // status
    BOOL ArrayDone;
    // Creation
    void AddElement(long NewPos, long NewLen);
    void MakeArray(void);
    // Access
    long GetCount(void);
    long GetLength(long Ix);
    long GetPosition(long Ix);
    // construction and destruction
    CWordList();
    virtual ~CWordList();
};
```

Figure 12-15   The CWordList Class

all words have been found, the *MakeArray function* must be called to reorganize the list of words into an array of words. The *ArrayDone* variable is used to ensure that the *MakeArray* function is called once and only once. When a new line of text is supplied to the component, the existing **CWordList** object will be deleted and a new one will be created. The *GetLength* and *GetPosition* functions will not return legitimate values until the *MakeArray* function has been called.

The property design table for the word-extractor Cache is given in Figure 12-16. The *Line* property is used to supply the line of text, while the *Word* property is used to extract individual words. The *WordCount* property can be used to determine the number of words in the line.

Property Design Table		
Name	**Type**	**Function**
Line	String Default=Empty	Provides a line of text to be parsed into words.
Word	String Array Default=Zero Size	Returns the individual words in the line. **Restrictions:** Read-Only
WordCount	Long Integer Default=0. Maximum=None Minimum=0	Returns the count of the number of words in the line. **Restrictions:** Read-Only

Figure 12-16   The Word-Extractor Property Design Table

When a new value is assigned to the *Line* property, the *MakeList* function is called to create a new **CWordList** object. For the purposes of this example, a word is considered to be a string of alphanumeric characters. All other characters are ignored. (What's wrong with this?) The *MakeList* function is given in Figure 12-17.

The implementation of the *Word* property is given in Figure 12-18. This property acts like a simple array; however, if there is an error in the request, the *ErrorMessage* event is fired, and the empty string is returned.

```
void CWordExtractorCtrl::MakeList()
{
    if (WL != NULL)
    {
        delete WL;
        WL = NULL;
    }
    if (m_line.IsEmpty())
    {
        FireErrorMessage("Empty String Given to Control");
        return;
    }
    WL = new CWordList;
    long WordPos = 0;
    long WordLen = 0;
    for (int i=0 ; i<m_line.GetLength() ; ) // work until EOL found
    {
        // Skip any "white space"
        while (i<m_line.GetLength() && !isalpha(m_line[i])
                && !isdigit(m_line[i]))
        {
            i++;
        }
        WordPos = i; Found beginning
        WordLen = 0;
        // Find the end of a the word
        while (i<m_line.GetLength() && (isalpha(m_line[i])
                || isdigit(m_line[i])))
        {
            WordLen++;
            i++;
        }
        if (WordLen > 0) // We may have found EOL
        {
            WL->AddElement(WordPos,WordLen);
        }
    }
    WL->MakeArray();
}
```

Figure 12-17   The *MakeList* Function

```
BSTR CWordExtractorCtrl::GetWord(long Idx)
{
    CString strResult;
    if (WL == NULL)
    {
        FireErrorMessage("No data to return");
        strResult.Empty();
    }
    else
    {
        long Pos = WL->GetPosition(Idx);
        long Len = WL->GetLength(Idx);
        if (Pos == -1 || Len == 0)
        {
            FireErrorMessage("Word Not Found");
            strResult.Empty();
        }
        else
        {
            strResult = m_line.Mid(Pos,Len);
        }
    }
    return strResult.AllocSysString();
}
```

Figure 12-18   The *GetWord* Function

7. THE SGE CACHE

The SGE Cache is used to hold several drawings created by the Simple Graphical Editor. Each drawing is identified by name and can be retrieved explicitly by its name. It is possible to enumerate all items in the cache and to selectively delete items from the cache. The items contained in the cache can be obtained from a number of different sources, including the SGE editor, the SGE background editor, and the SGE serializers. Internally the SGE Cache maintains a list of name-value pairs which consist of a name and a pointer to a **CGraphicList** object. The **CGraphHolder** object given in Figure 12-19 is used to maintain a name-value pair. The name-value pairs are stored in a simple linked list. The list is doubly linked because name-value pairs can be selectively deleted.

As with our other examples, the linked list of name-value pairs is encapsulated in a header object that performs most of the work. This object, **CHolderList**, is given in Figure 12-20. It has three data items for maintaining the list: (1) *Head*, (2) *Tail*, and (3) *Count*. The *Current* item is used during enumeration operations. The *AddItem* function is used to add new items to the list. It returns an error code if the item already exists. Items can be deleted from the list using either the name of the object or the address of the **CGraphicList** object. There are two ways to delete an item from the list. The *DeleteItem* functions remove an item from the list and destroy the associated **CGraphicList** object.

```
class CGraphHolder
{
public:
    // linking: doubly linked because
    // we anticipate deletions from the middle of the chain
    CGraphHolder * Next;
    CGraphHolder * Prev;

    // The object and its name
    CString Name;
    CGraphicList * Item;

    // Construction and destruction
    CGraphHolder();
    virtual ~CGraphHolder();
};
```

Figure 12-19 The CGraphHolder Object

```
// Main list-handler object
class CHolderList
{
protected:
    // List pointers and item count
    CGraphHolder * Head;
    CGraphHolder * Tail;
    long Count;

    // current iterator item
    CGraphHolder * Current;

public:
    // construction and destruction
    CHolderList();
    virtual ~CHolderList();

    // adding items
    long AddItem(LPCTSTR NewName,CGraphicList * Address);

    // removing items
    long RemoveItem(CGraphicList * RemAddress);
    long RemoveItem(LPCTSTR RemName);

    // removing items with model delete
    long DeleteItem(CGraphicList * DelAddress);
    long DeleteItem(LPCTSTR DelName);

    // searching by name and address
    CGraphicList * Find(LPCTSTR FindName);
    CString GetName(CGraphicList * FindAddress);
```

Figure 12-20 The CHolderList Class

```
    // iterators and accessor functions
    long FindFirst(void);
    long FindNext(void);
    CString GetCurrentName(void);
    CGraphicList * GetCurrentAddress(void);
    long GetItemCount(void);

protected:
    // Finds in anticipation of further manipulation
    CGraphHolder * FindItem(CGraphicList * FindAddress);
    CGraphHolder * FindItem(LPCTSTR FindName);
};
```

Figure 12-20   (*Continued*)

The *RemoveItem* functions will remove the item from the list without destroying the **CGraphicList** object. All of these functions will return an error code if the item cannot be found.

If we know the name of an object, the *Find* function can be used to retrieve the address of the associated **CGraphicList** object. Similarly, if we have the address of a **CGraphicList** object, we can use the *GetName* function to retrieve the name of the object. These functions return NULL, or the empty string, if the item cannot be found.

All objects in the cache can be enumerated using the *FindFirst* and *FindNext* functions. These functions use the *Current* item to enumerate the items in the cache. *FindFirst* sets *Current* equal to *Head*, while *FindNext* sets *Current* equal to *Current->Next*. No other forms of enumeration are provided. Once *Current* has been set, the functions *GetCurrentName* and *GetCurrentAddress* can be used to retrieve the name and address of the current object. *FindFirst* and *FindNext* will return an error code if *Current* does not contain a valid object. (This usually indicates the end of the list.) If *Current* is not valid, *GetCurrentName* will return the empty string, and *GetCurrentAddress* will return NULL. The function *GetItemCount* can be used to obtain a count of the number of items currently being stored in the linked list.

The **CHolderList** object also has two utility functions, both of which are named *FindItem*.

Four error codes are used in the implementation of the **CHolderList** class: SGE_NO_ERROR, SGE_DUPLICATE_NAME, SGE_NAME_NOT_FOUND, and SGE_ADDRESS_NOT_FOUND. Most of the functions of the **CHolderList** class are straightforward, so we will provide only a few representative examples. Figure 12-21 gives the implementation of the *AddItem* function. This function searches the list for the new name; if it is not found, it creates a new name-value pair from its operands. The new pair is added to the tail of the linked list.

Figure 12-22 shows the implementation of the *Find* function. A simple linear search is done to locate objects. If it is anticipated that a very large number of objects will be present in the cache, a more efficient method of organizing objects should be used.

```
long CHolderList::AddItem(LPCTSTR NewName, CGraphicList *Address)
{
    // check for duplicate name
    if (FindItem(NewName) == NULL)
    {
        // if new name is unique
        // create new graph holder and fill data fields
        CGraphHolder * Temp = new CGraphHolder;
        Temp->Item = Address;
        Temp->Name = NewName;
        // link graph holder into list
        if (Head == NULL)
        {
            Head = Temp;
        }
        else
        {
            Tail->Next = Temp;
        }
        Temp->Prev = Tail;
        Tail = Temp;
        // All OK
        return SGE_NO_ERROR;
    }
    else
    {
        // Error
        return SGE_DUPLICATE_NAME;
    }
}
```

Figure 12-21   The *AddItem* Function

```
CGraphicList * CHolderList::Find(LPCTSTR FindName)
{
    // Linear search for specified name
    for (CGraphHolder * Temp = Head ; Temp != NULL ; Temp = Temp->Next)
    {
        if (Temp->Name == FindName)
        {
            // terminate loop early if name is found
            return Temp->Item;
        }
    }
    // name not found
    return NULL;
}
```

Figure 12-22   The *Find* Function

```
long CHolderList::RemoveItem(LPCTSTR RemName)
{
   // find the graph holder containing the specified name, if any
   CGraphHolder * Temp = FindItem(RemName);
   if (Temp == NULL)
   {
      // error
      return SGE_NAME_NOT_FOUND;
   }
   else
   {
      // unlink found item
      if (Temp->Prev == NULL)
      {
         Head = Temp->Next;
      }
      else
      {
         Temp->Prev->Next = Temp->Next;
      }
      if (Temp->Next == NULL)
      {
         Tail = Temp->Prev;
      }
      else
      {
         Temp->Next->Prev = Temp->Prev;
      }
      // delete the holder, but not the model in it
      delete Temp;
      return SGE_NO_ERROR;
   }
}
```

Figure 12-23   The *RemoveItem (LPCTSTR)* Function

The *RemoveItem(LPCTSTR)* function is given in Figure 12-23. This function searches the list for the name, and if the item is found, it delinks the name-value pair and destroys it, without destroying the object pointed to by the name-value pair.

The *FindNext* function is given in Figure 12-24. This function first checks *Current* to see if it is non NULL; if it is, it advances the pointer to the next item. If the result is a NULL pointer, the function returns zero; otherwise it returns one. The *FindFirst* function must be called first for the *FindNext* function to operate properly.

The properties and methods of the SGE Cache are essentially wrapper functions for the **CHolderList** object. Rather than providing formal definitions for the properties and methods of the component in Figure 12-25, we will simply list them and indicate the associated function of the **CHolderList** class.

```
long CHolderList::FindNext()
{
    // Go to next item, if any
    // Return 0 if End of List found, return 1 if object is usable
    if (Current == NULL)
    {
        return 0;
    }
    Current = Current->Next;
    if (Current == NULL)
    {
        return 0;
    }
    else
    {
        return 1;
    }
}
```

Figure 12-24   The FindNext Function

Name	Type	Associated Function
AddItem	Method	*AddItem*
CurrentAddress	Read-Only Property	*GetCurrentName*
CurrentName	Read-Only Property	*GetCurrentAddress*
DeleteAddress	Method	*DeleteItem(CGraphicList *)*
DeleteName	Method	*DeleteItem(LPCTSTR)*
Find	Method	*Find*
FindFirst	Method	*FindFirst*
FindNext	Method	*FindNext*
GetName	Method	*GetName*
ItemCount	Read-Only Property	*GetItemCount*
RemoveAddress	Method	*RemoveItem(CGraphicList *)*
RemoveName	Method	*RemoveItem(LPCTSTR)*

Figure 12-25   Property/Method Association Table

8. A REVIEW OF THE METHODOLOGY

The design of a Cache component has four elements: (1) specifying the input view of the data, (2) specifying the output view, (3) designing the internal storage mechanisms, and (4) specifying the access methods for the data. Specifying the input view of the data is essentially the same as specifying the type of the data that will be placed in the component. Typically, a single type of data will be input—strings, integers, floats, objects of a specific type, and so forth. Specifying the output view is a little more complicated. Naturally, it is necessary to specify the type of the output data, but we must also define the relationship between the input data and the output data. Will the input items be passed through the Cache unchanged, or will they be transformed or combined in some way? Will they be disassembled into their individual parts, or combined with other data items to create more complex objects? These questions must be answered when specifying the output view of the data.

Next, it is necessary to specify the access methods of the component. Will data items be accessed sequentially or randomly? If they are accessed sequentially, in what order will they be accessed? If they are accessed randomly, how will we specify the desired item? Will a name of some sort be used, or will access be by an index number? If an index number is used, in what order will the items be stored? Once these questions have been answered, it is possible to proceed to the design of the internal storage mechanisms.

In one sense, the cache is simply a wrapper for its internal storage mechanisms. The design of the input and output views as well as the design of the access methods simply gives information about how the internal storage mechanisms must be organized.

The interface structure of the Cache is quite simple, usually consisting of nothing more than a *Value* property. If the Cache supports several different access methods, there may be multiple *Value* properties and perhaps some configuration properties and methods.

9. CONCLUSION

A Cache is particularly useful when it is necessary to manage a diverse collection of objects of the same type. The Cache provides a convenient place to store and organize data. The internal design of most Caches is relatively simple, so specialized Caches can easily be developed for specific applications.

EXERCISES

1. Create a cache that allows you to save e-mails. An e-mail message will have four parts: (1) date and time of receipt, (2) sender's name, (3) subject, and (4) content. You should be able to sort messages by date/time or by sender's name, and retrieve them in either order.

2. Create a cache that will store a list of strings (great sayings, insults, jokes, etc.) and permit you to retrieve them in random order.

3. Create a cache that will allow you to store a list of lines. A line consists of two points, and a point consists of two integer coordinates, which may be negative. The lines must be retrieved in descending order by length.

Chapter 13

Filters

1. PREREQUISITES AND OBJECTIVES

Before starting this chapter, you should have

1. A knowledge of programming in C++.
2. A knowledge of component interface design.

After completing this chapter, you will have

1. A knowledge of how to transform batch programs into filter components.
2. A knowledge of the principles of hot and cold Filters.
3. A knowledge of the Filter-Component design methodology.

2. INTRODUCTION

Prior to the advent of graphical user interface (GUI) programming, virtually any program that was written was a filter. Today, many of the most sophisticated programs in existence are filters: A compiler is a filter that transforms source files into object files; a link-editor is a filter that transforms object files into executable programs; a report generator is a filter that transforms database tables into printed reports; a database query engine is a filter that transforms a collection of database tables into a new table. In the area of image processing, there are innumerable filters for processing images or segments of images. Filtering is one of the first things that a programmer learns. Many of the exercises in introductory programming courses are filters.

Defined in the simplest terms, a filter is a program that transforms an object into a different object. The new object may be of a different type, or it may be of the same type but with more desirable properties. For the most part, the transformation algorithms themselves are beyond the scope of this book (but they are a widely discussed topic in computer science). However, most filters have similar frameworks. The purpose of this chapter is to demonstrate the principles of constructing frameworks for various types of filters. The application of these principles to other problems is straightforward.

3. THE METHODOLOGY

With the possible exception of configuration parameters, the external interface of a Filter is quite simple. A file-to-file filter generally accepts two file names, and uses one for input and the other for output. An object filter has mechanisms for supplying objects and for retrieving the transformed objects. The input and output mechanisms can be implemented as properties or methods.

Once the input and output mechanisms have been chosen, the configuration parameters, if any, must be designed. Depending on their complexity, there is a wide range of methods that can be used to specify configuration parameters. Simple parameters can be specified using a set of properties. (Methods can also be used, but properties are the preferred mechanism.) More complex parameters may be supplied as configuration objects or configuration files. In some cases, the configuration parameters are so complex, that a separate program must be used to create them. (Such is the case for report generators.)

In most cases the configuration parameters are very simple or even nonexistent. In any case, once the input and output mechanisms have been chosen and the configuration parameters have been designed, development can then proceed along the same lines as an ordinary command-line program.

4. HOT FILTERS AND COLD FILTERS

The Filter category can be further subdivided into hot Filters and cold Filters. The principles of these two types of filters are quite different. A cold Filter transforms its input in a predictable way. Its operation is frozen and unchanging. An example of such a filter is a C++ compiler. Regardless of which parameters are set, the filter transforms C++ files into object files. No change of parameters can "convince" the C++ compiler to transform Pascal files into object files.

A hot Filter has a function that must be programmed prior to its use. An example of such a Filter is a report generator. Before it can generate a report, it must be given the format of the report. In many cases hot Filters have self-defining input. This is certainly the case for a report generator since the definition of the report will generally include the name of the data base and the table or query from which the input data must be taken. Other types of hot Filters do not define their own input. An example of such a filter is an image processor that can apply a convolution transformation to a bit-mapped image. Before the filter can be used, it must be supplied with the definition of a transformation, but once this is done, the input can come from virtually any source.

5. FILE TRANSFORMERS

For the purposes of this book, we will further divide filters into file transformers and object transformers. File transformers operate in file-to-file fashion, while object transformers operate in memory-to-memory fashion. (Filters that operate between files and memory are known as Serializers; they are discussed in Chapter 9.) Although we feel that the distinction between file transformers and object transformers is somewhat artificial, it is useful for our purposes.

There are many traditional programs that fit into the category of file transformers, and it is generally a simple matter to convert such programs into Filter components. In this chapter, we will demonstrate two file Filters that are based on UNIX/DOS programs. The first of these will transform text files between UNIX and MS Windows, while the second will analyze the words in a text document and produce a report suitable for printing. (The report will be stored in a text file.)

5.1 Unix-to-PC Transformation

In a UNIX text file, every line must end with a linefeed character, a character that serves as a line terminator. In a DOS text file, lines must be separated from one another using a return character and a linefeed character. It is not necessary for the last line in the file to be terminated by a return/linefeed pair, but it is common to do so. (Technically, if the last two characters in a text file are a return and a linefeed, the file ends with a blank line.)

MS Windows programs do not handle UNIX text files well. Many of them do not recognize the single linefeed as an end-of-line marker and will attempt to treat the entire file as a single line. Similarly, UNIX programs do not know what to do with the extra return characters and will normally treat them as if they were ordinary text characters. Because C++ programs are stored in text files, porting C++ programs between MS Windows and UNIX can be a problem, and the compilers may not recognize the lines properly. (It is also true that many compilers *do not* have this problem.)

We want our component to be able to transform files in both directions, from MS Windows to UNIX and from UNIX to MS Windows. Furthermore, if the component is asked to transform a UNIX file into a UNIX file, or an MS Windows file into an MS Windows file, it should produce the correct output, even though the input is of the wrong type.

The Filter component will be built around two functions: (1) *MakeUnixFile* and (2) *MakePCFile*. Both of these functions take two arguments: (1) the name of the input file and (2) the name of the output file. With minor modifications, these functions are similar to those that might be found in a typical DOS or UNIX program. We could have used the *stdio.h* package or the *iostream.h* package, but we cannot be sure that these packages handle their global variables in a manner that is consistent with the requirements of a component.

The use of global variables can cause serious problems in a component. Because two or more instances of a component can run together in the same address space, we must be very careful to make sure they do not share their global and static variables. One way to avoid problems is to move all global and static variables into the support object for the component. By doing this, we can assure ourselves that every instance of the component has its own copy of the variables.

Once global variables have been moved into the support class, the functions that access them must be made members of the class. The transformed functions must also

Property Design Table		
Name	**Type**	**Function**
InputFile	String Default = Empty	Provides the name of the input file. Causes no other action. No restrictions.
PCOutput	String Default = Empty	Provides the name of the PC output file. When a new value is supplied, the input file is transformed into DOS/Windows format and written to the output file. Must not be the same as *InputFile*.
UNIXOutput	String Default = Empty	Provides the name of the UNIX output file. When a new value is supplied, the input file is transformed into UNIX format and written to the output file. Must not be the same as *InputFile*.

Figure 13-1   The Properties of the Text File Transformer

Event Description			
Name	ErrorMessage		
Description	Reports errors in the file transformation process.		
Triggers	Open errors or I/O errors. Occurs only when assigning a new value to *PCOutput* or *UNIXOutput*. Also triggered if *PCOutput* or *UNIXOutput* is assigned a value before assigning a value to *InputFile*.		
Arguments	**Name**	**Type**	**Description**
	Msg	String	Verbal Description of Error

Figure 13-2   The Text Transformer *ErrorMessage* Event

be made members of the support object to ensure that they have access to the global variables. The main difficulty that arises with this process is handling global variables with complex initializations. Since members of a class cannot have static initializers, these initializations must be moved into the constructor for the support class.

The text file transformer has three properties and one event; it has no methods. This simplicity in structure is typical of a file filter. Figure 13-1 gives the property design table for the component, while Figure 13-2 gives the formal definition of the event.

The *MakeUnixFile* function is given in Figure 13-3. In the Windows operating system, the functions to open, read and write files have become obnoxiously complicated, so we omit the details of them from Figure 13-3. The full details are available on the Web site.

The *MakePCFile* function is similar to the *MakeUnixFile* function. Characters are scanned one at a time, and when a linefeed character is encountered, the function checks to see if the preceding character was a return. If it was not, it inserts a return character into the output file. The *MakePCFile* function is shown in Figure 13-4.

Note that the functions given in Figures 13-3 and 13-4 are essentially the same sort of functions found in a typical batch program.

```
void CUnixToPCTxtCtrl::MakeUnixFile(CString &InFileName,
                                    CString &OutFileName)
{
  … // open input and output files, fire event and terminate if error
  // allocate buffers
  char * InBuffer = new char[10000];
  char * OutBuffer = new char[10000];
  // I/O control variables
  unsigned long BytesRead,BytesWritten;
  // output bytes used
  long OutC = 0;
  // state variables
  BOOL LastR = FALSE;
  BOOL LastN = FALSE;
  … // Read 10,000 bytes, terminate with error event if I/O error
  while (BytesRead > 0) // scan input buffer
  {
    char * tc;
    unsigned long i;
    for (tc = InBuffer,i=0 ; i<BytesRead ; i++,tc++)
    {
      LastN = FALSE;
      if (*tc == '\r') // if \r not before \n, don't delete
      {
        LastR = TRUE;
      }
      else if (*tc == '\n')
      {
        LastR = FALSE; // if there is a preceding \n, zap it
        LastN = TRUE;
        OutBuffer[OutC] = *tc;
        OutC++;
        if (OutC >= 10000)
        {
          … // write output buffer
          OutC = 0;
        }
      }
      else
       {
         if (LastR)
         {
           OutBuffer[OutC] = '\r'; // \r not before \n keep it
           OutC++;
           if (OutC >= 10000)
           {
             … // write output buffer
```

Figure 13-3   The *MakeUnixFile* Function

```
                OutC = 0;
            }
        }
        LastR = FALSE;
        OutBuffer[OutC] = *tc;
        OutC++;
        if (OutC >= 10000)
        {
            … // write output buffer
            OutC = 0;
        }
      }
    }
    … // read 10,000 more bytes
  }
  if (!LastN)
  {
    OutBuffer[OutC] = '\n';
    OutC++;
  }
  if (OutC > 0)
  {
    … // write output buffer
    OutC = 0;
  }
  // close files
  CloseHandle(InFile);
  CloseHandle(OutFile);
  // delete buffers
  delete [] InBuffer;
  delete [] OutBuffer;
}
```

Figure 13-3   (*Continued*)

```
void CUnixToPCTxtCtrl::MakePCFile(CString &InFileName,
                                  CString &OutFileName)
{
  … // open input and output files.
  … // Report any errors using ErrorMessage Event.
  // allocate buffers
  char * InBuffer = new char[10000];
  char * OutBuffer = new char[10000];
  // read/write control variables
  unsigned long BytesRead,BytesWritten;
  // output character count
  long OutC = 0;
```

Figure 13-4   The *MakePCFile* Function

```
                // State variable
                BOOL LastR = FALSE;
                … // Read 10,000 bytes
                while (BytesRead > 0) // while not EOF
                {
                  char * tc;
                  unsigned long i;
                  // scan each byte
                  for (tc = InBuffer,i=0 ; i<BytesRead ; i++,tc++)
                  {
                    if (*tc == '\r')
                    {
                      // record the presence of a return character
                      LastR = TRUE;
                      OutBuffer[OutC] = *tc;
                      OutC++;
                      if (OutC >= 10000)
                      {
                        … // write output buffer
                        OutC = 0;
                      }
                    }
                    else if (*tc == '\n')
                    {
                      // if the last character wasn't a return, add one
                      if (!LastR)
                      {
                        OutBuffer[OutC] = '\r';
                        OutC++;
                        if (OutC >= 10000)
                        {
                          // write output buffer
                          OutC = 0;
                        }
                      }
                      LastR = FALSE;
                      OutBuffer[OutC] = *tc;
                      OutC++;
                      if (OutC >= 10000)
                      {
                        … // write output buffer
                        OutC = 0;
                      }
                    }
                    else
                    {
                      // ordinary character
```

Figure 13-4   (*Continued*)

```
            LastR = FALSE;
            OutBuffer[OutC] = *tc;
            OutC++;
            if (OutC >= 10000)
            {
                … // write output buffer
                OutC = 0;
            }
        }
    }
    … // read 10,000 more bytes
    }
    if (OutC > 0)
    {
        … // write output buffer
        OutC = 0;
    }
    // close files and delete buffers
    CloseHandle(InFile);
    CloseHandle(OutFile);
    delete [] InBuffer;
    delete [] OutBuffer;
}
```

Figure 13-4   (*Continued*)

5.2 The Word Counter

We next illustrate a typical read-file-and-print operation. However, instead of printing the output, we will store the output in a text file. The resultant component is a file-transformation component. The Word Counter component will read a text file and count the number of times each word occurs in the text. The result will be an alphabetical list of unique words with a count of the number of times each word is used, and a similar list sorted by frequency of use.

The heart of this component is the **CWCount** class, which encapsulates the functionality needed to count word frequencies. Each unique word is represented by an object of the class **CWCItem**. Figure 13-5 gives the definition of **CWCItem**. Each object contains the word in lowercase, and a count of the number of times it occurs. These objects will be stored in a hash table that is implemented as a collection of singly linked lists.

The **CWCount** class is given in Figure 13-6. The user of the **CWCount** object must break the input text into words and call the *Word* function for each word. The **CWCount** object will keep track of unique words and count the occurrences of each. A hash table is used to keep track of the words. For the hash table to work properly, each entry in the array must be initialized to the NULL pointer by the class constructor. Each entry in the hash table is treated as the head of a stack. The hash-table key is computed by treating the characters of the word as unsigned 8-bit integers, computing their sum, and extracting the low-order eight bits of the result. The *Clear* function is

```
class CWCount;
class CWCItem
{
    friend CWCount; // container class
protected:
    CWCItem * Next;
    CString Word; // the word in lower case
    long Occur; // occurrences
public:
    CWCItem();
    CWCItem(LPCTSTR NewWord); // sets Occur to one
    virtual ~CWCItem();
};
```

Figure 13-5   The CWCItem Class

```
class CWCount
{
protected:
    long UniqueWords; // count of unique words
    long WordCount; // count of total words
    // Hash key is obtained by converting word to lower case
    // and adding up the letters as unsigned 8-bit integers.
    // The last 8 bits are trimmed off and used as a key.
    CWCItem * HashTable[256];
public:
    BOOL IsEmpty(void);
    // construction, destruction
    CWCount();
    virtual ~CWCount();
    // input functions
   // add word to hash table, or increment count
    void Word(LPCTSTR InWord);
    // delete all words from hash table & set counts to zero
    void Clear(void);
    // output functions
    // produce the totals line in text format
    void GetTotalsString(CString &Out);
    // produce the text of the list sorted by usage
    void GetUsageString(CString &Out);
    // produce the text of the list sorted alphabetically
    void GetAlphaString(CString &Out);
protected:
    // utilities
    // array of words in usage order
    CWCItem ** GetUsageArray(void);
```

Figure 13-6   The CWCount Class

```
    // array of words in alphabetical order
    CWCItem ** GetSortedArray(void);
    // compute hash-table key
    long Hash(LPCTSTR InWord);
};
```

Figure 13-6   (*Continued*)

used at the beginning of each operation to empty the hash table for a new operation. Once the input text has been processed, the usage report can be obtained by calling the three functions *GetTotalsString*, *GetUsageString*, and *GetAlphaString*. The function *GetTotalsString* produces a multiline text message giving the total number of unique words and the total word count. The *GetUsageString* produces a multiline text string containing the list of unique words, along with a count of the number of times that word occurs in the text. Each word is on a separate line. The list is sorted in descending order by the number of occurrences. The *GetAlphaString* function produces a string identical to that of the *GetUsageString* function, except the words are sorted into ascending sequence alphabetically. For both functions the words are listed in lowercase letters.

The *Word* function, which performs most of the real work, is given in Figure 13-7. Figure 13-8 shows the computation of the hash-table index.

```
void CWCount::Word(LPCTSTR InWord)
{
   WordCount++; // count total number of words
   CString Work = InWord; // place word in a convenient wrapper
   Work.MakeLower(); // convert to lower case
   long HIndex = Hash(Work); // compute hash index
   // search linked list for this hash table entry
   for (CWCItem * Temp = HashTable[HIndex];
        Temp != NULL && Temp->Word != Work;
        Temp=Temp->Next);
   if  (Temp != NULL)
   {
     // if word already in table, increment occurrences
     Temp->Occur++;
   }
   else
   {
     // if word not in table, create new entry and link into table
     UniqueWords++; // count unique words
     Temp = new CWCItem(Work); // sets occurrences to one
     Temp->Next = HashTable[HIndex];
     HashTable[HIndex] = Temp;
   }
}
```

Figure 13-7   The *Word* Function

```
long CWCount::Hash(LPCTSTR InWord)
{
   long rv = 0;
   for (const char * tc = InWord ; *tc != '\0' ; tc++)
   {
     rv += (unsigned char)(*tc);
     rv &= 0xff; // trim each time to avoid overflow
   }
   return rv;
}
```

Figure 13-8   Computing the Hash-Table Index

The remaining functions of the **CWCount** object are straightforward. For interested readers, they can be found on the Web site.

The Word Counter component is quite simple, having two properties and one event. These are documented in Figure 13-9.

The entire component is implemented within the access routines for the properties *InputFile* and *OutputFile*. (This is typical for a file-transformation component.) The routines for these properties are lengthy but straightforward. The code can be found on the Web site.

Property Design Table		
Name	**Type**	**Function**
InputFile	String Default = Empty	Used to provide the name of the input file. File will be read and processed immediately upon assignment to this property. **Restrictions:** Write-Only, Run-Time Only
OutputFile	String Default = Empty	Used to provide the name of the PC output file. When a new value is supplied, the accumulated totals are formatted and written to this file. **Restrictions:** Write-Only, Run-Time Only

Event Description			
Name	ErrorMessage		
Description	Reports errors in the file transformation process.		
Triggers	Open errors I/O errors, assignment to *OutputFile* with no prior assignment to *InputFile*.		
Arguments	**Name**	**Type**	**Description**
	Msg	String	Verbal Description of Error

Figure 13-9   The Word Counter Interface

6. OBJECT TRANSFORMERS

Object transformers are similar to file transformers in that they generally implement standard, nongraphical algorithms. The primary difference is that the input to an object transformer is already in a form that is readily usable by an algorithm. In most cases the input will be a pointer to a complex object obtained from another component. The object transformer either transforms the existing object to "improve" it in some way or creates a new object from the existing object. The most interesting examples of such components are far too complicated to be presented here, so we will concentrate instead on a few simple examples.

In all of our examples, it is necessary to work around a fundamental weakness in the ActiveX technology—namely, that it is impossible to define a property with an object type or an object pointer type. For that reason, we will coerce all object pointers into long integers and pass the addresses as integers. In general, this is a poor programming technique because long integers and addresses are not guaranteed to be the same length on all future systems. In fact, the memory sizes of many existing computers far exceed the limitations of a 32-bit address. There are other difficulties with passing object addresses from component to component, but we will save that discussion for Chapter 19.

In the first example, we will show how to embed a simple algorithm in a Filter component. In the second example, we will show how to create a hot filter that is configurable at run-time. For the third example, we will discuss a text-to-object transformer.

6.1 The Integer Sorter

Unlike file transformers, which can operate as stand-alone components, object transformers must be coupled with other components to provide the input and process the output of the object transformer. In the integer sorter, we will embed a simple insertion sort algorithm in its own component. However, to test the component, we must create two other components: one that will provide the input to the integer sorter and another that will display the output of the integer sorter in human-readable form. Figure 13-10 shows the relationship of these three components. This structure is typical for most object transformers.

In Figure 13-10 the communication between the three components is via an object called a dynarray—an object that serves as a wrapper for a dynamic array of integers. The definition of the **CDynarray** class is given in Figure 13-11. The implementation of this class is straightforward.

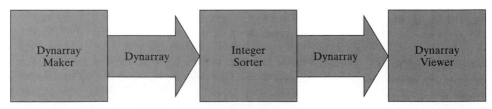

Figure 13-10   Component Relationships for Object Transformers

```
class CDynarray
{
public:
    // dynamic array implementation
    long * Data;
    long Count;
    // construction and destruction
    CDynarray(long NewCount, long * NewData);
    CDynarray(const CDynarray &x);
    CDynarray();
    virtual ~CDynarray();
};
```

Figure 13-11   The CDynarray Class

Property Design Table		
Name	**Type**	**Function**
Unsorted	Long/Pointer Default = NULL	Supplies the address of the *CDynarray* object to be sorted. No action is taken as a result of the assignment. The input object will not be modified by this component; however, the object is owned by the component and may be deleted by the component. **Restrictions:** Write-Only, Run-Time Only
Sorted	Long/Pointer Default = NULL	Provides the address of the sorted *CDynarray* object. This is a new object created by the Integer Sorter component. The sort operation is performed as part of the implementation of this property. The component does not own this new object and will not delete it. **Restrictions:** Read-Only, Run-Time Only

Figure 13-12   The Integer Sorter Interface

```
void CIntSorterCtrl::SetUnsorted(long nNewValue)
{
    if (SortItem != NULL)
    {
      delete SortItem;
    }
    SortItem = (CDynarray *)nNewValue;
    SetModifiedFlag();
}
```

Figure 13-13   The *SetUnsorted* Function

The interface of the integer sorter is quite simple, consisting of just two properties, *Sorted* and *Unsorted*. The formal description of these properties is given in Figure 13-12.

The implementations of the *Sorted* and *Unsorted* properties are given in Figures 13-13 and 13-14. The *SetUnsorted* function receives a pointer to a **CDynarray**

```
long CIntSorterCtrl::GetSorted()
{
    if (SortItem == NULL)
    {
        // if nothing to sort, return NULL
        return (long)SortItem;
    }
    if (SortItem->Count == 0)
    {
        // if object is empty, create empty object and return it
        CDynarray * EmptyItem = new CDynarray;
        return (long)EmptyItem;
    }
    // create duplicate object, sort it and return pointer to it
    CDynarray * NewSort = new CDynarray(*SortItem);
    InsertSort(NewSort);
    return (long)NewSort;
}
```

Figure 13-14   The *GetSorted* Function

object in the form of a long integer. The component assumes ownership of the object, in the sense that is permitted to delete the object when it no longer needs it. The sorting operation is performed when the sorted object is requested through an access to the *Sorted* property. Instead of sorting the existing **CDynarray** object, a copy of the object is created, sorted, and returned to the requester. The requester then assumes ownership of the returned object.

The *GetSorted* function calls the *InsertSort* routine to sort the **CDynarray** object. This routine, which is illustrated in Figure 13-15, is essentially the standard textbook version of the InsertSort algorithm. It is obvious that virtually any sort algorithm could be embedded in this component in the same fashion as the InsertSort algorithm, illustrating the manner in which standard algorithms can be embedded in filter components.

Although the integer sorter is a stand-alone component, it requires some source for the **CDynarray** objects. By the same token, if the output of the component is to be useful, it requires some consumer of the sorted **CDynarray** objects it creates. In an actual application, there would be natural producers and consumers of these objects. However, since we are dealing with this component in isolation, we must create our own producers and consumers specifically for the purpose of testing. Thus we have created two additional components which will serve as the producer and consumer of the **CDynarray** objects. Since these two components are artificial, we will merely give the definition of their interfaces, not complete details. The *DynarrayMaker* component has two properties, *NewValue* and *Unsorted*, and one method, *Clear*. *NewValue* is used to add a value to the **CDynarray** object being created, while *Unsorted* is used to retrieve the address of the newly created **CDynarray** object. The *Clear* method is used to begin a new **CDynarray** object. The property descriptions are given in Figure 13-16, and the

```
void CIntSorterCtrl::InsertSort(CDynarray *Item)
{
   if (Item == NULL)
   {
      return;
   }
   if (Item->Count == 0)
   {
      return;
   }
   if (Item->Data == NULL)
   {
      return;
   }
   for (long i=1 ; i<Item->Count ; i++)
   {
      long x = Item->Data[i];
      for (long j = i-1 ; j >= 0 && Item->Data[j] > x ; j--)
      {
         Item->Data[j+1] = Item->Data[j];
      }
      j++;
      Item->Data[j] = x;
   }
}
```

Figure 13-15   The *InsertSort* Function

Property Design Table		
Name	**Type**	**Function**
NewValue	Long Integer Default = None Maximum = None Minimum = None	Used to add a new value to the CDynarray object being created. All values assigned to this property will be accumulated into a CDynarray object. **Restrictions:** Write-Only, Run-Time Only
Unsorted	Long Integer Default = NULL	Contains the address of a newly created CDynarray object. The CDynarray object will contain all integers assigned to the NewValue property since the last call to the Clear method. **Restrictions:** Read-Only, Run-Time Only

Figure 13-16   Property Table for CDynarrayMaker

method description is given in Figure 13-17. When the *Unsorted* property of the *DynarrayMaker* is accessed, a new copy of the **CDynarray** object is created. The requester then becomes the owner of the newly created object.

The *DynarrayViewer* component subclasses a multiline text box and presents the list of sorted integers in ASCII form. This component has a single property, *Sorted*.

Method Description			
Name	Clear		
Return Value	Void		
Description	Deletes all elements from the queue.		
Arguments	**Name**	**Type**	**Description**
Void			

Figure 13-17   *Clear* Method of CDynarrayMaker

Property Design Table		
Name	**Type**	**Function**
Sorted	Long Integer Default = NULL	Must contain the address of a CDynarray object. The CDynarray object will be displayed in ASCII form. **Restrictions:** Write-Only, Run-Time Only

Figure 13-18   Property Table for Dynarray Viewer

When the address of a **CDynarray** object is assigned to this property, it will be displayed in the subclassed text box. Despite the property name, the **CDynarray** object does not have to be sorted. The *DynarrayViewer* assumes ownership of the objects assigned to it, in the sense that it is permitted to delete the object when it is no longer required. The description of the *Sorted* property is given in Figure 13-18.

6.2 Polynomial Evaluator

The polynomial evaluator is an example of a hot filter. The purpose of this component is to filter floating-point numbers using the rule $y = P(x)$. The filter is passed a stream of x values, and produces a stream of y values. The coefficients of the polynomial P determine the nature of the transformation. Both the coefficients and the degree of P can be changed at run-time, but they are assumed to be somewhat stable once they have been assigned.

Although this component can give the flavor of a hot filter, the more interesting hot filters are much more complicated than this. For example, we have created several circuit simulator filters in our research. The purpose of these filters is to transform a sequence of binary inputs into a sequence of binary outputs. Before feeding input vectors to the simulator, it is necessary to configure the filter by passing it the description of a digital circuit. The digital circuit description is itself created by a series of filters. Although the polynomial evaluator is nowhere near this level of complexity, its basic principles are similar to those of the circuit simulator.

In a hot filter, the properties and methods are divided into two distinct categories: (1) those used for configuration and (2) those used for filtering. The design processes for the two sets are more or less independent of one another. The polynomial evaluator has two properties—*Degree* and *Coefficient*—that are used for configuration. Both properties are read-write in nature. *Coefficient* is an array of floating-point

Property Design Table		
Name	**Type**	**Function**
Degree	Long Integer Default = 0 Minimum = 0 Maximum = None	Sets the degree of the polynomial. The coefficient array is destroyed when a new value is assigned to this property. This property must be assigned a value before the coefficients of a new polynomial can be supplied. **Restrictions:** Run-Time Only
Coefficient	Floating Point Array Default = 0.0 Minimum = None Maximum = None	Contains the coefficients of the current polynomial. The maximum index is equal to the degree of the polynomial, and the minimum index is zero. **Restrictions:** Run-Time Only

Figure 13-19   Property Table for the Polynomial Evaluator

numbers that is indexed from zero through the value of the *Degree* property. The *Degree* property must be assigned a value before the coefficients can be supplied. The description of these two properties is given in Figure 13-19.

The implementation of the *Degree* property is given in Figure 13-20, while the implementation of the *Coefficient* property is given in Figure 13-21. The implementations are straightforward.

In most hot filters, the properties and methods used for configuration will be more complex than those used for filtering. The polynomial evaluator is no exception. For filtering, we have one method, named *p*, that will be used to evaluate the current polynomial on a floating-point operand. The method description is given in Figure 13-22, and the implementation, which is the standard Newtonian algorithm, is given in Figure 13-23.

```
void CPolyEvalCtrl::OnDegreeChanged()
{
   if (m_degree < 0)
   {
     m_degree = 0; // Enforce minimum value
   }
   if (A != NULL)
   {
     delete [] A; // delete existing coefficient array
   }
   A = new float [m_degree+1]; // create new coefficient array
   for (long i = 1 ; i <= m_degree ; i++)
   {
     A[i] = 0.0; // initialize all coefficients to zero
   }
   A[0] = 1.0; // set constant coefficient to 1
}
```

Figure 13-20   The Implementation of the *Degree* Property

```
float CPolyEvalCtrl::GetCoefficient(long Idx)
{
   if (Idx <= m_degree)
   {
     return A[Idx];
   }
   return 0.0f;
}
void CPolyEvalCtrl::SetCoefficient(long Idx, float newValue)
{
   if (Idx <= m_degree)
   {
     A[Idx] = newValue;
   }
}
```

Figure 13-21   The Implementation of the *Coefficient* Property

Method Description		
Name	p	
Return Value	Floating Point	
Description	Evaluates the current polynomial on its argument and returns the result.	
Arguments	**Name**	**Type**	**Description**
	x	Floating Point	Value for polynomial evaluation.

Figure 13-22   Description of the *p* Method

```
float CPolyEvalCtrl::p(float x)
{
   float rv = A[m_degree];
   for (long i = m_degree - 1 ; i >= 0 ; i--)
   {
     rv = rv*x + A[i];
   }
   return rv;
}
```

Figure 13-23   Implementation of the *p* method

6.3 The SGE Scriptor Control

For our final example, we will return to the Simple Graphical Editor first introduced in Chapter 7. Suppose you have created a similar editor and wish to create a series of Web pages explaining how to use your component. You may want to illustrate some of the drawing features of your component by embedding the component directly in the Web page and drawing the objects in response to button clicks or other user input. This would, of course, require that you have some sort of background editor to create the drawings programmatically. You can certainly use a background editor similar to the SGE background editor described in Chapter 8, but if you want to illustrate complex drawings, this will require a large number of function calls and some prior experimentation with the parameters to make sure that you get the drawing just right. A simpler alternative is to use a scripting component—a two-way filter that can transform a **CGraphicList** object into an ASCII script or transform an ASCII script into a **CGraphicList** object. The scripts can be used incrementally to create a drawing in stages. This component is based on the serialization components described in Chapter 9.

You would use this component by first creating a drawing program in Visual Basic or some other language and adding a scripting component to it. You would first create a drawing, and then use the scripting component to transform the drawing into an ASCII script. The script could be displayed in a multiline text box and then cut and pasted into your Web page. Your Web page would also have a scripting component, which would be used to transform the script back into a drawing. It is possible to separate these two functions into two different components, but for simplicity we have integrated them into a single component.

Like the other SGE components, the *SGEScriptor* component has a set of model manipulation properties and methods. These include the *ModelHandle* property, the *ReleaseModel* method, and the *DeleteModel* method. Because these are identical to the properties and methods of the other SGE components, their descriptions are omitted here. In addition to these, the *SGEScriptor* component has a *New* method to create a new drawing. When a new script is processed by the component, all drawing objects in the script are added to the current drawing. The *New* method is used to terminate the existing drawing and start a new one. The description of this method can be found in Figure 13-24. It is not necessary to call this method before adding scripts.

The SGEScriptor is both a hot and a cold filter. When transforming drawings into scripts, it acts as a cold filter, but when transforming scripts into drawings, it acts as a hot filter with the model manipulation features playing the configuration role. The filtering itself is done using the *Script* property.

The implementation of the *Script* property is quite complex. When the value of the property is read, the existing model is serialized and the resultant string is returned as the value of the property. (An empty string is returned if there is no model.) When the value of the property is written, the script is parsed into lines, and each line is

Method Description		
Name	New	
Return Value	Void	
Description	Deletes the existing model and creates a new empty model. Use *ReleaseModel* prior to calling this method to prevent deletion of the existing mode.	
Arguments	**Name**	**Type**	**Description**
Void			

Figure 13-24   Description of the *New* Method

Property Design Table		
Name	**Type**	**Function**
Script	String Default = Empty	When read, transforms the existing drawing into a script and returns the script. When written, deserializes the input script and adds the drawing objects to the existing drawing. If there is no existing drawing, an empty drawing is created before adding objects. **Restrictions:** Run-Time Only

Figure 13-25   Property Table for the *Script* Property

```
// serialize model and return resultant string
BSTR CSGEScriptorCtrl::GetScript()
{
   CString Buffer;
   Buffer.Empty();
   if (Model != NULL) // Normally Supplied by ModelHandle
   {
       Model->SSerialize(Buffer);
   }
   // still empty if model is null
   return Buffer.AllocSysString(); // convert CString to BSTR
}
```

Figure 13-26   The Read Portion of the *Script* Property

passed to the deserialization function used by the serialization components of Chapter 9. The resultant drawing objects are added to the current drawing. If there is no current drawing, then a new empty drawing is created. The description of the *Script* property is given in Figure 13-25.

Figure 13-26 contains the implementation of the read portion of the *Script* property. The majority of the work is done by the *SSerialize* function of the **CGraphicList** object.

The majority of the write portion of the *Script* property is devoted to parsing the input script into lines. When the new objects are added to the drawing, they will be added as part of the selection. It will be possible to undo the addition, and the dirty flag of the drawing will be set. The implementation of the *write* portion of the *Script* property is given in Figure 13-27.

```
// deserialize new Script property value, and add to current model
// create new model if necessary
void CSGEScriptorCtrl::SetScript(LPCTSTR lpszNewValue)
{
   if (Model == NULL) // Create model if there isn't one
   {
```

Figure 13-27   The Write Portion of the *Script* Property

```
            Model = new CGraphicList;
    }
    // deselect everything so we can add new script to selection
    Model->ClearSelect();
    long BP = 0;
    long BufferBytes = strlen(lpszNewValue);
    CString S;
    S.Empty();
    // standard before adding a new UNDO
    Model->ClearRedo();
    // we will permit script to be undone
    Model->NewUndoCommand();
    // scan each byte of the new script
    // when an end of line is found, pass the line to
    // SDeserialize (global function, part of model)
    while (BP < BufferBytes)
    {
        // accumulate current byte
        S += lpszNewValue[BP];
        if (lpszNewValue[BP] == '\n')
        {
            // EOL found, deserialize S, and erase it
            CGraphicObject * Obj = SDeserialize(S);
            S.Empty();
            // if format OK, add new object to model,
            // with UNDO, with Dirty bit, added to selection
            if (Obj != NULL)
            {
                Model->InsertObject(Obj);
            }
        }
        // Next byte
        BP++;
    }
    if (!S.IsEmpty())
    {
        // If there are bytes left over in S, it is probably an
        // unterminated line, so go ahead and process it.
        CGraphicObject * Obj = SDeserialize(S);
        S.Empty();
        // if format OK, add to model
        if (Obj != NULL)
        {
            Model->InsertObject(Obj);
        }
    }
}
```

Figure 13-27   (*Continued*)

7. A REVIEW OF THE METHODOLOGY

Since most of the complexity of a Filter lies in its internal implementation, we must begin with a careful design of this portion of the component. Except for the simplest Filters, this will entail a detailed object-oriented design of the component internals. The component interface is used only for input and output.

The main interface decision is whether to use file-level or object-level input and output. Some combination of the two can also be used. In the case of object-level input and output, the input can be supplied in a single block (as it is in our examples) or it can be streamed. In general, file-level input and output permits larger amounts of data than object-level input and output. Streaming the input and output can provide a compromise between the two. In streamed input, a method call or property assignment is used to start the input process. When input becomes exhausted, the component issues an event requesting more input. Streamed output works the same way, with the component issuing events when a portion of the output is available.

Once the design of the input and output interfaces has been completed, the rest of the development proceeds as if the component were an ordinary program.

8. CONCLUSION

Because they contain general algorithms of arbitrary complexity, Filters are the mainstay of heavy-duty computing. Virtually any algorithm can be embedded in a Filter, allowing filters to act as a bridge between program-level and component-level design. Many traditional sorts of programs can be turned into components by embedding them in a file Filter wrapper.

Despite these advantages, there are few Filters on the market today. The most commonly available filters are those that provide some sort of image processing. For experienced programmers who are not familiar with component-level design, Filters are the best way to break into component level programming. In the future, we should expect to see Filters for many different applications appearing on the market.

EXERCISES

1. Select your favorite algorithm from your algorithms course and implement it as a filter. Create the required generator and display components to test your filter.
2. Take a project that you completed for another course, and embed it in one or more filter components.
3. Create a text filter that converts text strings to uppercase.
4. Create a hot filter that accepts a list of words as configuration data. The filter will filter strings searching for the words in the list. When one is found, it will be replaced by the string *(deleted)*.
5. Create a filter that reverses the characters of a string.

Chapter 14

UI Widgets

1. PREREQUISITES AND OBJECTIVES

Before starting this chapter, you should have

1. A knowledge of programming in C++.
2. A knowledge of component interface design.

After completing this chapter, you will have

1. A knowledge of how to design user interface components.
2. A knowledge of the UI Widget design methodology.

2. INTRODUCTION

At one time, virtually all components were User Interface (UI) Widgets. Even today, the UI Widget is the predominant type of commercial component. Some UI Widgets, like the list box, have programmable behavior, while others, like the button, do not. Because so many UI Widgets are available, it is unlikely that you will need to implement any of your own. However, it is still good to understand the principles of such components. Many interesting programs can be created using nothing but UI Widgets.

The primary function of a UI Widget is to transform mouse clicks into programmable events. (Do not be confused by text boxes. Text boxes are editors, not UI Widgets.) In addition to firing events, UI Widgets can display useful information and provide visual feedback regarding the events they are creating. Consider, for example, the scroll-bar component. The slider portion of the scroll bar provides useful information about the current position in a document, and it also provides visual feedback about scrolling operations.

In this chapter we will give examples of both configurable and nonconfigurable components.

3. THE METHODOLOGY

The first step in designing a UI Widget is the design of the visible display. You must decide between using a predrawn bitmap or drawing the display using drawing functions. If useful information is to be displayed along with static pictures, we must determine the source of that information. The typical way to handle this is by supplying the data through a property, but complex data can also be supplied through a series of method calls.

The second step is to determine how the user will interact with the display. You must specify the hot spots of the display—the spots that will produce events when clicked by the user. If keyboard shortcuts are to be used, you must determine the meaning of the individual keystrokes and how these keystrokes will equate to mouse clicks on the display. For example, if your UI Widget displays a left-pointing arrow, pressing the left arrow button might be the equivalent of clicking the left-pointing arrow.

The final step is to design the event structure of the UI Widget. The primary purpose of a Widget is to transform and transmit user input to the host program. This must be done through events. At the very least, it is generally necessary to analyze the mouse coordinates to determine which portion of the display has been clicked. The result of this design step will be a list of events, a set of parameters for each event along with the meaning of each parameter, and a list of conditions that trigger each event.

4. THE CROSS CONTROL

Our first example is a model of the four-way button that is available on some video-game controllers. Shaped like a cross, this button permits movement in four directions: up, down, left, and right. For some controllers, diagonal movement is possible by pushing two buttons at the same time. We will use the simple drawing shown in Figure 14-1 to represent the control. The figure shows the component as it would appear in a Visual Basic program. Normally, the programmer would adjust the white area to be the same size as the cross; however, this is not necessary. The component window, which includes the entire white area and the cross within it, is divided into 11 "hot zones," each of which

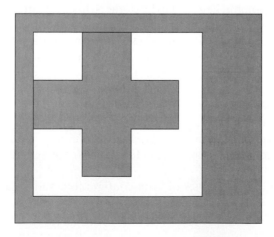

Figure 14-1 The Cross Component

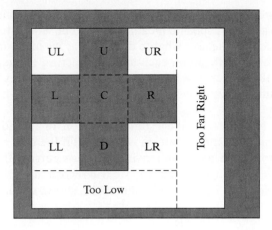

Figure 14-2   The Cross Component
Hot Zones

is associated with a particular event. These zones are shown in Figure 14-2. Clicking in one of the hot zones will produce the associated event.

Unlike most of the other types of components, for which events are almost incidental, the event description is the most important part of the definition of a UI Widget. Because the cross component has so many different events, we will use an event table to describe them, instead of an individual description for each event. Figure 14-3 gives the event table for the cross component.

Because the UI Widget provides a visual interface with the user of the program, considerable effort should be made to create a pleasing display. (Admittedly, we have

Event Table	
Description	These events report hot-zone clicks.
Arguments	Void
Name	**Triggers**
Center	Mouse click in the center of the cross.
Down	Mouse click on the lower arm of the cross.
Up	Mouse click on the upper arm of the cross.
Left	Mouse click on the left arm of the cross.
Right	Mouse click on the right arm of the cross.
DownLeft	Mouse click between the lower arm and the left arm.
DownRight	Mouse click between the lower arm and the right arm.
UpLeft	Mouse click between the upper arm and the left arm.
UpRight	Mouse click between the upper arm and the right arm.
TooFarRight	Mouse click to the right of the extension of the right arm.
TooLow	Mouse click below the extension of the lower arm.

Figure 14-3   Event Table for the Cross Component

failed somewhat in this regard.) In many ways, the drawing of the component is more important than the event structure. If specific meanings are to be associated with certain user actions, it must be clear to the user what to do. One way we might improve the cross component is to draw an arrowhead on each arm of the cross. However, we will leave this as an exercise for the reader. The drawing routine that produces the cross is given in Figure 14-4. This routine draws the outline of the cross and flood-fills the interior with gray.

We will make the cross buttons work like a standard button. In a standard button, the click event is not issued until the mouse button is released. If the user clicks on the button, holds the mouse button down, and then moves the mouse cursor off the button, no click event is issued. When the button goes down, we will record that the button has been pressed and then wait for it to be released. Figure 14-5 shows the actions taken when the button is pressed.

```cpp
void CCrossCtrl::OnDraw(
        CDC* pdc, const CRect& rcBounds, const CRect& rcInvalid)
{
    // set background to white
    pdc->FillRect(rcBounds, CBrush::FromHandle(
                    (HBRUSH)GetStockObject(WHITE_BRUSH)));
    // set up colors
    CBrush * GreyBrush = CBrush::FromHandle(
                    (HBRUSH)GetStockObject(LTGRAY_BRUSH));
    CBrush * OldBrush = pdc->SelectObject(GreyBrush);
    CPen * BlackPen = CPen::FromHandle((HPEN)GetStockObject(BLACK_PEN));
    CPen * OldPen = pdc->SelectObject(BlackPen);
    // draw outline
    pdc->MoveTo(50,0);
    pdc->LineTo(100,0);
    pdc->LineTo(100,50);
    pdc->LineTo(150,50);
    pdc->LineTo(150,100);
    pdc->LineTo(100,100);
    pdc->LineTo(100,150);
    pdc->LineTo(50,150);
    pdc->LineTo(50,100);
    pdc->LineTo(0,100);
    pdc->LineTo(0,50);
    pdc->LineTo(50,50);
    pdc->LineTo(50,0);
    // fill center -- RGB(0,0,0) is color to be replaced
    pdc->FloodFill(75,75,RGB(0,0,0));
    // clean up color selections
    pdc->SelectObject(OldBrush);
    pdc->SelectObject(OldPen);
}
```

Figure 14-4   The *OnDraw* Function of the Cross Component

```
void CCrossCtrl::OnLButtonDown(UINT nFlags, CPoint point)
{
    // record the fact that the mouse button has been pressed
    ButtonIsDown = 1;
    // we want to see the mouse-up, even if it happens outside
    // the control window.
    CWnd::SetCapture();
    // continue with normal event processing
    COleControl::OnLButtonDown(nFlags, point);
}
```

Figure 14-5   *Button-Down* Processing for the Cross Component

The real event processing takes place when the button is released. Figure 14-6 shows the processing for the button-up event. Note that because of the mouse capture, this event will be processed, even if the mouse button is released outside the component window. The mouse-up routine first tests to see if the mouse was clicked inside the component window, in which case *ButtonIsDown* will be set to one. If it was not, no

```
void CCrossCtrl::OnLButtonUp(UINT nFlags, CPoint point)
{
    // do nothing if Mouse-Down did not occur inside component window
    if (ButtonIsDown)
    {
        // release mouse capture
        // strange stuff will happen if we forget this
        ReleaseCapture();
        RECT R;
        CWnd::GetClientRect(&R);
        // do nothing if mouse-up is outside the component window
        if (point.x >= R.left && point.x <= R.right &&
                point.y >= R.top && point.y <= R.bottom)
        {
            // first check for the illegal positions
            if (point.x > 150)
            {
                FireTooFarRight();
            }
            else if (point.y > 150)
            {
                FireTooLow();
            }
            // Now find out which column the mouse is in
            else if (point.x >= 0 && point.x < 50)
            {
                // Left column, now check for the row
                if (point.y >= 0 && point.y < 50)
```

Figure 14-6   The *Button-Up* Routine for the Cross Component

```
            {
                FireUpLeft();
            }
            else if (point.y >= 50 && point.y <= 100)
            {
                FireLeft();
            }
            else
            {
                FireDownLeft();
            }
        }
        else if (point.x >= 50 && point.x <= 100)
        {
            // Middle column, now check for the row
            if (point.y >= 0 && point.y < 50)
            {
                FireUp();
            }
            else if (point.y >= 50 && point.y <= 100)
            {
                FireCenter();
            }
            else
            {
                FireDown();
            }
        }
        else
        {
            // Right column, now check for the row
            if (point.y >= 0 && point.y < 50)
            {
                FireUpRight();
            }
            else if (point.y >= 50 && point.y <= 100)
            {
                FireRight();
            }
            else
            {
                FireDownRight();
            }
        }
    }
}
```

Figure 14-6   (*Continued*)

```
    // weirdness will happen if we forget this
    ButtonIsDown = 0;
    // continue with normal event processing
    COleControl::OnLButtonUp(nFlags, point);
}
```

Figure 14-6   (*Continued*)

processing takes place. It next checks to see if the current mouse cursor position is inside the component window. If it is not, no processing takes place. Finally, the mouse position is analyzed. The first check is for the *Too Low* and *Too Far Right* zones. If the mouse is not in either of these zones, it must be within the drawing of the cross. The first check determines the horizontal position of the mouse. Once that has been determined, an additional check is done to determine the vertical position of the mouse within the column. These two pieces of information will determine the zone in which the mouse appears. The appropriate event for the zone is then fired.

An additional feature we could add to this component is visual feedback about which portion of the cross has been clicked. This will require tracking the mouse-move events, because the event that is eventually fired will be that corresponding to the final position of the mouse rather than its initial position. The visual display of the cross component is its greatest weakness. A considerable amount of work will be required to bring the display up to commercial quality.

5. THE CARDS COMPONENT

Unlike the cross component, the cards component will provide a useful visual display. This is accomplished by borrowing some drawings from an existing operating system component. The Windows operating system includes a file named *cards.dll* which contains high-quality drawings of a deck of playing cards, along with several designs for the backs of the cards and a couple of other useful drawings. This file has been used by many programmers to create interactive card games. Rather than provide a simple wrapper for the *cards.dll* drawings, we will add features that enhance the utility of the component, particularly for creating stacks of cards.

To begin with, we will specify two modes of operation for our component: (1) single-card mode and (2) multiple-card mode. In single-card mode, we want the user to be able to specify the card to be displayed. We also want the component to size itself to a single card, so that there will be no extra white space as there was with the cross component. Figure 14-7 shows what the display should look like for four single-card components.

Since many card games require the user to select a card before moving it, we also want some visible indication that a card is selected. To do this, we will add a *Selected* property to the component and invert the colors of the card when it is displayed. (This is a fairly simple graphical operation.)

In multiple-card mode, we want the cards to be displayed as a stack, as shown in Figure 14-8. We will permit the user to determine the amount of space between each card, which will determine the visible portion of the lower cards. When a stack is selected,

Figure 14-7 Single-Card Mode

Figure 14-8 A Card Stack

we will invert the display of the top card only. (Modifying the component to permit the selection of a particular card in the stack is an exercise left for the reader.)

In multiple-card mode, we want to be able to add and delete cards from the stack, and we want the component to resize itself when we do this to fit the new stack of cards. Of course, we want to be able to access the members of the stack to determine which card is in a particular position, and we especially want to be able to access the top card in the stack. We also want to be able to determine how many cards are in the stack. To accomplish our goals, we have created a set of properties that will allow us to control the display of the component. Figure 14-9 gives the description of these properties.

Because we are creating a UI Widget, we also need to be concerned about the event structure. We will provide a single event, *Click*, which will notify the container that the component has been clicked. It would make sense to add a parameter to this event to determine which card in a stack has been clicked, but we will leave this as an exercise for the reader. The event description for the *Click* event is given in Figure 14-10.

In addition to providing default values for properties and other support class variables, the initialization step of the Cards component must also load the *cards.dll* file. This is done in three steps: (1) the initialization routine attempts to load *cards.dll*; (2) if that fails, it tries to load *cards32.dll*; (3) if that fails, it uses the default images in the Cards component. Initialization also sets the size of the component and flags the component as nonresizable. If the initialization step loads *cards.dll* or *cards32.dll*, the termination step will unload the file.

Property Design Table		
Name	**Type**	**Function**
Multiple	Boolean Default = FALSE	Determines whether the component is in single-card mode (FALSE) or multiple-card mode (TRUE).
Selected	Boolean Default = FALSE	Determines whether the card or the stack is selected. This property will invert the colors of the card or the top card in the stack.
CardValue	Long Integer Default = 1 Minimum = 0 Maximum = 100	Determines which card face will be displayed. Each suit is numbered in ace, 2–10, jack, queen, king order. The suits are in bridge order: clubs, diamonds, hearts, spades. 1 is the ace of clubs, 52 is the king of spades. Numbers higher than 52 display card backs and placeholders.
CardCount	Long Integer Default = 0 Minimum = 0 Maximum = None	Determines the number of cards in the stack when in multiple-card mode. This property is active regardless of the current display mode.
Card	Long Integer Array Default Size = 0 Element Default = 0 Element Minimum = 0 Element Maximum = 100	Determines the value of each card in the stack. The size of the array is equal to the CardCount property. The array is indexed from 0, with Index 0 being the lowest card in the stack. The top card in the stack is Card[CardCount-1].
Offset	Long Integer Default = 30 Minimum = 0 Maximum = 100	Determines the number of pixels between the tops of each successive card in the stack. The offset of 30 is enough for the number and suit of the lower cards to be visible. Some games pack the cards more tightly.

Figure 14-9   The Cards Component Property Design Table

Event Description			
Name	Click		
Description	Notifies the container that the component has been clicked.		
Triggers	Mouse-click anywhere in the component window.		
Arguments	**Name**	**Type**	**Description**
Void			

Figure 14-10   *Click Event* Description for the Cards Component

The drawing routine is somewhat complicated but straightforward. The first step is to determine the current drawing mode. In single-card mode, the drawing routine loads a single bitmap and copies it into the component window. In multiple-card mode, this step is repeated for each card. As each card is drawn, the upper and lower edges of the target rectangle are incremented by the value of the *Offset* property. The standard Windows operating system function *BitBlt* is used to copy the bitmap images into the component window. This function has several drawing modes, two of which are *Source-Copy* and *Invert-Source-And-Copy*. For nonselected components, only the *Source-Copy* mode is used. For selected components (with the selected property equal to **TRUE**), the *Invert-Source-And-Copy* mode is used for the last card drawn.

Although the property implementations are straightforward, the *write* portion of many of them is complicated by the necessity of resizing the component. The resize operation is required when changing the value of the *Multiple, CardCount*, and *Offset* properties. (See the Web site for details on how this is done.)

The *write* portion of the *CardCount* property is especially complicated, because the internal array of card values must be destroyed and recreated. To avoid placing too many demands on the user of the component, the data in the existing card value array must be copied into the new card value array. If the new array is smaller than the old, the extra values are discarded. If the new array is larger than the old, the new positions are filled with zeros.

At this point the Cards component has everything it needs to be used as a component in a card-game program. However, there is one additional feature that we would like to add to enhance its utility in such programs. In the real world, virtually every game of cards begins with a shuffle and a deal. This is also true for simulated card games, so anyone who constructs a card-game program must also provide some method for shuffling and dealing cards. We can greatly enhance the utility of the Cards component by building such a feature into it. To this end, we add two methods to the Cards component. *Deal* and *DrawCard*. The *Deal* method shuffles a deck of 52 cards and deals them into an array. The formal description of these methods is given in Figure 14-11. The *DrawCard* method draws cards from the array one at a time. These functions can be used to deal bridge hands using the Visual Basic routine shown in Figure 14-12. In this routine, *Deck* is an instance of the *Cards* control, while *North, East, West*, and *South* are instances of the Queue component described in Chapter 12.

The implementation of the *Deal* method appears in Figure 14-13. This method first checks for the existence of the *CardDeck* array. (*CardDeck* is a support-class variable.) If it does not exist, it is created. The array is initialized with the numbers 1 through 52 in ascending order. A second 52-element array, *Work*, is initialized by assigning a random number to each element. (Since *Work* is a local variable, it will be destroyed when the *Deal* method terminates.) The two arrays are then sorted in parallel, using the *Work* array as the key. The *Insert Sort* algorithm is used to perform the sort. The random number seed is initialized from the system clock when the component is initialized, so each call to *Deal* will produce a different randomization of the deck.

Method Description			
Name	Deal		
Return Value	Void		
Description	Creates a 52-element array containing the numbers 1–52, and sorts the array into random order.		
Arguments	**Name**	**Type**	**Description**
Void			

Method Description			
Name	DrawCard		
Return Value	Long Integer		
Description	Draws a card from the randomized array of card numbers created by the *Deal* method. The *Deal* method must be called before calling *DrawCard*.		
Arguments	**Name**	**Type**	**Description**
	SlotNumber	Long Integer	Element of the randomized array of card numbers. *SlotNumber* must be taken from the range 0–51. If *Deal* has not been called or if the *SlotNumber* is not in the range 0–51, zero will be returned.

Figure 14-11   Method Descriptions for *Deal* and *DrawCard*

```
Deck.Deal
For i = 0 To 12
    North.Value = Deck.DrawCard(i)
Next i
For i = 13 To 25
    East.Value = Deck.DrawCard(i)
Next i
For i = 26 To 38
    West.Value = Deck.DrawCard(i)
Next i
For i = 39 To 51
    South.Value = Deck.DrawCard(i)
Next i
```

Figure 14-12   Dealing Bridge Hands

```
void CCardsCtrl::Deal()
{
    long Work[52]; // key for the random sort
    if (CardDeck == NULL)
    {
        CardDeck = new long [52]; // create if it doesn't exist
    }
    for (long i=0 ; i<52 ; i++)
    {
        Work[i] = rand();      // random key
        CardDeck[i] = i+1;     // card number
    }
    for (i=1 ; i<52 ; i++) // sort by the random key
    {
        long x = Work[i];
        long y = CardDeck[i];
        for (long j=i-1 ; j>=0 ; j--)
        {
            if (Work[j] < x)
            {
                break;
            }
            Work[j+1] = Work[j];
            CardDeck[j+1] = CardDeck[j];
        }
        j++;
        Work[j] = x;
        CardDeck[j] = y;
    }
}
```

Figure 14-13   The *Deal* Method

6. THE DICE COMPONENT

Our final example is a simulation of a six-sided die. The actions of the die are modeled by the class **CDie**. The Dice component serves as a wrapper for the **CDie** class. It is not clear whether this component should be classified as a UI Widget or as a model. This serves to illustrate that the dividing line between categories is not always clear.

Figure 14-14 gives the definition of the **CDie** class. Each face of the die is represented by a short integer. The value of each face must be taken from the range 1–6, and it is necessary that the faces have the correct relationship to one another. A quick examination of a die will reveal the following properties. The sum of the numbers on two opposing faces is always equal to seven. Thus 1 must be opposite 6, 2 opposite 5, and 3 opposite 4. There are two different configurations of spots that will meet this requirement. The correct configuration can be determined by looking at the corner where 1, 2, and 3 meet. When looking down at this corner, the numbers must appear in

```
class CDie
{
protected:
    short Back;
    short Front;
    short Right;
    short Left;
    short Bottom;
    short Top;

public:
    CDie();
    virtual ~CDie();

    short GetBack(void);
    short GetFront(void);
    short GetRight(void);
    short GetLeft(void);
    short GetBottom(void);
    short GetTop(void);

    void SetFront(short Face);
    void SetTop(short Face);

    void Reset(void);

    void SpinRight(void);
    void SpinLeft(void);
    void RollBack(void);
    void RollFront(void);
    void RollRight(void);
    void RollLeft(void);
};
```

Figure 14-14   The CDie Class

counterclockwise order. Thus, if the die is in front of you with 1 at the top and 2 to the left, 3 must be facing you.

All operations on the die, including initialization, must maintain these relationships. To enforce these rules, the six faces are maintained in protected variables. The *Get* functions can be used to obtain the value of each face. The *Reset* function, which is called by the class constructor, puts 1 at the top and 3 to the front with all other faces initialized consistently. The functions *RollRight*, *RollLeft*, *RollFront*, *RollBack*, *SpinLeft*, and *SpinRight* turn the die 90 degrees in the indicated direction. For *RollRight* and *RollLeft*, the front and back are left unchanged; for *RollFront* and *RollBack*, the left and right are left unchanged; for *SpinLeft* and *SpinRight*, the top and bottom are left unchanged. The *SetTop* and *SetFront* functions can be used to put the die in any desired position. Both functions must be called, with *SetTop* being called first. *SetTop* moves the specified number to the top, while *SetFront* spins the die without changing the top or bottom. *SetFront* will fail if the specified face is on the top or the bottom. We will omit the implementation details of this class because they are straightforward and somewhat tedious. The full implementation appears on the Web site.

The *Dice* control provides properties to access each face (*TopFace*, *RightFace*, etc.) as well as wrapper methods for each of the class manipulator functions. In addition to these, it provides two properties, *DotColor* and *FaceColor*, to set the dot color and the face color of the die, and a method, *Toss*, that can be used to simulate a random throw of the die. The only interesting implementation is that of the *Toss* method illustrated in Figure 14-15. The *Toss* method uses the *SetTop*, *SpinLeft*, and *SpinRight* functions of the **CDie** class to randomly position the die. The top is chosen randomly by generating a random number in the range 1–6. The front face is positioned randomly by generating a random number in the range 0–3. This number is used to select one of the four faces—*Front*, *Back*, *Left*, and *Right*—as the new front face. The spin functions are used to bring the selected face to the front.

```
void CDiceCtrl::Toss()
{
    Die.SetTop((short)((rand()%6)+1));
    long Move = rand()%4;
    switch (Move)
    {
        case 0:
        {
            Die.SpinLeft();
        }
        break;
        case 1:
        {
            Die.SpinRight();
        }
        break;
        case 2:
        {
            Die.SpinLeft();
            Die.SpinLeft();
        }
        break;
    }
    CWnd::Invalidate();
}
```

Figure 14-15   The *Toss* Method

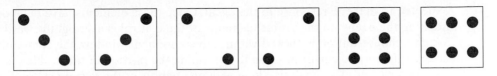

Figure 14-16   Die Face Orientations

Event Description			
Name	Click		
Description	Notifies the container that the component has been clicked.		
Triggers	Mouse click anywhere in the component window.		
Arguments	**Name**	**Type**	**Description**
Void			

Figure 14-17   *Click* Event Description for the Dice Component

There is one additional problem that we face if we are to provide an accurate simulation of a real die—namely, the configuration of the dots on faces 2, 3, and 6. These faces can be drawn in two different ways. (Faces 1, 4, and 5 are symmetric and do not have this problem.) Figure 14-16 illustrates the different drawings for the 2, 3, and 6 faces.

To determine which drawing to use in each case, it is necessary to examine a real die. Such an examination will reveal the following. When 1 is at the top, 3 will slant to the right, and 2 will slant to the left. These are the second and third drawings in Figure 14-16. Furthermore, the open ends of the 6 point at 3 and 4. The drawing routine will draw only the top face of the die. To determine which orientation of 2, 3, and 6 must be drawn, it is necessary to examine the front face. Apart from these details, the drawing of the die is simply a matter of drawing a few circles.

The die component has one event, *Click*, that is fired when the user clicks anywhere in the component window. The description of this event is given in Figure 14-17.

7. A REVIEW OF THE METHODOLOGY

Most UI Widgets combine information display with user interaction. (Buttons are the exception, but we already have a lot of those.) In the design of a UI Widget, we must answer three questions: (1) What information will be displayed? (2) How will it be displayed? and (3) How will the user interact with the display? The first step is to design the visible elements of the component and the properties and methods used to control the visible interface. Next it is necessary to design the event structure of the component. When designing an event, it is necessary to have a clear picture of how the programmer will use the event, to know what information the programmer will need to process the event, and to understand what actions the programmer would normally be expected to make in response to the event. Once these elements have been designed, hooking the events to the visible elements of the control is a straightforward process. When a mouse button is clicked within the component window, the component must analyze the mouse-cursor position to determine the portion of the visible display that has been clicked. This analysis, along with an analysis of the current state of the component, will permit the component to select and fire the proper event.

8. CONCLUSION

The UI Widget is the most common type of component available today. There are so many UI Widgets available, that it is difficult to find something that has not already been done. The wide availability of existing components makes it unlikely that the component designer will need to create many new ones.

EXERCISES

1. Create a UI Widget for an automatic transmission indicator. The user should be able to "shift gears" by clicking on one of the following characters: P, R, N, D, 1, or 2.

2. Create a three-way selector control that permits the user to select one of three states by clicking on one arm of a T. The T should look something like the one in Figure 14-18. Draw a black square on the arm that is currently selected.

Figure 14-18

3. Create a component similar to the cross control but use an 8-point star to indicate directions. Clicking on the appropriate point makes a move in the indicated direction.

4. Modify the cross control so the display is three-dimensional and moves down when pressed.

5. Modify the cross control so that holding the mouse button down in a particular location will create a series of events instead of a single event. The events should occur at a rate of 10 per second.

Chapter 15

Decorations

1. PREREQUISITES AND OBJECTIVES

Before starting this chapter, you should have

1. A knowledge of programming in C++.
2. A knowledge of component interface design.

After completing this chapter, you will have

1. A knowledge of how to design Decoration components.

2. INTRODUCTION

Decorations are similar to UI Widgets but normally do not provide user interaction. Despite their name, decorations often provide the user with useful information. Those that are purely decorative in nature tend to be the exception rather than the rule. For example, a label that reads "Warning. If you proceed, your hard disk will be erased!" provides extremely useful information, despite the fact that the label component providing the information is a Decoration. Most decorations can be configured in some way.

We will provide two examples of decorations: an LED component and a flashing label component.

3. THE METHODOLOGY

Because Decoration components are seldom, if ever, purely decorative in nature, the first step in the design of a decoration is to have a clear idea of its purpose. For example, the purpose of a label is to provide static textual information, while the purpose of a progress bar is to indicate what percentage of a task has been completed. Once a purpose has been clearly specified, the next step is to design a visual display to meet that purpose. It is generally useful to complete a set of drawings during this step.

Decorations are not always static. If some form of data input is required (such as text for a label), it should be specified through properties. State changes should also be specified using properties. The use of properties allows these values to be specified at design time. Generally speaking, once the visible elements of the component have been designed, the rest of the design is quite simple.

4. A SIMPLE LED COMPONENT

The LED component displays a picture of an LED. The bitmaps for this component were created on a white background. Because the bitmap editor anti-aliased the outline of the bitmaps with the white background, the LEDs look strange on any background that is not white. On the other hand, they look *excellent* on white backgrounds.

The LED component has two properties: one to set the color of the LED and one to set the color of the background. The LED bitmaps are circular but are drawn in a square background just large enough to contain the component. Figure 15-1 shows the three different bitmaps used to display the LED, while Figure 15-2 gives the description of the LED properties.

The drawing routine performs the following operations. It determines the current value of the *LedColor* property and loads the proper bitmap for the color. (The bitmaps are stored as resources in the component module.) The bitmap is copied into the component window, and the white border is flood-filled with the background color. Because the implementation of the component is straightforward, we omit the details. The code for the LED component is available on the Web site.

Figure 15-1   The LED Bitmaps

Property Design Table		
Name	**Type**	**Function**
BackColor	Color Default = Gray	Determines the background color of the rectangle containing the LED bitmap.
LedColor	Enumerated Led_Red = 0 Led_Green = 1 Led_Yellow = 2 Default = Led_Red	Determines the color of the LED. If a value other than 0, 1, or 2 is assigned, the value will be assigned.

Figure 15-2   The LED Property Design Table

5. THE FLASHING-TEXT CONTROL

The flashing-text control is a text label that has the capability of flashing to call attention to the text message. The programmer has the capability of changing the background color as well as the *on* and *off* text colors. The default state of the text message is on. When the text is flashing, the message alternates between the on and off state. The programmer can set separate text colors for each state or specify that the text is invisible in either the on or the off state. The programmer can also set the state of the text to *Flashing* or *Not-Flashing*.

When the *Flashing* state is first set, the component starts a system timer with an interval of 250 ms (1/4 sec.). This timer fires an event each time the 250 ms interval expires. This event is used to toggle the on/off state of the text. When the *Flashing* state is set to *Not-Flashing*, the text returns to the on state.

The **CTextControl** class given in Figure 15-3 was created to simplify the development of the Flashing-Text component. This class encapsulates all information about the flashing text. The variables of this class are modified directly by the component routines.

With two exceptions, the elements of the **CTextControl** object are available as properties of the Flashing-Text component. The variable *TimerID* is used to communicate with the system timer that controls the flashing, while the variable *NowOn* is set during the flashing process to control the display of the text. The heart of the Flashing-Text component is the drawing routine that is given in Figure 15-4.

Each time the component is redrawn, the existing text is erased and redrawn. The current on/off state of the text determines the color that is used to draw the text. The flashing state of the component is controlled by the *Flash* property, the implementation of which is given in Figure 15-5.

The *OnTimer* routine of the support class is used to process events from the timer and to control the flashing of the text. While the text is flashing, these events will occur

```
class CTextControl
{
public:
    COLORREF BackColor;
    UINT TimerID;
    BOOL OffInvis;
    BOOL OnInvis;
    BOOL Flashing;
    BOOL NowOn;
    COLORREF OffColor;
    COLORREF OnColor;
    CString Value;
    CTextControl();
    virtual ~CTextControl();
};
```

Figure 15-3   The CTextControl Class

```
void CFlashTextCtrl::OnDraw(
        CDC* pdc, const CRect& rcBounds, const CRect& rcInvalid)
{
    // paint the background
    CBrush MyBack;
    MyBack.CreateSolidBrush(Txt.BackColor);
    CBrush * OldBrush = pdc->SelectObject(&MyBack);
    pdc->FillRect(rcBounds, &MyBack);
    // save text-related colors
    COLORREF OldColor = pdc->GetTextColor();
    COLORREF OldBackClr = pdc->GetBkColor();
    // set text background color
    pdc->SetBkColor(Txt.BackColor);
    // set text foreground color and draw
    if (Txt.NowOn)
    {
        if (!Txt.OnInvis)
        {
            pdc->SetTextColor(Txt.OnColor);
            pdc->TextOut(0,0,Txt.Value);
        }
    }
    else
    {
        if (!Txt.OffInvis)
        {
            pdc->SetTextColor(Txt.OffColor);
            pdc->TextOut(0,0,Txt.Value);
        }
    }
    // restore drawing state.
    pdc->SelectObject(OldBrush);
    MyBack.DeleteObject();
    pdc->SetTextColor(OldColor);
    pdc->SetBkColor(OldBackClr);
}
```

Figure 15-4   The Flashing-Text *OnDraw* Routine

```
void CFlashTextCtrl::SetFlash(BOOL bNewValue)
{
    if (bNewValue)
    {
        if (!Txt.Flashing)
        {
            Txt.Flashing = TRUE;
```

Figure 15-5   Implementation of the *Flash* Property

```
                Txt.TimerID = CWnd::SetTimer(1,250,NULL);
                Txt.NowOn = TRUE;
                CWnd::Invalidate();
            }
        }
        else
        {
            if (Txt.Flashing)
            {
                Txt.Flashing = FALSE;
                Txt.NowOn = TRUE;
                CWnd::KillTimer(1);
                CWnd::Invalidate();
            }
        }
        SetModifiedFlag();
}
```

Figure 15-5   (*Continued*)

```
void CFlashTextCtrl::OnTimer(UINT nIDEvent)
{
    if (Txt.NowOn)
    {
        Txt.NowOn = FALSE;
    }
    else
    {
        Txt.NowOn = TRUE;
    }
    CWnd::Invalidate();
    COleControl::OnTimer(nIDEvent);
}
```

Figure 15-6   The Flashing-Text *OnTimer* Routine

at a rate of approximately four times per second. The implementation of the *OnTimer* routine is given in Figure 15-6.

Except for the *Flash* property, the implementations of the other properties of the Flashing-Text component are straightforward. Figure 15-7 describes the properties of the Flashing-Text component.

All of the properties listed in this figure are persistent properties. This implies that the text may be in the flashing state when the component is initialized, which in turn implies that the timer that controls the flashing must be started during the initialization process rather than as a consequence of assigning a value to the *Flash* property. The *OnCreate* routine of the support class is called after the values of persistent

Property Design Table		
Name	**Type**	**Function**
BackGround	Color Default = Gray	Determines the background color of the rectangle containing the text.
OnColor	Color Default = White	Determines the color of the text when it is not flashing.
OffColor	Color Default = Black	Alternates text color between the *OnColor* and the *OffColor* when flashing.
Value	String Default = "Flashing Text"	Displays the text by the component.
InvisibleWhenOn	Boolean Default = FALSE	If true, makes text invisible when the component is not flashing and when the state of the text is *on*.
InvisibleWhenOff	Boolean Default = FALSE	If true, makes text invisible when *off*. The text will appear to flash on and off.
Flash	Boolean Default = FALSE	If true, causes text to flash; if false, the text is in the *on* state.

Figure 15-7   The Flashing-Text Property Design Table

```
int CFlashTextCtrl::OnCreate(LPCREATESTRUCT lpCreateStruct)
{
    if (COleControl::OnCreate(lpCreateStruct) == -1)
    {
        return -1;
    }
    if (Txt.Flashing)
    {
        Txt.TimerID = CWnd::SetTimer(1,250,NULL);
        Txt.NowOn = TRUE;
        CWnd::Invalidate();
    }
    return 0;
}
```

Figure 15-8   The *OnCreate* Routine of the Flashing-Text Component

properties have been restored but before the component is displayed. This is the ideal place to start the timer. The *OnCreate* routine is illustrated in Figure 15-8.

6. A REVIEW OF THE METHODOLOGY

The main design element for a decoration is the design of the visual display. The main question you want to answer is, "What will it look like?" In your formal design documents you should have a clear English description of the visual aspects of the component, accompanied by hand drawings, if necessary. (Hand drawings would be good for the LED component but pointless for the Flashing-Text component.)

Next, it is necessary to determine whether the display will be static or configurable. If the display is static, virtually no component interface will be required. If it is configurable, then a set of configuration properties and methods must be designed. Persistent properties are preferred for this purpose, because this allows the component to be configured at design time.

For many decorations, the design of the visible elements will be the most time-consuming portion of the design. (This was certainly the case for the LED component.) Once the visible elements have been designed, the rest of the component design should be straightforward.

7. CONCLUSION

The primary purpose for a decoration is to supply information to the end user of a program. There are Decoration components that serve a purely decorative function, but these tend to be the exception rather than the rule. If you have some new, interesting way of passing information to the user that does not require any user interaction, then you should create a Decoration component to present the information. Decorations have the most in common with Display components.

EXERCISES

1. Create a speedometer component that will display a picture of a speedometer with markings from 0 to 100. A configuration parameter will be used to set a value from 0 to 100 indicating the position of the needle. The *OnDraw* routine will draw the picture with the needle in the correct position.

2. Create a progress bar component similar to that which you see when you install software or download something.

3. Create an invisible decoration that can be used to produce several different "beep" tones.

Chapter 16

Function Libraries

1. PREREQUISITES AND OBJECTIVES

Before starting this chapter, you should have

1. A knowledge of programming in C++.
2. A knowledge of component interface design.

After completing this chapter, you will have

1. A knowledge of how to design Function Library components.

2. INTRODUCTION

A function library is a component that provides a number of useful functions but has little or nothing in the way of internal state. Function Library components are extremely rare for two reasons. First, there are a number of different ways to provide function libraries, most of which are much more efficient than using a component. Second, function libraries are more closely associated with functional programming than with object-oriented programming. The object-oriented components described in the preceding chapters are likely to be far more useful than a pure function library.

Nevertheless, we have found at least one application where function libraries are quite useful. This is in the implementation of wizards and common dialog boxes. Even so, these are "information collectors," not pure function libraries. When a function is called, a dialog box, or a series of dialog boxes is displayed. The user supplies information to the dialog boxes, which is then recorded in the properties of the component. When the function completes its execution, the calling program extracts the information from the properties. These properties are also used to provide initialization values for the dialog box controls.

3. THE METHODOLOGY

No special methodology is used to create components of this type. The same principles apply here as would apply to any function library. We must make a collection of functions that are useful, and related in some way. There is the added dimension of having multiple instances of a common environment for all functions in the library, but this is useful only in specialized contexts. In many cases, it is more efficient to use a standard compile-time library or a dynamic run-time library.

4. THE VDAL COMMON DIALOGS COMPONENT

The Virtual Design Automation Laboratory (VDAL) Common Dialogs component was created to provide a set of dialog boxes for a set of Web-based design automation applications. Several of these applications require the user to enter circuit descriptions and other data in text format. A commercial text-editing component was used to support these operations. The VDAL Common Dialogs component contains a set of dialog boxes that were specially designed for use with this component. Some of these boxes are similar to those provided by the Windows Operating System common dialogs. These dialogs are shown in Figures 16-1 through 16-5.

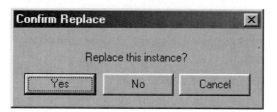

Figure 16-1   The *Confirm Replace* Dialog

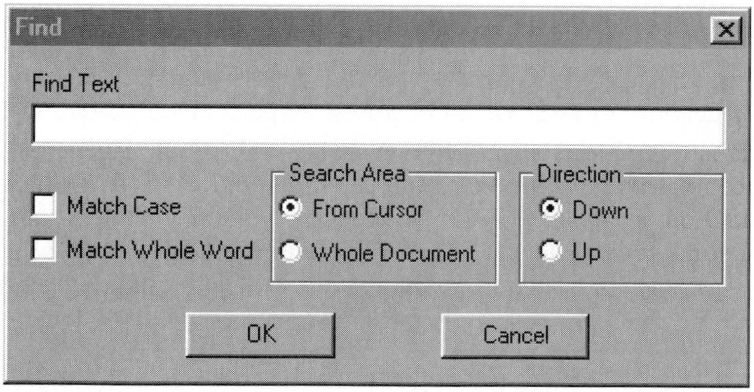

Figure 16-2   The *Find* Dialog

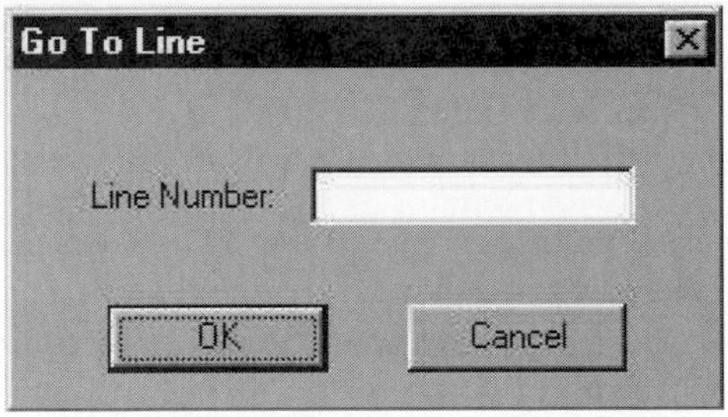

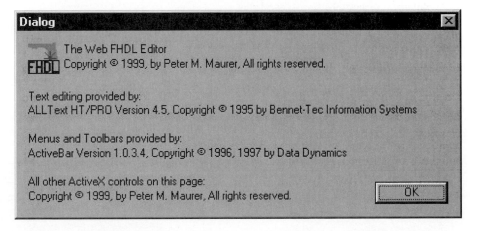

Figure 16-3   The *Go To* Dialog

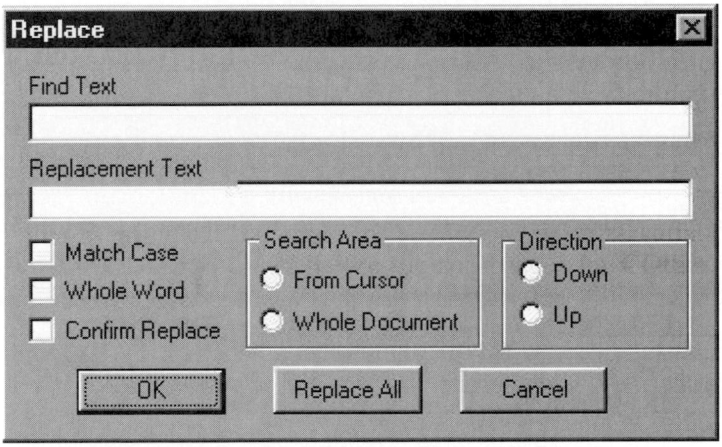

Figure 16-4   The *Replace* Dialog

Figure 16-5   The *About* Dialog

Each of the dialogs has an associated method that is used to display the dialog and an associated set of properties to hold the values of the text boxes and other controls on the dialog. The descriptions of these functions are given in Figures 16-6 through 16-10.

The component properties are used to supply initial values for the dialog boxes and to retrieve the values entered by the user. These properties are listed in Figure 16-11.

Method Description			
Name	ShowConfirm		
Return Value	Void		
Description	Shows the *Confirm Replace* dialog.		
Arguments	Name	Type	Description
Void			

Figure 16-6   The *ShowConfirm* Method

Method Description			
Name	ShowFind		
Return Value	Void		
Description	Shows the *Find Text* dialog.		
Arguments	Name	Type	Description
Void			

Figure 16-7   The *ShowFind* Method

Method Description			
Name	ShowLineNumber		
Return Value	Void		
Description	Shows the *Go To Line* dialog.		
Arguments	Name	Type	Description
Void			

Figure 16-8   The *ShowLineNumber* Method

Method Description			
Name	ShowReplace		
Return Value	Void		
Description	Shows the *Replace Text* dialog.		
Arguments	Name	Type	Description
Void			

Figure 16-9   The *ShowReplace* Method

Method Description			
Name	ShowWebFHDL		
Return Value	Void		
Description	Shows the *About* dialog.		
Arguments	**Name**	**Type**	**Description**
Void			

Figure 16-10   The *ShowWebFHDL* Method

Property Design Table		
Name	**Type**	**Function**
LineNumber	Long Integer	Holds *Go To* dialog text-box value.
FindText	String	Holds *Find/Replace* dialog target text.
ReplacementText	String	Holds *Replace* dialog replacement text.
MatchCase	Boolean	Holds value of *Find/Replace Match Case* check box.
SearchArea	Enumerated From Cursor = 0 Whole Document = 1	Holds value of *Find/Replace Search Area* radio buttons.
SearchDirection	Enumerated Up = 0 Down = 1	Holds value of *Find/Replace Search Direction* radio buttons.
WholeWord	Boolean	Holds value of *Find/Replace Whole Word* check box.
ConfirmReplace	Boolean	Holds value of *Replace Confirm* replace check box.
UserCancelled	Boolean	Set when cancel button is clicked on any dialog.
SearchAll	Boolean	Set when *Replace All* button is clicked on the *Replace* dialog.
LastFind	Enumerated None = 0 Find = 1 Replace = 2	Used to support "*Repeat Last Find*" operations. Keeps track of the last find/replace operation.
ConfirmYes	Boolean	Set when *Yes* is clicked on *Confirm Replace* dialog.
ConfirmNo	Boolean	Set when *No* is clicked on *Confirm Replace* dialog.
ConfirmCancel	Boolean	Set when *Cancel* is clicked on *Confirm Replace* dialog.

Figure 16-11   The VDAL Common Dialogs Property Design Table

The implementation of the VDAL Common Dialogs component is straightforward and will not be presented here. The source code for the component is available on the Web site. The component has additional features that are not described here because they do not fit the paradigm of a function library.

5. CONCLUSION

Because function libraries do not fit well with modern object-oriented design techniques and because they are available in many other forms, they are the least commonly encountered type of component. They do, however, provide a means of encapsulating and distributing sets of similar functions. Although function access is less efficient than it is with other types of function libraries, component function libraries do not require header files and may be somewhat easier to use for that reason.

EXERCISE

1. Make a list of your favorite functions, and combine them into a Function Library component.

Chapter 17

Service Wrappers

1. PREREQUISITES AND OBJECTIVES

Before starting this chapter, you should have

1. A knowledge of programming in C++.
2. A knowledge of component interface design.

After completing this chapter, you will have

1. A knowledge of how to encapsulate operating system functions in a programmer-friendly wrapper.
2. A knowledge of the Service Wrapper Component design methodology.

2. INTRODUCTION

A service wrapper is a component that provides access to operating system services. In most cases, these services are already available to the programmer in some form but are difficult to access or to use properly. The service wrapper is provided to simplify access to these services.

In commercial software, the service wrapper is probably the second most common type of component after the UI Widget. In the earlier versions of Visual Basic, it was difficult or impossible to access certain operating system services. In many cases, service wrappers were the only way to access these services. (An example of such a service is the font selection dialog.)

The quintessential example of a service wrapper is the Microsoft Common Dialogs component, which provides access to the *open, save as*, and *color selection* dialogs, in addition to several others. Commercial service wrappers are available for accessing Internet services—from FTP to telephony services such as autodial and terminal emulation. In this chapter we will provide a service wrapper for the INI (initialization) file services.

In most of today's software, these services have been replaced with registry services. We could have provided a service wrapper for registry services. However, registry information tends to be quite sensitive to tampering, and we chose not to enhance the student's ability to damage this information.

3. THE METHODOLOGY

The first step in the methodology is to examine the operating system service to be encapsulated to determine if the existing interface is adequate. In most cases, the features that are to be encapsulated are already accessible to the host program in some fashion, and it is important to determine whether a component-level wrapper will be an improvement. If the existing access methods require the use of callback functions or function calls with a large number of parameters, then a component-level interface will probably be an improvement.

The component should provide all required callback functions, and it should reduce the number of function parameters, either by supplying standard defaults or by using properties to set the value of parameters that are used repetitively. The component should provide events to report any asynchronous conditions that occur.

Where possible, functions should be reduced to variables. A function that supplies data to the operating system can usually be reduced to a variable. (Recall that a variable can be viewed as a pair of *Get/Set* functions.)

In some cases, it may be necessary to use pass-through functions—methods that merely pass a set of arguments through to an operating system function without changing the list or adding to it. (If a service wrapper consists only of pass-through functions, it is probably not worth the effort.)

4. THE INI FILE MANAGER

Figure 17-1 shows the format of a typical INI file. The file is broken into sections, each of which is preceded by a string in square brackets. The name in the square brackets is

```
[DBDATA]
DATADIR=E:\TESTDB
MEMBERS=MEMBERS.MDB
FINANCE=FINANCE.MDB
PRINTDIR=E:\CHURCHDB

[ProgLoc]
Household=E:\CHURCHDB\HOUSHOLD.EXE
People=E:\CHURCHDB\PEOPLE.EXE
RecordAttend=E:\CHURCHDB\RECATTND.EXE
ViewAttend=E:\CHURCHDB\CHKATTND.EXE
```

Figure 17-1   A Typical INI File

known as the *Application Name*. Each section consists of a series of name-value pairs of the form *MEMBERS=MEMBERS.MDB*. The string to the left of the equal sign is known as the *Parameter Name*, while the string to the right is known as the *Parameter Value*. To locate a particular parameter value, it is necessary to specify the file name, the application name, and the parameter name.

The Windows operating system provides functions for accessing INI files. Although the programmer may call these functions directly, we can simplify the access by encapsulating the functionality of these functions into a component. We will provide persistent properties for the file name, application name, and the parameter name. Assuming that these properties have been assigned values, reading and writing the parameter value can be reduced to a simple property access, as illustrated in Figure 17-2.

The four INI file functions are (1) *GetProfileString*, (2) *GetPrivateProfileString*, (3) *WriteProfileString*, and (4) *WritePrivateProfileString*. Figures 17-3 and 17-4 show the parameters of these functions and their usage. *GetProfileString* and *WriteProfileString* are used to access the WIN.INI file, while *GetPrivateProfileString* and *WritePrivateProfileString* are used to access other INI files. The functions *GetProfileString* and *GetPrivateProfileString* have two forms. If the parameter name is the constant NULL, the function returns a list of all parameter names in the section. If the parameter name is not NULL, the function returns the parameter value. If a list of

```
' Write parameter value
INIWrapper.Value = "New Parameter Value"
' Read parameter value
MyString = INIWrapper.Value
```

Figure 17-2 INI File Access

```
GetProfileString(Application,Parameter,Default,Buffer,Size)
GetPrivateProfileString(Application,Parameter,Default,Buffer,Size,
                        FileName)
```

Application	A null-terminated string containing the application name
Parameter	The constant NULL or a null terminated string containing the parameter name
Default	A null-terminated string that will be returned if the parameter does not exist
Buffer	A pointer to a storage area where the parameter value or name list will be stored
Size	The size of the storage area pointed to by *Buffer*
FileName	The name of the INI file to be read. If a full path name is not supplied, the file is assumed to be in the *Windows* directory

Figure 17-3 *GetProfileString* and *GetPrivateProfileString* Parameters

```
WriteProfileString(Application,Parameter,Value)
WritePrivateProfileString(Application,Parameter,Value,FileName)
```
Application	A null-terminated string containing the application name
Parameter	The constant NULL or a null-terminated string containing the parameter name
Value	The constant NULL or a null-terminated string containing the parameter value
FileName	The name of the INI file to be read. If a full path name is not supplied, the file is assumed to be in the *Windows* directory

Figure 17-4 *WriteProfileString* and *WritePrivateProfileString* Parameters

Property Design Table		
Name	**Type**	**Function**
FileName	String Default = Empty	Names the INI file. If this property contains the null string, operations will be performed on WIN.INI.
Application	String Default = Empty	Names the INI file section.
Parameter	String Default = Empty	Names the parameter. If this string is empty, the *Value* property will return a list of parameter names in the section specified by *Application*.
Value	String Default = value of Default property	Returns or sets the value of the parameter specified by *Application* and *Parameter*
Default	String Default = Empty	Serves as default value for parameters that do not exist.
DeleteApp	String Default = None	Names the section to be deleted from the INI file. **Restrictions:** Write-Only, Run-Time Only
DeleteParm	String Default = None	Names the parameter to be deleted from the section specified by *Application*. **Restrictions:** Write-Only, Run-Time Only

Figure 17-5 The INI Service Wrapper Property Design Table

parameter names is returned, each parameter name is terminated by the null character ($\backslash 0$), and the list is terminated by two consecutive null characters. *WriteProfileString* and *WritePrivateProfileString* have three different functions. If both the parameter name and the value parameters are specified as NULL, the section specified by the application name is deleted from the INI file. If a parameter name is specified with a

NULL constant for the value, then the name-value pair for the parameter is deleted from the section; otherwise the specified name-value pair is written to the specified section.

Our INI Service Wrapper will allow the user to perform all INI file operations, including deletes, by assigning values to properties. The properties of the INI Service Wrapper are listed in Figure 17-5.

Most of the functionality of the INI Service Wrapper is contained in the implementation of the *Value* property. The *read* portion of the implementation is given in Figure 17-6. If no application name is specified, this function returns the value of

```
BSTR CIniManagerCtrl::GetValue()
{
    CString strResult;
    static char StringBuffer[1024];

    if (m_application.IsEmpty()) // no application, return default
    {
        strResult = m_default;
    }
    else
    {
        if (m_fileName.IsEmpty()) // no file name, use WIN.INI
        {
            if (m_parameter.IsEmpty()) // no parameter, return name list
            {
                GetProfileString(m_application,NULL,m_default,
                                 StringBuffer,1024);
                strResult = StringBuffer;
            }
            else
            {
                GetProfileString(m_application,m_parameter,m_default,
                                 StringBuffer,1024);
                strResult = StringBuffer;
            }
        }
        else // file name has been specified, use it
        {
            if (m_parameter.IsEmpty()) // no parameter, return name list
            {
                GetPrivateProfileString(m_application,NULL,m_default,
                                        StringBuffer,1024,m_fileName);
                strResult = StringBuffer;
            }
```

Figure 17-6   The *Read* Portion of the Value Property

```
        else
        {
            GetPrivateProfileString(m_application,m_parameter,
                          m_default,StringBuffer,1024,m_fileName);
            strResult = StringBuffer;
        }
    }
}
// convert CString to BSTR
return strResult.AllocSysString();
}
```

Figure 17-6   (*Continued*)

the *Default* property. If no file name is specified, the *GetProfileString* function is used to access the WIN.INI file. Otherwise, the *GetPrivateProfileString* function is used to access the specified file. If no parameter name is specified, the *GetProfileString* or *GetPrivateProfileString* function is called with a NULL parameter name to obtain the list of parameter names in the section specified by the *Application* property. If either the application name or the parameter name does not exist in the file, the value of the *Default* property is returned. Returned strings are limited to 1024 characters.

The *write* portion of the *Value* property, which is given in Figure 17-7, is simpler than the *read* portion. Before assigning a value to the *Value* property, it is necessary to

```
void CIniManagerCtrl::SetValue(LPCTSTR lpszNewValue)
{
    // Both application name and parameter name must be specified
    // deletes are not permitted here.
    if (!m_application.IsEmpty() && !m_parameter.IsEmpty())
    {
        if (m_fileName.IsEmpty()) // no file name, use WIN.INI
        {
            WriteProfileString(m_application,m_parameter,lpszNewValue);
        }
        else // file name exists, use it
        {
            WritePrivateProfileString(m_application,m_parameter,
                                    lpszNewValue,m_fileName);
        }
    }
}
```

Figure 17-7   The Write Portion of the Value Property

```
void CIniManagerCtrl::SetDeleteApp(LPCTSTR lpszNewValue)
{
    if (m_fileName.IsEmpty()) // no file name, use WIN.INI
    {
        WriteProfileString(lpszNewValue,NULL,NULL);
    }
    else // file name exists, use it
    {
        WritePrivateProfileString(lpszNewValue,NULL,NULL,m_fileName);
    }
}
```

Figure 17-8   The *DeleteApp* Property

```
void CIniManagerCtrl::SetDeleteParm(LPCTSTR lpszNewValue)
{
    // application name must be specified or nothing happens
    if (!m_application.IsEmpty())
    {
        if (m_fileName.IsEmpty()) // no file name, use WIN.INI
        {
            WriteProfileString(m_application,lpszNewValue,NULL);
        }
        else // File name exists, use it
        {
            WritePrivateProfileString(m_application,lpszNewValue,NULL,
                                      m_fileName);
        }
    }
}
```

Figure 17-9   The *DeleteParm* Property

assign values to the *Application* and *Parameter* properties. If either of these is empty, no action will be taken. If no *FileName* is specified, the *WriteProfileString* function will be used to access the WIN.INI file; otherwise the *WritePrivateProfileString* function will be used.

We conclude here by presenting the implementations of the *DeleteApp* and *DeleteParm* properties in Figures 17-8 and 17-9. Assigning a value to the *DeleteApp* property causes the section specified by the new value to be deleted. Assigning a value to the *DeleteParm* property causes the specified parameter to be deleted from the section specified by the *Application* property. If the application property has not been set, assigning a value to *DeleteParm* will do nothing.

5. A REVIEW OF THE METHODOLOGY

Because a service wrapper is designed to enhance the programmer's access to something that is already available, it is first necessary to determine whether a component is needed for a particular service. You must begin by listing those features of the service that will be encapsulated. For each feature, describe the user access both with and without the component. Make sure to include any required header file access, initialization steps, and termination operations for each case, and also make sure to consider the case where a particular feature is used several times. If, on the whole, the access is simpler using the component, then a component is needed.

The most important simplification that a service wrapper can provide is reducing a function to a variable. In the case of the INI manager, the functions used to access a parameter are reduced to accessing the *Value* property. The access functions become transparent, and the user appears to be storing and retrieving the parameter value directly from the INI file.

The next most important simplification is reducing the number of required function parameters. This is especially useful if a control block is required for the service. Examples of services that require control blocks are listing files in a directory and obtaining the current time. The required control blocks can be embedded in the component and made invisible to the user. Some services require callback functions to be supplied as function parameters. Embedding these callbacks in the component is an important simplification. (Some languages do not support callbacks, and cannot give access to the service without a component to provide the callback functions.)

The least important simplification is providing straight-through access to service functions. The number of parameters is not reduced, and the parameters do not undergo transformation before being passed to the service function. Despite appearances, this is still a simplification, because components do not require header files.

6. CONCLUSION

As mentioned above, the service wrapper is probably the second most commonly encountered component after the UI Widget. This is because accessing these services in Visual Basic—the most widely used language for component programming—was difficult or impossible in the earlier versions. Many services that were already accessible in Visual Basic, such as common dialog access, were encapsulated to speed the development of programs using them. Service wrappers can be provided to specialize service access to specific needs. For example, a company may have a certain location in the registry where all initialization parameters are stored. A component could be used to simplify access to that portion of the registry, without giving access to the entire registry. Because operating system services are always expanding, there is still a great deal of development going on in this area.

Chapter 18

Containers

1. PREREQUISITES AND OBJECTIVES

Before starting this chapter, you should have

1. A knowledge of programming in C++.
2. A knowledge of component interface design.

After completing this chapter, you will have

1. Some knowledge of Container components.

2. INTRODUCTION

A Container is a component that can have other components embedded in it. The embedding can be static or dynamic. In static embedding, the collection of subcomponents is fixed when the Container is compiled. In dynamic embedding, new components can be added by the programmer after the component has been compiled. It is possible to embed one container in another to create arbitrarily complex hierarchies.

Although hierarchy is a useful concept in most kinds of programming, its usefulness in component-level programming has yet to be firmly established. Nor is it clear that existing methods for developing component hierarchies are adequate to support true hierarchical programming. In the ActiveX technology, for example, it is possible to create a simple container component, but the components embedded in the container will appear to be embedded in the container's host. Because the container does not establish a new name space, true hierarchical programming is not supported. Other technologies, most notably JavaBeans, do a better job of supporting hierarchy, but it is still not clear whether this hierarchy is of any benefit to the programmer.

It is likely that hierarchy will become increasingly important as we learn more about component-level programming. For that reason, we will demonstrate a dynamic container that permits programmers to group components in another component window. This will permit components to be moved as a group, but this organization is purely visual in nature. The components embedded in this container must be accessed as if they were embedded in the container's host.

3. THE METHODOLOGY

At the present time, the concept of hierarchy has not established itself well enough in component-level programming to permit the exposition of a reasonable methodology for container design. We will give an example to illustrate the straightforward design of this type of component.

4. A SIMPLE CONTAINER

Because adding container support to a component is handled by the component design tools in Visual C++, the simple container has roughly the same complexity as a "Hello, World" component. We will add two properties, *Caption* and *BackColor*, and create a suitable drawing routine. Beyond that, little or nothing is required. When creating the project, we will check the *Acts as a simple frame control* check box on the second page of the MFC ActiveX wizard. This will include the necessary features to support component embedding. The entire implementation of the component is given in Figure 18-2. Figure 18-1 contains the description of the *Caption* and *BackColor* properties.

Property Design Table		
Name	**Type**	**Function**
Caption	String Default = "Drop Controls Here"	Displays caption across the top of the container component.
BackColor	Color Default = White	Sets the background color of the component.

Figure 18-1 The Simple Container Property Design Table

```
void CSimpleContainerCtrl::OnBackColorChanged()
{
    CWnd::Invalidate();
    SetModifiedFlag();
}

BSTR CSimpleContainerCtrl::GetCaption()
{
    return m_caption.AllocSysString();
}
```

Figure 18-2 Implementation of the Simple Container

```
void CSimpleContainerCtrl::SetCaption(LPCTSTR lpszNewValue)
{
    m_caption = lpszNewValue;
    CWnd::Invalidate();
    SetModifiedFlag();
}

void CSimpleContainerCtrl::OnDraw(
        CDC* pdc, const CRect& rcBounds, const CRect& rcInvalid)

{
    CBrush MyBrush;
    COLORREF BackC;
    OleTranslateColor(m_backColor,NULL,&BackC);
    MyBrush.CreateSolidBrush(BackC);
    // paint the background
    pdc->FillRect(rcBounds, &MyBrush);
    if (!m_caption.IsEmpty())
    {
        // paint the text
        pdc->SaveDC();
        pdc->SetBkColor(BackC);
        pdc->TextOut(0,0,m_caption);
        pdc->RestoreDC(0);
    }
    // clean up
    MyBrush.DeleteObject();
}
```

Figure 18-2   (*Continued*)

5. CONCLUSION

Although containers are useful at present for physically grouping components in a layout, it is not yet clear whether hierarchical design will be useful at the component level. Presently containers are not particularly important, but this may change as we learn more about component-level programming.

Chapter 19

Semipersistent Objects

1. PREREQUISITES AND OBJECTIVES

Before starting this chapter, you should have

1. A knowledge of programming in C++.
2. A knowledge of component interface design.
3. A thorough knowledge of the Simple Graphical Editor and its family of components.

After completing this chapter, you will have

1. A knowledge of how to pass objects safely from one component to another.
2. A better understanding of how to integrate a number of components into a component family.

2. INTRODUCTION

The preceding chapters contain several examples of components that use semipersistent objects. In formal terms, a semipersistent object is any object whose lifetime exceeds the life of its creator but is never written to persistent storage. Semipersistent objects exist only in RAM storage, but because they can be passed from one computer to another, their lifetime is unlimited. In our examples, the most extensive use of semipersistent objects is in the Simple Graphical Editor (SGE) family of components. Figure 19-1 shows the SGE components that produce and use **CGraphicList** objects. The components outlined with heavy lines are both producers and consumers of **CGraphicList** objects; the others are consumers of **CGraphicList** objects.

In designing this system of components, we have paid little attention to a number of important issues. As a result of ignoring these issues, programs created with

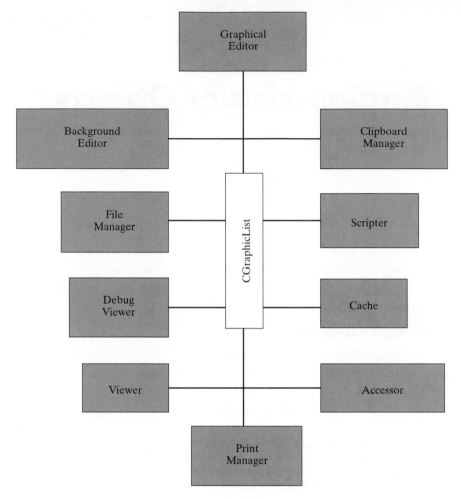

Figure 19-1 The Simple Graphical Editor Components

these components can be unreliable unless extreme care is taken when passing **CGraphicList** objects between components. The three most important issues that we must address are (1) object ownership, (2) object validation, and (3) the management of virtual functions.

3. OBJECT OWNERSHIP

The issues of object ownership are essentially the same as those for any shared object. The most serious problem occurs when two or more components have pointers to the same object and one component deletes the object without informing the other. For example, suppose we are using the Simple Graphical Editor to create **CGraphicList** objects, and the SGE Viewer to display three different views of the objects. This configuration is illustrated in Figure 19-2. If the editor deletes the object, the *OnDraw*

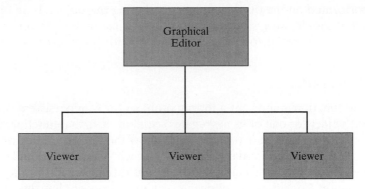

Figure 19-2   Sharing a CGraphicList Object

routines of the SGE Viewer components will probably fail. The programmer must be careful to call the *ReleaseModel* function for each of the viewers before taking any action that will cause the graphical editor to delete its object. Managing semipersistent objects is error-prone and would clearly benefit from some formalization of the object-deletion process.

One solution to the shared ownership problem illustrated in Figure 19-2 would be to add a reference count to the object and delete the object only when its reference count reaches zero. To guarantee that the reference count is handled properly, a special delete function for **CGraphicList** objects should be created that will decrement the reference count and delete the object only when the count reaches zero. This function should be declared as a friend of the **CGraphicList** class, and the destructor of the **CGraphicList** object could be made private. (Making the destructor private prevents a delete statement from being used to delete the object.)

Because the applications we have been dealing with are single-threaded, we can pretty much ignore the problem of object consistency. However, if a shared object is used by components on more than one thread, it will be necessary to protect objects with semaphores.

Completely apart from the issues of shared objects is the issue of object ownership. For the integer sorter described in Chapter 13, objects are passed by value rather than by reference, so the issue of shared objects does not exist. (When a request is made for a **CDynarray** object, the component makes a copy of the object.) If we had decided instead to pass objects by reference, it would be necessary to clearly identify the owner of each object and clearly specify the conditions under which it is permissible to delete an object. Even when passing objects by value, it is necessary for the designer of each component to know whether it is permissible to delete the objects it receives through its properties.

When semipersistent objects are used to pass data between components, the rules for passing objects must be clearly specified in the design documents before development starts. If objects are to be shared, the owner of the object must be clearly specified, and the rules for deleting the object must be clearly specified. Any operations that delete objects must be clearly identified along with the required operations that must be performed on the other components sharing the object. If an operation deletes an object, it should *always* delete the object, not just under certain conditions. (Here the term *operation* refers to reading a property, writing a property, or calling a method.)

4. VIRTUAL FUNCTIONS

Virtual functions represent a thorny problem for semipersistent objects. If a semipersistent object (or one of its aggregates) contains a virtual function, you can experience program failures even if you carefully follow the rules of object ownership. The problem is that the object contains a pointer to each virtual function. These pointers are set up by the object constructor, and normally reside within the module containing the constructor. Consider the following scenario. Suppose that the semipersistent object was developed as a separate project. (Our recommended approach.) Suppose further that the methods of the object and its aggregates are compiled into a function library that will be included in each component using the semipersistent object. Under these conditions, *each component will have its own copy of the virtual functions*. In fact, each component will have its own copy of every function it references, but *virtual functions are always referenced*. Let's suppose that a dynamically created component creates a semipersistent object, passes the object to another component, and then relinquishes ownership of the object. If the creator of the object is destroyed, all virtual function pointers may become dangling pointers, *even though the current owner has its own copy of the functions!*

Virtual functions can also cause peculiar problems when debugging a set of components. Suppose a virtual function F is used only by component X, but component X receives all its objects from component Y. If you find a bug in function F, it will manifest itself during the execution of component X. However fixing function F and recompiling X will not make the problem go away. The object was created by component Y, therefore the execution of function F will use the copy in component Y, not the copy in component X. In fact, it is not necessary to recompile X at all. The only thing you need to do is recompile Y. (You can spend *hours* figuring this out on your own.)

One way to avoid this difficulty is to avoid using compile-time libraries for semipersistent objects. You can instead create an independent load library for the component and use the library for each component you create. (In the Windows operating system these are known as DLLs.) This will give you a single copy of the virtual functions that will be used by all components, but it will complicate the deployment of your components because each component that uses the semipersistent object must have access to the run-time library.

5. OBJECT VALIDATION

As yet, we have not addressed the problem of receiving an invalid address for a semipersistent object. In all of our examples, we have naively assumed that every address we receive is valid. Naturally, this can have disastrous consequences, but the problem of object validation is not straightforward. At the very least, it is necessary to observe the following conventions.

Every property that is used to pass addresses to a component must be *run-time only*. If it is not, it is inevitable that some programmer using the component will attempt to assign a value to the property at design-time, which will probably cause immediate failure, not just of the component but of the entire development system. It is also inevitable that this will happen only after the programmer has completed six hours of changes without saving them.

No property that is used to pass addresses should be persistent. Addresses are not valid from one invocation to the next, and attempting to restore an address from persistent storage will probably make the module containing the component completely inaccessible. (The development system will fail every time the module is accessed.)

One method of performing a sanity check on an object address is to require all semipersistent objects to contain a class signature identifying the class to which they belong. Naturally, we would want this signature to be at the beginning of the object, just in case we get the address of an invalid object that is much shorter than the one we were expecting. Unfortunately, in C++ it is difficult to be certain of the location of data items within an object. Visual C++ guarantees the order of data items *only between public/protected/private labels*. If an object contains both public and a private variables, it is difficult to determine which comes first in the object, and the relative order is not guaranteed to be consistent between different compilers or different versions of the same compiler. As a practical matter, most compiler writers want function libraries to be consistent over versions and they also want their function libraries to be usable with other products, so the problem is not as bad as it might first appear. We recommend placing a private signature variable at the beginning of the class description. This variable should be of type long (no object is shorter than four bytes) and should contain a "magic number" that identifies the class of the object. If you are using a large number of semipersistent objects, make sure each magic number is unique. The value of the magic number should be tested using a nonvirtual member function.

6. CONCLUSION

The main problem with using semipersistent objects is that virtually all programming practices associated with memory-based objects assume that they are ephemeral and contained within a single invocation of a single program. While it is true that this view is changing rapidly, the problems discussed in the preceding section suggest that there is still much work to be done. Indeed, the mere fact that we must coerce object pointers to long integers suggests that we are straining the design parameters of the underlying technology.

While it is impossible to predict the future, we can at least suggest some innovations that would facilitate the use of semipersistent objects. We find that the current state of the art of compiler technology to be insufficient to support semipersistent objects. In the functional view of programming, all functions belong to a program or to a module. This leads to the problems with virtual functions described in the preceding section. The use of dynamic link libraries to bypass the problem is only a stopgap measure. The real problem is that the functions of an object, especially the virtual functions, must be treated as part of the object and must be independent of a particular module. When an object is instantiated, its functions must be instantiated in a way that is independent of the module creating the object. This would enable the object to have an existence that is independent of its creator.

It would be helpful to have some operating system support for object validation. It would be nice to be able to ask the operating system, "Does this address point to an X?" and receive an accurate reply. Ideally, every object that is created anywhere should have its own unique address. When the object is destroyed, the address would be discarded and never reused. Of course, this would require extremely wide addresses, probably on the order of 200 bits or more, but such a practice would simplify the sharing of objects between address spaces and between different machines. Existing technology is quite capable of copying complex objects between address spaces and even between different machines, but this requires changing pointers into a machine-independent form and reconstituting them when the object reaches its final destination. (Transferring functions from one machine to another is another matter.)

These issues are the subject of intense ongoing research both in academia and in the commercial world. It will be interesting to see what the future brings.

Chapter 20

The Future

1. PREREQUISITES AND OBJECTIVES

Before starting this chapter, you should have

1. A thorough knowledge of the material in Chapters 1 through 19.

After completing this chapter, you will have

1. Some knowledge of future trends in component-level technology and design.

2. INTRODUCTION

Although component-level programming is enormously successful, it still remains in its infancy. As our experience with component-level programming grows, we will see significant changes in existing technologies, and perhaps entirely new technologies coming into existence. This chapter will focus on those areas that I believe should have the highest priority.

3. DIRECT COMPILER SUPPORT

Few programming languages provide direct support for component-level programming. Although we have used Visual C++ extensively in our examples here, the only thing "visual" about Visual C++ is its name. In most respects, it is an ordinary C++ development system. In C++, regardless of the compiler, it is not possible to declare a variable X of type *TextBox* and then access the *Text* property X using syntax of the form $S=X.Text;$. Such features need to be incorporated into the C++ standard.

Java has a similar problem. Elaborate mechanisms must be used to access properties and to fire and process events. Both C++ and Java would benefit by borrowing a few features from Visual Basic.

At present, Delphi is the language that best incorporates component-level programming into its structure. The language not only supports direct access to components but also provides language features for the development of components. In Delphi, it is possible to declare a class variable to be a property, and it is even possible to declare virtual properties that have access functions but no variable. Event declarations could use a bit of work, but in general the features of the Delphi language greatly simplify the development of components. Both C++ and Java could benefit from the incorporation of such features.

4. REMOTE OBJECTS

Because component-level programming is inextricably tied to object-oriented programming, any research that improves our ability to handle objects remote or otherwise will directly benefit component-level programming. Remote access to objects is one of the most exciting developments in the area of object-oriented programming. Although the data portion of an object can be passed between different address spaces and even between different machines, objects are not just data. Objects are data plus behavior. Unfortunately, there is no simple answer to the problem of transferring functions between different machines, especially machines with incompatible instruction sets. I believe that a combination of just-in-time compilation of object methods and independent caching of both object data and functions will contribute to the solution of this problem.

5. ENVIRONMENTAL SERVICES

In existing component systems, the environment provides a number of services to the component. At the very least, the environment must create component instances. If the component requires a window, it must provide the window and the necessary support functions. In addition, the environment must implement the mechanisms used to properties, methods, and events. Events place the most strenuous demands on the environment. When a component declares an event, this is a demand to the environment that a particular function be created. Furthermore, this function must be different for each instance of the component. In terms of objects, event declarations are a demand by the component that the environment perform the following steps:

1. Create a new class for the component. This class will contain a number of functions but no variables. The functions correspond to the events defined for the component.
2. Create an empty body for each function.
3. For each instance of the component, derive a new class from the component class and override a number of functions to provide unique behavior for the instance.
4. Create one instance of the derived class to handle the events for the component.

It is our contention that since a component can demand that one sort of object, there is no reason why other sorts demands should not be made as well. In a sense, we can consider the method for handling properties and methods to be a demand on the environment. Each component has an associated class containing data members that correspond to properties and function members that correspond to methods. For each instance of a component, the environment must construct an object of the corresponding type.

In the future, we expect that components will be able to make more complex demands on their environment. For instance, let us suppose that components are permitted to make three different types of demands: (1) a demand for a function, (2) a demand for a variable, and (3) a demand for an object.

When a variable is created in response to a component's demand, it must be created within the proper scope. Several different scopes should be available. For example, if the scope is *Instance*, then every time a new instance of the component is created, a new instance of the variable should also be created. If the scope is *Component*, all instances of the component share the same variable. If the scope is "Global," then all components that demand the variable will share the same variable. If the scope is *Group*, then the variable will be shared by all components in the same group. (A component group is a mechanism that will be used for defining a hierarchy of scopes within the environment.) There should also be mechanisms for creating hierarchies of scopes within the environment.

It should also be possible to specify the location of demanded variables. The location can be *Internal*, which will make the variable equivalent to an ordinary property, or *External*, which requires that the variable be explicitly created and maintained by the environment. If the location is declared to be *Remote*, the variable will be maintained within a different component. (We believe that this is a more systematic way to handle component/component interactions such as those performed by the Visual Basic data component.)

Demands will probably also specify the variable's implementation, *Nullable* or *Required*. If a variable's implementation is *Nullable*, the container is free not to create the variable. All write accesses to the variable will be discarded, and all read accesses to the variable will return a specified default value.

Like variables, function demands will have a specified scope, location, and implementation. A function demand that has scope *Instance*, location *External*, and implementation *Nullable* corresponds to the notion of an event. A function demand that has scope *Instance*, location *Internal*, and implementation *Required* corresponds to the notion of a method. (When a function is declared to be *Nullable*, this implies that the environment is free to create an empty body for the function.)

These concepts will probably be extended to include object-demands, which are a demand for an object with specified variables and functions. It is possible that each member of the object will have its own set of specifications, so an object could be created in "mix and match" fashion.

6. LAYERED STANDARDS AND PROTOCOL INDEPENDENCE

It has been recognized for many years that communication protocols should be specified as a set of hierarchical layers. It has been further recognized that the layers of a standard are independent of one another, and the implementation of a particular standard at one layer does not preclude the implementation of a different standard at a different layer.

There are actually three distinct layers that appear in component-level programming, although in all existing technologies these layers are blended together in such a way as to make them very difficult to pinpoint. At the lowest level is the interprogram communication layer that is used to implement properties methods and events. In the ActiveX technology, this consists of the COM technology. The next layer is the host-component interface, which consists of properties, methods, and events. These two layers are actually distinct and should be independent of one another. It should be possible to implement an ActiveX look-alike based on message passing, shared memory, or some other interprogram communication mechanism. The third layer is the program layer. At this level, a program consists of a set of Accessors, Editors, Service Wrappers, UI Widgets, and so forth. Much of what we have studied in this book is an attempt to bring some organization to the third layer of the component technology. As we have pointed out several times, the third layer is independent of the other two layers.

7. CONCLUSION

Component-level programming is the "stealth revolution." It developed, almost overnight, as a new and powerful way of organizing complex programs. It has become an essential tool for the development of new programs of virtually every kind, and its use grows every day. The lessons of component-level programming go beyond any one technology or programming language. If ActiveX and C++ were to vanish, new languages and technologies would instantly step in to fill the gap. Despite the success of component-level programming, there are many new developments waiting on the horizon. Regardless of what the future brings, it is certain to be exciting.

Object-Oriented Design

A.1 INTRODUCTION

A thorough grounding in the principles of object-oriented design is invaluable in component-level design. A complete discussion of this topic is beyond the scope of this book, but we offer a few tips that will simplify the design process for those who have not yet taken a course in object-oriented design. The information provided here will allow you to create objects in a consistent way and will permit you to complete the exercises in this book without too much difficulty. Please remember that this is a collection of programming tips, not a substitute for a course in object-oriented design.

A.2 PRIVATE, PROTECTED, OR PUBLIC VARIABLES: WHEN TO USE THEM

One problem that many programmers have is trying to decide when to make class variables private, when to make them public, and when to make them protected. As a general rule of thumb, you should make all variables private unless there is an overriding reason not to do so. Initially, the temptation will be to make all data items public, and then selectively make some of them private or protected. This is the precise opposite of the approach you *should* take. The reason people take the wrong approach is because they are used to thinking in terms of functional languages and structures. Classes are not structures, nor should they be treated as structures. That being said, here are a few guidelines to help you decide between public, private, and protected.

A.2.1 Public Variables

A variable that is an object should *never* be made public. A pointer to an object can be made public if it is not the head of a linked list or some other complex structure. The only reason for making such a variable public is to allow the outside world to "give" a subobject to an object of your class. It is never permissible to allow the outside world to manipulate the internal elements of subobjects. When in doubt, *do not* make the pointer public.

Regardless of the type of the variable, if the value of the variable has any required relationship with any other class variable, including implicit variables like the drawing window, it *must not* be made public. If there are any restrictions on the value of the variable other than those imposed by its type, it *must not* be made public. If the variable is a member of a collection of variables that are normally changed as a group (for example, *Height* and *Width*), then the variable *must not* be made public. If the variable is read-only after it has been initialized, it *must not* be made public. If the variable should not be modified even by member functions after it has been initialized, it should be declared to be a constant.

Public variables are variables of simple types, whose values can be changed without restriction and whose values have no relationship to the value of any other variable in the class. Needless to say, such variables are uncommon.

A.2.2 Protected Variables

If a variable has access restrictions but can be manipulated in an arbitrary way by member functions, then it should be made protected. If the value of the variable has a required relationship to other variables but this relationship can change in derived classes, then the variable should be made protected. However, if the value of the variable has unchanging relationships with other variables, then it should be made private, and derived classes should use accessor and mutator functions to access the variable. Typically, variables that are subobjects should be made protected as long as there are no additional restrictions in the way the subobject is accessed.

A.3 OBJECTS VERSUS CLASSES

Many authors are careful to distinguish between objects and classes. A class is a formal description containing definitions of variables and functions. The distinction is generally expressed as follows: an object is an instance of a class that has storage allocated for it and values assigned to its variables. This distinction is useful, but it ignores the fact that the structure of some objects cannot be described using a single class. A singly linked list, for example, has a head, a tail, and a list of items chained together with pointers. The description of the linked list requires at least two classes: one to define the head and tail pointers and one to describe the items in the list. Nevertheless, the linked list is a single object.

There are various ways to handle multiclass objects in C++, none of which is completely satisfactory. Using the linked list as an example, let us assume that we wish to create a queue of (x,y) values using a singly linked list. The class declarations of Figure A-1 could be used for this purpose. There are several design flaws in this figure. First, users of these classes can create **CElement** objects if they wish. This violates the spirit of these declarations, since together they represent the design of a single object. Furthermore, the rules for variable access permissions given in the preceding section have been violated. In class **CElement**, x and y are normally set as a group and thus must not be public. In class **CQueue**, *Head* and *Tail* have a required relationship and cannot be made public. Furthermore, *Head* points not to a simple object but to a list of objects. Let us first make these corrections and then proceed with tying the two classes together. The corrections appear in Figure A-2.

```cpp
class CElement
{
public:
    CElement * Next;
    double x;
    double y;
    CElement( );
    ~CElement( );
};

class CQueue
{
public:
    CElement *Head;
    CElement *Tail;
    CQueue();
    ~CQueue();
};
```

Figure A-1   Two Coordinated Classes

```cpp
class CElement
{
public:
    CElement * Next;
private:
    double x;
    double y;
public:
    CElement( );
    CElement(double NewX,double NewY);
    ~CElement( );
    void GetValues(double &RetX, double &RetY);
};

class CQueue
{
private:
    CElement *Head;
    CElement *Tail;
public:
    CElement();
    ~CElement();
    void Push(double NewX,double NewY);
    void Pop(double &RetX, double &RetY);
};
```

Figure A-2   Corrected Classes

```
void CQueue::Push(double NewX, double NewY)
{
    // constructor will set Next to NULL
    CElement *NewElem = new CElement(NewX,NewY);
    if (Head == NULL)
    {
        Head = NewElem;
    }
    else
    {
        Tail->Next = NewElem;
    }
    Tail = NewElem;
}
```

Figure A-3   The CQueue Class

Once the two class descriptions have been corrected, it is necessary to add accessor functions to access the values of the protected elements and constructors to assign them values. For the **CQueue** class, the two functions *Push* and *Pop* will be used to add and delete elements from the queue. The implementation of the *Push* function is given in Figure A-3.

The *Next* data item of **CElement** is declared as public to permit the statement

```
Tail->Next = NewElem;
```

to compile properly.

This will allow the queue to function properly, but will not reserve the class **CElement** for the exclusive use of the **CQueue** class. (This can be good or bad, depending on your requirements.) There are two ways to tie the two classes together so that **CElement** belongs only to **CQueue**. The first is to move the definition of **CElement** inside of the definition of **CQueue** and to declare the **CElement** class to be a private member of class **CQueue**. This works just fine, but tends to be a bit unreadable. If this is done, the function body of the default constructor would be declared using the syntax `CQueue::CElement::CElement()`. Other function bodies would require the same syntax. Note that **CQueue** does not gain any special permissions within the **CElement** class by virtue of the containment.

Another more readable way to do the same thing is to declare all functions of **CElement** to be private, including all constructors. This will make *any* use of the **CElement** class illegal, because no external entity, including the global environment, has permission to call the default constructor or any other constructor for **CElement** objects. We can then explicitly give **CQueue** permission to access the **CElement** class by declaring **CQueue** to be a friend of **CElement**. Figure A-4 shows how this is done. This solution is not completely satisfactory either, because **CQueue** now has permission to access *all* data items of **CElement**, not just the *Next* pointer.

```
class CQueue; // forward reference required.
class CElement
{
    friend CQueue;
private:
    CElement * Next;
    double x;
    double y;
    CElement( );
    CElement(double NewX,double NewY);
    ~CElement( );
    void GetValues(double &RetX,  double &RetY);
};
```

Figure A-4   CElement with Friend Declaration

A.4 PARAMETERIZED CONSTRUCTORS

Proper use of private, public, and protected attributes can complicate the initialization process for derived objects when a parameterized constructor is used. Consider the two classes shown in Figure A-5.

When an object of type **COther** is created using the constructor *COther(long,long)*, there is no way to assign the value of *NewSize* to the *Size* variable. Although the constructor for **CThing** is called before the constructor for **COther**, it is the *default*

```
class CThing
{
private:
    long Size;
public:
    CThing();
    CThing(long NewSize);
    ~CThing();
};

class COther : public CThing
{
private:
    long Quality;
public:
    COther();
    COther(long NewSize,long NewQuality);
    ~COther;
};
```

Figure A-5   An Initialization Problem

```
CThing::CThing(long NewSize)
{
    Size = NewSize;
}
COther::COther(long NewSize, long NewQuality) : CThing(NewSize)
{
    Quality = NewQuality;
}
```

Figure A-6   Initializing Base Classes

constructor, *CThing()* that is called, not *CThing(long)*. It is possible to override the se-lection of the default constructor in the body of *COther(long,long)*. Figure A-6 shows how to do this.

A similar method can be used to initialize aggregate classes within an object. Consider the class shown in Figure A-7.

The constructor *CMore(long,long)* should be defined as shown in Figure A-8. If a class has constant items, they must be initialized using the syntax shown in this figure—namely, **Variable-Name(Value)**. Any number of initializers can be used after the colon separated by commas. The base class initializers can be mixed with the member initial-ization items.

```
class CMore
{
private:
    CThing First;
    CThing Last;
public:
    CMore();
    CMore(long FirstSize, long LastSize);
    ~CMore();
};
```

Figure A-7   An Aggregate Initialization Problem

```
CMore::CMore(long FirstSize, long LastSize) :
                              First(FirstSize), Last(LastSize)
{
}
```

Figure A-8   Initializing Aggregate Classes

A.5 PURE ENCAPSULATION

In most functional programs it is possible to classify the various subroutines into categories. There are routines that perform file management, others that handle internal storage, and so forth. In object-oriented design, each category of subroutines should be implemented as a class. If there are global variables associated with the functions, they must be made members of the class. In many cases the functions grouped in this manner will not change significantly. When this happens, it is known as pure encapsulation. The class serves only to group similar functions together. Grouping functions in this manner will generally make the code much easier to read and to modify. An example of pure encapsulation is the mouse handler used in the Simple Graphical Editor (see Chapter 7).

A.6 VIRTUAL BASE CLASSES AND MULTIPLE INHERITANCE

Suppose you are creating a set of classes that will be used by other programmers to create *Useful Objects*. There are three features that may be incorporated into a *Useful Object*, which we will call *Feature A, Feature B*, and *Feature C*. These features are completely independent of one another. A particular *Useful Object* may have any combination of these features. Regardless of the features that a *Useful Object* has, there are certain data items that it must incorporate. To implement *Useful Objects*, we create four classes: (1) **CUseful**, which contains the basic data items; (2) **CUsefulA**, which inherits from **CUseful** and implements *Feature A*; (3) **CUsefulB**, which also inherits from **CUseful** and implements *Feature B*; and (4) **CUsefulC**, which inherits from **CUseful** and implements *Feature C*. To create a new *Useful Object*, our client programmers will create a new class and derive the class from **CUsefulA**, **CUsefulB**, or **CUsefulC**, depending on which features they need. If they need more than one feature, they will use multiple inheritance and derive their new class from two or more of **CUsefulA**, **CUsefulB**, and **CUsefulC**. Under normal circumstances, this would create multiple copies of the basic data items. However, we had the foresight to declare class **CUseful** to be a virtual class, as shown in Figure A-9. When a virtual class is inherited from more than one class in multiple inheritance, only a single copy of that class is created. Thus in a multiple inheritance that derives from **CUsefulA** and **CUsefulB**, there is a single copy of the

```
class CUseful
{
    ...
}

class CUsefulA : virtual public CUseful
{
    ...
}
```

Figure A-9 Virtual Base Class Declarations

```
class CUsefulB : virtual public CUseful
{
    ...
}
class CUsefulC : virtual public CUseful
{
    ...
}
```

Figure A-9   (*Continued*)

base class **CUseful**. Note that *virtual* is a property of the inheritance, not a property of the base class.

A.7 THE DEFICIENCIES OF C++

C++ is an excellent language for object-oriented programming. Nevertheless, there are some additional features that would make life easier for object-oriented programmers. The section that follows lists the features that I would like most to see added to C++.

A.7.1 Read-Only and Write-Only Data Items

The choice between public and private for a variable is too restrictive. Consider Figure A-10, which defines a variable-sized array class. In this figure, it is necessary to make both variables, *Size* and *Data* private, because they have a required relationship—namely, that *Size* must contain the size of the array pointed to by *Data*. However, not every access to these variables would destroy this relationship. In fact, only a write access would be a problem. Unfortunately, there is no way to declare these variables to be read-only. The problem is particularly annoying when attempting to access the elements of the array. An access of the form *X.Data[i]* should be legal regardless of whether it is a *read* access or a *write* access. It would be more helpful to separate the *read* and *write* portions of the access and declare each one separately, as in Figure A-11.

Unfortunately, the example given in Figure A-11 is not legal C++.

```
class CVarIntArr
{
private:
    long Size;
    int * Data;
};
```

Figure A-10   A Variable-Sized Array Class

```
class CVarIntArr
{
private-write:
    long Size;
    int * Data;
public-read:
    long Size;
    int * Data;
};
```

Figure A-11   Separated *Read/Write* Access

Naturally, we can provide (or *not* provide) accessor and mutator functions for a private variable to restrict access rights to it. We can (and should) also declare these functions to be inline so that there is no function-call overhead when using them, but having separate read/write access rights would be a more convenient and natural way to program the same thing.

A.7.2 Friend Access Rights

When you declare a class B to be a friend of class A, class B immediately gains read/write access to everything in class A. This is a little bit like taking a new friend home and immediately giving him or her permission to go into your bedroom and dig through your underwear drawer. I am very much in favor of limited friendships where the access rights of friend functions and classes are clearly defined. In the specification of friend access rights, it would be nice if the read and write access to variables could be specified separately. Figure A-12 shows what I have in mind. Lets assume that the keyword *grant* is used to grant specific rights, and the keyword *restrict* is used to remove access rights.

```
class B
{
    ...
}
class A
{
    friend class B grant (read X, write Y, call F);
    ...
}
class C
{
    friend class B restrict(write Size, write Data);
    ...
}
```

Figure A-12   Restricted Friend Access Rights

In Figure A-12, *class B* would be able to read variable *X*, write variable *Y*, and call function *F*, but it would be unable to access the members of *A* in any other way. Class C has full access to the members of *B*, except for *Size* and *Data*, which are read-only. Unfortunately, the syntax of Figure A-12 is illegal.

This sort of access can be designed into a class using the existing features of C++, but it is quite cumbersome to do so. One technique is to separate the data items and functions into different sets, depending on the access rights we wish them to have. Each separate set could then be placed in its own subclass, each with its own friend declarations. The subclasses would then be aggregated into a containing class, which would have universal friend access to all of them. This becomes even more cumbersome if the member functions of one subclass must access the data items of another subclass. Each subclass could contain a pointer to the aggregated object, but the result would be a complicated mess that is best avoided.

On the whole, I feel that it is best to avoid friend functions and classes unless it is absolutely necessary to use them.

A.7.3 Metamorphic Objects

The primary use for polymorphic objects is to avoid the cumbersome decoding of type codes. We have made use of this fact in designing the Simple Graphical Editor of Chapter 7. When calling the *Draw* function of a **CGraphicalObject**, it is actually the *Draw* function of the subtype that is called. In essence, the virtual functions of the object take the place of the type code. We could probably use virtual function pointers *exactly* the way a type code is used if we had it in mind to brutalize ourselves. However, the virtual function gives us immediate access to the routine that the type-decoder would select, and it is thus significantly more useful than a type code for identifying an object.

Unfortunately, type codes are not the only state variables in an object. Consider the Simple Graphical Editor. The support class variable *Mouse.Code* is a state variable that determines the action that will be performed the next time the *OnLButtonUp* function is called. The *OnLButtonUp* has a decoding routine that determines what action will be taken based on the value of *Mouse.Code*. However, when the value is assigned to *Mouse.Code*, the future action of the *OnLButtonUp* function is completely known. We find ourselves in the position of losing that information, only to regain it later by decoding the *Mouse.Code* variable. It would be far simpler to be able to replace the *OnLButtonUp* function with one that did exactly what we wanted. If we could replace the *OnLButtonUp* function and the *OnMouseMove* function, we could eliminate the *Mouse.Code* variable entirely, along with the decoding routines. This process is referred to as *Metamorphosis* because the identity of the object is being changed by replacing its virtual functions.

Of course, we could use function pointers to achieve the same thing, but this technique permits the unconditional replacement of a virtual function with another function of the same type. We wish to restrict the replacement to a set of predefined functions.

True metamorphosis can be achieved using polymorphic subobjects. (I believe that C++ should support metamorphosis directly, but until that happens, polymorphic subobjects are a workable substitute.) To achieve our goal, we first define a base class

```
class CMouseHandler
{
public:
    virtual void OnMouseMove(UINT nFlags,CPoint point,
                                CSGEditorCtrl *Base)=0;
    virtual void OnLButtonUp(UINT nFlags,CPoint point,
                                CSGEditorCtrl *Base)=0;
}

class CMouseHandlerMDMove : public CMouseHandler
{
public:
    void OnMouseMove(UINT nFlags,CPoint point,CSGEditorCtrl *Base);
    void OnLButtonUp(UINT nFlags,CPoint point,CSGEditorCtrl *Base);
}

void CMouseHandlerMDMove::OnLButtonUp(UINT nFlags,CPoint point,
                                CSGEditorCtrl *Base)
{
    // undraw the selection rectangle
    Base->DoSRect();
    // move the selection.
    long XDelta = Base->Mouse.EndPoint.x - Base->Mouse.StartPoint.x;
    long YDelta = Base->Mouse.EndPoint.y - Base->Mouse.StartPoint.y;
    Base->Model->MoveSelection(XDelta,YDelta);
    Base->CWnd::Invalidate();
}
```

Figure A-13   Derived Classes for Emulating Metamorphosis

of type **CMouseHandler**. To this class we add two pure virtual functions named *OnMouseMove* and *OnLButtonUp*. We place no data items in the class. We then proceed by deriving new classes from **CMouseHandler**, one for each value of *Mouse.Code*. In the definitions of the *OnLButtonUp* and *OnMouseMove* functions, we place the code to handle that particular value of *Mouse.Code*. Figure A-13 shows the definition of **CMouseHandler** and the derived class used to handle the *Mouse.Code* **MDMove**. The definition of the **MDMove** *OnLButtonUp* function is also given in Figure A-13. The functions *OnLButtonUp* and *OnMouseMove* must have the same parameters as the original *OnLButtonUp* and *OnMouseMove* functions as well as one additional pointer that will point to the support object. Unlike true metamorphic functions, our new *OnMouseMove* and *OnLButtonUp* functions do not have automatic access to the variables of the support class.

Several changes must now be made to the support class. Each of the classes derived from **CMouseHandler** must be declared as friends of the support class, **CSGEditorCtrl**. We must also add a public variable, *MH*, of type *CMouseHandler*[*] to the **CMouse** class. In the constructor for the **CMouse** class, we must allocate a new object of type **CMouseHandlerMDNone** and assign its pointer to *MH*. We must alter the *Down* and *Up* functions of the **CMouse** class as shown in Figure A-14.

```
void CMouse::Down(CMouseHandler * NewHandler)
{
    delete MH;
    MH = NewHandler;
}
void CMouse::Up()
{
    delete MH;
    MH = new CMouseHandlerMDNone;
}
```

Figure A-14   Changes to the CMouse Functions

The calls to the **CMouse** *Down* function must now be altered to reflect the change in the operand. A former call of the form *Mouse.Down(MDMove)* must be replaced with *Mouse.Down(new CMouseHandlerMDMove)*. Finally, we replace the switch statement of *OnMouseMove* with *Mouse.MH->OnMouseMove(nFlags,point,this)* and similarly replace the switch statement of the *OnLButtonUp* function.

Once these changes have been made, we can eliminate the *Code* member of the **CMouse** class. We leave it to the reader to decide which implementation style is preferable.

A.8 CONCLUSION

The material presented in this appendix represents object-oriented programming and design tips. There are a number of important issues that we have not mentioned. The reader is strongly encouraged to take a course in the subject.

Programming the Windows GUI

B.1 INTRODUCTION

Many of the examples given in this book contain Windows operating system drawing functions. In this appendix, we give a brief introduction to using these functions, some of which can be quite complicated.

B.2 DEVICE CONTEXTS

In the Windows operating system, all functions are associated with a device context. The device context is actually an object-oriented concept that was introduced into the Windows operating system before object-oriented programming was widely used. For MFC components, the **CDC** class encapsulates the functionality of the device context, making drawing operations completely object-oriented. From time to time, however, it is necessary to make a call to a non–object-oriented function.

The device context, for the most part, allows a single drawing routine to be used for several different purposes. For example, the same drawing routine can be used to draw the component window, print a copy of the component window, and copy the component window drawing into the clipboard.

B.2.1 Window Device Contexts

A device context to the component window is provided as an operand of the *OnDraw* function. This parameter is named "*pdc*" and is a pointer to an object of type **CDC**. This pointer must be used for all drawing functions called by the *OnDraw* routine. The **CDC** address can be passed to other subroutines, but it *cannot* be saved in the support object for use by other routines.

If you need to draw to the component window from some place other than the *OnDraw* routine, you will first need to obtain the address of the device context for the component window. This is done by executing the following statement within any support-class function:

```
CDC * MyDc = CWnd::GetDC();
```

When you are finished with the device context, you must give it back. If you fail to do this, you can gobble up system resources and eventually lock up your system. To give the device context back, you execute the following statement:

```
CWnd::ReleaseDC(MyDc);
```

In the *OnDraw* function, the *rcBounds* argument will give the size of the window. In most cases the *Top* and *Left* members of this rectangle will be zero, but this may not always be the case. To obtain this rectangle outside the *OnDraw* routine, execute the following statement:

```
CRect MyRect;
CWnd::GetClientRect(&MyRect);
```

B.2.2 Memory Device Contexts

A memory device context allows you to draw into a bitmap that is not visible to the user. This can be done for a number of different reasons, but the most common is for smoothing animation. In such a case, you want to make sure that your bitmap is compatible with the frame-buffer memory, and that your device context is compatible with the device context of the component window. To draw into a bitmap that will eventually be copied into the component window, execute the statements shown in Figure B-1. We assume that these appear in the *OnDraw* function.

After executing the code in Figure B-1, all drawing with the device context *Mydc* will be directed into the bitmap *Xmap*. Once the device context and bitmap are no longer required, they must be destroyed using a procedure similar to the one shown in Figure B-2.

```
CBitmap XMap,*OldMap;
// create a bitmap with the same properties as the frame buffer
XMap.CreateCompatibleBitmap(pdc,rcBounds.Width(),rcBounds.Height());
CDC WorkDC;
CDC *Mydc=&WorkDC;
// create a device context with the same properties as the component
// window device context
MyDc->CreateCompatibleDC(pdc);
// associate the bitmap with the device context.
OldMap = Mydc->SelectObject(&XMap);
```

Figure B-1   Creating a Memory Device Context

```
    // select out the bitmap
Mydc->SelectObject(OldMap);
    // delete the bitmap
XMap.DeleteObject();
    // delete the device context

Mydc->DeleteDC();
```

Figure B-2   Deleting a Memory Device Context

B.2.3 Metafile Device Contexts

A metafile is a recorded list of drawing commands that can be replayed to create a drawing in several different locations. Metafiles are used to copy drawings to the clipboard and to save drawings to disk as well as for various other purposes. To create a device context for a metafile, execute the following two statements:

```
HDC MfHdc = CreateMetaFile(NULL);
CDC * MyDc = CDC::FromHandle(MfHdc);
```

After executing these two statements, you can use the device context *MyDc* to draw into the metafile. You can use the same drawing routine that you use for window and memory device contexts. Once you are finished drawing, you need to create a metafile handle for the metafile you have just created. To do this, execute the following statement:

```
HMETAFILE MHandle = CloseMetaFile(MfHdc);
```

The metafile handle can now be used by various metafile processing functions. This statement destroys the metafile device context.

B.2.4 Printer Device Contexts

A printer device context works like other device contexts but is used to create output for a printer. There are a few additional function calls that must be used with a printer device context.

Once you have the device context, you must start the printing process by calling the *StartDoc* function. The *StartDoc* function has one argument, which must be a pointer to a **DOCINFO** structure. (This structure is documented in the MSDN library.)

To start each page, you must call the *StartPage* function. At the end of the page, you must call the *EndPage* function, and at the end of the document, you must call the *EndDoc* function. Figure B-3 shows how to print a one-page document with a large X on it. On a 600 DPI printer, the code of this figure will print an X that is 5 inches on a side.

```
MyDc->StartDoc(&MyDoc);
MyDc->StartPage();
MyDc->MoveTo(0,0);
MyDc->LineTo(3000,3000);
MyDc->MoveTo(3000,0);
MyDc->LineTo(0,3000);
MyDc->EndPage();
MyDc->EndDoc();
```

Figure B-3   Printing an X

B.3 PENS AND BRUSHES

In addition to being associated with a particular device, the device context also contains a collection of drawing resources. We have seen one of these already. The memory device context owns the bitmap into which the drawings are made. Two additional types of drawing resources are pens and brushes. The pen determines how lines are drawn, while the brush determines the fill color for closed figures like rectangles and ellipses.

Figure B-4 shows how to create a green pen. After executing these statements, all lines drawn using the device context *Mydc* will be drawn using green lines of minimum width. To use a larger width, the second argument of *CreatePen* should be set to something larger than zero. The third argument determines the color of the pen, while the first argument is a system-defined constant that specifies solid lines (as opposed to dotted or dashed lines.)

If you create a pen, you must destroy it when you have finished using it. Figure B-5 shows how to destroy the green pen that we created in Figure B-4. Before the pen can be destroyed, it must be selected out of the device context.

Creating a brush is quite similar to creating a pen. Unlike a pen, a brush does not have a width or a style specification. Figure B-6 shows how to create a brush, and Figure B-7 shows how to delete it when you are finished with it. When this brush is selected into the *Mydc* device context, all rectangles and ellipses will be filled with the color magenta. To prevent filling of these shapes, use the stock object *HOLLOW_BRUSH*. (See *GetStockObject* in the C++ documentation.)

```
CPen MyPen;
MyPen.CreatePen(PS_SOLID,0,RGB(0,255,0));
CPen * OldPen = Mydc->SelectObject(&MyPen);
```

Figure B-4   Creating a Green Pen

```
Mydc->SelectObject(OldPen);
MyPen.DeleteObject();
```

Figure B-5   Deleting the Green Pen

```
CBrush MyBrush;
MyBrush.CreateSolidBrush(RGB(255,,255));
CBrush * OldBrush = Mydc->SelectObject(&MyBrush);
```

Figure B-6   Creating a Magenta Brush

```
Mydc->SelectObject(OldBrush);
MyBrush.DeleteObject();
```

Figure B-7   Deleting the Magenta Brush

The main use of pens and brushes is to set the line and fill colors for drawing shapes and lines. There are other uses for these objects, and these objects have many functions that we have not described. See the C++ documentation for more information.

B.4 USEFUL DRAWING FUNCTIONS

Line drawing is performed using the **CDC** functions *LineTo(NewX,NewY)* and *MoveTo(NewX,NewY)*. Every device context has a current pen position. The *LineTo* function moves the pen from the current position to the position defined by *(NewX,NewY)* and draws a line between these two points. The function *MoveTo* moves the pen in the same way but does not draw a line.

The **CDC** function *Rectangle* is used to draw a rectangle with the current pen and to fill it using the current brush. Rectangle has four parameters—*Left, Top, Right*, and *Bottom*—that define the bounds of the rectangle. The **CDC** function *Ellipse* works exactly like the *Rectangle* function but draws the inscribed ellipse of the rectangle rather than the rectangle itself.

Other **CDC** functions can be used to draw Polygons, Polylines (non-closed polygons), to perform Bitblt operations, and to fill rectangular areas with color. One additional function that has been used in a few examples in this book is the *FloodFill* function. An example of a call to this function is **pdc->FloodFill(2,2,RGB(0,0,0))** This function call begins a flood-fill operation at point (2,2) in the component window, and replaces all black pixels in the flood-fill area with pixels of the current brush color.

Another function that is widely used in the examples is the FillRect function, which is generally used to paint background areas a single color. To use the FillRect function, we must create a brush or obtain a stock brush (see *GetStockObject* in the C++ documentation). Figure B-8 shows how to fill an area with a green brush.

There are a few text functions that are used in the examples in this book, the most important of which is *TextOut. TextOut* has three parameters, the first two are the coordinates of the upper-left corner of the rectangle that will contain the text, and the third is the text itself in the form of a null-terminated string of characters. All text drawn with the same Y coordinate will have the same base line.

If we want to know the size of the rectangle required to contain a particular text string, we can use the **CDC** *GetTextExtent* function. We can draw text in different fonts

```
CBrush MyBrush;
MyBrush.CreateSolidBrush(RGB(0,255,0));
Mydc->FillRect(&rcBounds,&MyBrush);

MyBrush.DeleteObject();
```

Figure B-8   Painting the Background

by selecting a font resource into the drawing context. We normally obtain the font re-source from the stock font property. We can change the text foreground and background colors by using the **CDC** *SetTextColor* and *SetBkColor* functions. The *SetBkColor* applies only to the background of the rectangle in which text is drawn.

B.5 SCALING AND SCROLLING

The capability of the Simple Graphical Editor would be greatly enhanced if it had the ability to scale and scroll drawings. Both processes can be done fairly simply using stan-dard Windows operating system functions. This section will explain how to perform some of the basic operations.

B.5.1 Scroll-Bar Management

For scrolling features to be useful, it is first necessary to enable the scroll bars in the component window. This is done by adding a *PreCreateWindow* function to the support class. This function is added using the first tab of the class wizard menu. In this func-tion, you can add a vertical scroll bar, a horizontal scroll bar, or both. Figure B-9 (which is taken from Chapter 10) shows how to add both a horizontal and a vertical scroll bar. To create a single scroll bar, *OR* just one of the constants into *cs.style*.

Once the scroll bars are added, it is up to your program to determine how they will be used. A scroll bar is a UI Widget that does nothing more than pass operating system messages to your component. You must determine how the scroll bars will af-fect the display, and you must handle all scrolling operations yourself. The first thing you must do is set the range of each scroll bar. The default range is 0–0, which will not permit the user to move the slider. The scroll bar ranges are set using the following functions:

```
CWnd::SetScrollRange(SB_VERT,0,VMax);
CWnd::SetScrollRange(SB_HORZ,0,HMax);
```

```
BOOL CTextViewerCtrl::PreCreateWindow(CREATESTRUCT& cs)
{
    cs.style |= WS_HSCROLL | WS_VSCROLL;
    return COleControl::PreCreateWindow(cs);
}
```

Figure B-9   Adding Scroll Bars to a Control Window

The first operand of the *SetScrollRange* function determines which scroll bar will be affected. The second operand is the minimum value, and the third is the maximum value. Either value may be negative. The size of the range determines the number of allowable slider positions. These functions are normally called from a spot where the size of the document being displayed is known.

The next step is to set the scroll bar position. Never assume that the position will be set for you automatically. Regardless of how a new scroll bar position is determined, you should always set the position yourself. You do this using the following two function calls:

```
CWnd::SetScrollPos(SB_HORZ,HPos);
CWnd::SetScrollPos(SB_VERT,VPos);
```

The first operand of the *SetScrollPos* function determines which scroll bar will be affected. The second gives the absolute position of the slider. The second operand must be an integer in the current range of the scroll bar. You normally start by setting both scroll bar sliders to their minimum position and then change the position as scroll-bar messages are processed.

To process scroll-bar messages, you must add an *OnVScroll* function and an *OnHScroll* function to your support class. (If you have only one scroll bar, you should add only the function you need.) These two functions are added using the first tab of the Class Wizard dialog box. The functions themselves will not appear in the list of available functions. You must add handlers for the Windows operating system messages WM_HSCROLL and WM_VSCROLL.

The first operand of the *OnVScroll* and *OnHScroll* functions is a code telling you what operation the user has performed on the scroll bar. The name of this operand is *nSBCode*. You should code a switch statement to decode this operand. There is a set of predefined constants that you can use to make this job somewhat easier. Some of the codes are different for horizontal and vertical scroll bars. Figure B-10 gives a complete list of the codes and their meanings.

It is best to keep track of the current scroll bar position using a tracking variable, but you can also query the scroll bar for its current position. Your response to most of the message codes will be to change the value of your tracking variable, reset the scroll bar position using the *SetScrollPos* function, and then invalidating the display to force a redraw with the new scroll bar position. Handling the SB_THUMBTRACK message usually requires special drawing techniques to avoid flicker. Such techniques are beyond the scope of this appendix.

The amount of change in the scroll-bar position for the codes SB_LINEUP, SB_LINEDOWN, SB_LINERIGHT, SB_LINELEFT, SB_PAGEUP, SB_PAGE-DOWN, SB_PAGELEFT, and SB_PAGERIGHT must be determined by you. Normally, you will adjust the slider position by a constant value for each of these codes. It is sometimes necessary to experiment with the values to achieve a pleasing result.

B.5.2 Window and Viewport Origin

If your document is relatively small, you can do all of your scrolling using the **CDC** *SetWindowOrg* function. Normally, the upper-left corner of the component window is at the coordinates (0,0). The *SetWindowOrg* function changes the coordinates of the

Code	Meaning
SB_TOP	The user has moved the slider of the vertical scroll bar all the way to the top.
SB_LEFT	The user has moved the slider of the horizontal scroll bar all the way to the left.
SB_BOTTOM	The user has moved the slider of the vertical scroll bar all the way to the bottom.
SB_RIGHT	The user has moved the slider of the horizontal scroll bar all the way to the right.
SB_LINEDOWN	The user has clicked the button at the bottom of the vertical scroll bar.
SB_LINERIGHT	The user has clicked the button at the right end of the horizontal scroll bar.
SB_LINEUP	The user has clicked the button at the top of the vertical scroll bar.
SB_LINELEFT	The user has clicked the button at the left end of the horizontal scroll bar.
SB_PAGEDOWN	The user has clicked in the slider area of the vertical scroll bar but below the slider.
SB_PAGERIGHT	The user has clicked in the slider area of the horizontal scroll bar but to the right of the slider.
SB_PAGEUP	The user has clicked in the slider area of the vertical scroll bar but above the slider.
SB_PAGELEFT	The user has clicked in the slider area of the horizontal scroll bar but to the left of the slider.
SB_THUMBPOSITION	The user has dragged the slider of either scroll bar to a new position. The new position is given in the second operand of the function, *nPos*.
SB_THUMBTRACK	The user is in the process of dragging the slider of either scroll bar. This message allows you to synchronize the display with the movement of the scroll bar. The current position of the slider is in the second operand of the function, *nPos*.
SB_ENDSCROLL	Signals the end of a set of SB_THUMBTRACK events. Will normally be followed by an SB_THUMBPOSITION event.

Figure B-10   Scroll Bar Message Codes

upper-left to whatever coordinates you specify. If you set the coordinates to values larger than zero, this has the effect of moving a different portion of your document into the visible portion of the window. After calling *SetWindowOrg*, you draw your document normally. The apparent movement of the document is handled automatically.

Suppose you have a component window that is 200 pixels wide and 100 pixels high, and suppose your document is 400 pixels wide and 200 pixels high. If you draw

`pdc->SetWindowOrg(0,0)`	`pdc->SetWindowOrg(200,0)`
`pdc->SetWindowOrg(0,100)`	`pdc->SetWindowOrg(200,100)`

Figure B-11   The Effect of *SetWindowOrg*

this document without calling *SetWindowOrg*, only the upper-left quadrant of the document will be visible. Figure B-11 illustrates the four quadrants of the document, and the *SetWindowOrg* call that must be used to make each quadrant visible.

If you use tracking variables for your scroll bars, these variables can be used as *SetWindowOrg* operands.

B.5.3 Window and Viewport Extent

Just as the origin can be used for scrolling, the window and viewport extents can be used for scaling. These extents provide a pair of numbers that are used to scale output to a device context. The ratio of the extents is important, the absolute value of the extents is not. (To avoid overflow problems, both values should be as small as possible.) Normally, the window and viewport extents are the same. When they are not, the coordinates of all drawn objects are multiplied by the viewport extent and then divided by the window extent. A different scale can be used for the *X* and *Y* directions. Let's suppose we want to change the size of our drawing, to make it appear 200 percent of its original size. We would make the following function calls before drawing our document:

```
pdc->SetWindowExt(1,1);
pdc->SetViewportExt(2,2);
```

If instead we wanted to draw our document at 50 percent of its original size, we would use the following function calls:

```
pdc->SetWindowExt(2,2);
pdc->SetViewportExt(1,1);
```

Scaling is especially important when drawing graphical objects to a printer. When doing this, use the function calls shown in Figure B-12. (Assume that *MyDc* is a printer

```
long PixX = MyDc->GetDeviceCaps(LOGPIXELSX);
long PixY = MyDc->GetDeviceCaps(LOGPIXELSY);
// Start a document and a page
MyDc->StartDoc(&MyDoc);
MyDc->StartPage();
// This stuff MUST DEFINITELY follow StartDoc and StartPage
// MM_ANISOTROPIC allows independent scaling of X and Y dimensions.
MyDc->SetMapMode(MM_ANISOTROPIC);
MyDc->SetWindowExt(100,100);
MyDc->SetViewportExt(PixX,PixY);
```

Figure B-12   Scaling Print Output

device context.) The *GetDeviceCaps* function calls are used to determine the horizontal and vertical resolution of the printer. The display has a logical resolution of 100 pixels per inch. If you wish, you can use similar function calls to determine the precise resolution of the display, but things will look right if you use 100.

Instead of using the window and viewport extents, you could perform all scaling operations yourself. This is fairly simple for graphical objects but is nightmarishly difficult for text. If your document contains text, do not try to scale it yourself.

B.6 BITMAPS, ICONS, AND OTHER RESOURCES

The *Cards* and *LED* examples used bitmap resources to draw their displays. To use a bitmap resource, first draw the bitmap using the Visual C++ bitmap editor or some other tool, and save it as a *.bmp* file. (This is done behind-the-scenes in the Visual C++ editor.) Be sure to include the bitmap in your component as a resource. (It is fairly obvious how to do this.) Bitmaps drawn in the Visual C++ editor get added to your resources automatically.

Once you have your bitmap stored as a resource, you need to load it into memory and then map it into your component window. This is done using a memory device context. You first load the bitmap from your resources using the following statement:

```
CBitmap MyMap;
MyMap.LoadBitmap(IDB_MYMAP);
```

The operand IDB_MYMAP is the name of the resource as it appears in the resource editor. Once the bitmap has been loaded into memory, it must be selected into a device context. The device context must be compatible with the display. This is done using the following statements:

```
CDC MyDc
MyDc.CreateCompatibleDC(pdc);
CBitMap *OldMap = MyDc->SelectObject(&MyMap);
```

To draw the bitmap at position (X, Y) of your component window, use the following function call:

```
pdc->BitBlt(X,Y,Width,Height,&MyDc,0,0,SRCCOPY);
```

In this function call, *Width* and *Height* are the width and height of the bitmap in pixels.

Before exiting your *OnDraw* function, you should select the bitmap out of the *MyDc* context using the following function call:

```
MyDc.SelectObject(OldBitmap);
```

The destructor of the **CBitmap** class will take care of removing the bitmap from memory.

There are several standard resources that are created when you use the MFC ActiveX wizard. The first is the bitmap that will be used to represent your component in the Visual Basic toolbox. The default is the letters OCX in purple on a gray background. If you make more than one ActiveX component, these bitmaps can quickly become confusing. You should edit this bitmap to identify your component. You do not need to be creative; a few meaningful letters will do. You can enlarge the bitmap if it is too small. Note that the color of the edge of the bitmap will be treated as the background color and will be replaced by gray when the bitmap appears in the Visual Basic toolbox.

The next standard resource is the about-box icon, which is the standard MFC building blocks icon. This icon will appear in your about box and wherever the Windows operating system needs an icon to identify your component. (This happens only rarely.) You should edit this icon to provide some useful information.

Another standard resource is the about-box dialog. You should change the copyright notice and provide the long name for your component. You can provide additional lines of text as necessary. The property page dialog is discussed in Appendix C.

The string table is a standard resource that gives the names that will be used for your component in the registry. It is seldom necessary to change the defaults. The intent of the string table is to provide translated names for components that are distributed in other countries.

The version resource is discussed in Appendix D.

B.7 CONCLUSION

This appendix has given a brief outline of Windows GUI programming, which will be sufficient for most simple ActiveX components. As you gain experience, you will want to enhance your knowledge of the GUI drawing functions. The Visual C++ documentation contains an enormous amount of material that will help you broaden your knowledge of this subject.

MFC and ATL

C.1 INTRODUCTION

All of the examples given in this book were created using the MFC ActiveX Control Wizard. By this time, you should be quite familiar with the MFC tools. The one topic that we still need to cover is the creation of property pages. These are quite useful and in some contexts are almost essential for setting the default values of persistent properties. Many of our examples contain property pages, even though we have not discussed them.

Another important topic that we have not covered is ATL components. ATL can be used to create ActiveX components and can also be used to create COM and DCOM components. We will focus here only on ActiveX components. (ActiveX components are actually a special case of COM components.)

ATL components are usually smaller and faster than MFC components, but they are somewhat more complicated to program. In any case the differences between the ATL and MFC programming styles are significant. We will cover the most important differences between these types of components.

C.2 MFC PROPERTY PAGES

A property page allows the default values of a component's persistent properties to be set without using a development system like Visual Basic. Property pages are quite useful when designing Web-based applications. The property page is a dialog box with conventional controls for setting property values. Numeric and string properties are set using text boxes, Boolean properties are set using check boxes, and enumerations are set using either radio buttons or combo-boxes. (A combo-box is a drop-down list.)

The first step in creating a property page is to draw the dialog box using the Visual C++ editor. Provide a control (or a set of radio buttons) for each persistent property. To edit the size of the drop-down list for a combo-box, click on the button. To make a set of radio buttons act as a group, display the properties of each button, and click the *GROUP* check box for everything except the last radio button in the set. The tab order of the buttons in the group is important. To see the tab order, go to the layout menu and select the tab-order command. The tab order of the radio buttons must be a contiguous range of numbers, with all but the last control in the tab order having the GROUP property set. When the tab order is displayed, set the order of your controls by clicking on them in the correct order. Select the *Layout Tab Order* command again to turn off the Tab Order display.

Right-click on each control to display its properties. Change the name of each component to something you can remember. (This name is only for *your* use.) It is best to leave the first four characters (IDC_ etc.) unchanged. For radio buttons, it is the name of the first button in the tab order that is important. The others can be left unchanged.

After assigning mnemonic names to all controls, right-click on the dialog box and select the ClassWizard command. Go to the second page of the Class Wizard, which is entitled *Member Variables*. You will see a list of your controls on the left-hand side of the dialog box. Select the top one by clicking on it, and then click on the button *Add Variable*. In the *Add Variable* dialog box, type a variable name. This variable name has nothing to do with anything else in your component. It is a brand-new variable name in a new class. Use whatever name you wish. *Do not change the category*. In the *Optional Property Name* box, type the name of the persistent property in your component. This is the property name itself, not the name of the variable holding the property. Click *OK*, and go on to the next variable. When you've finished with all the variables, compile your component, and you're all set. Test the property page in Visual Basic to make sure you've specified the property names correctly.

Although property page dialog boxes are supposed to all be the same size, there are two acceptable sizes, one large and one small. The MFC ActiveX gives you the smallest one, which may not give you enough room. If this happens, just make the dialog box bigger. Do not attempt to set it to the correct size. The first time you test your property page you will receive a warning dialog box that says it is the wrong size. It will also give you the correct dimensions. Write down the dimensions of the largest, and exit from the Visual C++ development system. Open your project directory, and find the file with the *.rc* suffix. Edit this file using the windows notepad. In this file you will find an entry for your property page dialog box. This line will contain the dimensions of the box. Replace these with the dimensions you wrote down, and save the file. (This is the *only* way I know of to get the dimensions correct.)

C.3 THE DIFFERENCES BETWEEN ATL AND MFC

The MFC ActiveX wizard creates an ActiveX component with every possible feature implemented. The ActiveX standard will actually allow you to pick and choose among the features that are implemented. To some degree, ATL allows you to design an ActiveX component in this fashion. In most cases, however you will want to implement as much of the ActiveX standard as possible to maintain the versatility of your component.

The first step in designing an ATL ActiveX component is to create a new project of type *ATL COM AppWizard*. Do not change any of the default selections in the wizard; just click *Finish*. This creates a project with almost nothing in it. You can now populate your project with COM objects.

Add a single COM object of type *Full Control* to your project. Go to the *Insert* menu and select the command *New ATL Object*. This will produce a dialog box with two panes. In the category pane, select *controls*. From the objects pane select *Full Control*, and click on the *Next* button. *Be very careful at this point.* Type in a short name for your component. Now click on the *Attributes* tab and find the check box labeled *Support Connection Points* and make sure it is checked. If you do not do this, your component will not be able to have events. There is a way to fix this after the fact, but it is not easy.

Go to the stock properties tab and select all of the stock properties you want your component to support. The Class Wizard is not usable with ATL projects, so you've got to make the decision about stock properties *now*. On the miscellaneous tab, you can select a standard windows control to subclass, if you want to do this. There is also one other important check box on this tab, the one that is labeled *Windowed Only*. Normally ATL components do not have their own window but share a portion of the host's window. This can cause problems because the *CWnd::* functions will not work without a window. If you anticipate using a lot of *CWnd::* functions, check this box; otherwise leave it unchecked. Windowless activation is faster and usually more efficient than windowed activation. (For containers that do not support windowless activation, all ATL ActiveX components will have a window.)

Check over all tabs to make sure everything is correct, and then click *OK*.

C.4 ATL PROPERTIES, METHODS, AND EVENTS

Let's suppose that when you created your ATL component, the simple name that you typed into the ATL dialog box was *MyCtl*. In the class-name pane to the left of the Visual C++ window, you will see two items beginning with the letter "I." These are **IMyCtl**, and **_IMyCtlEvents**. (The second actually begins with an underscore.) This is where you add properties methods and events to your component. To add properties and methods, right-click on **IMyCtl**, and select either *Add Method* or *Add Property*, depending on which you want. Let's first create a property named *First* of type *long*. Right-click on **IMyCtl**, and select *Add Property*. Type in the name of the property, *First* and select *long* from the list of types. Leave the parameters box blank, and click *OK*. This creates two functions in your support class: *get_First* and *put_First*. To find the bodies of these functions, click on the + in front of **CMyCtl**. You will see a second line starting with **IMyCtl** under **CMyCtl**. Click on the + in front of this line to display the *get* and *put* function names. Double-click on the function names to see the function bodies. The generated function bodies are given in Figure C-1. Note that both functions return the value *S_OK*. This is necessary—do not change it. To return a value from the *get_First* function, you must assign the value to *pVal*. In ATL components, all property functions should return *S_OK*.

Creating a method is somewhat more complicated. Let's create a method, *Second*, that returns a long integer and has one long integer operand. Right-click on IMyCtl and select *Add Method*. In the *Add Method* dialog box, type in the method name *Second*. In the parameters box, type the following line:

```
[in] long InVal, [out, retval] long * OutVal
```

```
STDMETHODIMP CMyCtl::get_First(long *pVal)
{
    // TODO: Add your implementation code here
    return S_OK;
}
STDMETHODIMP CMyCtl::put_First(long newVal)
{
    // TODO: Add your implementation code here
    return S_OK;
}
```

Figure C-1 *Get* and *Put* Functions

```
STDMETHODIMP CMyCtl::Second(long InVal, long *OutVal)
{
    // TODO: Add your implementation code here
    return S_OK;
}
```

Figure C-2 Second Function Implementation

The generated function, which can be found in the same way you located the *get* and *put* functions, is shown in Figure C-2.

Note that, the direction indicators *[in]* and *[out, retval]* in this figure are missing. Even though the method returns a value, the implementation function is not permitted to do so. It must return a success/failure code. In most cases this will be *S_OK*. The return value for the method must be placed in the location pointed to by *OutVal*. When declaring the operands, each must be preceded by a direction indicator. All but the last must have the direction indicator *[in]*. If the return value is void, the last parameter will also have the direction indicator *[in]*. Otherwise it will have the direction indicator *[out, retval]* and it will be a *pointer* to the return value type. The return value of the method must be placed in the location indicated by this pointer.

In ATL, events are the methods of the **_IMyCtlEvents** interface. To create an event, right-click on **_IMyCtlEvents** and select *Add Method*. Suppose that you want to create an event named *Third* with one long integer parameter *Note*. You define the event just as if it were a method, except the return value must be void. (That is, there must be no parameter with a direction indicator *[out, retval]*. All parameters must have a direction indicator of *[in]*.)

To create the event, we right-click on **_IMyCtlEvents**, select *Add Method*, and type *Third* as the method name. We then type *[in] long Note* in the parameters box and click *OK*. Technically, this is all you need to do to define an event, but firing the event will be nightmarishly difficult without a wrapper function. Visual C++ can create the wrapper function for you, but the procedure is somewhat complicated and subject to weird errors. To create the wrapper functions, perform the following steps:

1. Create all your events by adding methods to **_IMyCtlEvents.**
2. Compile your program. Fix all errors until you get a clean compile.
3. Right-click on **CMyCtl** and select *Implement Connection Point*.
4. In the resultant dialog box, click the check box in front of **_IMyCtlEvents**.
5. Click *OK*.
6. Compile your program again. If it works, you will be all set; in most cases, however, you will get six compile errors.
7. Double-click on the first error message. This will take you to a line containing the defined constant IID__IMyCtlEvents. Change this constant to DIID__IMyCtlEvents. (Just add a capital letter "D" to the front.)
8. Compile your program again.

After completing these steps, your support class will have the wrapper function *Fire_Third*, which can be called to fire the *Third* event.

C.5 WINDOWS NATIVE GRAPHICAL FUNCTIONS

For the most part, the ATL drawing functions are the same as those for MFC drawing with a few parameter changes. Nevertheless, these are Windows native drawing functions, not members of some class. In general, a drawing function of the form

```
pdc->DrawFunc(P1,P2, …, PN);
```

is replaced with

```
DrawFunc(di.hdcDraw,P1,P2, …, PN);
```

There are usually fewer choices as to parameters as well. The one notable exception is the line drawing function *MoveTo*. This existed in Windows 3.1 but no longer exists in Windows 95 and above. You need to replace this with *MoveToEx*, and set the fourth (and last) parameter of this function to NULL.

C.6 WINDOWLESS ACTIVATION

The default windowless activation of ATL components can cause several problems. First, even though the drawing routine has an apparent window and device context in which to draw, what it actually has is a portion of the container's window and a handle to the container's device context. In most cases, the upper-left corner of the drawing window will not be (0,0). If your component assumes that the upper left corner is (0,0), your drawings will not display correctly.

The second problem is that *CWnd::* functions do not work in windowless activation. The most commonly used of these is *CWnd::Invalidate*. Replace this with *FireViewChange* and everything will work. If you need more extensive access to the *CWnd::* functions, you should avoid windowless activation. Although there are ways to duplicate the actions of these functions, they are not always as efficient as using a window.

C.7 FIXED-SIZED MFC COMPONENTS

Creating a fixed-sized component is not particularly difficult, but you can spend (literally) weeks digging through the documentation trying to figure out how to do it.

Let's suppose you want to create a control of fixed size 32 × 32. The first step is to add the following line to the constructor of your support class:

```
SetInitialSize(32,32);
```

Then, using the first page of the ClassWizard, add the *OnSetExtent* function to your support class. Comment out the body of this function, and return a zero instead. Keep the body of this function as a comment to remind yourself how to resize a control if you want to resize it yourself later.

For an example of a fixed-sized ATL component, see the Cards component. (Although the example was presented as an MFC component, it is implemented as an ATL component on the Web site.)

C.8 CONCLUSION

There are many books on MFC and ATL programming that can be used to extend your knowledge of these subjects. In addition, there is extensive documentation on both MFC and ATL in the Microsoft Developer Network Library.

Using ActiveX Controls on the Web

D.1 INTRODUCTION

The most intriguing feature of ActiveX components is that they can be incorporated into a Web page and used as if the Web page itself were a program. (This works only with the Internet Explorer browser, however.) Before you can begin using ActiveX components on the Web, there are a number of things you must do. This appendix goes through the steps that you must complete to use your ActiveX components on your Web site.

D.2 MARKING CONTROLS AS SAFE

You must begin by marking your components as safe. There are two kinds of safe: (1) safe for scripting and (2) safe for initialization. The first means that scripts written in either VBScript or JScript are allowed to assign values to the properties of your component and to call its methods. What you are saying when you mark a component as safe is that there is no way that a pirate Web site could use your component to damage a user's system. (In other words, if you have a method that reformats the user's hard drive, *do not* mark the component as safe.) Safe for initialization means that the browser is allowed to assign the initial values to your persistent properties. You will normally use both markings or neither of them. In both cases, think about what could happen if a malicious person included your component in his or her Web page. If your component could be used to damage the user's system, it is *not safe*.

If you plan to use your components on your Web site, you definitely want to make your components safe and mark them as safe. (Putting an unsafe component on the Web can cost you a lot of money in lawsuits.) To mark a component as safe, you must replace the default *CMineCtrl::CSGEditorCtrlFactory::UpdateRegistry(BOOL)* function of your support class. (Replace "Mine" with the name of your component.) You will find this function in the *MineCtl.cpp* file. (If you are using ATL instead of

MFC, there is an entirely different procedure that must be followed. Skip ahead to Section D. 3, which discusses safe marking of ATL components.)

Before you do this, you will need to add the helper files to your project. These helper files—named *helpers.h* and *helpers.cpp*—are included in every project on the Web site. You can obtain them from there or from the Microsoft Developer Network. Copy these files into your project directory, and make them part of your project. Now add the following two lines to your *MineCtl.cpp* file. Make sure these lines *follow* the other *#include* lines.

```
#include "helpers.h"
#include <objsafe.h>
```

The final step is to replace the body of your *UpdateRegistry* function with the code shown in Figure D-1. *Be careful*: There are three lines of the existing function

```
if (bRegister)
{
    BOOL retval = AfxOleRegisterControlClass(
        AfxGetInstanceHandle(),
        m_clsid,
        m_lpszProgID,
        IDS_SGEDITOR,        // COPY FROM OLD FUNCTION BODY
        IDB_SGEDITOR,        // COPY FROM OLD FUNCTION BODY
        afxRegApartmentThreading,
        _dwSGEditorOleMisc,   // COPY FROM OLD FUNCTION BODY
        _tlid,
        _wVerMajor,
        _wVerMinor);
    // mark as safe for scripting—failure OK
    HRESULT hr = CreateComponentCategory(CATID_SafeForScripting,
        L"Controls that are safely scriptable");
    if (SUCCEEDED(hr))
    {
        RegisterCLSIDInCategory(m_clsid, CATID_SafeForScripting);
    }
    hr = CreateComponentCategory(CATID_SafeForInitializing,
        L"Controls safely initializable from persistent data");
    if (SUCCEEDED(hr))
    {
        RegisterCLSIDInCategory(m_clsid, CATID_SafeForInitializing);
    }
    return retval;
}
else
{
    return AfxOleUnregisterClass(m_clsid, m_lpszProgID);
}
```

Figure D-1   Safe-Marking Code

body that you need to copy into this new function body. These lines refer to #*define* statements and variables that contain the name of your component. They are commented in Figure D-1.

If you neglect to mark your component as safe, anyone accessing your Web page will receive a warning about unsafe controls every time your Web page is accessed. This will make your page extremely unpopular.

D.3 SAFE MARKING OF ATL COMPONENTS

The procedure for safe marking of ATL components is much simpler than that for MFC components. To mark an ATL component as safe, first find the line *END_PROP_MAP( )* in your *MineCtl.h* file, where *MineCtl* is the name you used when you added the control to your ATL project. Add the four lines of Figure D-2 after this line.

D.4 SUPPORTING PROPERTY BAGS IN ATL

By default, ATL controls do not implement enough of the ActiveX specification to be usable in a Web page. Fortunately, the only deficiency is in the support for persistent properties. (If you do not have any persistent properties, you can ignore this section.) In Web pages, the initial values for persistent properties are stored in something called a *Property Bag*. (I don't make up these names!) You need to add property bag support to your ATL component before the persistent properties will be initialized properly. Before you do this, make sure you have downloaded and installed the latest updates for your version of Visual C++, because there is a flagrant bug in ATL property bag support in some of the released versions of Visual C++.

The first step is to add the following to the list of derived classes for your class **CMineCtl**, where *Mine* is the name of your control:

```
public IPersistPropertyBagImpl<CMineCtl>
```

Next, find the COM map for your control. (It should be the next thing in your *.h* file.) The COM map starts with the macro *COM_MAP(. . .)* and ends with the macro *END_COM_MAP( )*. Add the following line to the end of your COM map.

```
COM_INTERFACE_ENTRY(IPersistPropertyBag)
```

Adding these two lines to your project will make persistent properties work on a Web page.

```
BEGIN_CATEGORY_MAP(CAPentCtl)
  IMPLEMENTED_CATEGORY(CATID_SafeForScripting)
  IMPLEMENTED_CATEGORY(CATID_SafeForInitializing)
END_CATEGORY_MAP()
```

Figure D-2   ATL Safe-Marking Code

D.5 CREATING AN INF FILE

A big part of putting your component on a Web page is preparing your component for distribution. Before your ActiveX component can run on someone else's system, it must be downloaded and installed. The INF file contains instructions for installing your component on a new user's system. The INF file will then be packaged with your object file or files and downloaded as a unit. The INF file for an ATL component is much simpler than that for an MFC component. The problem is that MFC components require three additional files in addition to your object file. If you are using MFC, your object file will be named *Mine.ocx*, where *Mine* is the name of your project. (More on this in the next section.) If you are using ATL, your object file will be named *Mine.dll*.

The INF file for an MFC component (the Simple Graphical Editor) is given in Figure D-3. The file in this figure shows the correct way to include the three additional files with your component. I have seen other recommendations about how to do this, but as far as I can tell, none of them work. This version has been tested and does indeed work correctly.

I would recommend using this file and modifying it to install your component. Every line starting with a semicolon is a comment, so you can safely ignore those lines. Make the following changes:

1. Modify the initial comment to document your file. Describe your component as accurately as possible.
2. Change the line that reads *SGEditor.ocx = SGEditor.ocx*. Put your own *ocx* name in both places.

```
; Install SGEditor.ocx

[Version]
Signature="$CHICAGO$"
AdvancedINF=2.0

[Add.Code]
SGEditor.ocx=SGEditor.ocx
mfc42.dll=mfc42.dll
msvcrt.dll=msvcrt.dll
olepro32.dll=olepro32.dll

[SGEditor.ocx]
file-win32-x86=thiscab
clsid={DCAFB66A-1D94-4D8B-8D4F-1DDF2E5AF7C4}
DestDir=11
FileVersion=1,0,0,1
RegisterServer=yes

; dependent DLLs
[msvcrt.dll]
```

Figure D-3   An MFC INF File

```
; This is an example of conditional hook. The hook only gets processed
; if msvcrt.dll of the specified version is absent on client machine.
FileVersion=6,0,8168,0
hook=mfc42installer

[mfc42.dll]
FileVersion=6,0,8168,0
hook=mfc42installer

[olepro32.dll]
FileVersion=5,0,4261,0
hook=mfc42installer

[mfc42installer]
file-win32-x86=http://activex.microsoft.com/controls/vc/mfc42.cab
; If dependent DLLs are packaged directly into the above cabinet file
; along with an .inf file, specify that .inf file to run as follows:
;InfFile=mfc42.inf
; The mfc42.cab file actually contains a self extracting executable.
; In this case we specify a run= command.
run=%EXTRACT_DIR%\mfc42.exe
```

Figure D-3   (*Continued*)

3. Change the line that reads *[SGEditor.ocx]*. Put your own *ocx* name here.

4. In the section under *[SGEditor.ocx]* change the line that reads. *clsid= {DCAFB66A-1D94-4D8B-8D4F-1DDF2E5AF7C4}*. You need to replace the string between the braces with the GUID of your own component. To find out the GUID of your component, open your project and then open the source file that has the suffix *odl*. You will find this in your list of source files. Scroll down to the end of this file. You will find several GUIDs in this file. The one you want is the *last* one in the file. Copy the string from your ODL file into your INF file.

5. In the section under *[SGEditor.ocx]* find the line that reads *FileVersion = 1,0,0,1*. Change this to match the version number of your *ocx* file. Do not guess at the version number! There are two ways to find out the version number. The first is to open your project and look at the version resource. This is the best way. The second way is to right-click on your *ocx* file and call up the properties window. Record the version number correctly.

6. Once you have made these modifications save the file under the name *Mine.inf*, where *Mine* is the name of your *ocx* file.

Figure D-4 gives the format of an ATL INF file. You modify it in the same way that you would modify the MFC INF file. The only difference is in how you locate the GUID. For ATL projects, this can be found in the *idl* source file. Suppose the support class for your ATL component is named **CMine**. Find the line in this file that reads *coclass Mine*. The GUID you want is the one *just before* this line. Don't forget to modify the version number, and make sure you get it correct.

```
; Apent.ocx
; Advanced Pentominos

[Add.Code]
Apent.ocx=Apent.ocx

[Apent.ocx]
file-win32-x86=thiscab
clsid={6764E70D-6016-11D4-A057-00104B5FBF5B}
DestDir=11
FileVersion=1,0,0,1
RegisterServer=yes
; end of INF file
```

Figure D-4 An ATL INF File

D.6 CREATING A *cab* FILE

Before creating your *cab* file, you must have two things: your INF file and the *release version* of your OCX (or DLL) file. You cannot distribute the debug version of an MFC control. It will not work on a user's system unless the user just happens to have C++ installed. Even then it still might not work right. So you must first create the release version of your OCX. Go to the *Build* menu, and select the *Set Active Configuration* command. This command will bring up a window that will allow you to select a configuration. The default for both MFC and ATL is *Debug*. For MFC change to *Release*. For ATL change to *Release MinDependency*. Rebuild the project (it will most likely recompile from scratch). You should now have a *Release* directory (*ReleaseMinDependency* for ATL.) *You must have an* ocx *file in this directory to proceed!*

Create a new subdirectory in your project directory, and place both the INF file and the release-version *ocx* file in it. Create a new *txt* file in this directory and add the following single line to it:

```
cabarc -s  6144   n  sgeditor.cab   SGEditor.ocx   SGEditor.inf
```

Change the string *SGEditor* to match the name of your OCX. I recommend making the name of the *cab* file all lowercase. If your HTTP server is a UNIX server, case will make a difference and all lowercase will cause fewer problems. Save the *txt* file, and change the suffix from *txt* to *bat*. Double-click on the file to create your *cab* file. In most cases, this will fail the first time you try it because Windows will not be able to find the *cabarc* program. Search your system for *cabarc.exe*. If you find it, copy it (Do not move it!) into your Windows directory. If you cannot find it, go to the Microsoft Web site and search for *cabarc.exe*. You may need to search around a bit, but it is part of several different System Development Kits (SDK), and eventually you will find one containing it. (If I give you the URL, it will be out of date by the time you read this.)

D.7 SIGNING

Once you have *cab* files, you are almost ready to begin distributing your ActiveX components. The last thing you need is to sign your ActiveX component. Unfortunately, there is no cheap way to do this. Before you can sign ActiveX components, you must have something called a *Cert*. You can get these from several different places (Verisign is one of them). Unfortunately, they are rather expensive. If you are a college student, your school may be able to provide you with one free of charge, but as of this writing only a few universities provide this service.

If you do manage to obtain a *cert*, this is how you use it. Your cert will actually consist of two files: (1) a file with the suffix *spc* containing the *cert* itself, and (2) a file with the suffix *pvk* containing your private key. (The C++ SDK has programs that allow you to create these two files, *but they are fakes!* You can practice signing files with these fake files, but the user's Web browser will not be able to recognize the signature.) If you have a real *cert* from a recognized certificate-issuing authority, the two files are used by the *SignCode* program to insert a digital signature into your *cab* file. You should also sign your *ocx* file before creating your *cab* file. First create an empty file named *signocx.txt*, and add the following line to it:

```
signcode -spc mycert.spc -v mykey.pvk -n "My OCX" -i "http://…"
mine.ocx
```

Next create a file named *signcab.txt* and add the following line to it:

```
signcode -spc mycert.spc -v mykey.pvk -n "My OCX" -i "http://…"
mine.cab
```

You may need to specify a full path name for the files *mycert.spc* and *mykey.pvk*. You may also need to specify a full path name for the *signcode exe file*. Replace the *http://* ... string with the Web address providing documentation for your component. Replace the *My OCX* string with an English description of your component. After creating these two *txt* files, change the suffix of both to *bat*. You may now double-click on the files to sign your code.

You can distribute your components without signing them, but if you do this, your users will have to change the default security settings of their browsers to download them. You should warn your users about this. If at all possible, sign your *cab* files.

D.8 VERSIONING

In the section on INF files, we warned you several times to "get the version number right." Once you have placed your component on your Web site, the version number becomes *very important*. (Version numbers are important any time your component is being used by someone other than yourself.) Once the component is on your Web site, *you cannot change it without changing the version number*. This is not just a teacher's warning about something nice that you *ought* to do. It is an absolute and inescapable requirement for your Web page to function correctly. The software at the user's site will key on the version number to ensure that things are functioning correctly—so if you mess up the version numbers, you mess up your users.

Before distributing your component, edit the version resource, and *fill in all the fields*. The version number appears in two places. *Make sure they are the same.* You *should* change the fourth part of the version number every time you build it for testing. You *must* change the version number every time you distribute it. Make sure the new version number is *larger* than the previous.

ActiveX components are downloaded and installed once. After the first access, all accesses to the component are made to the downloaded component, not the component on your Web site. The component will be downloaded and installed again when the version number changes. The version number change is the *only way* to get your changes to your users.

D.9 HTML TAGS AND EDITORS

To include an ActiveX component in a Web page, place the tags shown in Figure D-5 in your HTML file. (These tags are for the SGEditor component.)

The *classid* parameter of the object tag must contain the GUID of your component. This must be the same GUID specified in your INF file. The *codebase* parameter of the object tag contains the URL of the CAB file containing your component and the current version of your component. *The version number must be correct.* There are four places the version number appears. It appears twice inside your ActiveX component, once in your INF file, and once in your *codebase* parameter. *All four numbers must match.*

If you have several instances of the same component on a single Web page, the *codebase* parameter is required only on the first (but to be safe, you should put it on all of them).

The *param* tags are used to supply the initialization values for your persistent properties. You must have one *param* tag for each persistent property. The first four lines in Figure D-5 are properties provided by the browser, not properties defined by the component. The easiest way to get all of this right is to use an ActiveX aware HTML editor. Most colleges and universities purchase Visual Basic and Visual C++ as part of a larger package called Visual Studio, which includes an ActiveX-aware HTML editor.

```
<object classid="clsid:DCAFB66A-1D94-4D8B-8D4F-1DDF2E5AF7C4"
id="SGEditor1" width="100" height="50"
codebase="http://www.mydn.com/mine.cab#version=1,0,0,1">
  <param name="_Version" value="65536">
  <param name="_ExtentX" value="2646">
  <param name="_ExtentY" value="1323">
  <param name="_StockProps" value="0">
  <param name="DrawMode" value="0">
  <param name="FillColor" value="0">
  <param name="LineColor" value="0">
  <param name="HandleRadius" value="4">
</object>
```

Figure D-5   HTML Tags for ActiveX Components

D.10 SCRIPTS

Scripting is beyond the scope of this appendix, but with a few tips you can probably accomplish everything you want to accomplish in VBScript. You can begin by creating a Visual Basic program that does the same thing you want your Web page do. Take the code of the Visual Basic program, and embed it in a VBScript in your Web page. To do this, place the following two lines between the *</head>* and *<body>* tags in your HTML file.

```
<script language="VBScript"><!- -
- -></script>
```

Put your Visual Basic code between these two lines. You will need to make the following changes. Remove the *Private* keyword from all function definitions. Local variable definitions are not used, so remove them also. (All variables are untyped variants.) Global variables and function parameters may not have a type, so remove the *AS INTEGER* (or other type) from all declarations. Save the file and then run the script. Remove whatever else the browser complains about. Almost anything that will work in Visual Basic will also work in VBScript.

D.11 LICENSING

The full details of licensing are beyond the scope of this appendix, but we nevertheless want to at least discuss the basic issues. When using an ActiveX component in Visual Basic, many commercial components will refuse to run in design mode unless you have paid the licensing fee. The MSDN library that comes with Visual Studio will explain how to incorporate such a feature into your own components. What licensing does is allow programmers to distribute commercial components with their applications. Users of the application cannot use the distributed components to create their own applications without paying the license fee.

This scheme does not work for components distributed with Web pages because there is no design mode. HTML files can be created with virtually any text editor, including the Windows Notepad. To protect your component from unauthorized use, you must also include some sort of run-time license. The way this normally works is to provide license-checking features that will permit a component to execute in a Web page only if that page, the *cab* file, and a special licensing file have been downloaded from a common server. The license file is a special file that is tied to a particular system and cannot be easily faked. For more information, see the Microsoft Developer Network (MSDN) index under "LPK files." If you purchase third-party components for use on your Web pages, you will need to learn how to create and use LPK files. The MSDN documentation provides detailed information on creating and using LPK files.

D.12 CONCLUSION

The best way to learn about using ActiveX components in Web pages is to practice. For some examples of Web pages containing ActiveX components, see the URL http://cs.baylor.edu/~maurer/vdal.

Index